D1249840

FATED DESTINY

FATED DESTINY

BLITZ EDITIONS

Copyright © Bookmart Ltd 1994

All rights reserved. No part of this publication may be reproduced,
stored in a retrieval system, or transmitted in any form or by any
means, electronic, mechanical, photocopying, recording or otherwise,
without prior written permission from the publishers.

Published by Blitz Editions
an imprint of Bookmart Ltd
Registered Number 2372865
Trading as Bookmart Ltd, Desford Road, Enderby
Leicester LE9 5AD

This book was produced
by Amazon Publishing Ltd

Cover design: Peter Dolton
Text design: Jim Reader
Production Manager: Sue Gray
Editorial Manager: Roz Williams

Printed in the Slovak Republic
51740

ISBN 1 85605 197 8

Every effort has been made to contact the copyright holders for the pictures.
In some cases they have been untraceable, for which we offer our apologies.
Thanks to the following: Ancient Art & Architecture Collection, Janet & Colin Bord, EPA Photo Library,
Mary Evans Picture Library, Express Newspapers, Fortean Picture Library, Fotomas Index, Frank Spooner,
Hulton Deutsch Collection Ltd, Illustrated London News Picture Library, Library of Congress,
Mander & Mitchenson Theatre Collection Ltd, Midsummer Books, Press Association Photo Library,
Peter Newark's American, Historical, Military and Western Americana Pictures, Popperfoto, Portfolio,
Rex Features Ltd, Ian Drury, Syndication International, Topham Picture Source and Roger Viollet.

Cover: The main picture supplied by the Royal Observatory, Edinburgh/AATB/Science Photo Library.
The front left by Rex Features Ltd and the rest, including the back cover, by the Hulton Deutsch Collection Ltd.

The Authors
Karen Farrington is a journalist who has worked for both national newspapers, and as a freelance, for the best
selling weekly women's magazines. Her broad experience has brought her into contact with some of the most
intriguing mysteries, compelling crimes and moving animal stories of recent times.

Nick Constable, also a journalist, has spent many years working in Fleet Street and covered top stories including
the famine of Ethiopia, the government-backed assassinations of street children in Brazil and the Gulf War.
He has also worked extensively to expose cruelty to animals in Britain and around the world.

Contents

FATED DESTINY

Whether we want to or not, at times we all wonder if there is some strange destiny shaping our lives. We may choose to deny the influence of some force greater than ourselves, and claim that our lives are in our own hands to make of them what we will. Or we may play safe, and admit the possibility that there might be something, somewhere, even if we don't know precisely what or where.

This book looks at some of the more inexplicable aspects of our lives, and seeks to uncover the truth behind the stories that have become popular currency in our sceptical culture. Its investigations encompass a vast number of unanswered questions that have tormented some of the most brilliant intellects in recent years. If you want to know the latest information about the death of Marilyn Monroe, the existence of Atlantis and the malign power of curses, you will find all the facts here, presented in an objective manner so that you can make up your own mind.

Fated Destiny presents the truth and nothing but the truth. It does not seek to sensationalise – but then it doesn't need to. At times, the facts are sensational enough.

RAGS AND RICHES

DREW BARRYMORE
A bright and burning star

Drew Barrymore's amazing performance in *E.T.* proved she was a true Barrymore – tragically so, since she was unable to escape the sordid destiny that had cursed America's greatest acting dynasty.

When she leant forward to kiss the alien from outer space on the tip of its pug nose, it seemed Drew Barrymore had the world in the palm of her innocent, baby-soft hand.

Cute and charismatic, the six-year-old was starring in one of cinema's biggest blockbusters, *E.T.* No heart could fail to melt at the tender tale of a bug-eyed creature from the stars who was stranded on Earth and fell into the arms of an American family.

And no one could resist the fair-skinned, wispy sensation who played Gertie, one of the three youngsters involved in the unearthly adventure to get E.T. safely home.

On-screen Drew made a bigger impact even than the endearing E.T. Director Steven Spielberg gently coaxed and cajoled an extraordinary performance from the youngster. She grasped the role with an instinctive talent and made it her own.

Pundits forecast a brilliant future for the starlet: surely she would be the Greta Garbo or Meryl Streep of her generation? But as the critical acclaim poured in, no one could foretell the personal hell that fate held in store for Drew.

At 6 she was on top of the world. By 9 she was a heavy drinker; a year later she smoked cannabis for the first time and before she was 13 she was a cocaine addict.

The world watched in horror as the girl with so much promise was sucked into the twilight world of alcohol and drugs at an age when she should have been playing in the park or doing homework.

It would take every ounce of courage she could muster to haul herself out of the mire. Hers was a shocking story in which history played an eerie part.

THE BURDEN OF THE BARRYMORES

Drew was a Barrymore, perhaps the greatest acting dynasty of America, and too many members of that highly talented family had fallen foul of drink or drugs or

both, and marched down a path to self-destruction. Along with success came a hopeless taste for excess.

A little older and Drew herself could have looked back at her ancestors to see how they had wreaked havoc living life in the fast lane. Perhaps she'd have summoned the strength of character which has since become one of her hallmarks, and side-stepped the road to hell. But she was much too young to understand what her father and grandfather before her had undergone. She was destined to take the rocky route they had trodden.

'Drew has always been overwhelmed by being part of such a glorious heritage and wanted to continue the tradition,' says a friend. 'She is a sweet girl and I think that

Opposite: Despite her problems Drew blossomed into one of Hollywood's most beautiful women. Perhaps success just came a little too soon.

Above: Aged 4, Drew was pleading to be allowed to audition for film roles. Two years later she was, for a while, the world's biggest child star.

A BRILLIANT FUTURE
BECKONED – BUT DREW
WANTED TO LIVE LIFE
IN THE FAST LANE THAT
LED TO HELL.

Above: *Drew was the fourth generation of an acting dynasty.*

she has been led astray by the movie and TV business. This is an industry that has often led to tragedy for the children of the famous.'

In the end, she proved a match for any of her hard-drinking, fast-living relatives from the past.

The Barrymores' roots were in England: that's where Herbert Albert Blythe punched his way into the history books by becoming the amateur middleweight boxing champion of the nation. He was the best and he loved being top of the pile.

But there was little the old country could offer him when his prowess in the ring started to fade. Casting around for a new direction, Herbert fell into acting. There was only one place where he could realize his high ambitions – America.

He set sail for New York and soon found success on Broadway with a new name, Maurice Barrymore. It seemed the faith he had in his own abilities was not misplaced.

In the final gay decades of the 19th century, he was riding high on a string of stage successes and had married America's top comedienne, Georgia Drew.

Together they had three children, two boys called Lionel and John and a girl called Ethel, but their joy was not to last. Georgia died suddenly from illness and

Maurice couldn't stand the pain. He consoled himself with a bottle. Maurice died in 1905 in a clinic, suffering from alcoholism and insanity.

Although the writing was on the wall, all three children eventually took up an acting career.

The eldest, Lionel, first studied art. It wasn't until talking movies were made that he really found top form. He won an Academy Award for best actor in the film *A Free Soul* in 1930, ironically playing a drunk when he himself was the black sheep of the family as he hardly touched the hard stuff. But it was as Dr Gillespie in the series of films about the strife and times of dashing Dr Kildare that he is best remembered.

The ravages of arthritis and the effects of a serious fall left him wheelchair-bound when he was still a young man, but it didn't end his fame or popularity. His enduring success proved a tough act to follow for younger members of the clan. He died aged 76 in 1954.

Ethel, meanwhile, had shunned the allure of Hollywood in preference for a life on the stage which brought her considerable wealth. She also showed her personal mettle when she headed the actors' strike against Broadway

Right: *Acting together for the first time in 1912, John and Ethel Barrymore both went on to find fame on the silver screen.*

management at a time when union power carried flimsy weight. It dented her popularity with the impresarios of the day, of course. But she fought back to continue her career which ended only two years before her death in June 1959, aged 80.

Her greatest accolade was an Academy Award for being the best supporting actress in the film *None but the Lonely Heart* in 1944 during one of her brief flirtations with the film industry.

But history probably remembers her best for launching the career of her firebrand brother John, Drew's infamous grandfather.

Youngest of the trio, he had resolved not to enter acting. Instead he strived to be a journalist or artist. But destiny had other ideas. When he found himself aged 20 and out of work, his sister Ethel found him a job as a bit part actor in the stage show she was in at the time.

It was enough to give the handsome charmer the acting bug. And his considerable skills earned him national stardom when a play called *Glad of It* swept to fame on Broadway.

He was the toast of the town. But John Barrymore was already drinking to success all night and all day. His huge appetite for life, like his father before him, led to booze binges which won him notoriety before he reached 30.

However, it seemed nothing could stop the steamroller that was John Barrymore's career. The age of movies was beginning and he was ready to seize the opportunities it could offer a handsome, go-ahead actor.

He made his film debut as early as 1913 in a silent film called *An American Citizen*. When talkies took cinema by storm, his silky tones were ideal and it assured his future as a matinee idol who could set pulses racing with a flashing smile and smoothly delivered words of love.

Off-screen he was wilder and more tempestuous than any of the roles he played. He married four times, fathering a daughter, Diana, by his second wife, and son, John Junior, by his third wife Dolores Costello.

As a child, John Junior saw little of his well-known dad. Soon the name John Barrymore was synonymous with drunken womanizing and he became loathed for his outrageous ways across Hollywood. And that was the only role model John Junior knew.

In 1932 John Senior was caught urinating in a ladies' toilet by the shocked wife of a producer. 'Excuse me, this is for ladies,' she uttered with a blush. 'So, Madam, is this,' said the unrepentant Barrymore buttoning his trousers.

Another incident which compounded his infamy was when he hurled a 10-year-old actress across the set because she had upstaged him during a scene. Luckily she was caught by some stage-hands without sustaining injury.

Alcohol soon took its toll. Once a brilliant interpreter of Shakespeare, the swashbuckling hero became dependent on reading cue cards because his memory was failing. In and out of sanatoriums, he was finally reduced to playing ham comedy and was the stooge on a radio show playing

Above: *John Barrymore Junior, the debonair actor who loved the high life – with catastrophic results.*

ON-SCREEN THE MATINEE IDOL WOULD SEND WOMEN INTO A SWOON; OFF-SCREEN HE WAS MORE LIKELY TO SEND THEM CRASHING ACROSS THE ROOM.

Above: *John Barrymore Junior and his first wife, Cara Williams. Their relationship was turbulent and sometimes violent.*

opposite Rudy Vallee. It was while he was rehearsing for one of these shows that he died in 1942, aged 60 and with hardly a dollar to his name.

The mercurial heart-throb left a ruinous inheritance to his children.

John Junior grew up with this tainted view of fatherhood. While he may have longed for a dad who would play baseball or read stories, he witnessed a fallabout drunk with no respect for women or the establishment.

Diana blamed her father's neglect for a failed acting career and inner turmoil which led to three wrecked marriages. She also turned to drink, attempted suicide and was found dead in her New York home in 1957, aged 38, killed by the effects of alcohol.

VOLCANIC RAGES

John Junior tried to establish himself in films but was overshadowed by the ghost of his more famous father and more popular uncle. He found himself avidly watched by newspapers, not because of his acting achievements, but for the boozing, brawling and violent rows he had with his first wife, Cara Williams, which led him into trouble with the police.

After a jail term for possessing cannabis he secluded himself in the Californian desert, returning after some years to play in unremarkable low-budget European films.

Against this stormy background, Drew entered the world carrying the burden of the Barrymore clan on her fragile, velvety shoulders.

Her mother, Hungarian actress Ildiko Jaid, was Barrymore's third wife. Even when she was pregnant, Ildiko suffered from the volcanic rages which erupted without warning in her heavy-drinking husband. It was no surprise that this union also failed when Drew was only a few months old.

When she was 3, Drew can recall her dad storming into the kitchen, pushing her mum to the floor, hurling her across the room and charging off with a bottle of drink. This was their reunion after more than two years apart.

At school, the young Drew quickly learned another of life's harsh lessons. Other children reckoned she had a boy's name. It was the kind of ammunition that kids love and they made her life a misery with constant barracking.

In the end, she left school to have an alternative education at home. While other children settled down to *Sesame Street*, Drew rebelled. She now admits she was scared at the sight of outsized puppet Big Bird.

Her bedtime stories were not nursery rhymes or Disney tales but complex tomes by Dostoyevsky and Henry Miller. Lullabies were by Janis Joplin or the Doors. Perhaps this early sampling of glitz and grit armed her for later exploits.

With her breeding, it was no surprise she was going to act and at just 11 months she made her screen debut, starring in a dog-food commercial. Concerned at the bizarre life-style led by child stars, her mother stopped auditioning her when she was 2. But by 4 Drew herself asked to be allowed to resume her career.

It was a matter of months before the chance for international fame came with auditions for the new Steven Spielberg film. Already a celebrated director, Spielberg was determined that this project would be the epic he dreamed of.

Carefully he scrutinized the 31 nervous hopefuls who lined up yearning for the part

of Gertie. One stood out as having enough sparkle and innate expertise for the demanding role. It was Drew.

For a while, Spielberg became the father-figure she yearned for.

'I wanted so badly to be accepted by him – and when I was, it meant so much to me,' said Drew later.

'I was thrilled when he invited me to his Malibu house. We'd run along the beach and build sandcastles. It was so much fun to be with him. But working with Steven was even better. Often he let me do whatever I wanted.

'He would often take me aside and ask if I could do something a different way. It made me feel so good. For once I didn't feel like some stupid kid. I felt important and useful.'

She recalls that making the film was the best time of her life. Her young head was brim-full of fantasies and make-believe, so it was a dream come true to be with the Spielberg creation E.T. every single day. It wasn't important that he was a studio-made dummy, reliant on special effects to come alive. To her eyes, he was real and she believed in him.

WITH A DRUNKEN FATHER, AND BULLIED AT SCHOOL, DREW'S LIFE WAS A MISERY.

Left: *Drew enjoyed few of the pleasures open to other children of her age after she was thrust into the limelight.*

Below: *Spielberg and E.T. The blockbuster film grossed more than $700 million and was seen by at least 240 million cinema visitors after its release in 1982.*

Above: *The screen kiss that sealed Drew's fate. Thousands were captivated by her, but the pressure of superstardom nearly wrecked her life.*

'On lunch breaks I'd take my food into the room where he was kept, sit down beside him and carry on a conversation while I ate.'

She stayed at the Universal Sheraton Hotel before the release of the film with her screen brothers Henry Thomas and Robert McNaughton, by now her closest friends.

At night they would keep themselves awake by telling each other ghost stories. During the day they would chase each other around and have wild food fights. They were larking about together when the TV flashed up how record cinema queues were forming to see the new hit film, *E.T.* 'We're in that,' screamed Drew breathlessly, but she had no idea how that one film would change her life for ever.

For Drew those happy months during and shortly after filming were the last vestiges of childhood that she could cling to.

NIGHTMARE FAME

When the film opened, it was a roaring hit. She describes it as like walking into a thunderstorm. Drew became public property with an army of fans made up of children and adults alike.

Every time she ventured out she found swarms of autograph-hunters at her heels. As she walked down the street people would point and stare. Some even called her E.T.

There was no all-embracing family life to protect her. Drew Barrymore's childhood was swallowed up by stardom.

'I was expected to be a role model after *E.T.* Kids loved me and I had thousands of fan letters. But the kids didn't know what I was going through. After *E.T.* it was like an earthquake. People wanted things from me and expected me to be much older. It was very frightening,' she explained.

The wrinkly alien she had once adored

turned into a spectre which was to haunt her. She was living the glittering life of a superstar – but deep inside she knew she would have swapped the trappings of Hollywood for the comfort and security of two loving parents.

Her father ignored the international acclaim won by his young daughter. He failed to acknowledge the heights to which she had been catapulted.

Meanwhile her mother, once a hard-working actress, gave up her career to become Drew's manager. Was the girl simply an unloved meal ticket?

Of course, her mother was only doing her level best to support young Drew, but through the child's eyes, it seemed a calculated and manipulative move. By now Drew was unmistakably different from other girls of her age, set apart by her life-style and her character. It wasn't long before she embarked on the addictive behaviour which seemed to be born to the Barrymores. At first, she got hooked on behaving outrageously, almost certainly to attract the attention of her mum.

Without the discipline of school, there was little to curb her wilful ways. And with estimated annual earnings of £100,000, it seemed no one could stop Drew from going her own way.

Aged 9 she was a pert young madam acting like a 29-year-old and relishing the opportunity to sample champagne. With that first glass of bubbly started a long-term addiction to drink. It was in the same year that she learned to drive and started smoking.

At 10 she was booked to fly to Germany for a three-hour television film called *Babes in Toyland*. She teamed up with pop legend Rod Stewart who had a gig in town and was thrilled to travel on his tour bus back to a hotel.

BLIND DRUNK

While the gravelly-voiced singer retired, Drew stayed up with members of the entourage and got blind drunk. At 4 am they decided to play musical instruments including trumpets and drums as loud as they could. The impromptu session ended when the hotel manager blazed at them, threatening to throw them out if the racket continued. In league with the rest, she made sure her mother didn't find out about

the incident. But at home with mum her life was far from normal.

Together with friends in the same jet-setting world, she would dress up in seductive mini-skirts, black lace blouses, high heels and make-up. Her mum mistook

the temptress garb as innocent dressing up. She would even compliment the girls on how lovely they looked. Then together they would visit a swish club. Parents instructed the youngsters to stay on a balcony overlooking the action while they danced below.

However, it gave the girls ample opportunity to sample the delights of the adult world. They would take it in turns to raid drinks left on the bar by unsuspecting clubbers. They would knock back anything that came their way.

And, of course, they took their place on the dance floor with the rest of the

THE WRINKLY ALIEN SHE'D ONCE ADORED TURNED INTO A GRUESOME SPECTRE WHICH RUINED HER YOUNG LIFE.

Above: *Drew giving an interview. While most children of her age were doing schoolwork, she became the darling of the media.*

Right: *Drew in make-up. She looked and behaved far older than her years.*

Below: *A sophisticated Drew out on the town.*

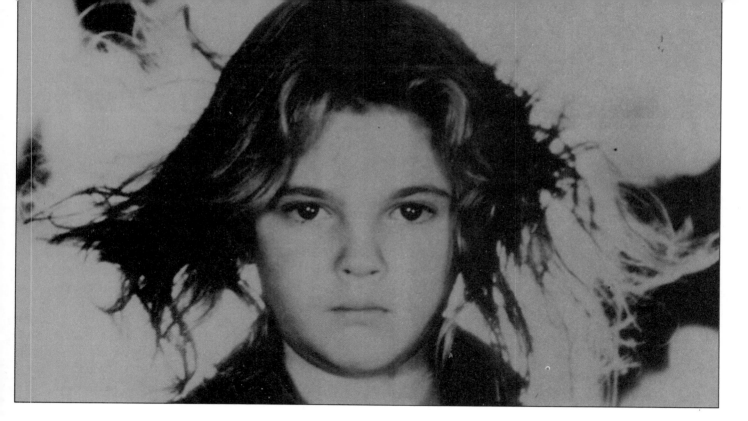

revellers, imitating the sexy swaying of the older women in the room.

It led to a banner headline: 'Drew Barrymore dancing at 2 am. Shouldn't she be in bed?'

But far from chastising the youngster, the headline made her determined no one would tell her what to do or how to do it.

It was on her way home from a club that she took her first marijuana. In the early hours she was going to spend the night at a friend's house when the young pal's mother lit up a pot-smoking pipe. Glancing around with a serene smile, the woman asked if anyone wanted to try it.

Without hesitation, Drew volunteered and soon mastered the technique of using the drug.

A few puffs left her helplessly giggling although she insisted between spasms of laughter that it was having no effect. Sure that she was in control, she wondered what taking cocaine would be like. She could not resist the prospect of experimenting.

Addiction to cocaine was no different for little rich kids like Drew than for ordinary drop-outs on the street. Quickly she was hooked and she craved her next fix of the designer drug. Without it, her palms began to sweat and she cannot remember without flinching how her head was filled with a flashing sign saying: 'Coke, get Coke'. The nightmare was well and truly under way.

A CRY FOR HELP

In her early teens Drew made a desperate bid to escape her private torment with a dramatic attempt at suicide.

It followed a row with her mum who then flew to New York. Drew found herself sobbing uncontrollably as she realized she was alone and totally lonely. Her mother's parting words were echoing in her ears: 'I have washed my hands of you, I don't give a damn what you do.' Drew was too distraught to understand the words were said on the spur of the moment and meant nothing. In an almost defiant gesture she took a knife from the kitchen and pulled it across her pale, vulnerable wrist.

She was saved by a friend who was alerted by Drew's hysterical telephone call. As Drew says later in her autobiography, *Little Girl Lost*, it was a cry for help. 'I wanted to get the most attention and sympathy. I didn't want to die.'

A family friend said at the time: 'Drew is a child who never was a child. She gets herself into adult situations. Everyone forgets she is only 14 years old.'

It was inevitable that she would end up in a clinic. Her admission into a therapy centre came after a noisy and violent row with her mother. Ignoring a midnight curfew, Drew drank, took drugs and then took exception to her mother. She rang and told her to get out of the house.

Left: *Little girl lost? In her autobiography, written when she was 14, Drew spoke frankly about her drug and drink dependency.*

THE KITCHEN KNIFE CUT ACROSS THE PALE, SOFT FLESH OF HER WRIST AND THE BLOOD SPURTED OUT.

Above: *Drew eventually found happiness after kicking drink and drugs. She once told reporters with a smile: 'I'm a girl who has lived a lotta life.'*

a regime of rules and regulations. It was easy to sneer at the soul-baring sessions to begin with and Drew only grudgingly joined in. But by the time she left a fortnight later to start a new film, she resolved to abandon the bottle.

It was easy enough at work to fight the urge for a drink – there were constant distractions, not to mention her mother's watchful gaze.

But at play the temptations were always at hand. Even friends who knew she was fighting against a drink-and-drugs habit would offer her alcohol and cocaine. The consequences were disastrous.

A fine record of 76 days without a drink was wiped out in one late-night session. With it went Drew's painfully constructed self-esteem. She vowed to escape by flying off to Hawaii.

When she returned home to pack some clothes she found a stranger in her room who snapped on some handcuffs. Her concerned mum had called agents from a drug centre who were willing to intervene to stop Drew's recklessness.

It wasn't the last time Drew would go to a centre to help control her addictive ways. And each time Drew was brought a bit closer to the realms of clean living that were her goal.

She began to learn that she had to face up to problems rather than hide behind drink and drugs. While they may have shielded her from the pain, they certainly didn't solve anything. In therapy she met other girls like herself who were running wild. It made her realize that, contrary to her beliefs, she was not isolated and alone.

The fact that Drew could write an action-filled autobiography when she was 14 is an indication of how extraordinary her early years were. She was fortunate in that her highly publicized descent from grace didn't end her career. In time producers got back in touch and she remained a hot property in Hollywood. In recent years she has proved she is no longer driven by drink. And she has reaped the rewards with major film roles including a sinister belle in *Gun Crazy* and a trickster in *Poison Ivy*.

Today she is more likely to stay at home lying on her sunflower bedspread and reading books or painting T-shirts than she is to go cavorting in clubs. The only

When she returned home just before dawn Drew was incensed to find her still there. She started throwing anything she could lay her hands on at her mum who looked on helplessly.

Suddenly, Ildiko picked up the telephone and called a friend. Drew, overcome by the drink and emotion, didn't resist their bid to take her to a clinic.

For the first time in years she was facing

addiction she has not been able to kick is a love of Camel cigarettes. She cherishes the time she spends with friends.

But it has taken years to reach this happy plateau. The hell-raising days didn't stop when the therapy was over. She was 15 when she paid £1,000 for four tattoos on her breast, backside, arm and ankle. And she continued to attend wacky parties despite her pledge of clean living.

She put her house on the market after being plagued by a night stalker who breached her home's security fences and peered in at the windows. At the time she revealed she frequently walks around California in disguise because the pressure of being recognized is so great.

BETRAYED

Her love life has been another disappointing tangle. She was paired with Balthazar Getty at 15, the son of ill-fated oil empire heir John Paul Getty III. He was there to listen and advise when she first began emerging from the haze of the addiction years. There were other more fleeting associations and finally an engagement to an engineer, but at 17 it fell apart because of the binding ties of her job.

Her life's major romance was to actor Jamie Walters. They too marked their love with a ring and dreamed of days growing old together. But their relationship floundered.

The film industry that she is mostly wedded to still pulls no punches. She played the lead role in *The Amy Fisher Story* about a Lolita who shot her lover's wife. She enacted a 10-second sex scene fully clothed.

Without her knowledge, the makers used a body double to spice up the story with lurid romps. Viewers believed the wild child was back to her old ways.

The betrayal enraged her. 'I'm not like that,' she insisted afterwards. But it seems unlikely that she will abandon her acting heritage despite the knocks it has dealt her.

'I was thrown into so much so soon. It was expected of the Barrymores.

'And I have to admit I couldn't cope with it all. Drugs and booze were both available. So I thought, why not?

'Everybody has to touch the stove to see how hot it is. I was never one of those people who could just hear about it. I always had to touch.'

> SHE SOUGHT PEACE BUT IT ELUDED HER: A NIGHT PROWLER STALKED THE GROUNDS OF HER HOME AND SPIED ON HER.

Below: *Drew won critical acclaim in* **Gun Crazy,** *a love-on-the-run story of murder and mayhem.*

VIV NICHOLSON
From spend, spend, spend
to scrub, scrub, scrub

Viv Nicholson had known only poverty and drudgery when a spectacular win on the pools transformed her life. But as she tried to spend her way to happiness, she discovered that money buys tragedy as well as joy.

The winners come and go. The jackpots get bigger every year. But for millions of Britain's ever-hopeful pools punters only one name lingers as 'the' winner who cornered the market in fame.

Her name is Viv Nicholson. Her edict was 'spend, spend, spend'. And perhaps more than any other living Brit she has gone from rags to riches and back in record time.

Viv was born in a two-up-two-down terrace home – No 38, Walling Street, Wheldon Lane, Castleford – on 3 April 1936. She was working from the moment her little limbs were strong enough, picking coal off the local pit-head tip or pea-picking in the nearby fields.

Her dad George, an epileptic, worked occasionally down the pit after failing to make it as a policeman and as a soldier in the Guards. For many of those early years Viv remembers the family income (his sick pay) disappearing behind the bar of the local.

At school she was good at art, sport and Bible classes but admitted she 'got the stick a lot on my backside'. She'd often play truant, spending her dinner money at the flicks or posing in front of the boys she fancied outside their school. Weekends she'd work in her Aunt Liz's shop, help her mum look after the younger kids and then make the evening trek to the pub to pick up her dad's beer.

Even her first wages from the nearby Liquorice Allsorts factory were handed over to the old man. She'd get back half-a-crown pocket money – if she was lucky – and had to supplement her wages working at the Queens, the town cinema, until 11 pm. It was there she met a soldier called Barry and began necking with him. He would write her explicit and raunchy love-letters and in her biography *Spend, Spend, Spend*, she vividly recalls the beating her dad handed out when he discovered them.

'He hit me on the ribs at the side which he knew would cave me in anyway. Then he picked me up and he hit me again on the other side. I kept falling. I had a bloody lump on the side of my head where I'd hit the corner of this oak chair and my eye hit the other side of it.

'... Afterwards I was bad: I was vomiting all night, my head hurt, I didn't know which part of me to hold.'

After that Viv decided that if you got beaten for NOT having sex she might as well go ahead and try it. She lost her virginity to a young miner called Matthew Johnson – he would become her first husband – in his bedroom. Quickly she got pregnant from the affair and, despite her father's grumbles, decided to marry. She was 16, he was 23.

The relationship turned into a sham almost overnight. Viv rejected Matt's advances even as she waited to have his baby, Stephen. She said later that the

Opposite: *Viv Nicholson in 1971. Her image graced Fleet Street tabloids for years.*

Below: *Viv, second husband Keith and Bruce Forsyth at the cheque-presentation ceremony.*

Above: Viv borrowed the brolly and bowler belonging to Littlewoods' chief Cecil Moore for this famous pose.

THEY WERE SO POOR THAT VIV'S DINNER WAS A SLICE OF BREAD, USED TO WIPE THE KIDS' PLATES CLEAN.

---

prospect of raising children frightened her, though she stressed she loved the child deeply, and later admitted: 'At 17, stuck in that bleeding house baby minding I was only a kind of kid myself.

'I thought what a fool I was. But I'd enjoyed what I'd done so that is what you get for what you enjoy. That's what I told myself.'

BEG, STEAL OR BORROW

Things improved slightly when she and Matt moved out of his mother's place into a council house in Duke Street, but it wasn't to last. Viv had spied the handsome young miner living next door, called Keith Nicholson, and set about seducing him. Just as quickly she became pregnant with Sue and the marriage to Matt finally broke down.

More children followed – Timmy and Howard – and Viv and Keith moved out to a bigger house shortly before the divorce

was sealed. They married, but found the going tough. Keith's trainee wage was barely enough to see them through the week.

Viv said: 'The little bit he did get wasn't blinding worth it. It didn't go far.

'But I made sure those kids really had their fill. I'd only have what was left, even if it was just a little bit of mashed potato. I'd make about four potato sandwiches out of it for me and I'd really thoroughly enjoy it.

'Then I'd get my bread and chase it round their plates for a bit of dip. I hardly once sat down to a good square meal.

'... Keith thought he was providing money for us. You see, he didn't care how I managed. He brought home £7 or £8 a week clear, and I never told him I had to beg, steal or borrow.

'He thought we were doing great guns on it because although I hardly had enough to eat we had a three-piece suite, nice red carpet, nice little table lamp, a rented TV, eventually, and a standard lamp – all got on tick, of course.'

On 23 September 1961, Keith was, as usual, keeping an ear on the Saturday afternoon football results. He knew the numbers he'd picked but was also realistic enough to know the enormous odds stacked against him getting a big win.

He was shaving ready to go out that evening and as the fifth draw came up – he needed eight for a possible jackpot – remarked to Viv: 'It's a start love, eh?'

He'd cut his chin when number 5 was announced and he cut it again when 6 came up. At 7 he was grabbing a towel to staunch the blood pouring from the neck wounds and shouting 'That's it, that's it!'

He was celebrating what he thought would be a payout of a few hundred pounds but he was way out in his calculations. Excitedly he and Viv recovered their crumpled copy of the coupon from his trousers. Then she rushed to get her dad, who returned with the local Saturday sports paper. He and Keith lay on the floor as the old man checked the numbers.

'Tha's right Keith, there's seven draws, lad.'

Then a short pause and, almost as an afterthought: 'Tha's got the eighth too, Keith.'

Viv said: 'We wanted to celebrate and we had £1 between us.

'So I borrowed a few quid from my dad, who hadn't cared much for Keith till then, extracted the family allowance from my mother and off we all went to the local.'

THE TASTE OF FAME

Viv could take none of it in, not even when they sent off the telegram claim. It wasn't until 1.45 pm the following Monday that she began to believe she could be rich beyond imagination. She was making chip butties at the time.

There was a knock on the door and a fat man with grey hair asked: 'Does Keith Nicholson live here? I'm sorry we are a bit late but we are from Littlewoods Pools.'

Keith had ticked the no-publicity box on his coupon but got talked out of it by the PR men. The Nicholsons were taken to the Metropole Hotel in Leeds, out of the way of the hunting press men, before catching a train to London on the Wednesday.

Littlewoods, who had already paid out £200,000 to a winner in 1957, knew they were in for a good press, but even the most optimistic of their marketing people could never have dreamt so much free publicity was about to come their way.

So it was that when the 7 am train from Leeds pulled up in London Viv Nicholson tasted fame for the first time. A throng of reporters and photographers besieged her on the platform. One asked the inevitable question: 'What are you going to do with the money, Viv?'

Quick as a flash back came the reply: 'I'm going to spend, spend, spend.'

And spend they did. The only thing that stopped them starting right away was the insatiable demand of Fleet Street. Viv was photographed smiling at Bruce Forsyth, who presented her with the cheque, and then close to tears when she realized it was made out for £152,319. She was snapped dancing, jumping, hugging, even high-kicking in a famous pose which used Littlewoods' chief Cecil Moore's brolly and bowler as props.

Then it was an expensive hairdo (pink champagne blonde) followed by a trip to the Palladium to see Sammy Davis Junior and a Soho nightclub. Finally she and Keith returned to their suite at the Grosvenor Hotel and bathed in champagne and brandy.

From there it was back to Castleford and a free drinks party at their local pub, the Miners' Arms. It cost £200 – eight months' wages then – and Viv later described it as a

> **THEY CELEBRATED BY BATHING IN CHAMPAGNE AND BRANDY – AND THAT WAS ONLY THE BEGINNING OF THEIR WILD SPENDING SPREE.**

Below: *There was a lot of sneering and sniping in the press after Viv bought her dream home. But she didn't care.*

Above: *The sweet-factory girl made good. Fur coats and fast cars were suddenly no more than a signed cheque away for Viv and she realised every opportunity to unload her winnings.*

bloody battlefield. But that was only the start. Viv bought a new car – an American Chevrolet, a £500 organ and a new house, No 11 Grange Avenue. She watched the begging (and hate) letters come and go and entertained hundreds of total strangers who'd start by buying her a drink and then expect the next ten rounds to be hers. Generous to a fault, Viv never failed to disappoint them.

By now the kids were in a private boarding school and Keith and Viv were free to throw party after party, to the chagrin of their new middle-class neighbours. Many would go on for days, lubricated by a seemingly unending supply of booze.

Keith, meanwhile, could indulge his love of fast cars. He also bought racehorses and top-of-the range shotguns and would laugh at the notion of rubbing shoulders with the nobs at Ascot or blazing away at grouse on some remote northern moor.

They were halcyon days and son Tim would later recall: 'It was like living on the edge of a volcano.

'Me and the other kids never knew what she was going to do next. There would be late-night parties, with Sparrow – we all call her that – bringing people she hardly knew in for free drinks. I don't resent her getting rid of all the money although, like everyone else, I would sooner be in a nice house with a decent car outside.

'They were only living on £7 per week when they won the pools. It's no wonder it went to their heads but it's no use worrying now the money is gone. My mother is kind and generous. I've seen her spend her last pound on a round of drinks.'

In her book Viv recalled: 'I was becoming an alcoholic ... it would always be somebody's birthday or something.

'We'd even throw a party for a dog's birthday because we needed people.'

Only months after the big win had sunk in the money was draining away. Viv had taken little heed of the advice offered by the financial consultants put forward by Littlewoods. Her idea of investment was putting money into fun and she was not planning to waste time.

By 1964 Viv and Keith had spent around one-third of the money. The pressure of getting rich quick was now telling on

Right: *The serious-looking gentlemen with Viv were her financial advisers. They had every reason to look serious. As fast as they tried to invest her 'luvverly lolly' she blew it.*

Keith. He couldn't understand why the bank was hassling him over an overdraft when he had £100,000 invested. In anger and frustration he'd tell Viv: 'Why don't they just take it out and stop pestering me and do what the hell they have to do with it? I've my life to lead.'

He would refuse even to open bank statements and would sometimes burn tax demands. And still neither of them wanted to put the brakes on their spending.

That year they chose just about the most expensive – and lengthy – holiday they could find. Viv wanted to see Dallas on the first anniversary of President John Kennedy's death, but they also took in Los Angeles and New York, and the bills kept on coming.

By the standards of the nineties their windfall was worth more than a million, to them a bottomless pit of cash. But it couldn't last. In 1965 the pit of cash was replaced by the pit of despair.

In later interviews Viv always insisted the loss of the 'luvverly lolly' didn't worry her. She'd set out to have a good time and that's exactly what she'd done. After all nothing was for ever, was it?

DISASTER STRIKES

Then that year Keith was killed in a car crash and Viv discovered the true meaning of loss. Her world fell apart. She later spoke of him as the only one of her five husbands she'd ever truly loved.

Keith had been on his way back from Wetherby races when it happened. By astonishing coincidence – Viv later believed it was a sign from beyond the grave – her own brand-new Chevrolet broke down at almost exactly the same moment as she drove to see relations in Sheffield. In her grief she took to drinking and popping the occasional sleeping pill. On one occasion the memories overwhelmed her and she packed the kids into a car to go and visit Keith's grave at midnight, a kind of crude but heartfelt therapy to assuage the tremendous loss they all felt. Later she admitted: 'I was so bad tempered. Talk about Jekyll and Hyde.'

In those difficult months Viv found herself living off a widow's pension and social security benefit. Keith's death meant his £100,000 estate was frozen. Even the £10 they found on his body was taken away. The bank called her and told her that all she had was £10 per week to live on from a trust fund.

She recalled how one bank official told her: 'Well, what a life.

'You've had three different kinds of lives: you've had poverty, you've had the very rich and what's this got to be? It's got to be the middle class, hasn't it?'

Viv, who now owed the bank £4,000, decided to fight to get her share of the will. She survived by bouncing the occasional cheque and selling what possessions she could. It wasn't until months later that she was awarded £34,000 by a court for proving that the stake money was hers. She put £14,000 into the kids' school trust fund and blew the rest: a holiday in Malta while she searched to buy a business, another new car, and then a fashion shop in Castleford.

It was a disastrous venture and by the time the VAT and tax people had taken

THE FRIGHTENED CHILDREN WERE BUNDLED INTO THE CAR FOR A MIDNIGHT VISIT TO KEITH'S GRAVE.

Below: *Viv could never resist posing for a camera and she made the most of her numerous wedding days. Here the lucky man is Graham Ellison. She thought he was terribly handsome … but the marriage lasted just six months.*

Above: *With fourth husband Brian Wright on their wedding day. He proved a jealous lover.*

Right: *With Gary Shaw, husband number 5. He and Keith were her true lovers.*

HAUNTED BY THE PAST, VIV TOOK ONE PILL, AND THEN ANOTHER, AND THEN ANOTHER …

---

their share, Viv Nicholson was back where she started. Living in Castleford. And broke.

Lonely – but determined not to be – Viv set out to seek true love once more. It proved a fruitless search that saw her take on, and lose, a string of husbands. As she put it: 'Falling in love … that's what life is all about, isn't it?'

Throughout the rest of the sixties and early seventies Viv tested that theory to its limits. Sadly, true love always seemed to be one step away. Marriage number 3 was to car salesman Graham Ellison, but they stayed together for only six months. 'He was terribly handsome,' Viv would admit later. 'He used to call me Mags Diamond.'

Fourth husband was nightclub doorman Brian Wright. He proved to be a jealous lover and the relationship was marked by almost constant bickering. Wright later died, again in a car crash.

Fifth – and last – spouse was Gary Shaw. He died in her arms from a drugs overdose just seven weeks after they exchanged their vows. It left her totally distraught. Gary was later buried beside her beloved Keith.

In 1978 all the anguish of those difficult years came to a head. By now Viv was getting the first warnings from doctors to kick her 20-a-day smoking habit and give up alcohol. They argued it would be better for her health and help control her arthritis and stomach ulcers.

She did, in fact, try to go on the wagon but later declared: 'They were the most miserable three weeks of my life.

'Doctors told me I would end up in an emergency ward if I did not change my ways.

'There is no fun at all in going out for a night and sipping orange juice with a long face. I have taken my life into my own hands.'

They were brave words but Viv's past still haunted – and taunted – her. On 4 February 1978 she came within a whisker of following three of her husbands to the grave. From her Castleford home she telephoned a friend and revealed she'd taken some sleeping tablets. The friend didn't like the sound of her voice and decided to call an ambulance, just to be on the safe side.

When the crew dashed into her house at 4 am they found her lying unconscious in a bedroom. She was immediately admitted to hospital as an emergency, but later Viv insisted she hadn't deliberately taken an overdose. In one remarkably frank interview she said: 'There is a 36-hour gap in my life. I have no idea what happened.'

A SECRET FEAR

She speaks of waking up in the Pontefract Infirmary with a 'secret fear' engulfing her. It had been brought on by the glimpse of an old lady in a nearby bed. In that woman's tired, worn face Viv saw herself in years to come and began to realize her own mortality. She told of feeling a desperate urge to escape, of an obsession about getting old and of the anguish she endured watching her father take two years to finally die at the age of 60. Perhaps most telling of all she spoke of 'getting out' while she still looked good.

Viv added: 'I want to be remembered as a striking lady with sex appeal.

'When I look at actresses like Bette Davis and see how they have wilted I think it is a pity that somehow their beauty couldn't be preserved. I want the impossible. I want time to be stopped. I want to turn the clock back.'

In the interview Viv returned again and again to her 'hobby horse' – the fears felt by women as they grew older and realized that sex appeal had a shelf life. Men, she said, could still pull the birds when they got old and wrinkly. Women saw this happening and feared being left alone.

She spoke of herself as being 'halfway to Paradise' at 41 and admitted it was the 'decay of the body' that scared her.

She added: 'I know it's time I started settling down. I don't want to get to 50 and meet some guy who will just be a fireside companion.'

She spoke of how fame, and her reputation for walking on the wild side of life, had made her almost an oracle in the eyes of some young men. 'Guys come up to me with problems about their wives,' she said. 'They are mainly young men. They complain that their wives won't even discuss sex problems with them. I have to answer the best way and show that I am interested. Women who are having trouble with their husbands also expect me to know all the answers.

'In fact, I sometimes feel like the Marje Proops of Castleford.'

Released from hospital Viv returned home with a new-found optimism, yet she had hardly had time to fully recover from the overdose scare before the next crisis developed. She was stopped by police on

suspicion of drink-driving and accused of failing to provide a specimen for lab tests. In fact, a court later found her not guilty of driving while unfit through drink.

But magistrates still ordered her to pay £294 in fines and compensation and banned her from driving. Viv was outraged and promptly vowed to go to prison rather than stump up the cash for what she saw as trumped-up charges. She claimed she was 'sick and tired of being harassed by the police'.

Sure enough the fines stayed unpaid and she was given a 6-week sentence at the 'Grisly Risley' remand centre near Warrington, Cheshire. It was perhaps the lowest point of her amazing life. Stories appeared in the papers describing how she was given a job cleaning the floor of a prison corridor known among inmates as the Golden Mile.

Under the headline 'Scrub, Scrub, Scrub Viv' it was claimed she worked for just 49p per week to buy cigarettes. Yet once the sentence was over she was quickly back to her old self … and again looking for love.

JINXED

Twice she thought she'd found husband number 6. Each time her hopes were sadly dashed. First came a 25-year-old divorcé,

Above: *Viv's children Steve and Sue call at 'Grisly Risley' remand centre, where Viv was taken to serve her sentence.*

Above: *Viv and Bernard Curran. But wedding number 6 never happened.*

Son Howard Nicholson later revealed there had been a last-minute disagreement between the couple. It was two years before Viv tried again, this time to a man she met in a whirlwind romance. She accepted his proposal but then ditched him when she found out he was already married.

He pleaded that he was separated and had planned to wed her after his divorce came through. But it was no good. Viv declared he'd tried to make a fool of her and he was kicked out of her life.

It seemed, in her own words, that she was just 'a born loser' in love and marriage. In the past she had often talked of a jinx on her life, a belief heightened when the actress Susan Littler (who played her in the award-winning TV play *Spend, Spend, Spend*) succumbed to cancer aged just 33. Yet by now a subtle transformation was beginning in Viv Nicholson. For the first time in her life she had begun to take a genuine interest in religion and found she could look beyond the frustrations and pain that so dominated her days as Britain's best-known pools winner.

She was persuaded to go along to the local Kingdom Hall meeting of Jehovah's Witnesses. And she later recalled: 'Everyone was so happy I just cried.'

In August 1982 Viv appeared on the BBC 1 series *Sin on Saturday* to talk about the deadly effects of covetousness. In an interview published that day she joked that she didn't even know what covet meant until she joined the Witnesses.

Bernard Curran, 16 years her junior. He was a market trader in children's clothes and Viv would joke that she'd finally managed to marry into money.

But on the big day – fixed for 13 May 1978 – neither of them turned up. A congregation of around 600 had to kick their heels outside the Castleford register office before eventually giving up and going home.

Right: *Viv with her sons Steve and Howard in March 1977.*

Through them, she said, almost all traces of her old existence had disappeared.

'I was always the one to go from the sublime to the ridiculous,' she said. 'I've never been the halfway type. At a crossroads I've always wanted to go all four ways. I'd probably have finished up in a mental home if I hadn't let it all hang out. I was always rebelling against my father. But Jehovah accepts you when you're ready to give up your past and I've finally found the real me.

'It's hard work coveting things, believe me. I couldn't sleep at night for worrying about things I wanted. Jehovah's Witnesses's beliefs are contrary to everything I've ever done. But I've never been as happy in my life. You don't give up the seven deadly sins to be unhappy, do you?'

She made it clear she no longer accepted the idea of a jinx on her life, even though she'd been through a recent cancer scare (two aunts died of the disease). The cancer tests were clear and she regards the whole upsetting episode philosophically as the will of Jehovah.

As for publicity and the TV appearance – no, she didn't much like publicity, she said, but she'd made an exception for *Sin on Saturday*.

'I love Jehovah and thought I'd have a go at witnessing for Him on TV since the Witnesses never get a plug on the Sunday religious shows.'

Viv speaks with pride of the 'services' she carries out – door-to-door preaching aimed at persuading more people to join her religion. Far from the popular belief that Jehovah's Witnesses are used to slammed doors, she remembers only one rebuff that really hurt.

'It was many years ago; a lady came to the door who'd had a recent bereavement, she'd lost her father.

'I said: "Don't worry, Jehovah will return him." She said: "You can talk; how many husbands have you had back?"

'I suppose she was reacting to the bad profile the press has given me over the years. I keep a chart of the man-hours I put in. If someone new is baptized I don't take it as a personal compliment but as a sign that God is working through me.

'It's good that we work with the angels who guide us to the right doors. We are taught to be humble.'

THE SIMPLE LIFE

In one interview, in 1989, she revealed: 'Sometimes people ask: "Aren't you Viv Nicholson?" I reply: "Yes, what's left of her." But people still talk about me because I know how to live life and they've never tried it.

'They need a psychiatrist. I don't because I've worked out my problems. I studied the Bible and found it was the truth.'

Viv's life is now a world apart from that of the excitable extrovert who first shot to fame so many years ago. She now speaks with fondness of the simple pleasures in her life – completing *The Sun* crossword, reading her copy of the Witnesses' journal, *Watchtower*, or spending time with her grandchildren. She enjoys ironing and vacuuming, household chores which she finds soothe her thoughts.

And she's not too proud to work – a part-time post in a perfume shop, paying less than £100 per week, has been among the jobs she's taken.

'People ask me if I still do the pools,' she says. 'Of course I don't, it's against my religion. I miss absolutely nothing from the past. I mean, once I could drink in the pub all evening, get through money like there was no tomorrow.

'True, I had a lot of fun but it's hard work having money and I certainly did spend.

'I wouldn't want it again.'

'THE ANGELS GUIDE US TO THE RIGHT DOORS. WE ARE TAUGHT TO BE HUMBLE.'

Below: *In 1984, with the money long gone, Viv is just another grandmother.*

MARLENE DIETRICH
Falling in love again

She'd dreamed of being a concert violinist but fate put paid to her dreams. Instead Marlene Dietrich was destined to become one of Hollywood's most famous actresses, and notorious for her outrageous love life.

A bowed figure patiently pressed the bell of an apartment block in a Parisian avenue.

His hair was grey, his lean face lined, but there was no mistaking the identity of the caller. It was James Stewart, matinee idol and Hollywood legend. Even in his 70s, his presence was enough to cause a stir.

He waited for the door to open. He could reasonably have expected it to be flung wide for a greeting of kisses and joyous exclamations. But the welcome he had hoped for was not forthcoming. Instead the door was opened just a few inches. Peering out from the shadows was an equally famous face from Hollywood's heyday, but there were no smiles, no embraces, no warmth at all.

No, he could not come in. And no, she would not come out. After a tense exchange, James Stewart departed, bemused and anxious.

For half a century they had been friends. Now screen goddess Marlene Dietrich was refusing to meet him. As she closed the door in his face, her pain was palpable. She couldn't bear a man who had once surveyed her fabulous body with pleasure and longing to see it raddled by old age. Brittle bones beneath a withering skin were frequently fractured and left her in constant distress. The lines of agony were etched on to a face which was once as smooth as an apple. The hair was now limp and lacklustre thin. None of this was surprising.

Marlene was born at the turn of the century. Now it was the closing quarter and

she had aged in the same way as the world about her, but Marlene had no time for the toll of the rolling years.

Seven years after she kept Stewart on the doorstep he returned with fellow actor Roddy McDowall. This time they were graciously allowed an audience. Afterwards she commented bitterly: 'James has a beer belly, I can hardly walk. We are both ancient ruins.'

He wasn't the only pal she refused to acknowledge. She met film director Billy Wilder in 1928 – he was her oldest surviving associate from the film industry – but even he received a cold shoulder. 'I call her up whenever I'm in Paris. She answers in a different accent every time, either French, Polish or Czech, telling me Miss Dietrich has gone to Switzerland.

'I always call her bluff. I say: "For Christ's sake, Marlene, cut the bull. I know it's you." She then either hangs up or invents some phoney reason why she can't see me. She doesn't want to be reminded of the past.'

For 15 years the performer and party-goer who was escorted by some of the

Above: *Billy Wilder, one of Marlene's oldest friends. He said of her: 'I call her up whenever I'm in Paris. She answers in a different accent every time ... telling me Miss Dietrich has gone to Switzerland. I always call her bluff.'*

Opposite: *Marlene, the screen goddess.*

century's most adored men shunned the public's gaze. Fiercely private, she allowed only a few chosen people to witness her physical degeneration. They included her secretary, a radio producer and her butcher. The lonely and frugal life she led in the years leading up to her death in 1992 were a stark contrast to her opulent existence as screen queen during some four decades.

Marlene was born as the world bade farewell to the 19th century. A consensus of opinion puts the date at 27 December 1901. She contradicted herself on numerous occasions about the date, finding pleasure in feeding the confusion.

DIVIDED LOYALTIES

Her father was a police lieutenant, Louis Erich Otto Dietrich, former Cavalry major who served with honours in the Franco-Prussian War of 1870–71. His courage in the field won him the Iron Cross. The household reflected his military background. It was well ordered and respectful, and the abiding memory Marlene had of her father was his shiny leather boots and the whip he cracked regularly to instil discipline in his daughters.

In 1883 he took a 17-year-old wife, Wilhelmina Elisabeth Josephine Felsing, the daughter of an eminent watchmaker, who bore him a daughter, Elisabeth, followed a year later by the little Marlene.

Her full name was Marie Magdalene Dietrich – the stage name she adopted telescoped her pretty Christian names – and she entered the world in Schoneberg, Germany. Later, she lived in both Berlin and the attractive district of Weimar.

At the knee of their forthright and fierce mother, Elisabeth and Marlene learned the skills of which Prussian women were most proud – cookery, needlework, flower arranging and the art of running a household. They were talents she took pride in throughout her sparkling career into her old age. Wherever she went neighbours grew used to the sight of the elegant and stylish Miss Dietrich, unrecognizable in a headscarf and pinny, on her knees scrubbing her own front doorstep.

Also in the home, she was introduced at an early age to the literary greats so beloved by the Germans: Goethe, Schiller and Heine were the favoured writers in the Dietrich household. Marlene and her sister learned their masterpieces by rote and read aloud to each other on long, quiet Sunday afternoons. It was an ideal grounding for the profession she chose much later.

She went to a well-thought-of girls' school where she was shy, religious and a dedicated pupil. While she abhorred games, her favourite subjects were French and literature. She was also an accomplished violin player. Paradoxically, she became

Below: *The Wintergarten theatre in Berlin, where Marlene spent much of her early life.*

furious when people repeatedly thought her younger than her years.

In 1911 her father died. Her mother married again, another military man who perished in the carnage of World War 1. During the war, Marlene joined other womenfolk knitting clothes for soldiers, humming patriotic songs and never complaining about the food shortages. But in her heart she was divided. The nation's enemy was France, yet French-speaking Marlene adored all that was Gallic and always had done.

It was with relief that she greeted the end of the conflict when her loyalties were no longer split. She decided to study the violin at the Konservatorium in Weimar. There, her teacher was Professor Paul Elgers. Wolfgang Rose – nephew of the composer Gustave Mahler – who was also there later recalled: 'I will never forget the sensation Marlene caused when she arrived to study the violin with Elgers. Her beauty astonished us all and the young men were lining up to take her out. But she was not at all flighty. She was very modest and shy and seemed almost unaware of her loveliness.'

An injury to her finger put an end to any dream of becoming a concert violinist. Despite opposition from her family, she plumped for a career as an actress instead.

She moved alone to Berlin where she took lessons from an eccentric English woman called Elsie Grace. In her spare time she earned commission as a gloves saleswoman and found some popularity as a dancer and singer in the town's swinging cabaret clubs. Her aim was to join the prestigious Max Reinhardt drama school but she failed her audition and had to make do with private tuition from a teacher.

OUTRAGEOUS LIFE-STYLE

Soon she was trying her luck at auditions across the city. It was during one such reading – for a part in a silent film called *The Tragedy of Love* starring idol of the era Emil Jannings – that she met her husband.

Rudi Sieber was a production assistant, aged 25 and tall with blond hair and a muscular frame. The instant she entered the building he noticed her – it was difficult not to. Marlene had honed an outrageous dress sense which had her wearing red fox furs or wolf skins instead of the plain woollen coats more usual on the streets of Berlin at the time. Not only that, she arrived at the studio holding a puppy which tugged her this way and that on its lead.

With help from Rudi she won the part of the svelte girlfriend of a prosecutor in a murder trial. Although her time on screen was limited, it was enough to sow the seeds of a legend. For her role she donned a monocle which had belonged to her father. The image was instantly seized by the underworld of gays and lesbians as a trademark.

The marriage of Sieber and Marlene was followed eight months later with the arrival of a daughter, Maria. For some eight

THE MODEST GIRL WAS QUICKLY SEDUCED BY THE DECADENT NIGHTLIFE OF BERLIN.

Below: *Marlene with her daughter, Maria, whom she loved and left.*

Above: *Marlene in top hat and tails, the garb which became her trademark.*

MARLENE FLAUNTED HER SEXUALITY AND BOTH MEN AND WOMEN LUSTED AFTER HER.

months Marlene gave up her ambitions to look after the baby which bewitched her. Aged 22, she found joy in feeding, dressing and walking her lovely baby.

But her contentment which grew from the homemaker skills she had learned as a girl did not provide sufficient satisfaction for a woman with a destiny.

Her place was on the big screen where her elemental appeal would explode like a storm. When she went back to the world of theatre and film, Rudi stayed at home to care for their child and he quickly realized his wife would never be tamed. Marlene struck up various liaisons, apparently discussing her infidelity openly at home.

By 1927 Rudi had fallen in love with Russian dancer Tamara Matul – she became Marlene's unofficial replacement for both little Maria and Rudi. But Rudi and Marlene never divorced. Indeed, he remained a loyal ally until his death, when she mourned as any widow would.

In her diary in later years she wrote: 'My husband is an extraordinary man and I want to pay all my homage to him. He has guided me through all my turbulent life, never thinking of himself, only for me and our daughter. He said *"merde"* to all the dirty insinuations and kept on his chosen way to be all he promised me and much, much more.

'We never lied to each other from the time we married. His love for me was greater than I understood then. I was not very bright when I was young … It had to do with his complete acceptance of me, all my faults included.

'He knows what is right and wrong which I don't, except in the basic rules of life. He would always steer me in the right direction: that is the essence of our relationship.

'Although we have been apart geographically we are tied eternally. I am certain no such relationship exists between any other two people.'

LESBIAN LOVE

Marlene, meanwhile, was becoming an enigma in the Germany of the 'Roaring Twenties'. As Germany shed the austerity of its Prussian past and World War 1 defeat, a liberation spread among its young, vibrant people. Marlene was part of the sexual revolution, and it appears she, ranking alongside many leading figures of the day, was flagrantly bisexual.

She was the only woman allowed to attend the annual male transvestite ball in Berlin, arriving in top hat and tails. As well as socializing with transvestite clubs, she became infamous for her performance of a duet with another woman actress clutching a bunch of violets, the floral symbol of lesbian love in the city.

Rumours about her sexuality gained momentum throughout her career. There were hordes of male admirers, of course, but her name was romantically linked with cabaret star Claire Waldoff, actresses Claudette Colbert and Lili Damita – later Mrs Errol Flynn – and society darling Mercedes de Acosta.

Biographer David Brett insists: 'Marlene denied any lesbian affairs. In fact, she was virulently anti-gay.'

Yet her own daughter Maria Riva, whose book wasn't published until after Marlene's death, details how she took women as well as men to bed.

Sailing to America at the start of the thirties, she is said to have invited a fellow woman passenger to her cabin to woo her with champagne and violets. When Marlene produced a book on lesbian love the woman stalked out. Marlene merely shrugged and said: 'In Europe it doesn't matter if you're a man or a woman. We make love with anyone we find attractive.'

She told critic Kenneth Tynan the lesbian rumours were merely a useful diversionary tactic which added to her allure. Yet her former secretary Bernard Hall is certain where her tastes lay. 'Emotionally, she was a man. She went to bed with men to give them pleasure but her strongest feelings were for women.'

At any rate, she refused to deny the lesbian rumours. Mostly, when confronted, she would roar with laughter at the suggestion of having women lovers. The sexual grey mists she created clearly amused her.

Her first film role earned her accolades in Germany. Offers of work came pouring in, and already she was earning a reputation for being stroppy on set. On one film she refused to do profile shots because it revealed a tilt at the end of her nose. The director was furious but she remained stubborn and won the day.

But there was an appealing vulnerability in her brittle, ambitious character too. Her love of music, for example, endeared her to fellow actors. Often she would give impromptu recitals on the musical saw which she mastered in those early Berlin years. She was also known for carrying a Negro doll given to her in childhood as a good-luck charm.

Before long, the biggest break of her career offered itself in the form of the sleazy singer Lola-Lola in *The Blue Angel*. Joseph von Sternberg, an eminent Austro-American director in charge of the film, was captivated by Marlene's beauty, but he also saw a sensual talent which was tailor-made for the part. While other leading actresses were tipped for the coveted part, it was Marlene who was triumphant.

The film had Emil Jannings in the part of a stuffy professor who falls head over heels for a cabaret singer-cum-trollop. They wed but soon she is bored. Heartbroken and humiliated, the professor returns to his classroom to die.

In the film Marlene was mesmerizing in a top hat, silk stockings and black suspenders. She also first crooned the

melody which became her hallmark. 'Falling in Love Again' was instantly memorable and much admired, thanks to the guttural style which was all her own. Emil Jannings was bitter at being upstaged. A scene which had the professor attacking Lola-Lola became all too real when an enraged Jannings gripped Marlene by the neck, leaving finger-marks in the soft skin for weeks afterwards. He

was dragged off by stage-hands. The tension between them reverberates through the film.

At the time of its release *Variety* said: 'It will undoubtedly do splendidly in the whole of Europe and should also appeal strongly in the States ... its only fault is a certain ponderousness of tempo which tends to tire.'

Ponderous or not, it was a huge hit and had American star spotters knocking at

Above: *Marlene as Lola-Lola in* **The Blue Angel,** *a role she grew to despise.*

HITLER WANTED HER TO BE HIS LOVER – BUT SHE LAUGHED IN HIS FACE.

Marlene's door. She signed for Paramount Pictures and set sail for the USA, leaving Rudi and Maria in Germany.

THE HORRORS OF NAZISM

It was a well-timed exit. Her homeland was in the grip of burgeoning Nazism which spiralled during the early thirties until Hitler was finally in command. Marlene herself had no time for his brand of national socialism and was sympathetic to the Jews he persecuted.

Later she would not only turn down a personal invitation from Hitler to return to Germany – which many might have taken as an order – but also spurned the opportunity to become his lover. Her pet name for the Führer was 'that horrible little dwarf'. She commented lazily: 'He promised me a triumphal entry into Berlin. I'm afraid I laughed.'

She was furious with her fellow Germans for allowing the dictator to hold sway and bring ruination to the country and its people. At the end of the war she discovered her own sister Elisabeth was a victim of the harsh regime. The modestly living teacher had been confined as a privileged prisoner in the death camp, Belsen. Marlene ducked out of her high-flying career to nurse her sister back to health. She also supported Elisabeth financially until her death. Much later she visited the house of Anne Frank, the Dutch girl killed by occupying Nazis, and emerged wordless with her eyes red-rimmed from crying.

The horror of the Nazis was a world away, though, as she sailed from Germany in 1930. She may not have been fêted on her arrival – newspapers hardly carried a line – but she soon whipped up a storm. Marlene, who wore trousers in Berlin without raising an eyebrow, generated shock waves when she slipped into slacks in the conservative USA. In fact, she insisted on wearing them when the dismay of the studio bosses became apparent. It was a gamble which she won hands down. Before long women across the country were imitating the casual style.

Teaming up with her in the USA was Von Sternberg, who soon added to her notoriety by having her kiss a fellow actress full on the lips in her first American

Above: Von Sternberg, the director who helped to launch her career.

Right: Marlene and her husband Rudi, bound for the United States on the SS Berengaria in 1937.

film, *Morocco*. She was the manipulative cabaret singer who finally fell in love. She was reluctant to repeat the role of good-time girl but Von Sternberg was insistent. And he was right. One review read: 'A definite step forward in the art of motion pictures' while another enthused: 'Brilliant, profuse, subtle and at almost every turn inventive'. It earned Dietrich and Von Sternberg each an Academy Award nomination.

But Von Sternberg was a tyrant to Dietrich. Frequently his rantings in their native German reduced her to tears and sent her fleeing to her dressing room.

Despite their fierce battles, Von Sternberg was besotted by Marlene, to the consternation of his wife Riza. By 1931 she was suing him for divorce and Dietrich for alienating her husband's affections. And there was a libel writ after a magazine interview in Germany reported Marlene as saying Riza was an undutiful wife.

Rudi was summoned from Germany and the family – complete with Maria – put on a united front. Paramount Pictures, embarrassed at the commotion, paid Riza $100,000 to drop proceedings.

Marlene's public agony was not at an end, however. A year later a crank sent her an anonymous note threatening to kidnap her beloved daughter. Frantic, she told the police, who kept guard on her Californian home and staged a ransom drop to catch the villain. The cash, however, was never collected. Marlene put bars on the windows, employed bodyguards and armed the nanny. In the end her daughter became a prisoner in her own home, lonely, frightened and bored in turns.

The partnership with Von Sternberg was not to last. Although they made several more films together, his popularity with studio bosses waned while hers soared. He was tortured when she embarked on a series of relationships which read like a *Who's Who* in Hollywood and were to keep Tinseltown gossips working overtime for years to come.

PARAMOURS

There was Gary Cooper, her co-star in *Morocco*, who boasted a magnificent physique. Their liaison was carried out in tandem with an affair with French singer

Above: *Maurice Chevalier signing autographs. He refused to admit to an affair with Marlene.*

Maurice Chevalier. Later he branded their fling as 'simply camaraderie' but his wife did not agree. She used the evidence of an association as the basis for a divorce. Much later Marlene said of Chevalier: 'I adored him. He was the finest man I ever loved.'

John Wayne was among her paramours, too. The Duke was invited into her dressing room. After locking the door behind him, Marlene purred: 'What's the time?' She went on to answer her own question by provocatively raising her skirt to reveal a garter watch around her thigh. 'It's very early, darling. We have plenty of time,' she cooed at him.

Author Erich Maria Remarque, who wrote the powerful anti-war epic *All Quiet on the Western Front*, was a suitor as well as Douglas Fairbanks Junior and Frank Sinatra. During World War 2 she bedded Generals Paton and Gavin. She freely admitted she had never felt a strong sense of possession about anyone.

Ernest Hemingway was a close confidant. Although he was apparently never a lover, his picture was kept at her bedside and they corresponded in affectionate terms.

Her greatest love of that period was brooding French actor Jean Gabin whom she met in 1939. A real-life tough guy, he wanted to abandon his Hollywood career to fight Hitler with the Free French army. He even slapped Marlene powerfully both in public and behind closed doors, sending her reeling across the room. But she adored him. At home she would cook and launder

Above: *With Jean Gabin, the macho French actor she adored.*

Right: *By the mid-thirties Marlene was ranked the third-biggest earner in the US.*

DESPERATE FOR HIS LOVE, MARLENE HAUNTED THE STREET WHERE HE LIVED, HOPING TO CATCH A GLIMPSE OF HIM.

---

later, Dietrich haunted the street where he lived just to catch a glimpse of him, such was her continuing infatuation.

She felt she was mother and lover to Gabin and that was the role she favoured above all. All too frequently, she felt an urge to cherish and care for emotionally damaged men who crossed her path. It normally ended between the sheets.

Her life-style was lavish by any standard. By the mid-thirties she was earning an estimated $350,000 a year, making her the third-highest earner in the country. She would fly food from her favourite bakeries or delicatessens in Europe to her table in America. For 30 years she paid $300 a month to store a 16-cylinder Cadillac in Hollywood where she never rode in it.

for him. Star Tyrone Power was astonished to see her bow down to remove his shoes and massage his feet before sliding on some slippers.

The pull of duty was too strong for Gabin to counter. He returned to Europe in 1943 to join the ranks against Hitler, but their affair continued in Paris after the war. It only foundered when Gabin, then 55, grew weary of her infidelities which continued in the face of her devotion to him. He finally ended the affair to marry French actress Mauban.

In 1963 she told Senator Robert Kennedy that Gabin was the most attractive man she had ever known. Why had they split? 'Because he wanted to marry me. I hate marriage. It is an immoral institution. I told him that if I stayed with him it was because I was in love with him and that was all that mattered.' Years

But then age began to be an issue. Her lovers were all much younger, her rivals more juvenile. In her middle years she courted two men who were later to wed Elizabeth Taylor.

Michael Wilding, the foppish Englishman, was 11 years younger than Dietrich when they starred together in Hitchcock's *Stage Fright*. She was devastated when their love affair ended so he could marry Elizabeth Taylor, some 30 years her junior.

Wealthy producer Mike Todd, tragically killed in a plane crash in 1958, was the other man she was to share with Taylor, to her fury.

She then became obsessed with one lover, Yul Brynner, during a 6-year-long affair. He was married with a child and refused to leave his wife.

In her 1954 diary Marlene wrote: 'How can I stand this much longer? It will be four years in May. I must ask him to be more definite. As always I'm depressed when he leaves without anything personal being talked about.'

At last Marlene knew what it was to yearn for one love – and not to win it.

Later in the sixties, composer Burt Bacharach was the subject of her attentions. Although he was 27 years younger than she, the relationship flourished for a while with Dietrich once again in the role of *hausfrau*. Dietrich was acerbic when he abandoned her later to marry blonde actress Angie Dickinson.

'He might as well marry Julie Andrews,' she spat.

She was concerned enough about ageing to visit a Swiss clinic for rejuvenating therapy. Three times the cells of a lamb foetus were injected into her bottom, causing maximum discomfort. As she discovered, the effects, if any, were purely temporary.

THE TRAGEDY OF AGE

Afterwards she was shaken by two tragedies. She was touring in Poland in 1967 when she met 39-year-old Zbigniew Cybulski, a home-grown heart-throb with legions of fans around the country. Although bisexual, he became devoted to Marlene and she to him, the vast age difference not withstanding.

She was booked to leave on the midnight express train from Wroclaw to Warsaw. The parting was an emotional one, rendering both in tears. In an impetuous gesture, Cybulski decided to join her and aimed to leap on the moving train. It was a stunt he had carried out successfully many times on film.

But as she watched breathlessly, he slipped between the platform and the train, falling to his death. Emotionally she was scarred by the shocking experience and refused to talk about it.

Above: *With Burt Bacharach before he left her to wed actress Angie Dickinson.*

AS THE HELICOPTER DITCHED INTO THE SEA, THE WHIRRING BLADES SLICED OFF HER LOVER'S HEAD.

The following year she visited Australia and met journalist Hugh Curnow, of the same physical stamp as Jean Gabin but aged about 30. Quickly she snapped him up to work on her biography. Although a grandmother, she still tingled at the challenge. The relationship fell apart somewhere between Australia and Paris where she whisked him away. He returned full of stories about the woman who spent evenings poring over scrapbooks reminding herself of a glorious past.

When she went back to Australia to take part in the Adelaide Festival of Arts, he was covering an oil discovery off the coast of Victoria. A helicopter being used to photograph the rig suddenly ditched and the whirring blades decapitated Hugh in an instant. The grim news was broken to Marlene just before she went on stage. Unflinchingly she gave her performance, but the incident wounded her irreparably.

For many, reaching 70 would have been a time to retire gracefully from the public eye to enjoy some well-earned rest. Marlene continued on the showtime beat, mainly because she needed the money.

But her health was not good. The aches

Right: *Leaving London Airport after falling on stage in 1974. Her body became increasingly frail.*

Opposite: *On stage in London, 1973, on one leg of a gruelling world tour.*

and pains of old age and hardening arteries in her legs made her scratchy. Never was it more striking than when she toured Japan and a violinist played a wrong note. Viciously, she turned on the orchestra and sizzled: 'Don't think I have forgotten Pearl Harbor.'

On stage she wore a rubber body suit to enhance her fading figure. A strenuous world tour sapped her energies. There followed a series of disastrous falls including one in which she broke her hip and another when she fractured a thigh bone.

Depressed by the deaths of Von Sternberg, her husband Rudi and Gabin, she faded from public view at last. Then the inducement of earning $250,000 for two days' work on the film *Just a Gigolo* enticed her back to the screen. The movie was savaged by critics. It was taken as a sign, if any were needed, and Dietrich hid herself away in penury.

Behind the doors of her Paris flat, she laced her morning cup of tea with whisky to help dull the pain of her tender limbs. She would avidly read newspapers from across Europe or devour Dick Francis novels and spend hours on the telephone to friends all over the world.

Marlene continued a disorderly approach to eating and drinking. As she had done throughout her working life, she would often forgo food during the day to feast around midnight, troubled as she was with insomnia.

Bizarrely, she used a police whistle to summon her staff at any hour. Often the crack of a gunshot would ring out. Reclining on her pillows, she used a starting pistol to scare pigeons from her window boxes.

A photographer who lurked outside her apartment in the hope of snatching a picture was treated to a whack around the head with her handbag. Another who hired a crane snapped the outraged recluse hidden behind a writing pad.

Dietrich was a proud if distant grandmother who refused to brook any talk of *The Blue Angel*, the film which carved out her career and which she grew to loathe.

She collapsed and died while looking at family snaps, alone save for a paid helper. It's probably just as she would have chosen.

CHRISTIAN BRANDO
Rich kid loser turned killer

Scarred by the traumas of a desperately unhappy childhood, addicted to drugs and obsessed with guns, Christian Brando was a killer-in-waiting. The writing was on the wall for the son of the famous filmstar.

He fancied himself as an aspiring titan of Hollywood, just like his father.

The same smouldering good looks, the hypnotic eyes, the effortless charm so few women could resist. Yet when Christian Brando finally fulfilled his craving to become a household name it was the crime reporters – not the Tinseltown critics – who penned the front-page stories.

In a scene which could have been culled straight from father Marlon's most acclaimed picture, *The Godfather*, Christian stood accused of murder. He'd pumped a single bullet into the head of 26-year-old Dag Drollett, who was the lover of his pregnant half-sister Cheyenne, 20.

The fact that the killing happened at Marlon's sprawling 12-room mansion at Mulholland Drive, deep in California's South Monica Hills, added spice to the scandal. And from the moment the local night duty cop answered an emergency call to hear 'This is Marlon Brando. There's been a shooting at my house,' even the most jaded of Hollywood gossips sprang to attention.

Not since 1958 when Lana Turner's daughter stabbed to death Johnny Stompanato, her mother's lover, had the movie world become so engrossed in a crime story. And as the trial unfolded they would not be disappointed. Every nuance, every tragic twist of the Brando dynasty was finally laid bare.

How Christian was among nine children produced for Marlon by a string of wives. How he became trapped in a vicious custody battle, dropped out of high school and became sucked into a spiral of drug abuse and booze that perfectly fitted the classic 'poor little rich kid' syndrome.

And how, at 32, he pulled the trigger of an SIG-Sauer .45 pistol and threw away his future in a pique of rage.

EXOTIC PASSION

From the start, Christian's life seemed destined to be a roller-coaster ride.

What started as a passionate love affair between Marlon and the boy's mother, Anna Kashfi, ended in hostility and bitterness as they squabbled their way through the child custody courts. The couple had met in Hollywood in 1955, three years before Christian was born.

Brando was quickly transfixed by the beautiful, olive-skinned woman whose taste for sari dresses so ignited his passion

Above: *Marlon in a scene from perhaps his most famous movie,* **The Godfather.**

HE PUMPED A SINGLE BULLET INTO THE LOVER OF HIS PREGNANT HALF-SISTER.

Opposite: *Christian, aged 13, arrives at London's Heathrow Airport. Brando Senior had just brought his son back from the hippy commune in Mexico following Anna's kidnap attempt.*

Above: *The scene of the murder. In this house on Mulholland Drive, Hollywood, Christian gunned down Dag Drollett.*

IT WAS TO BE A FAIRY-TALE
ROMANCE – WITH THE
BITTEREST OF ENDINGS.

for the exotic. He promised her all the help he could in pursuing a film career and the pair began dating almost immediately. But within months they were faced with personal crisis. Anna contracted tuberculosis and was confined to a hospital bed. Once past the worst ravages of the disease doctors ordered that she must take time to convalesce and agreed to release her into Brando's care.

By now deeply in love, Brando bought her an engagement ring. She responded by telling him he was soon to become a father. A secret marriage ceremony in October 1957 appeared to have set the seal on the fairy-tale romance. In her own words Anna once recalled those halcyon first weeks as she waited for Christian to arrive.

'After we married I was like the queen of a strange castle at his house in Mulholland Drive.

'My days were spent in idle splendour. I had maids to wake me up and cook me lunch.

'I would spend the morning painting before driving in a Mercedes to my favourite restaurant for lunch with friends. In the afternoon I would laze around until it came time for the maids to dress me before I went out to some dazzling party.'

Anna described how she would be dressed by names such as Chanel, Yves St Laurent and Christian Dior, and how her pearls, hand-made shoes and designer accessories only ever needed to be signed

for – nothing so crude as a cheque or cash for Marlon's girl.

But if the seal on the romance ever truly existed, it was smashed to fragments within weeks. A newspaper published an exclusive story revealing the new Mrs Brando's claim of coming from Indian stock was pure fiction. In fact she was Welsh. Anna's father, factory worker William O'Callaghan, said his daughter had no Indian blood and was merely brought up there while he worked on the Indian railways.

BRUTAL REJECTION

Brando's blind love turned to blind rage. His personal aides were ordered to wring the truth out of Anna by testing her life story at every opportunity. At first she was aloof and dismissive, but as the questions kept firing in she became hysterical, then rambled incoherently and finally wrapped herself even deeper in a cloak of inventions and half-truths.

Brando responded in typical style – by rejecting her company at home for his old bachelor life-style and the hordes of Hollywood beauties falling over themselves to attract his attentions. Anna hit back by publicly accusing him of flirtatious behaviour.

But despite it all, Brando stayed with her until Christian was born. Soon afterwards she packed her bags and left, taking the baby with her, and then collapsed, suffering from a nervous breakdown.

Before baby Christian was a year old, Anna had dragged Brando into court claiming he had physically abused her. He meanwhile accused her of trying to break into his home. It was the start of a marathon legal tussle in which Christian would be torn between his warring parents like a rag doll. By the time the boy was 6, however, Brando had established a clear advantage.

Anna admitted she had a problem with alcohol and drug abuse and her appearance before the court made it clear she desperately needed treatment. As she gave evidence she went on a violent rampage and was even arrested for attacking three people. The judge granted Brando temporary custody and further ruled that Anna could not even see her son unless there was a lawyer present.

With an apparent victory behind him, Marlon began weaving a new, tangled web to his personal life. He married – and divorced – Mexican actress Movita Castenada, with whom he had another son, Miko, and a daughter, Rebecca.

Then, while playing his role in *Mutiny on the Bounty*, he met a Tahitian woman who totally captivated him. Actress Tarita Teriipia – to whom he is still married – gave him two more children. The youngest, a girl, they named Cheyenne.

By 1971 Christian Brando was seeing his mother again, but her joint custody agreement was blown apart in spectacular style when she paid $10,000 for her boy to be kidnapped and brought to a hippy commune she had joined in Mexico.

A team of crack private detectives eventually returned a bemused Christian to his father. For a couple of years the young Brando was destined to enjoy a stable – and utterly idyllic – life on his father's Tahitian island. When Marlon was called away, either to film or pursue his interest in helping the American Indian human rights movement, hired nannies would take care of his needs.

As his teenage years moved on he was sent to a private Californian school where the darker side of his mixed-up personality soon began to show through. Far from trying to pitch in as just another ordinary kid, Christian would boast about his mega-rich life-style and loved to be known as 'the son of Marlon Brando'.

It was the one slice of self-respect he'd retained in a childhood that had lurched from trauma to crisis. At school he was, predictably, a failure. He hadn't the willpower to knuckle down to exams and had no desire to achieve independence through a career of his own.

He would even question his undoubted ability to attract girls, convincing himself they only wanted to make love to him because he had such a famous father.

In 1981, aged 22, he married a make-up artist called Mary McKenna, but hopes of a stable relationship and family life proved fanciful.

Christian became fascinated by guns – the bigger and more powerful, the better. He grew more and more dependent on booze and cocaine, drifting slowly down

Below: *Marlon and Tarita Teriipia. She totally captivated him.*

into the gutter with Hollywood's motley bunch of no-hopers and hangers-on.

A TIME BOMB

One gang he joined, the Downboys, were stunned at his passion for weaponry and desire to play 'death games'. One member of the gang later told reporters: 'We knew he'd kill one day.

'If only we'd turned him in to the police Dag might still be alive.

'Christian could have killed any of us at any time. When he's spaced out on drugs and booze he's a wild man, a time bomb waiting to go off.

'I saw him trying to kill four people and he didn't even know he was doing it.'

Others told how Christian would launch himself into fights using steel-capped boots and even a claw hammer. All the time the shady, third-rate agents were closing in – promising bit-parts in B-movies. Theirs was a secret agenda. The real aim was to cash in by securing some snippets on his personal life and flogging them to some trashy magazine.

When Christian finally got his 'big break' it verged on farce. He was to play a hitman in an Italian-made gangster movie called *The Issue at Stake*. But the funds ran out and the project collapsed in turmoil and recriminations.

Above: Christian and his half-brother Miko, who later worked for Michael Jackson.

CONVINCED THAT NO ONE COULD EVER LOVE HIM, HE RESORTED TO BOOZE AND COCAINE — AND VIOLENCE.

Right: Christian with a girlfriend, Laura Fuoni.

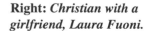

While in Italy, though, Christian did get a genuine chance to break free of the leeches and pushers that now monopolized his private life. He was an instant hit as a male model and drew high praise from leading agents around the world. One, New York-based Andreas Julietti, said of him: 'Christian had a rugged, boyish-yet-male Don Johnson style – a great formula.

'If someone came to me with his portfolio of pictures I would snap him up.

'He displays great character in modelling … and he has the physique.'

Modelling could have been Christian's ticket to the fame after which he still hankered obsessively. Sadly, addled by drink, and unable to control his coke habit, he turned his back on the opportunity and lurched back to life as a professional waster.

By 1983 he was languishing on Marlon's Tahitian island paradise, Tetioroa, entertaining friends who had both the money, and the will, to help finance his high-spending habits. And it was in the summer of that year that he delivered a treacherous blow to one of his closest friends.

Bill Cable, a bit-part actor had brought his wife Shirley to stay on the island. Christian decided it would be fun to seduce her. He would contrive to have the three of them running naked along the long, sandy beaches or to share drinks with Shirley at sunset.

In an interview she later admitted: 'Christian explained that he had only invited us so that he could get closer to me.

'There was an animal magnetism about him, a smouldering sense of danger. He had charm, but it was a rough kind of charm.

'Although I felt myself being drawn to him I didn't want to sneak off and have sex with Christian. I knew that ultimately it would destroy everything that Bill and I had together.'

NAKED SEDUCTION

Shirley related how she challenged Christian one evening as they strolled together, naked, along a beach. She wanted to know why he was trying to double-cross his best friend by romancing her.

With a grin Christian told her: 'To hell with Bill, I go for broke.'

> **CHRISTIAN LIKED TO PLAY IT ROUGH WITH HIS WOMEN – HE LIKED TO PROVE 'WHO'S BOSS'.**

Below: *Bar and beach, Tetioroa. Christian used the island as his personal paradise.*

Above: *Dag, his mother and Cheyenne. Cheyenne never took Christian's threat to kill her lover seriously.*

Then they made love at the water's edge.

Shirley always insisted she knew she was playing with fire. Her new-found lover had told her how he liked to play rough with his women and how sometimes he liked to prove to them 'who's boss'. Christian told her that on one occasion he was punching a girlfriend hard in the face while he held her by her twisted hair in the other hand.

Suddenly his father entered the room, alerted by her screams, and placed a huge hand on his shoulder to jerk him violently away.

Marlon told him: 'You punk! Touch this girl again and I'll flay your skin off your back.'

Shirley, however, insists: 'I'm a lady and he always treated me like one except towards the end.

'He did a lot of bad things but he never physically harmed me.'

As the days turned into weeks on Tetioroa the tension between Bill Cable and Christian built up into a full personal crisis. Shirley decided to leave, in the hope they could sort out the love tangle between them.

But when six weeks later the two men in her life followed her back to Los Angeles their friendship seemed in tatters.

The affair continued to simmer behind Bill's back, at cheap motels or Christian's

Hollywood Hills home, bought for him by his father.

Shirley would later describe him as 'an incredible lover, very sensitive to a woman's needs'.

Christian, she claimed, would melt into her arms after sex and regress to his childhood, calling her 'Mommy' and curling up into the foetal position.

'I think that's where a psychiatrist would say all his problems stem from,' she said.

'A deeply disturbed and unhappy childhood has left him scarred mentally beyond belief.'

'Christian,' she said, 'lost his virginity at the age of 13 to a 25-year-old stripper who hoped to use him as a way to get close to Marlon.'

Shirley went on: 'One day after we made love I asked him why he had never straightened himself out. He said: "Listen babe, the old man has blown a packet on shrinks for me and it ain't done any good for me.

"The problems I got no one can solve. There ain't anyone else like me."'

In the end it was drink that drove Christian and Shirley apart. He was cracking a six-pack of malt liquor for breakfast every day – no matter what state he'd arrived home in the night before.

He'd tell friends how his father desperately tried to dry him out, first by sending him to detoxification clinics, then by isolating him for six months on Tetioroa.

Both attempts failed. Christian would even boast how he learned to make his own hooch on the island using fermented coconut and banana juice. He proudly claimed the concoction would 'send an elephant loco'.

THE SMELL OF DEATH

Throughout the booze-and drug-induced haze of the late eighties Christian would increasingly look to his extended family as a rock in troubled waters.

He didn't know Cheyenne well but saw her as something of a fellow spirit – rebellious, independent and strong willed. In fact their lives shared an obvious parallel and each perhaps guessed a little of the other's torment. Christian would even admit to detectives that he was 'over protective' of his half-sister.

Cheyenne had grown to cherish her father's superstar reputation and spoke of him in glowing terms. But, like Christian, when it came to school she rejected his plea to study and became a teenage drop-out. If booze was Christian's weakness, drugs – especially marijuana, tranquillizers and LSD – were hers.

In 1989 she was severely injured when a car, driven by her lover of three years, Dag Drollett, crashed. It left her with deep psychological and emotional scars and as her father would later observe laconically: 'She's been doing a lot of strange things since then.'

When, in the autumn of that year, she became pregnant with Dag's child, Brando insisted that the couple fly to stay with him in Los Angeles. Tarita would come too, to care for the young mother-to-be, and Brando could be sure his grandchild would be given the best medical care money could buy. In truth, he had no confidence in Tahitian doctors. But Dag's parents were concerned. His father Jacques, a high-ranking retired government official, warned in striking terms that the union was doomed.

And in words that sounded chillingly like a premonition he told Dag: 'Stop this life with Cheyenne.

'She's not balanced. You're going to meet a tragedy with that girl. Your life

together smells of tragedy, it smells of death.'

Afterwards he would recall his strange feeling on the night of the killing – still unaware that a tragedy had taken place.

Jacques said: 'I cannot easily describe it. I just didn't feel well inside.

'I said to Françoise [his wife], "I have to go home."'

That fateful night, 16 May 1990, Jacques had been in the Tahitian capital Papeete to attend a reception in honour of the French President François Mitterand.

His overpowering sense of dread is still recalled by Polynesians as further proof of the magic of the South Seas. No one can

*Above: **Jacques Drollett.** He had some kind of premonition the night his son was shot.*

ever be sure if that feeling descended upon him at the very moment of Dag's death. But it is possible.

For as the limousines full of dignitaries drew up outside Papeete's Gauguin Museum in the mellow evening sundown, it was late in the evening over in Los Angeles.

The next day, Jacques discovered the awful truth in the worst possible way. An LA TV journalist rang him to say: 'Your son has been shot through the head. He's dead.'

'At first I thought it was a joke,' Jacques recalled. 'I thought that someone was having a sick joke on me. When I learned this was the truth I didn't know what to do.' Back in Los Angeles that 16 May night Cheyenne had decided to accept Christian's invitation to dinner to get a change of scene. She hoped it would give them a chance to know each other better, away from the influence of their family.

Dag meanwhile stayed at home to eat with Marlon and Tarita. At Musso & Frank's restaurant on Hollywood Boulevard brother and sister talked – and drank – and gradually opened up their innermost thoughts.

Christian asked her about her relationship with Dag. She told him it was good, but didn't all couples fight occasionally? Christian seemed to get angry even though she promised that the fights were only verbal. Suddenly he was talking about killing Dag.

THE LUST TO KILL

After dinner they drove to the apartment of Christian's then girlfriend, actress Laurene Langdon. Cheyenne recalled how he stormed into the bedroom and came out carrying a knife and a large gun. He again talked about killing Dag but, she later insisted to police, she did not take his threats seriously. On the way to Brando's home he vowed for a third time that he was bent on killing her lover. Cheyenne told how she followed her into the house and confronted Dag in the TV room. She heard a short conversation followed by a single shot. Christian then walked out holding the gun and said simply: 'I killed him.'

Later, brother and sister's accounts of

Above: *Tuki. He was born with his mother's dependency.*

Dag's final moments would be hopelessly at odds. Christian told police later: 'It was an accident.

'The gun was under the couch. I got it because he hit my sister. My sister is pregnant. Two guys with a gun wrestling. It goes off and he's dead.

'When we came back here it got crazy. He went nuts ... he grabbed the gun and we fought over it. The gun had a bullet in the chamber and it went off.

'Man, death is too good for the guy. If I am going to knock someone off it wouldn't be in the house. It was an accident. I told him to let it go. He had my hands then "Boom!" Jesus, man, it wasn't murder.'

Cheyenne's statement was quite different. With a frankness that delivered potentially explosive evidence to prosecutors she told one cop the killing was 'not an accident like everyone was trying to make it out to be'.

And she went on: 'It's a murder, in case you didn't know it.' Almost immediately she was put on a plane back to Tahiti with her mother – the travel arrangements were made by her father. Her claim was never tested in court and she refused to return. Later she would give birth to a baby boy, Tuki, born with his mother's drug dependency and looked after in his first weeks of life by Tarita.

Cheyenne, still vowing she would never forgive Christian, later took an overdose. She lapsed into a coma but recovered under the love and care of her mother.

So what of Brando himself? He had become the main witness to a drama more incredible than anything he'd played on screen. Within minutes of the shot ringing out he had dashed on to the scene of the killing. Frantically, pointlessly, he had tried to revive Dag. Then, at 10.58 pm, he made the call to his local police station.

An ambulance, a fire crew and two police cars were despatched to Mulholland Drive. Fire captain Tom Jefferson was first through the double gates to find Brando confronting him. 'He's in the TV den. I've tried mouth to mouth but I can't get a response.'

Jefferson and his men ran into a large white room dominated by a huge TV screen built into one of the walls. There, slumped on a luxury padded sofa, was Dag dressed in blue surfer shorts. A blanket had

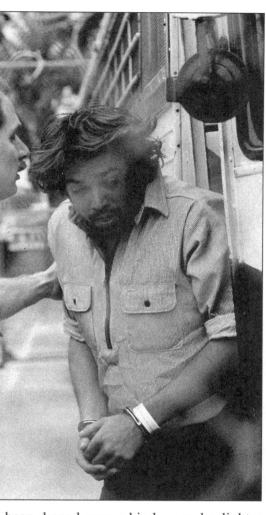

mean to shoot him,' he said. Seconds later his hands were handcuffed behind his back and he was hearing the words of a murder charge.

THE MESSENGER OF MISERY

As Dag's corpse was removed in a body bag the ambulancemen were halted by Brando and asked to open it. Then he gently bent forward to kiss the father of his unborn grandchild.

Later he would tell reporters: 'That night the messenger of misery came to my house.'

Suddenly Brando, the silver-haired screen genius who never really rated acting as a proper job, found his life turned upside-down.

> THE TV REMOTE CONTROL WAS STILL CLUTCHED IN HIS HAND AND HIS EYES LOOKED AS IF THEY WERE WATCHING THE FLICKERING SCREEN, BUT THERE WAS A GAPING BULLET-HOLE IN HIS HEAD.

Left: *Christian on his way to court.*

Below: *Dag's funeral turned into a media circus.*

been draped across his legs and a lighter and tobacco pouch were clenched in his left hand while a TV remote-control console was clutched in his right.

On the wall the TV remained on, channels flipping up constantly as though Dag was still trying to choose what he wanted to watch.

His eyes were still open and he seemed to be staring at the screen, but a bullet-hole gaped wide in his left cheek. Outside policeman Steve Cunningham leapt from his patrol car to be grabbed by a fireman.

'There's a guy in the house shot dead,' the man screamed. 'Brando's son is the suspect. He's still in there somewhere.'

Warily Cunningham pulled out his pistol and approached the open front door. The first person he met was Marlon.

'Where's your son?' he asked.

'I don't have any idea,' replied Brando. 'I can't believe Christian shot him.'

Cunningham found Christian in his half-sister's room sitting on the floor with his arm around her. She was crying. 'I didn't

Above: *Marlon in court. He said later, 'My son isn't a mad dog killer.'*

First he pledged his beautiful £3 million home to secure Christian's bail. Then he broke almost 40 years of media silence to call a press conference in his son's defence. In an often rambling monologue he said: 'It's tough for any of you to go through the experience of being famous.

'It robs you of your personality. Most people believe what is written about them. Let them call me names, it doesn't hurt me. But my children aren't used to that.

'My son isn't a mad dog killer and I hate to see him portrayed that way.'

Dressed immaculately in crisp white shirt, navy blue blazer and slacks, the two-times Oscar winner went on: 'Christian has been depressed and I don't think he should be punished simply because he has got a father who has been well known.

'It's become a zoo, or some kind of animal show, where my son is portrayed by the carrion press as the mad dog killer, but that picture has been run to death.

'There is another view. There is another Christian.'

Marlon said he'd had to fight to bring up his children 'with a sense of the real world'.

'They all work for a living,' he said. 'Christian is a welder. Miko works for Michael Jackson. My daughter Rebecca worked as a waitress.

'My other daughter,' here he paused, clearly forgetting her name, 'my other daughter Petra worked for a law office and wants to be a lawyer, and Teho is working.

'I've got nine children. You have to forgive me.

'They have all put in time. They're not all standing around waiting for my millions.

'I've had them open the door on their birthdays looking for the Porsche. And it's not even there. I couldn't even spell Porsche.'

Then, recalling the custody struggle he fought for years over Christian with Anna Kashfi – coincidentally at the same Santa Monica court where his boy was to be tried – he said: 'I fought like hell.

'I was in court about 15 times on visitation rights and custody and by the time he was 14 the judge let him make up his own mind who he wanted to live with. He didn't choose his mother.'

Asked directly if his son was innocent Brando replied: 'I believe Christian. He has never lied to me.

'You might think that every father will believe his son. But when I sat him down he said: "I've always told you the truth."'

Christian's trial, when it finished, produced a predictable result. He escaped the first-degree murder rap but pleaded guilty to voluntary manslaughter and was sentenced to ten years in the St Luis Obispo penitentiary, California.

Apparently he shows little remorse. When his appeal for a reduced sentence came up in 1991 a fellow prisoner told the judge Christian spoke often about the killing. He told other convicts: 'I'd do it again. Dag beat and abused my sister.'

Not surprisingly, sentence was upheld. But what of his mother Anna, the woman he'd railed so hard against during the case and whom he'd refused to even acknowledge? Like Christian, her story also became one of rags and riches.

The $800,000 settlement she got from Brando back in 1960 quickly dwindled into nothing. She claims the lawyers bled her dry. In recent years she has taken to living in a ramshackle trailer home, drawing a $60 per week social security cheque. And when she visited St Luis prison Christian turned her away. The irony is that as a kindergarten teacher she is adored by dozens of children. All she has to remind her of her son is a glazed pottery cast of his hand and an embroidered picture made for her by Christian before Brando won custody. A message on it reads: 'The best things can never be kept, they must be given away – a smile, a kiss and love.'

> **CHRISTIAN SHOWED LITTLE REMORSE FOR THE BRUTAL KILLING, BOASTING IN PRISON: 'I'D DO IT AGAIN.'**

Below: *Christian on trial. The verdict of the court was manslaughter.*

IVANA TRUMP
A fairy-tale romance?

Brought up under the miseries of Communism, the beautiful Ivana fought for her happiness and found love in the arms of a dashing American tycoon. But all her millions could not protect her from the ultimate betrayal.

Above: *At Ascot in 1991 Ivana's flamboyant clothes raised eyebrows.*

At the foot of a steep snowy slope, a 4-year-old Czech girl lay in a crumpled heap, skis awry, not knowing whether to laugh or sob.

The winding route at the centre of panoramic white mountains had looked so simple. It was an ambitious path on a sharp curve that might have daunted skiers twice her age, but this gutsy girl with sparkling eyes and skin like a cherub never thought of turning back.

At first her descent was precise and controlled, but suddenly she found herself out of control and racing at dizzy speed towards the foot of the slope. Her skis were like arrows shooting her into the unknown. Beyond the slope edge was a cliff where she would plunge into goodness knows what.

Unable to halt herself with a snowplough stop on skis, the youngster remembered her father's words of advice during earlier skiing tuition. She summoned her courage, let herself go limp and flopped on to the ice-hard ground.

She bruised her head and her bottom. More than that, her pride was dented. She longed to cry but feared it would mean the end of skiing on the adult runs where she craved to be. After just a few moments lying on the snow, the young body swathed in woollens began to flex. Realizing no bones were broken, she got back onto her feet and on to her skis ready to march back up the mountain and give it another go.

Ivana Zelnicekova could not have known it but those early tumbles in the picturesque mountain ranges of her native Czechoslovakia were symptoms of what destiny had in store for her later on. It was the first time Ivana found she had to pick herself up, dust herself off and start all over again – but not the last.

For Ivana has lived a fairy-tale life which has taken her from the heart of grim Communism into the headquarters of glossy capitalism on the arm of a dashing tycoon. To most people, the lives led by characters in American soaps like *Dynasty* and *Dallas* were a fantasy. For Ivana, a sumptuous US life-style of private jets, limousines and lavish parties was an everyday reality.

But just as it seemed she had her heart's desire, her charmed existence was smashed apart when her husband deserted her for another, younger lover. The public mud-slinging that followed would have been enough to make lesser women crumble but Ivana was from a determined mould. She

IVANA'S HAPPY FAMILY LIFE HAD BEEN PUBLICLY SMASHED TO SMITHEREENS AND IT SEEMED IMPOSSIBLE THAT SHE'D EVER BE ABLE TO PICK UP THE PIECES.

Opposite: *Ivana learned to ski in order to escape from Communist repression.*

Above: *Prague, capital of Ivana's native Czechoslovakia – a beautiful city dulled by Iron Curtain politics.*

THE DRAWN FACES OF HER FELLOW WORKERS ENSLAVED IN DRUDGERY FILLED HER WITH HORROR AND MADE HER DETERMINED TO ESCAPE.

Right: *A hearts-and-flowers romance led quickly to marriage after Ivana met Donald Trump.*

vowed to build her own empire on which her faithless husband could gaze with envy.

And that's just what she has done.

ESCAPE FROM MISERY

Looking at the little girl whose knocks on the ski slopes only made her more dedicated, it would be difficult to chart a more extraordinary life.

Ivana, now 45, was the daughter of an electrical engineer who grew up against the grey backdrop of Communism in post-war Czechoslovakia.

Under the knuckle of the Nazis during World War 2 the Czechoslovakian people had found little comfort. And there was no joy in store either when the war ended and another totalitarian regime held sway.

Those who ventured opinions about politics and the economy were swiftly dispatched by the Communist rulers. Ordinary folk were forced to look over their shoulders before speaking on even the most innocent of subjects. Religion was frowned on behind the Iron Curtain. Families which had sought solace in the embrace of the Catholic Church found themselves bearing the full weight of official opposition.

The street corners were haunted by the grey-coated policemen, their faces like sullen masks. They were the tools of the regime employed to keep good order at any price. Even now Ivana confesses to suffering an involuntary shiver when she sees a uniformed policeman.

The bleak way of life caged so many spirits but Ivana was convinced she would escape its clutches. Her early years were tinged with the kind of glamour hardly known in that grim era. She found herself by chance picked as a child actress by a popular director to appear in several films.

It was a thrilling time, but the young Ivana decided the excitement of make-up, lights and cameras paled against the adrenalin which came from torpedoing down a mountainside on a pair of skis.

Anxious to give their only daughter the best, her parents focused her on a sporting career from an early age. They reckoned it was the best chance she had of milking the Communist system which cosseted its sports stars, and might even give her a chance to escape.

Ivana was a natural athlete: her slender, strong limbs soon thrust her leagues ahead of other child skiers. Her devotion to the sport and an innate competitive edge marked her out as a winner.

As if she needed any convincing, she spent two weeks inside a shoe factory when she was 12 years old which left her petrified and full of resolve to flee the constraints of Communism. The drawn faces of fellow workers enslaved in drudgery filled her with horror.

'I promised myself that I was never ever going to do that kind of work again,' she recalled.

So she concentrated on her skiing, spending every weekend she could on the country's most challenging runs. By 1972 she was accomplished enough to be considered for the Czech Olympic skiing team.

Not surprisingly, her education was orientated around sport. She studied for a degree in physical education at the prestigious Charles University in Prague. Her glorious good looks were not wasted either. She worked as a model, well paid by Communist standards even if the frippery of the job was abhorred by the bull-headed rulers.

It was through her love of skiing that she seized her first chance to flee the repression

of Czechoslovakia. She met Austrian ski instructor Alfred Winklmayr through mutual friends. For the price of a pair of skis, he agreed to wed her – so providing a ticket out of her homeland. The service took place in Prague in November 1971. That night the couple returned to separate beds and he went back to Austria soon afterwards without consummating the marriage. It was ended in a Los Angeles divorce court the following year.

Now Alfred Winklmayr has remarried and lives modestly as an estate agent in a suburb of Sydney, Australia, where he emigrated after that first marriage of convenience. He remains intensely loyal to the woman whose career he helped to launch in the freedom of the West.

Tracked down by reporters in 1990 when the cracks in the Trump marriage began to show he said: 'She's certainly come a long way since I knew her but we are still friends. I've been trying to follow events but it's not easy to keep up with everything.

'Ivana's been receiving a lot of criticism lately but I can tell you she's not the kind of person to take it without a fight.'

A DREAM ROMANCE

Ivana used her newly found freedom from the Communist tentacles to live and work in Montreal where she was a successful skier and model. It was during the Olympics, held there in 1976, that she first laid eyes on Donald Trump, 48, the man who arguably made her, then tried to break her.

It was the stuff of which slushy romance novels are made. Their eyes met across a crowded room. A fizz of electricity left them both shaken. The busy reception they were at might as well have been empty of people – they only had eyes for each other.

After nine months' long-distance courting they were married in April 1977. Later Ivana revealed what thrilled her about Trump.

'What really attracts me is that fabulous energy. Donald is a great leader in the way he motivates people.

'Energy. He had a great head on his shoulders and that he was handsome didn't hurt either. Values, hard work. His sense of reality. Not smoking, taking drugs, drinking. No cheating, lying or stealing.'

He was embarking on a career in wheeling and dealing. He admitted he was hooked on what he called 'the power of the deal'. With clear-headed Ivana as wife and business ally, there would be no stopping them.

Such was his talent for making money, he went on to become America's 19th richest man. The empire of the man who became something of a billionaire boardroom showman was astonishing. The jewel in his crown was Trump Tower, a shiny skyscraper 58 storeys high in the heart of fashionable New York. It comprised apartments, offices and a luxury shopping mall. Also in New York were the prime-site developments of Trump Plaza and Trump Palace.

Add to that the Plaza Hotel, the Grand Hyatt Hotel and the city's ice rink and you

Top: *Donald in Trump Tower.*

Above: *The Trump shuttle airline service, just one arm of Donald's amazing money-spinning empire.*

Above: *Ivana and her three children: Donny, Ivanka and Eric.*

Above right: *Chef Anton Mosimann on his home ground with Ivana.*

Below: *Ivana's own hotel, which she steered to success.*

learn a fraction of what Trump owned in New York alone.

There were three casinos in Atlantic City, an estate in Florida, the Trump shuttle airline service, a splendid yacht and a weekend retreat in Greenwich. The list of his acquisitions seemed endless and all were hallmarked with the Trump name – as was a Monopoly-style board game, a television show called Trump Card, a Brazilian horse race, the Trump Cup, and the cycle race known as Tour de Trump.

'I believe I've added show business to the real-estate business,' he told *Playboy* magazine. 'That's been a positive for my properties and in my life.'

Ivana found herself at the hub of a world most can only wonder at. She slipped into the role of society hostess with relative ease. Apart from their three children, Donny, now 16, Ivanka, 13, and 7-year-old Eric, there were swanky charity bashes to support and lunch parties where she could gossip and giggle. But while it might have kept many women happy, Ivana was keen to make her mark.

Donald recognized the business asset he had in his gorgeous wife. 'She's incredibly good at anything she's ever done, a natural manager – she may be the most organized person I know,' he commented while they were still in harmony.

So Ivana was put in charge of Trump Castle, one of the trio of casinos in Atlantic City. As chief executive, she proved her worth as a money-spinner by rewarding him with a turnover of £20 million a year.

A year later he bought the fabulous Plaza Hotel and presented it on a platter to Ivana. She had big plans for the hotel, featured in the hit films *Funny Girl* and *Crocodile Dundee*.

'I want to make it one of the world's memorable experiences. I want it to represent the glamour of the New York of 1907 when it first opened.'

In came a team of designers who lavished marble on the bathroom suites and antiques in the hallways. Donald told the world she was running the 1,000-room landmark for 50 pence a year – and all the dresses she could buy.

In fact, her extravagant fashion spending had prompted some cutting criticism among society watchers. She is said to have paid $37,000 for a beaded Christian Lacroix jacket alone. The garish colours she favoured raised eyebrows too.

Then she did for American fashion what Princess Diana had done for Britain's top designers. Her European sprees came to an end and she bought quality imitations drawn and made in the USA at a fraction of the cost they commanded as originals in a French or Italian fashion house. The common-sense move won her friends at home, especially as she went on to lure top names in the rag trade to her revamped hotel, giving a stage to home-grown talent.

HER EXTRAVAGANCE ONCE PROVOKED JEALOUS CRITICISM — SHE PAID $37,000 FOR A SINGLE JACKET.

Left: *Setting the style for a generation of women, Ivana went to fashion shows with personalities such as Bianca Jagger.*

She revealed how her clothes would last for several seasons.

'A Christian Lacroix dress costs $24,000. I could buy a Porsche for that. At some point you have to draw the line.

'Usually I wear something two or three times and then I put it to sleep for a year with tissues and covers and bring it out a few seasons later.

'Or else I give it to my mother and she gives it to my friends in Czechoslovakia.'

In addition to a will to win, she admits her Czechoslovakian roots have helped her succeed.

'Most of the people there work and you either have the drive or you don't,' she admitted.

As a working mother, her day would start at 7 am with a work-out with her personal trainer before arriving at her office before 10 am. For efficiency, her appointments for the day were neatly typed on a sheet which she slipped into her bag.

At lunchtime she often missed the chatty lunches so loved by American society women in favour of a wholefood snack at her desk. 'I have a disciplined diet and I don't eat junk food,' she explained.

By 5.30 pm she would be on her way back to see her children, oversee their homework and preside at a family dinner. Both she and Donald were keen to instil decent values in their children. Pocket money was restricted and a huge emphasis was put on education. Sometimes in the evening she went clubbing with her husband. Often she would read in solitude or busy herself arranging fresh flowers which she adored around the apartment. Twice weekly she went to the hairdresser and, unlike many others in her income bracket, she applied her own make-up.

If 'The Donald', as she affectionately called him in her attractive East European accent, had a business trip abroad, she always found the time to go with him, providing invaluable assistance as hostess with business brains.

Home was a 50-room suite high in the imposing Trump Tower. There were handmade crystal chandeliers, a king-sized bed with gold canopy, a marble-paved dining room, 24 ct gold-leaf stencils, a solid bronze front door and even a 12 ft waterfall.

Below: *The 50-room suite in Trump Tower, opulent and splendid, which the Trumps called home.*

IVANA THOUGHT SHE HAD
EVERYTHING — UNTIL THE
RUMOURS MADE HER
SUSPECT SHE NO LONGER
HAD HER HUSBAND'S LOVE.

Come the weekend it was time to adjourn to an out-of-town retreat where she kept her figure in trim by playing tennis or swimming.

A CRUEL AWAKENING

Ivana clearly adored her husband and she was devoted to and fiercely protective of their handsome children. Under scrutiny from the public they seemed a model all-American family who might one day end up in the White House. At the end of the have-it-all eighties, Ivana did indeed seem to want for nothing.

Then rumours that Donald was being seen around town with another stunning blonde came to her ears. Catherine Oxenberg, actress and daughter of Princess Elizabeth of Yugoslavia, and former Olympic skater Peggy Fleming were mentioned in the press. But reporters were wide of the mark.

The object of his attentions was Marla Maples, a former Miss Georgia, fan of motorcycling and trampolining and former

girlfriend of football star Sean Landetta. She was quite unknown in the New York circles frequented by Ivana.

Matters came to a head shortly after Christmas 1989 when the two women in Donald Trump's life met at the swish winter resort of Aspen, Colorado.

Audaciously, Trump and Maples arrived at the jet-set playground in the same plane and left the airport together in an incongruous black limousine. Marla jumped out of the car to stay in a holiday home with a girlfriend while Trump met his wife.

Ivana gradually began to suspect that something was amiss. She overheard a telephone conversation between her husband and a friend relating to the illicit affair. She believed her rival to be called Moolah and didn't have a clue what she looked like. Finally she came face to face with Marla at a mountain-side café called Bonnie's Beach Club.

Marla asked her acidly: 'I'm Marla and I love your husband. Do you?'

Ivana told her to 'get lost', a statement she was later to regret for being unladylike.

Other diners saw the Trumps skiing away with Ivana wagging her finger and chastising the wayward Donald. He wearily replied: 'You're over-reacting.'

Despite his wandering eye, Ivana loved her husband and urged him to save their marriage by calling off the relationship with Marla.

Meanwhile, the American press got into a frenzy. In the USA the couple had been regarded as royalty. News of cracks in the institution of the Trump marriage was met with a huge volume of newspaper coverage which relegated other world events, like the release of South African Nelson Mandela, to corner slots.

At Ivana's 41st birthday lunch in a top New York restaurant – attended by 30 close friends, mother Matka and her mother-in-law Mary – crowds greeted her shouting: 'Take the money.'

As the wronged wife, she was earning more sympathy and respect across America than ever she could have expected as a brittle society beauty. Women who had previously looked on Ivana with envy and even loathing began to identify with her and the impossible position she found herself in.

Below: *Donald Trump with his pregnant mistress Marla Maples. She came face to face with Ivana at a Colorado ski-cafe and told her: 'I love your husband. Do you?'*

Friends encircled her during her pain and urged her to dry her tears, set her jaw and brazen out the agony of the very public split. Among her famous supporters were tennis player Martina Navratilova, designer Calvin Klein, TV personality Oprah Winfrey and actress Robin Givens.

Meanwhile, Donald found backing from boxer Mike Tyson, Cher, Liza Minnelli and Frank Sinatra.

For almost three months the couple tried to work out their differences – but to no avail. Trump had not fallen out of love with Ivana but had toppled head over heels for 27-year-old Marla. It was a hopeless triangle.

A sour clash began with Ivana demanding millions in cash, as well as the Plaza Hotel, of which she was president, and a Boeing 747 jet.

His response was to throw her out of the hotel office she ran.

By the end of March both sides signed a separation agreement along the lines of their 1977 nuptial agreement. Trump agreed to pay $350,000 in cash to Ivana, as well as an annual sum of $350,000 until she remarries, and $300,000 in child support.

A BITTER ENDING

Divorce came later that year in Manhattan Superior Court. In a swift hearing Judge Phyllis Gangel-Jacob declared: 'I grant you a divorce from Donald John Trump on the grounds of cruel and inhuman treatment and particularly Donald Trump's flaunting of his relationship with Marla Maples.'

Afterwards Ivana said: 'It's very sad for me, for the children, for our families and for everyone concerned.'

After 13 years, it was the start of the single life again for Trump, but it coincided with a disastrous slump in his business activities. It seemed his Midas touch was deserting him. Rumours that he would have to borrow heavily simply to survive in business were rife. He had a battle on his hands.

Ivana too was struggling with a crisis: she felt shattered by the split of the marriage she had held so dear. It came in the same year as her beloved father's death.

'It hurts, of course,' she explained. 'But my mother helps me tremendously. Maybe

because of my upbringing in a Communist country where you really did have to keep your thoughts to yourself, I don't open up very much. It still takes time until I open up, even with my friends.'

But a Manhattan journalist threw her a lifeline. Shirley Lord invited her to do a cover for *Vogue* magazine. At first it seemed a brutal suggestion.

'You must be joking. I'm going through the worst time of my life and I look terrible,' replied Ivana.

Dully she accepted the challenge, certain it would be a disaster, but she was reckoning without the talents of a make-up artist and hairdresser who together turned out a new woman. It was a woman Ivana liked the look of – softer colours on her face, quieter lipsticks – and she adopted the image to face the nineties.

She also lost an incredible 2 stones in weight. In 1992 she displayed the remarkable poise and flair she had re-created after the body blow of divorce when she took to a catwalk at a Paris fashion show, to gasps of appreciation from

Above: *After his divorce from Ivana many thought Donald would revel in a bachelor boy lifestyle. But his return to the single life after 13 years coincided with a devastating collapse in his business fortunes and Donald became a more subdued figure in society circles.*

WHEN DONALD TRUMP DESERTED HIS WIFE – THE MIDAS TOUCH DESERTED HIM.

Above: *Ivana causes a sensation on the catwalk in Paris.*

Above right: *Beautiful hair: 'the best revenge'.*

a delighted crowd. The picture was so breathtaking it appeared in *Penthouse*.

'I couldn't have gone out in front of 2,000 people if I didn't feel good about myself, about my body – and if I didn't have my sense of humour,' she said afterwards.

She still had Donald to contend with, however. He had won a victory which he had longed for – a gagging order on Ivana to stop her revealing details of their life together, uncomfortable in the knowledge that revenge was on her mind.

She had already taken a public swipe at him by recording an advertisement for Clairol shampoo in which she swung her

glossy mane and stated: 'Beautiful hair is the best revenge.'

Ivana published a novel called *For Love Alone*, written with former TV scriptwriter Camille Marchetta. It's about a Czech girl, Katrinka, who skis brilliantly, escapes her homeland and marries a tycoon. After an unhappy split following his affairs, they divorce and she marries an even richer man.

While admitting she wrote about things she knew, Ivana stoutly denied the novel mirrored her life with Trump. She would not give her ex the satisfaction of featuring in her drama, she announced.

He disagreed and sued her for $25 million. Months of bitter wrangling followed with accusation upon counter-accusation eagerly seized on and spat out again by the newspapers.

Trump accused her of violating their nuptial agreement by living with her boyfriend Ricardo Mazzuchili, a 50-year-old Italian engineer, and demanded that the divorce cash he paid her should be returned.

For her part, Ivana demanded the $4 million housing allowance which formed part of the now disputed agreement and claimed he had failed to pay her alimony.

It wasn't until 1993 that the couple managed to negotiate a secret deal which made peace between the parties.

Ivana had the satisfaction of watching her husband's fortune dwindle. After they separated she told interviewer Barbara Walters she thought she had Trump's last $9 million.

Refusing to be beaten, Donald made two business comebacks in typically flamboyant style, assuring his rivals he was still a force to be reckoned with.

Ivana was quick to drop her second name. It was a statement which said she no longer needed the man who was once her husband.

She launched a successful cosmetics, jewellery and clothing business, appearing on American TV to sell her wares. They are inexpensive copies of her favourite designs and have been a hit with the American public. During a weekend she sells about $3 million worth of merchandise. She is well rewarded for public speaking engagements and in huge demand. Also, she has more books in the pipeline including further love stories and a how-to book on going-it-alone following divorce.

'I am not poor and I don't mind work,' she declares. 'The divorce was very difficult but I am an optimistic person. You have to pick up the pieces and make the best of it. The money I received from Donald was put in trust for the children. I make my own money. Always have.'

In December 1993, Donald Trump and Marla Maples wed in a lavish ceremony. It took place at Trump's Plaza hotel and Marla wore a tiara worth more than £1 million to go with her designer wedding gown. Although top New York socialites were on the guest list, their daughter Tiffany, aged two months, did not appear. Neither did Trumps three children from his marriage to Ivana who preferred to continue a skiing holiday in Aspen, Colorado.

Above: *Ivana found happiness again with new love Ricardo Mazzuchili.*

JIMI HENDRIX
A tragedy in waiting

Once the brilliant and shocking Jimi Hendrix had excited a whole generation of kids with his unique brand of music and sexuality, but the burden of fame tore him apart as the fans who'd once screamed their admiration turned their backs on him.

To the flower children of the sixties Jimi Hendrix was the pop star turned prophet, a musical genius who could, literally, make his guitar talk.

Even more than Bob Dylan or the Beatles, Hendrix had a magical stage presence that entranced all those lucky enough to witness it. More than that, he was the figurehead who fuelled a million sex, drugs and rock 'n' roll fantasies for his adoring teenage fans.

There were the legendary three-in-a-bed sex sessions. All-night parties overflowing with heroin, cocaine or LSD. Delightful society-shockers like his faked orgasms on stage with an electric guitar. And, of course, his sheer ear-splitting, gut-wrenching exclusive brand of blues rock.

Like many a pop hero who came before – and after – him, Hendrix was both a magnificent showman and a master of his art. Yet he never came close to mastering his destiny.

His three years of fame would end in a lonely, pathetic death – the apparent victim of a large dose of sleeping pills which led him to inhale his own vomit. Some insist he committed suicide; others say he took an accidental overdose. Even more outlandish is the claim that he was somehow murdered.

Yet, however he passed away in his adopted London that September day in 1970, one thing is sure: Hendrix deserved a better end.

He had been born 28 years earlier in Seattle, Washington, a city he mostly loathed. His dad was a gardener and although money was tight James Marshall Hendrix grew up as part of the classic American middle-class culture attending predominantly white schools.

HIGH SCHOOL DROP-OUT

He and kid brother Leon had a sober, god-fearing father who perhaps

Opposite: *The wild man of rock. He virtually made his guitar talk.*

Below: *Pop star and prophet, Hendrix fuelled a million teenage fantasies.*

> JIMI CLAIMED HE WAS THROWN OUT OF HIGH SCHOOL FOR DARING TO HOLD A WHITE GIRL'S HAND IN CLASS.

over-compensated for the wild ways of their mum, Lucille, a woman of Cherokee Indian ancestry. Jimi would later tell how she would drink and engage his dad (also James) in blazing rows. Often as not he would be packed off to his grandma's place in Canada until things calmed down.

Lucille died when Jimi was 10, a personal trauma he never shook off.

Above: *Hendrix was a natural performer. He'd also picked up a few tricks from stars such as Little Richard, the Isley Brothers and Wilson Pickett.*

Despite her boozy, devil-may-care approach to raising kids he always referred to her fondly as his 'groovy mother'.

Not long after her death the young Hendrix began to show his first interest in rock 'n' roll. He'd already played around on harmonicas and violins from the age of 4. Now he would pick up an old kitchen broom and pose with it slung low across his thighs as a make-believe electric guitar. His father bought him his first, cheap, acoustic instrument when he was 11 and on his next birthday he was upgraded to an electric.

In those early days of endless practice sessions in his room, Jimi naturally found himself drawn to the great blues singers of the fifties and early sixties. B.B. King, Elmore James, Muddy Waters and, later, Bob Dylan all shaped his style. To James Senior (who had only ever managed to play the spoons) it was all an amazing revelation.

Jimi was kicked out of high school in 1957 – he later claimed it was 'for holding a white girl's hand in class' – and began picking up any casual work he could find. In summer he could work cutting grass for his father; in winter he took anything that would pay.

All the time he was getting better and better on the guitar, experimenting with wah-wah and feedback, the sounds that would later become his trademark.

His first gig was at a National Guard armoury where he and a few friends trotted out the Tamla Motown and rhythm and blues numbers their audience demanded. Later Jimi would observe: 'I dug listening to Top 40 R&B ... but that doesn't mean I like to play it every night.'

In 1963 he joined the US Army's 101st Airborne Division on the grounds that he might as well sign up sooner as later. Although he hated the Army he reckoned his National Service would be that much worse if it arrived just as he stood close to making a breakthrough in the music business.

Jimi made 25 jumps in what was regarded as one of the Army's toughest training grounds. Asked what made him do it he would delight in replying: 'The Sergeant ... and the fact you got more money.'

The 26th jump, however, went slightly wrong and Jimi took a bad landing, breaking his ankle. He was discharged after a 14-month stint and found himself quickly on the road as a professional backing musician. He worked with the likes of Little Richard, the Isley Brothers and Wilson Pickett, and also on some of the trendy star 'package tours' of the time.

These left him rubbing shoulders with B.B. King, Sam Cooke, Solomon Burke, Chuck Jackson, Ike and Tina Turner and the twisting sensations Joey Dee and the Starlighters.

THE BIG BREAK

It wasn't until 1965 in Greenwich Village that he finally formed his own band – Jimmy James and the Blue Flames – a name that later caused him to crack up in self-mocking laughter.

The following year Jimi got the big break he'd dreamed of.

Chas Chandler, bass player with the Animals, had decided to move into management and record production. He'd heard from Rolling Stone Keith Richard's girlfriend, Linda Keith, of a brilliant young guitarist who was setting the cafe bars of Greenwich alight with a fresh, raw talent. They watched him perform in the Cafe Wha, and Chandler was hooked.

He urged Hendrix to come back with him to England, then almost the centre of the pop world. Jimi liked the idea but was cautious. Were the backing musicians any good? What about the equipment? He didn't want to compromise his act by blowing second-rate amplifiers every night.

Chandler soothed his doubts but it was only when Jimi asked him about Eric Clapton that the deal was sealed. Jimi said: 'If you take me to England will you take me to meet Eric?'

Chandler told him: 'When Eric hears you play he'll be falling over to meet you.'

That night Chandler watched Jimi perform 'Hey Joe' several times. It was a song he'd recently discovered and had been itching to record. Hearing it pounded out in the Cafe Wha seemed to be an omen and he became convinced he was watching a future megastar.

In one later interview he admitted: 'Jimi wasn't known at all at this time but I hadn't any doubt in my mind. I thought he was fantastic.

'I thought there must be a catch somewhere. Why hadn't anyone else discovered him?'

In September 1966 Hendrix arrived in England and found himself tasting stardom for the first time in his life. He was booked into the swish Hyde Park Towers Hotel by Chandler and taken on a rapid tour of London's trendiest clubs, where almost the only clientele were musicians, agents and managers. Chandler knew he needed to find his protégé a backing band quickly, but the people had to be right. As it turned out everything fell into place.

That same month a bespectacled kid called Noel Redding arrived in London from his native Kent with 10shillings in his pocket. He'd read in the *Melody Maker* newspaper that the Animals wanted a new lead guitarist and he turned up at Chandler's Gerrard Street offices to offer his services. Chandler told him the job had gone, but how did he fancy trying to switch to bass and play with the still unknown Hendrix?

Jimi and Redding strummed together for a few hours and Jimi decided he'd got the right man. Redding ruefully admitted to Chandler: 'I'll switch to bass. I don't see anyone else playing lead guitar with this bloke.'

A few days later Hendrix had his drummer. Mitch Mitchell had just quit a band run by Georgie Fame and was looking for work.

The Jimi Hendrix Experience was born.

Below: *The Jimi Hendrix Experience was a band thrown together by chance. Noel Redding had arrived in London to audition as a lead guitarist but after playing with Hendrix he switched to base. 'I don't see anyone else playing lead guitar with this bloke', he told his manager.*

Above: *Hendrix, Mitchell and Redding show they can pose with the best of them.*

THEY WERE AT THE POINT OF GIVING UP – THE JIMI HENDRIX EXPERIENCE WAS A FAILURE.

Right: *Eric Clapton. He once said of Hendrix: 'Christ, nobody told me he was that good.'*

Their first single, 'Hey Joe', was rejected by a Decca Record company executive who tardily informed Chandler he didn't think Hendrix had 'got anything'. It was to be one of the greatest blunders in the history of rock.

Chandler took no notice and got the 45 distributed anyway through a newly launched company. He sold five guitars to pay for a promotions party at London's Bag O'Nails club.

Jimi got the offer of more support work but it was hardly big money – £25 a night. Chandler later confessed he was down to his last 30 shillings and when Jimi had his guitar stolen Chandler had to sell his last bass to replace it. For a while it looked like the Jimi Hendrix Experience was going to be a bad one for all concerned.

Then 'Hey Joe' stormed into the charts and their problems were solved. From £25 a gig the Experience was earning £1,000 a night by the spring of 1967. Redding and Mitchell got 25 per cent of the takings, with Hendrix himself getting 50 per cent.

THE WILD MAN OF ROCK

Jagger, Lennon and McCartney were among the first in the queue to watch them. Quickly Chandler capitalized on the publicity, designing an outrageous stage package for Jimi which was unveiled during a tour with the Walker Brothers. Apart from a sleazy sex romp with his guitar, Jimi began setting fire to it with the aid of lighter fluid – an act that filled theatre managers across the land with a sense of dread.

A concert in Monterey followed with the Experience acting as support for the Mamas and Papas and Otis Redding. The 7,000 fans had never heard of the black guy in the outrageous psychedelic gear, but after he played a stunning version of 'Like a Rolling Stone' they went berserk. It was almost half an hour before the fans had quietened down enough for the Mamas and Papas to take the stage.

From September 1967 to the summer of 1968 Jimi Hendrix was simply the biggest pop star in the world. His talents had at last been recognized in the USA following acclaimed gigs in San Francisco and New York. In London the album 'Are You Experienced' raced up the charts. Fashion magazines clamoured to get him on their covers, reporters jostled for interviews, photographers trailed the band everywhere and millions tuned in to *Top of the Pops* to see him strut his stuff.

Flower-power teenagers saved their pocket money to get kitted out in the Hendrix look. Typically this would include military-style embroidered jackets, bright silk cravats, frilly shirts, patterned bandannas, velvet purple waistcoats, ethnic bead pendants, long-fringed white leather jackets, bell-bottomed trousers with button leg detail and a large, floppy black fedora hat.

In Britain Eric Clapton – himself dubbed 'God' by rock fans – was at one time being lined up to perform a duet with Jimi.

He went to one gig and, with his usual modesty, politely declined, saying: 'Christ, nobody told me he was that good.'

Another big-name strummer of the time, Johnny Winter, summed up Hendrix's talents as well as anyone.

'He could create feelings nobody else could,' said Winter. 'His guitar was like an

extension of his soul. It wasn't even a guitar, or notes, or music. It was him. He was just projecting Jimi Hendrix.'

And Mitch Mitchell revealed: 'He had huge hands, his thumbs were nearly as long as his fingers. Like many blues players he could use this to his advantage – hooking it over the neck of his guitar as an extra finger.

'Jimi could, and did, play anything – left-handed, right-handed, upside-down, behind his back, over his head. He could even play with his teeth.'

Often those closest to Jimi's guitar genius were the roadies who watched him warming up for a gig. At that time amplifiers and speakers were crude by today's standard and the problems of feedback – the noise made when the electrical field generated by a guitar interferes with a sound system – were the bane of many a band's life on the road.

Jimi simply used it as just another way to make music. Combined with a fuzz box and wah-wah pedal the effect was genuinely unique.

His road manager Eric Barrett would tell how Jimi would wire up massive banks of speakers and souped-up amplifiers through a special box of gadgets, itself linked in to the fuzz and wah-wah systems. Sometimes Barrett would try to test a guitar on it – but all he got for his trouble was a wall of feedback noise.

Barrett said: 'Jimi could control it all with his fingers and I still don't understand to this day how he did it. It was all part of his genius.

'We carried two dozen fuzz boxes and two dozen wah-wah pedals. We had so many spare parts – 13 guitars and pieces of guitar that he had smashed. He enjoyed smashing guitars – it got his frustrations out and the kids went berserk.

'Out of all the bits I'd build another guitar and he'd go and smash it again.'

Despite the on-stage violence – a hallmark of live Hendrix – roadies and stage managers around him at the time spoke consistently of the gentle man behind the wild image that had been so carefully crafted on his behalf.

Jimi hated any of his entourage feeling left out, often insisting on introducing a newcomer personally to the rest of his team. This attitude also translated into his

attitude to fame. He was keen for Mitch Mitchell and Noel Redding to get their fair share of the glory.

Off-stage Hendrix's musical choice was inevitably Chicago, or Led Zeppelin – he was an admirer of Jimmy Page – Cream or Bob Dylan. He worshipped Dylan and even grew more confidant in his own vocals after realizing that Dylan's nasal whining was one of his greatest attributes. Jimi's all-time favourite song was rumoured to be 'All Along the Watchtower' but, according to Eric Barrett, he could never remember all the words and would often end up singing the first verse four times over.

His music ranged from the sad and tender, such as 'The Wind Cries Mary', to the bluesy 'Red House' or the driving rhythms of 'Can You See Me'. In almost everything he wrote, the first few bars made it unmistakably Hendrix.

FREAKING OUT

The band's outrageous reputation brought the predictable backlash from Conservative MPs and some over-zealous churchmen who considered him the devil incarnate. In June 1967 it was claimed no fewer than 30 Stockholm

Above: *The Experience fly in to Heathrow Airport in 1967. Jimi was then simply the biggest pop star in the world.*

THE VIOLENCE AND SEXUALITY OF HIS STAGE ACT DROVE THE KIDS BERSERK.

hotels had banned Hendrix from staying with them.

It was all superb publicity and, naturally, record sales rocketed. Hendrix even managed to shrug off the disastrous decision to tour America with the Monkees, a band billed as the New Beatles at the time. Their fans were mainly love-struck teeny-boppers; Hendrix's the rebel-student type. Unsurprisingly the teenies turned out in force to see their idol Davey Jones and the Experience died a death at the first few concerts. A way out had to be found and Chandler let it be known that a right-wing group called the Daughters of the American Revolution had demanded Hendrix be banned for his indecent act. The Experience were able to quit the tour with heads reasonably high while the Daughters carried on their campaign blissfully unaware of the unwitting part they had played.

Friends of Hendrix later claimed this tour was the first sign of what became known as 'Jimi's downer', a progressively blackening mood that led him to start flirting with LSD and drug cocktails.

Shortly after the New Year of 1968 the Experience arrived in Sweden on a three-day tour. The band booked into the Opelan Hotel in Gothenburg and it seemed all three were happy if tired from a round of almost constant live shows and recording stints.

Then on 4 January the world awoke to find Hendrix was in police custody. He was accused of damaging his room by smashing windows, mirrors and chairs. Night staff had reported screams coming from the room. Police said they arrested Hendrix after three members of the tour entourage sat on him to calm him down.

Jimi was taken to hospital to have stitches in the self-inflicted wounds on his hands, presumably caused where he'd struck the window. He had clearly been out of his mind on a drugs- and booze-induced rampage and claimed later he could remember nothing of what went on. But the incident clearly frightened and disturbed him, so much so that it formed the basis of his song 'My Friend' from the 'Cry of Love' album. Jimi had temporarily lost control of his mind and he didn't like the feeling.

He was fined the sum of his earnings in Sweden and left the country immediately to prepare for a new tour of the USA. That tour provided the first clear signs that Jimi was getting tired of his wild-man-of-rock image. There was none of the crazed guitar riffs or half-screamed-half-sung vocals. At one concert he played only four numbers in his second set, apparently infuriated that an amplifier had blown.

In the months ahead Chas Chandler realized Jimi was starting to drink far more than his usual three whiskies a day. It was also becoming obvious that he'd started taking the 'flower-power drug' acid, or LSD, at almost every opportunity. Chandler urged restraint, realizing Hendrix was tempted to 'drop' a tab of acid whenever it was available. Later the manager recalled: 'There were so many people hanging around him. He couldn't be himself.

'We had an argument about it and he said "OK, no more." Then someone would turn up at the studios with a bag of goodies and pour some more down his throat.'

Jeanette Jacobs, one of Jimi's closest and oldest friends, observed: 'He would say to me: "What do you want?"

'I would say: "What do you mean?" And he'd say: "In the next room you can get anything for free."

'I asked who they were and he said they were fans trying to get him stoned. Not to hurt him but to turn him on. There was anything you could think of – uppers, downers, white lightning, purple hearts, take your pick.

'You wouldn't believe it. They really thought he could take it all at once. It's a drag to think that the people who loved him could have killed him. Not intentionally, of course.

'He was an idol, maybe a genius, and they thought he could take everything. He enjoyed experimenting but I never saw him take anything except acid.'

It was too much for Chas Chandler. Sick of the studio hangers-on, whom he saw as parasites on Jimi's talent, he decided at the end of 1968 to quit as Jimi's manager. As he put it so succinctly later: 'All I was doing was sitting there collecting a percentage. ... He wouldn't listen to anyone. And I had no way of saying anything. He was tearing himself apart for no apparent reason. I wasn't wanted any more so I split and flew back to England.'

BUSTED

In November 1968 it was announced that the Jimi Hendrix Experience had split up. In an interview Jimi suggested Mitch and Noel wanted to do their own things, producing or managing other performers. Noel, it was said, was reluctant to spend hour upon hour in the studio when the band could be out playing live. Hendrix insisted he was not abandoning Britain and paid tribute to his UK fans for not forgetting him. At that time his single 'All Along the Watchtower' – the classic Dylan song – was bursting into the top 20. But it was far removed from Hendrix's new work and had not even been his choice of release. He seemed like a man full of ideas but desperately unsure how to translate them on stage or vinyl.

Money was by now almost meaningless to Hendrix. He'd give vast sums to his family and in Los Angeles once gave $3,000 – then almost a year's wages for ordinary folk – to two girls for a shopping expedition.

Another story had him buying a brand-new Stingray car, taking it on the road for a day and smashing it up. Without a second thought he headed straight back to the showroom to buy another, only for the same thing to happen again four days later.

Ironically the first time he was prosecuted for possession of drugs he was totally innocent. Customs officers at Toronto airport discovered heroin in his luggage. He was arrested and warned by lawyers that he could go down for ten years.

Fortunately police uncovered the truth. Hendrix had complained of a headache and one of his girl groupies had thrown a package in his bag, promising 'Here, this'll help your head'.

Jimi was acquitted and the fear of an innocent man facing punishment convinced him to be more discreet – at least temporarily – about his use of hard drugs.

By now America had really woken up to the boy from Seattle, heralded in the media as the Black Elvis. Leaders of the Black Power movement thought he would be the

Top: *Playing in Sweden, where he had a huge following.*

Opposite top: *Jimi and his road manager, Eric Barrett.*

Opposite below: *Another airport, another pose. Jimi arrives in London en route to the Isle of Wight Rock Festival.*

Bottom: *The Experience are interviewed by Godfrey Winn. Jonathan King lurks in the background.*

Above: *Performing in 1969. By now the strain was starting to show.*

HENDRIX WAS TAKING LSD AT EVERY OPPORTUNITY — THE FANS THAT ADORED HIM WERE KILLING HIM WITH DRUGS.

Right: *The Isle of Wight Festival. Hendrix had lost much of his genius but got through the concert.*

perfect figurehead and began courting him as an active supporter. Jimi turned out at a few functions but it was clear he couldn't be dealing with the politics of colour. Some say he found it inconceivable that any human being could really be racially prejudiced, and so felt the struggle was somewhat pointless.

But he did send a $5,000 cheque to the Martin Luther King Memorial Fund, a rare contribution to a current-affairs issue. Later he was quoted as saying: 'I just want to do what I'm doing without getting involved in racial or political matters. I'm lucky that I can do that … lots of people can't.'

By the end of 1969 Hendrix was based permanently in New York, venturing out only to play a couple of concerts at the Royal Albert Hall in London and the legendary Woodstock free festival. However, early in 1970 he re-emerged with a new backing group – the Band of Gipsies – featuring Bill Cox on bass guitar and Buddy Miles on drums.

They knocked out one live album in New York but to most fans it was a poor substitute for the previous Experience. At a later concert in the city Jimi stormed off in a huff after a few numbers, claiming the band wasn't working together well.

Afterwards he admitted he

was never happy with the Gipsies' album and suggested it had been a rushed affair brought out under pressure from record company executives who wanted the tracks he 'owed' them.

In August 1970 Jimi flew back to Britain for what was to be his last live appearance, at the Isle of Wight Rock Festival, perhaps still the most prestigious ever held in Europe.

Jimi was tired – he'd flown to London straight from a party to launch his Electric Lady recording studios in New York – and then found himself scheduled to go on stage at 3 am.

He, Bill Cox and Mitch Mitchell were left hanging around in straw-strewn tents for hours, then endured a further delay while equipment was tested and re-tested. Finally he appeared before a tense, expectant crowd under a starry sky with the words: 'Yes, it has been a long time, hasn't it?'

The first few numbers didn't work out well and Jimi was forced to take the mike again and murmur: 'Let's start all over again. Hello, England.'

At the end he got the thunder of applause befitting his pedigree but he knew, and every fan staring up from the

damp fields knew, that this was not the Hendrix of old. A month later he was dead.

Hendrix had been staying in London at the Notting Hill basement flat owned by his then girlfriend, German Monika Dannemann. She was a stunning blonde skating instructor whom Jimi had met a year earlier in Düsseldorf. Rumour had it that they planned to marry.

SUICIDE?

On 16 September Hendrix showed up without warning at Ronnie Scott's Jazz Club in Frith Street, Soho. He knew his old pal Eric Burdon was playing there with a new group, War, and Burdon had earlier hinted he wanted Jimi to play with them.

Burdon later recalled: 'We knew things weren't all that good with him but we did our best to let him know that we were there to help him.'

Jimi started poorly but his performance improved throughout the set. There was little to suggest he was overtly depressed or unstable.

The following day Monika called Burdon to tell him Hendrix was ill. He immediately reassured her and promised Jimi would be OK. Later he was to change his mind and urge her to call an ambulance.

That evening Monika and Jimi arrived home around 8.30 pm and shared a hot meal and bottle of wine. He washed his hair in the bath and then sat up with her talking and listening to music until the early hours. Then, at 1.45 am, Jimi suddenly announced he had to go to meet some people – he refused to call them friends – at a nearby house. He said he did not want Monika with him but agreed that she could drop him off there in the car.

After leaving him at the address Monika returned at 3 am to take him home to bed. She later told of making him a fish sandwich and then sitting and talking to him right through to 7 am. She finally took a sleeping tablet but woke again at 10.20 am to find Hendrix dozing. She left to buy some cigarettes but by the time she returned he had been sick. For the first time it occurred to her that he had swallowed sleeping tablets.

Monika checked his pulse and called an ambulance, which took about 20 minutes to arrive. There is little doubt that Hendrix

was still alive as he was ferried towards St Mary Abbotts Hospital, Kensington.

Monika would later maintain: 'He did not die from the sleeping tablets because he had not taken enough to be an overdose.

'The reason he died was because he couldn't get air. He suffocated on his own vomit.'

Above: *Monika Dannemann, Jimi's German girlfriend, arriving at the Westminster coroner's court for the inquest.*

DESPITE THE KIND APPLAUSE, JIMI READ THE SIGNS – HE WAS FINISHED.

The following day the headlines screamed the inevitable to a shocked world: 'Jimi's last, lost days', 'Jimi Hendrix dies in drugs mystery' and, inaccurately, 'Jimi Hendrix dies – drug overdose'. One Sunday paper even called him the 'prophet-in-chief of the drugs generation'.

Three days later Eric Burdon appeared to support the suicide claim. He told the BBC that Jimi had left a suicide note and that as one of the star's closest friends he intended to carry on the Hendrix legacy.

The theory was immediately pooh-poohed by Jimi's manager Mike Jeffrey who said: 'I've been going through a whole stack of papers, poems and songs …. many could be interpreted as a suicide note. I just don't believe it was suicide.'

The Kensington coroner, Dr Thurston, agreed. He said there was no evidence to suggest a deliberate attempt was made by Hendrix to take his own life. His report concluded: 'The question why he took so many sleeping tablets cannot safely be answered.'

Above: Shown here on his wedding day, Eric Burden claimed Jimi had left a suicide note. The coroner came to his own conclusion.

Detectives established that nine pills were missing from a bottle in Monika's flat. But why should Jimi have risked downing them when he was so aware of the dangers?

One theory is that he wanted to make a cry for help, to tell those around him that he was unhappy and didn't know how to break free from his cycle of despair. Others say he simply couldn't find sleep with one tablet and took a further eight in his impatience.

The effect on British musicians who knew him, and indeed the entire nation, was of deep shock combined with a sense of disbelief. Wasn't he so young, so famous? Hadn't he so much more to give?

THE END OF THE PARTY

Eric Clapton, it is claimed, cried for three days when he heard the news. And Chas Chandler, being met that day by his father at Newcastle station, remembers: 'I couldn't believe it. I was numb for days. But somehow I wasn't surprised.

'I don't believe for one minute that he killed himself. That was out of the question. But something had to happen and there was no way of stopping it.

'You just get a feeling sometimes. It was like the last couple of years had prepared us for it. It was like the message I had been waiting for.'

Noel Redding in his memoirs *Are You Experienced* suggests Hendrix was capable of killing himself. He claims Jimi slashed his wrists at the end of one particularly taxing US tour in 1968. Intriguingly, Redding also says he does not rule out foul play in the star's final hours.

'There is no question that Jimi was in a mess and involved with some pretty creepy people,' he said. 'Jimi's death was the most lucrative act of his sad career.'

That comment is at the root of Redding's anger and frustration at the way he and Mitch Mitchell were later treated. Hendrix's estate was estimated at more than $100 million by the early nineties, mostly the royalties from four studio albums and 15 compilations of concert recordings. But much of the money has been enmeshed in a series of highly complex legal arguments.

At one point even Jimi's father – the man surely first in line for a share of his son's wealth – was given a yearly allowance barely amounting to the price of a new car.

Redding says the mass confusion that

erupted around Jimi's fortune followed the death of his manager, Mike Jeffrey, in a plane crash in 1971. From then on, he and Mitchell have had to live in relative penury – despite their massive contribution to the success of the Experience.

In 1990 Mitchell was finally forced into parting with his most prized possession, the white Fender Stratocaster guitar that Hendrix gave him after playing that final Isle of Wight performance. It fetched a record £198,000 at the London auction house Sotheby's and Mitchell kissed it goodbye with the words: 'I would like to think it would get passed on to people who have access to play it.'

In death, as in life, Jimi milked every moment. Even the funeral in his Seattle home town turned into a massive knees-up with musicians such as John Hammond and Buddy Miles jumping on stage in a rented hall to pay tribute. As Mitchell later put it: 'We had a good party. It was the way he would have wanted. We gave him a good send-off.'

To a generation of sixties fans, Jimi Hendrix had been a hero among heroes. A musician who could at once show Jeff Beck's amazing speed, Eric Clapton's imagination and Pete Townshend's raw energy. His sad pathetic death was the final chapter in one of pop music's most moving stories.

Yet there may still be an epilogue. On Saturday 11 December 1993 the London based *Daily Mail* reported on its front page that Scotland Yard officers had sensationally re-opened their investigations into Jimi's death. They had received new evidence from another of his girlfriends, Kathy Etchingham, who had commissioned her own private detective. British Attorney General Sir Nicholas Lyell was said to be considering quashing the coroner's original open verdict and holding a new inquest.

For the fans it brought back memories of Hendrix's words in his favourite song 'All Along the Watchtower'.

Prophetically he sings: 'There's too much confusion.

'I can't get no release.'

Below: *Jimi Hendrix. 'The music will be played loud and it will be our music.'*

JUDY GARLAND
Born to sing

The future seemed rosy – fame and fortune were hers at an early age. Yet despite a wonderful voice, a powerful personality and hordes of adoring fans, Judy Garland was doomed to be trapped on the wrong side of the rainbow.

Audiences went wild for her, children were entranced by her and men fell at her feet. But although everybody loved her, she failed to love herself – or at least not enough to stop the slide into a drink-and-drugs oblivion.

Singer-actress Judy Garland was simply one of the most versatile and popular stars of the century and she loved her fans in return, from the bottom of her soul. She never failed to be genuinely moved by the public's displays of affection.

Despite her glorious voice, her impressive theatrical skills, an appealing face and hordes of devoted followers, she could not find the happiness she craved. The girl who won a million hearts as Dorothy in *The Wizard of Oz* found her own yellow-brick road was a path to self-destruction and distress.

At first it seemed nothing could halt the glittering career of the open-faced Judy who fizzed and effused over the screen. But then her own great talent enslaved her. She found herself on a treadmill, unable to stop the cycle of demands on her time, energy and money, addicted as she was to performing. She was dragged to the depths, eventually losing that amazing voice and dying in June 1969 aged 47. It was the end of a career marked not only by ovations and adulation, but also by a 30-year dependency on drugs and a string of nervous breakdowns.

How could a woman who commanded so much love and respect be the author of comments such as: 'If I am such a legend, why am I so lonely?' She also admitted: 'I seldom know who really likes me.'

In fact Judy was never given a chance to outgrow the childhood fears and insecurities that haunt us all. While everyone wanted to know about her singing and dancing act, no one was interested in the vulnerable, tortured person underneath.

A STAR IS BORN

That uneasy illusion of Judy being a commodity rather than a person with needs and desires was rooted in her childhood. Judy was the third daughter of Frank and Ethel Gumm, baptized Frances but known among the family as Baby.

The place was Grand Rapids, Minnesota, where her dad Frank ran a theatre and film house. Before her had come two sisters, Mary Jane and Virginia.

Already, Frank, Ethel, Mary Jane and Virginia were established entertainers at the theatre. Frank had inherited warm, lilting tones from his Irish ancestors which he duly passed on to his daughters. Ethel, meanwhile, was a piano player for both the film shows and the act. The Four Gumms, as they were known, were well received in Grand Rapids.

Opposite: *'Miss Show Business' at London's Dominion Theatre in 1957. Her powerful performances moved fans to tears.*

Above: *Dorothy in* **The Wizard of Oz** *tends to the Cowardly Lion, played by Bert Lahr. Judy was a 17-year-old yet convincingly portrayed a child of 9.*

HER FATHER'S
HOMOSEXUALITY WRECKED
THE YOUNG GIRL'S LIFE
WHEN SHE LOST THE HOME
SHE'D LOVED.

Above: *A superstar, yet Judy once said: 'If I am such a legend, why am I so lonely?'*

Above right: *In happier days, Judy celebrates her 18th birthday with her mother and movie mogul L.B. Mayer.*

From the moment she was born, little Frances was surrounded by the sights and sounds of showbusiness. She was the apple of her proud father's eye – he loved nothing better than to lull her off to sleep with the ballads of the day. From the first, the theatre was her playground and she was keen to join the family in their stage routine from the moment she could toddle.

Her first public performance was when she was 18 months old: her sisters let her sing 'Jingle Bells' in a neighbourhood talent show they were producing. She repeated the number soon afterwards when she sneaked up on stage at the theatre during a Christmas Eve show in 1924 for an unscheduled debut. Her bold voice and cute image earned her waves of applause from the audience. Her parents realized she was now in on the act so the Gumm sisters became a trio.

Soon their horizons spread beyond the theatre. Their mother was driven by a dream of her girls making it big, but there was no doubt the three loved to be on stage and performed with a delightful, confident charm which won them critical praise.

Little did they know there was more than just a vision of fame that kept Ethel pursuing new frontiers. She had a secret torment that she would never share with the girls. Ethel had been devastated to realize that her loving husband was in fact a homosexual whose covert activities threatened to have them run out of town.

Ethel had known about her husband's inclinations since before their youngest child was born. So upset and disgusted was she by what she discovered, she even sought to have an abortion but was talked out of it by a doctor friend.

It wasn't long before snippets of his gay exploits were the talk of the town. Until now, Ethel and Frank had been pillars of the community. A full-blown scandal would have made their previously comfortable, uncomplicated lives intolerable. In 1926 they decided to leave Grand Rapids and headed for Los Angeles.

It was the first proper tour the girls had undertaken. Frances relished this gypsy world of putting on a show in town after city until they reached their destination. They were thrilled by Los Angeles, its size and buzzing atmosphere. They returned to Grand Rapids only to sell up and move for good.

Frequently, Judy the star regretted the move which took her out of the close-knit community which she had loved. As shadows grew over her life, she wondered more than once if she might have been fulfilled had her family only stayed in the cosy town where she was born. She never fully understood that her father was a homosexual and that his leanings might have wrecked any semblance of happiness in small-town America.

Finally, Frank found a theatre to run in Lancaster, a town melded into the Southern Californian desert where cowboy legend John Wayne had gone to school. The Valley Theatre, as he called it, was the new venue for the Gumm sisters, and the townsfolk their new audience.

Later, residents remarked on the charisma and energy of the smallest sister which shone out to almost eclipse the talents of the other two. Her vibrant personality – which suffered not a fleck of affectation – soon made her popular with both young and old. Everyone could hear her practising in her loud, almost abrasive voice as they passed the house.

They would hear Frank perhaps joining in the singing with Ethel on the piano and

could smell the mouthwatering aroma of Grandma cooking up doughnuts in the kitchen. Amid this vision of homeliness, it was Grandma, all floury hands and sweet smile, who first christened bubbly Baby Gumm as 'Miss Leatherlungs'.

THE SEARCH FOR STARDOM

The energetic Ethel soon became discontented, however. She yearned for her girls to get the glory they seemed to richly deserve. She would take Frances into Los Angeles, some three hours distant, in search of the big break.

The effort wasn't in vain. When she was 6 years old, Frances, together with her sisters, was on KFI radio in Los Angeles. They were a hit and it paved the way for more performances. The trips to the city became more frequent, the partings from Frank longer and longer.

Eventually, the women of the family found a base in the city to give showbusiness their best shot, leaving an unhappy Frank running the picture house in Lancaster.

Their lives were perpetually unsettled after that. The girls hopped between Los Angeles and Lancaster, depending on the shows and slots in which they appeared. They were beginning to make sacrifices, reluctantly, for their budding careers. School dances were missed, friendships curtailed, family Christmases abandoned, romances put on the rocks by the continuing demands of the shows.

Neighbours began to remark unkindly that Ethel Gumm was neglecting her husband. Others felt she was forcing her children to perform and tour. One described her as 'a pushy movie-mother who thought she was better than the local yokels'.

Usually the girls would appear as second, third or fourth billing at vaudeville theatres around the area. Their popularity was only increasing at a moderate rate. Could it be because theatres were constantly misspelling their name so they appeared as the Glumm sisters? In a bid to improve their fortunes, they changed the surname to Garland. They were, said one theatre critic, as pretty as a garland of flowers and the image stuck.

After a performance in 1934, the *Los Angeles Times* read: 'The Garland Sisters scored a hit, with the youngest member of the trio practically stopping the show with

Top: *The brat pack.* **From left to right:** *Freddie Bartholomew, Peggy Ryan, Mickey Rooney, Deanna Durbin, Judy Garland and Jackie Cooper.*

Above: *With Mickey Rooney, another child star, who watched Judy crumble under the acute pressures of superstardom.*

Above: *With her first husband, orchestra leader David Rose. She was heartbroken when they split up a year after marrying.*

GRIEF-STRICKEN AFTER HER FATHER'S PREMATURE DEATH JUDY WAS FILLED WITH HORROR AND LOATHING BY HER MOTHER'S AFFAIR.

her singing.' Other newspapers carried on in the same vein during that year and the next. Each was to rave about the three sisters but most particularly the outstanding youngest girl.

The signs were pointing to a solo career. Frances's sisters were, in any case, courting and hoping to be married. It was only a matter of time before she came to the attention of an agent. Eventually she was summoned for an audition at MGM in September 1935, to belt out a melody in front of movie mogul L.B. Mayer himself. Well known for his keen eye for talent, Mayer instantly presented her with a 7-year contract which she signed with the new Christian name she had chosen for herself, Judy.

Her parents were delighted. Ethel said: 'Hollywood can't hurt my daughter! As long as Judy is the girl I know she is, movies or movie life can't hurt her. She is happiest when she is busy and you know the old saying "the devil finds uses for idle hands". Judy wants to go on making pictures, minding her own business, developing her mind, building a sane and normal future for herself.'

THE SHADOW OF DEATH

Her solo career started with an appearance on a radio show with star of the day Wallace Beery, but her bubble burst that November when her father Frank died suddenly after a short illness, aged 49. He was never to see the huge achievements of the daughter he helped to mould and make great.

It was devastating for Judy, who later called his death 'the most terrible thing that ever happened to me in my life'.

For her it was the start of an idolization which would last a lifetime. Recalling her father, Judy later said: 'I loved my father. He was a wonderful man with a fierce temper … and an untrained but beautiful tenor voice. He had a funny sense of humour and he laughed all the time – good and loud like I do. I adored him … And he wanted to be close to me too but we never had much time together.'

Little did she know that he had been forced to leave the theatre in Lancaster due to mismanagement which left him thousands of dollars in debt, nor that whispers of his indiscretions with schoolboys were echoing around the arid town. There was even talk of an arrest in Los Angeles. Her continuing promise at the start of the thirties was merely a good excuse for Frank to cut loose once more.

His death also helped to drive a wedge between herself and her mother. While blissfully unaware of her father's flings, she had found her mother during an assignation with another Lancaster man, to her horror and shame.

The seed of suspicion that Ethel was a dominant, pushy type who cared only to bask in her daughter's reflected glory began to grow. Judy once said of her mother: 'She was a lonely and determined woman and I guess I'm the same way.'

But she went on to blame her mother at least in part for much of her misery. They exchanged some contrary insults in an embittered battle of wills. Judy said Ethel was 'the real wicked witch of the West who was no good for anything but to create chaos and fear'. In turn, Ethel remained convinced she had done her level best for Judy and was simply assisting the girl's expressed ambition to become an actress.

By the time Judy was 30, mother and daughter were estranged. Ethel, the mother who had once called her youngest daughter loving, generous and unselfish, branded her as self-centred. 'That's my fault, I made it too easy for her,' she complained. 'She worked but that's all she ever wanted, to be an actress. She never said "I wanted to be kind" or "loved", only "I want to be famous."'

Ethel went to court to gain financial support from her by-now famous daughter. With a second, failed marriage behind her, she worked as a clerk at Douglas Aircraft in Santa Monica. Finally she had a heart attack in January 1953 and was found slumped between two cars, collapsing as she hurried to work.

Shocked, Judy went to the funeral with her sisters. Observers declared both mother and daughter always loved each other in their hearts.

However, only the germ of this personal disaster was forming when Judy was in those first heady days with the world's best-known film studio.

THE TRICKS OF THE TRADE

Her first movie was made in 1936; it was called *Every Sunday Afternoon* and starred Deanna Durbin. Judy then learned the tricks of the trade in a further six films alongside established stars including Betty Grable, Robert Taylor, Buddy Ebsen and Mary Astor.

In the same stable of child stars were Freddie Bartholomew and Mickey Rooney. The diminutive Rooney, who first met Judy at a Los Angeles stage school, struck up a lasting comradeship with her which he recalled in his autobiography, *Life is Too Short*.

'It was the perfect new name for the 15-year-old singer Frances Gumm. Judy was just right: cute, peppy and full of bounce. When I knew her at Ma Lawlor's Profession School she had more bounce than everyone else put together. Gumm was the wrong image: sticky, soft, chewy, tutti frutti, Garland was full of joy.

'And I will never forget her performance at the Pantages Theatre in Hollywood. She planted both feet wide apart as if she were challenging the audience then sang: "Zing went the Strings of my Heart" with the kind of verve that made all our heartstrings go bing, ding, ping, ring, ting and zing.'

He witnessed how Judy, the young individualist, was under pressure to conform to the likes of the leggy beauties who traditionally made it big in Hollywood.

'Judy ... was no glamour girl. In the first place she had a bad bite and her teeth were out of alignment. This, of course, was something MGM's dentists could fix.

'But there were some things about her that the studio couldn't fix. She was a little too short, a half inch under 5 feet tall. Her legs were long but they seemed to be hitched to her shoulders which were too broad for her body. She looked, well, different.'

When she saw herself in her second film with plaits and gingham dress, she described it as the most awful moment of her life. 'I'm like a fat little pig in pigtails,' she moaned.

Rooney pinpointed her fabulous physical attributes. 'In fact, Judy was an all-American beauty in more ways than one. She had marvellous, warm eyes that invited you to share her secret mirth and a cute little nose that wrinkled when she laughed.

'She had an expressive generous mouth that hardly ever uttered a line that wasn't funny, or, in her later years, outrageous or filled with feeling. If I had not been so tainted with the same phoney Hollywood notions about who was beautiful and who was not, I would have fallen in love with her myself.'

But Judy was learning young about the

Above: *Judy with Vincente Minnelli, the film director, who was 20 years her senior. He was the father of her first daughter, Liza, who also found fame in show business.*

AT 17, HOW COULD SHE HAVE KNOWN THAT THOSE HARMLESS TABLETS PRESCRIBED BY THE DOCTOR WOULD MAKE HER A JUNKIE FOR LIFE?

penalties of being different. The loyalty and allegiance she found in Rooney was a big comfort, but it wasn't enough. Even Mayer himself compounded her troubles. He would call her 'the fat kid' or even 'my little hunchback'.

Her big break came four years after joining the studio. She was picked to play Dorothy in *The Wizard of Oz* when rival studio Twentieth Century Fox refused to release Shirley Temple for the role.

Her confidence oozed all over the screen. That, alongside her moving rendition of the song: 'Somewhere Over the Rainbow', made Judy hot property.

FEAR OF FAILURE

But although at 17 she was little more than a child, the catapult to fame brought with it adult pressures. For about the first time in her life the effervescent kid whom neighbours found so natural and endearing became highly strung.

Perhaps it was the weight of performing in films, being the focus of the camera, lights, director and everyone else, that put her on edge.

Or maybe it was the constant invidious comparison to other svelte sex symbols of the day. Confused, the young Judy construed it was ideal to be thin, tall and sultry, none of which were her natural strengths.

To keep her nerves under control, she started popping pills prescribed at the studio. How could she have known then that those apparently harmless tablets would make her a junkie for life? By the time she was 20, she had suffered her first nervous breakdown. She had another the following year.

A lifetime of frustrating insomnia started. And the harder she worked, the less sleep she managed to achieve at night.

She considered herself plump and tried desperately to diet. She yearned for physical and dramatic perfection. It was a gilt-edged recipe for depression.

Much later she recalled how early fame had affected her: 'I had so many anxieties, so many fears. I'd had them as a child and they just grew worse as I got older and more self-centred. The fear of failure, the fear of ridicule. I hated the way I looked. I cried for no reason, laughed hysterically, made stupid decisions, couldn't tell a kind word from an insult.'

To escape the loneliness and insecurity, she married orchestra leader David Rose.

Right: *On stage, where she overcame her nerves to belt out songs which thrilled her audiences.*

Below: *With Lorna, aged 4, and Joseph, 2, in 1957.*

He was 12 years older and seemed to represent all that Judy was lacking in her world – stability, warmth and guidance.

But fate wasn't kind to the young romantics. Rose was drafted into the army within weeks. A year later he asked for a divorce on the grounds the pair had grown apart. Judy was wounded, despite his assurances she was in no way to blame for the collapse of the marriage. She continued working at a frenetic pace, finding time to entertain the troops when she wasn't making movies.

Within five years she was married again, this time to director Vincente Minnelli. Although 20 years older than her, he gave Judy time to mature and thrive. Her happiness was complete when she gave birth to a baby girl, Liza, in 1946.

BREAKDOWN

Still, Judy found the strain of working for the studio giants intolerable. Using pills as her prop, she was suffering poor health, but studio schedules and her own compulsion to perform wouldn't allow her to put her feet up. With the bouts of illness flared up tantrums and tears. Judy gained a reputation for being difficult on set.

It was during convalescence after a nervous breakdown in 1949 at the Peter Bent Brigham Hospital in Boston that her love of and dedication to children became obvious to herself and those around her. Judy spent hours at the bedside of a 6-year-old girl who refused to talk after being abused by her family. Quietly, comfortingly, Judy chatted about her life, her shows and the people she had met. The girl never said a word.

But when the day came for Judy to say goodbye, the youngster couldn't bear it. "Don't go. Don't go away," she pleaded as Judy prepared to leave, the first words she had uttered in months. Could Judy have found her niche if only she had stayed at home to be a full-time mother? It was another question that tormented her over the years.

Judy's contract expired in 1950 after 15 years and 30 pictures – and MGM decided she was too much trouble to take on again. At the same time, Minnelli decided to bring the curtain down on their marriage.

Judy was gutted by the double disaster.

It led to a frantic attempt to slash her neck and wrists, more a case of self-mutilation than suicide but enough to convince the Hollywood gossips she was finished.

And so it happened that when Judy was aged just 29, she was making her first 'comeback'.

It was to happen in London at the renowned Palladium in April 1951 in front of a buzzing crowd peppered with stars. Characteristically, Judy cowered in the wings – the prospect of performing in front of the excited throng terrified her. It was down to her friend Kay Thompson to get her onto the stage with a push from behind. But once on stage she sparkled.

COWERING IN THE WINGS, THE STAR WAS PETRIFIED WITH STAGE-FRIGHT.

To use a tired but apt statement, she took the place by storm. *The Daily Telegraph* said: 'It was not only with her voice but with her whole personality that she filled the theatre. Miss Garland's charm is a complete absence of affectation. She presented herself with no particular preparation and no preamble and just did what she must have been born to do … sing.'

It was followed by a country-wide tour where she received the same rapturous reception and then some dates back in the USA which also played to critical acclaim. The roller-coaster tour only stopped when Judy, exhausted and suffering critical pains in her chest, collapsed on stage during a matinee performance. Her body was pleading for a rest. Judy refused to listen and went back to work after only four days.

Above: *With Liza, Lorna, Joey and her third husband, pilot Sid Luft. Their stormy marriage lasted for 11 years.*

Above: *Judy gave a stunning performance in the film* **A Star is Born,** *which also featured James Mason.*

Below: *As one of the host of big-name stars, Judy packed a punch as the persecuted Jewish woman in* **Judgement at Nuremberg.**

Her new-found burst of energy was due in part to a fresh love in her life. In 1951 she became engaged to ex-test pilot Sid Luft and wed him the following year. They had two children, Lorna and Joseph, known as Joey.

Her stage revival an unqualified success, she found the courage to go back into the studios and record a movie, *A Star is Born.* James Mason was her co-star, although both Humphrey Bogart and Cary Grant had been sought for the role.

Word had it Judy was up to her old tricks of temperamental walk-outs and fainting fits which cost the production time and money. Afterwards Judy explained: 'I'd be the last to deny the picture took an awful long time and went way over budget. But there was a reason for all that.

'I'm a perfectionist; George Cukor [director] is a perfectionist and so is Sid. We had to have it right and to make it right took time. It was a good picture; as good as we'd hoped it would be.'

It won her one of two Academy Award nominations although the golden prize of an Oscar was to elude her.

Throughout the fifties Judy performed at dates in the USA, Britain and the rest of the world, but she was still dogged by ill health. First laryngitis threatened her shows after it consumed her voice. Then there was the constant struggle against weight gain, frequently caused by fluid retention. Finally, in 1959, her very life was in the balance when she contracted hepatitis. Many would have given up the bright lights and the glory for a life at home, but

Judy was a born trouper – she loved to do her stuff in front of audiences and cameras.

More than that, she was persistently plagued by cash worries. No matter how much she earned, there were always more bills and increased demands. The lovable tramp who performed 'Couple of Swells' so memorably seemed to have a permanent hole in her own pocket.

It is thought she earned $10 million during her career. Unfortunately her mother seems to have managed the starlet's income badly. Agents and managers carved off a slice of her earnings, as well as the expenses for her entire entourage. Then there were hefty back-tax demands – Judy had no idea why – and she was always broke.

Valiantly she went back to work, making a special effort to sing in support of John F. Kennedy, a valued friend.

In 1961, she filmed *Judgment at Nuremberg* and brilliantly portrayed the German woman persecuted by Nazis on a trumped-up charge.

A review in *Weekend* magazine described how fellow star Maximilian Schell was captivated by her performance.

'Max Schell's usually solemn face was alight with admiration. "She is fantastic," he said. "She is just a whole human being. Every dimension is there. And such warmth! It is as if she is enveloping you, as if she is trying to embrace the whole world."

'He was right. The magic, the old alchemy was very much present. This was no burned-out star staying airborne on a broomstick of temperament, laryngitis and law suits.'

The marriage to Sid Luft was a stormy one. They split and were reconciled three times before a final parting. It was after one of these break-ups that Judy fled to London with Lorna and Joey, terrified Sid was going to have the courts pronounce her 'an unfit mother'.

Although the threat came to nothing, it was another turn of the screw, putting her under extraordinary pressure. The marriage staggered on until May 1963 when it was finally finished. That was just before she embarked on her own television series, something she swore she would never do. The production of the shows was fraught with difficulty and received only mixed reviews. All Judy's old infamy came back to haunt her.

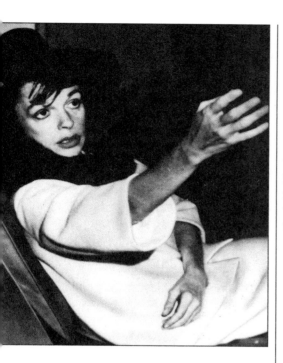

WHEN SHE TRIED TO SING JUDY DISCOVERED TO HER HORROR THAT THE OLD MAGIC HAD DESERTED HER.

CATASTROPHE

Judy was exhausted, from both work and continued ill health, including a painful kidney infection and a suspected heart attack. She was warned to temper her use of pills. Nevertheless, as her nightly quest for sleep ended in failure, she found herself reaching for a remedy in the long hours before dawn.

Her existence was getting more and more nightmarish too. She would ring up friends at all hours, starting impossible conversations about paranoid visions. Friends grew weary of soothing her panic attacks and few could blame them.

In May 1964 she undertook a series of tours in Australia. It started blindingly well in Sydney but the Melbourne date was a well-chronicled catastrophe. She was an hour late, tripped as she walked on stage and sang with a voice that could have scoured pans. She sang only a handful of songs before fleeing the stage in tears.

Quickly she moved on to Hong Kong to escape the publicity. Within days she was in a coma, struck down by broncho-pneumonia and pleurisy. Again she nearly died but fought back. Later she married Mark Herron, the man who discovered her unconscious and drove through a tropical typhoon to take her to hospital.

However, the marriage in November 1965 lasted only five months. Judy was hurt again, unable to understand how the relationship had collapsed, following as it did a year-long engagement.

There were more concerts at which she was croaky, tired and unable to finish. Lonely outside the theatre, she tried to write poetry to escape her problems but was stung by the bevy of criticism.

Judy had one final grab at happiness in the last months of her life. She met and married Mickey Deans, a discothèque manager who fell under her spell. He was touched by her vulnerability, enjoyed her tactile ways and realized she was not

Left: A feeble wave as Judy fled Australia after a disastrous show.

Above: Marriage to Mark Herron. The actor looks delighted to have wed Judy but the relationship floundered within six months.

unpredictable, just scared. It wasn't her temperament to blame for perpetual upsets but mostly her health. And he was outraged at the way showbusiness hangers-on would leech from her, helping to cause her cash problems.

Appalled when he discovered the extent of her dependency on pills, Mickey limited her to 40 a day. But he was helpless in the end – which came while they were visiting her favourite city, London, in June 1969. They had spent a lazy day, playing the piano and watching TV. They curled up in bed together and Mickey, suffering the

Above: *Judy and Liza, two show business legends, embrace in mutual admiration following a show in 1965.*

Right: *The final marriage, to Mickey Deans, came in March 1969. Just three months later he discovered her body after she died from a barbiturate overdose.*

ravages of a sore throat, knew nothing more until he woke up in an empty bed to the shrill ring of a telephone and tried to find her.

There was no response from behind the locked bathroom door. Judy had collapsed and died from the effects of too many barbiturates.

Her body was flown back to New York for a funeral. Before she was buried more than 20,000 people filed past her as she lay in a white steel casket at Campbell's Funeral Home in Madison Square Garden. Hundreds more turned out for the 20-minute service at which James Mason read the eulogy.

He read: '... I travelled in her orbit only for a while but it was an exciting while and one during which it seemed that the joys in her life outbalanced the miseries.

'The little girl whom I knew, had a curl right in the middle of her forehead; when she was good she was not only very very good, she was also the most sympathetic, the funniest, the sharpest and the most stimulating woman I ever knew. She was a lady who gave so much and richly, both to the vast audiences she entertained and the friends around her who she loved, that there is no currency in which to repay her ...'

Mickey Rooney said: 'Judy's not in pain any more but I am still sad about her leaving. There will never be another talent like Judy, never anyone who can sing with such heart. Other people sing the words. She never lost the thought behind the words, never lost the poetry.'

Liza recalls her legacy from her mother. 'My mother gave me strength and magic and humour. Her humour was so immense, people don't realize that. And she gave me my drive.'

Perhaps it was that drive which drove her to death.

SPECTACULAR FAILURES

GENERAL CUSTER
The last blunder

The ancient tribes, pushed to their limits by the land-hungry settlers, refused to surrender their holy lands. The arrogant General Custer was determined to make the Black Hills of Dakota run red with Indian blood.

George Armstrong Custer was a model soldier, the kind of man through whom wars are won and of whom legends are made. The legend of General Custer, however, is not one by which he would wish to be remembered.

Born on 5 December 1839 at New Rumley, Ohio, he graduated from the famed US Military Academy at West Point and was plummeted straight into the tragic American Civil War. He distinguished himself in this conflict by his pursuit of the Confederate Commander-in-Chief, General Robert E. Lee. By the age of only 23, he had rocketed to the rank of brigadier-general.

It was then that the vanity that eventually led him to an ignominious death first reared its arrogant head. He became a glory-seeker, desperate for mentions in dispatches. He grew his blond locks to shoulder length, and commissioned dozens of sketches and portraits of himself, with which he adorned his quarters.

His flamboyance and insufferable ego made him hated by his fellow officers, who were able to get their own back when, after the Civil War ended in 1865, he was relegated to the rank of captain. His driving ambition made him try all the harder, however, and he curried favour with senior officers until, within a year, he had regained the rank of lieutenant-colonel.

A LAUGHING STOCK

Custer was still a laughing stock among his peers. Perhaps it was one of them who reported him to his superiors for an offence that would have cost any other man his career. The long-haired egotist had found himself a wife, Libbie, and decided to spend a vacation with her – without troubling himself to seek permission from his senior officers. His absence from camp was discovered and Custer was hauled before a court martial. The sentence: suspension for a year without pay.

The delight back at camp must have been immense. It was the last anyone thought they would see or hear of the arrogant buffoon. In typical Custer style, he used his period of penury to write – about himself, of course! He portrayed himself in

Opposite: *George Custer; the truth about his bungling was kept hidden for years.*

Below: *Indian chief Sitting Bull, who had 50 pieces of flesh carved from his body to prove his courage in the preparations for Custer's last stand.*

GENERAL SHERIDAN'S
DIPLOMACY WAS SIMPLE:
THE ONLY GOOD INDIAN
WAS A DEAD ONE.

the role of hero in a series of adventures that bore more relationship to fiction than fact. Unfortunately, it is these writings that perpetuated his image and restored his reputation. The truth, however, was that while writing his early memoirs, he was running up bills which, as he later moved from fort to fort, he never quite managed to pay off.

Custer's luck remained with him. In 1868 he was reinstated. Unbelievably, he was given the exalted rank of general and placed in charge of the illustrious 7th Cavalry. He was also given a special mission, one that required the virtues of a diplomat as much as those of a soldier.

General Philip Sheridan, nicknamed the 'Angry Bear' of the frontier forts, is best known for his pronouncement that 'the only good Indian is a dead one'. He is certainly not remembered for his diplomacy or compassion. Perhaps that is why he appointed the newly promoted General George Armstrong Custer, who also had none of these virtues, to solve one of America's thorniest problems. At the tender age of 28, Custer was ordered to bring to heel the ancient tribes of the Plains Indians.

THE WHITE MAN'S GREED

For decades, the Indians (mainly Cheyenne and Sioux) had been slowly pushed westwards by land-hungry settlers. Land treaties allowed the native Americans freedom of movement but in the 1860s the greed of the white man produced an increasing number of clashes between the new and old residents of the plains. Wandering bands of Indian buffalo-hunters were becoming an annoyance to the authorities – because they wanted the land on which the buffalo roamed. For these wholly commercial reasons, it was decided to push the Indians into reservations. Many refused, preferring a precarious existence on the plains to mere survival on reservation handouts. The government wanted 'these renegades, these outcasts, these anti-socials' to be made to see the error of their ancient ways.

Why Custer should have been chosen as the man to get this message across can only be a matter of conjecture. His career as a soldier had been extremely patchy, and he was desperate to rehabilitate himself with the senior staff. He needed success and yearned for glory. It must have been made clear to him by General Sheridan that a handful of despised Indians must not be allowed to stand in his way.

In fact, Custer's mission was: 'To proceed to Washita River, the winter seat of the hostile tribes, and then to destroy their villages and ponies, kill or hang all warriors and bring back all women and children'.

The general was delighted to accept the task. In the autumn of 1868, he rode out towards the west, revelling in the nicknames the Indians had given him – 'Hard Backsides' because of the long chases he made without leaving the saddle, and the 'Long-Haired One' (or *Pahuska*) because of his flowing, straw-coloured locks.

His first foe was to be a peaceable old chief called Black Kettle, leader of the Southern Cheyenne, who had settled with his tribe of 200 families on the bank of the Washita River – the same river mentioned in Custer's secret orders.

Winter was about to set in and Black Kettle had asked to be allowed to move his tribe to the protection of the nearest white military outpost, Fort Cobb, about 100 miles distant. General William Hazen, the fort's commander, had refused, ordering Black Kettle and his deputation to return to the Washita. The general had, however, given them a firm assurance of safety. He had promised them that they would be allowed to remain by the river until after the snows had melted.

Did General Hazen know he was lying? Or did General Custer decide to overrule him? All that is certain is that before dawn on a foggy December morning, Custer's men surrounded the Cheyenne camp. Puzzled, Black Kettle saddled up and rode out through the mist to find the leader of the whites and talk with him.

SLAUGHTER OF INNOCENTS

As the Cheyenne chief left his camp, the cavalry charged. According to Indian legend, he was shot dead as he raised his hand to greet the approaching soldiers.

A massacre followed. Custer's secret orders were to kill the warriors, but it is estimated that only ten of the victims were warriors. The other 100 were men, young and old, women and children executed indiscriminately. Another 50 women and children were taken prisoner as a warning against retaliation. As a final blow, hundreds of ponies were slaughtered so that the survivors would have no means of flight.

This act of ignominy was but the first of a series of merciless campaigns throughout the winter against all other Indians in the area. Custer encouraged the reputation of himself as a pitiless warrior against whom no Indian dare stand. For a while, he succeeded. Then he met his match – in the Sioux chief Sitting Bull.

The word 'Sioux' is an alternative to Dakota, and in 1868 the Black Hills of Dakota had been given for all time to the Indians who lived there. This treaty suited the white man because the hills were thought valueless. But in 1874 Custer led an expedition into the region and reported: 'The hills are full of gold from the grass roots down.' The local military authorities tried to renegotiate a treaty but the Indians would not budge. Their hills, the 'Paha Sapa', were holy places, the centre of their spirit world, and they would not give them up.

A commission was sent from Washington to meet not only the Sioux but also the Arapahos and Cheyenne, all of whom had claims to the Black Hills. The tribes were unwilling to sell their land or to exchange it for other territory. Sitting Bull warned: 'We want to sell none of our land – not even a pinch of dust. The Black Hills belong to us. We want no white men here. If the white man tries to take the hills, we will fight.'

The reaction of the white man was predictable. The treaty was torn up and Custer pushed a trail through to open up the wealth of the Black Hills. In the Sioux language it was known as the 'Thieves Road'. The War Department leapt into action, issuing a hypocritical ultimatum that any Indians not on their official reservations by the end of January 1876 would be considered hostile and that 'military force will be sent to compel them'.

At this, Sitting Bull proved himself a better diplomat than the commissioners or the War Department. He protested in the

most measured terms that he had received news of the ultimatum only three weeks before the deadline. It would be impossible for his tribe to move camp in midwinter. The government was confounded. Genocide could not be sanctioned, and there was no good excuse to implement such a policy.

Instead of acting openly, the War Department resorted to subterfuge and deceit. On 7 February they ordered General Sheridan to attack the Indians. He entrusted the task to his fiercest commander, General George Armstrong Custer.

This was to be Custer's greatest hour. He left the safety of Fort Abraham Lincoln, in North Dakota, and journeyed westward. Every night of his journey, he sent a dispatch to New York newspapers, relating tales of his own courage and imagination. He also kept a 'private' diary – which he meant to be published later for his own self-glorification. In it he wrote: 'In years long-numbered with the past, my every thought was ambitious. Not to be wealthy,

Above: *One of Custer's scouts, Curley, a member of the Crow tribe. He was one of the few to survive the massacre at Little Big Horn though his life was not spared out of any racial loyalty. Sitting Bull's warriors were too busy slaughtering white men.*

THE GREEDY WHITE MEN THOUGHT THE HILLS WERE FULL OF GOLD AND WERE HAPPY TO MASSACRE INDIAN WOMEN AND CHILDREN TO GET THEIR HANDS ON IT.

Above: The *Battle of Little Bighorn, 1876.*

AT THE HEIGHT OF THE FEASTING AND CHANTING, SITTING BULL HAD 50 PIECES OF FLESH TORN FROM HIS BODY TO PROVE HIS COURAGE.

not to be learned, but to be great. I desired to link my name with acts and men, and in such a manner as to be a mark of honour, not only to the present, but to future generations.'

The campaign against the tribes settled around the Montana–Wyoming border began slowly. Cavalry would attack an isolated Indian encampment and burn its tepees. Often they would shoot the horses. Feeling increasingly isolated, the scattered Indians began to band together for safety in the Powder River and Tongue River basins. Eventually, a 'mega-tribe' came into being, comprising at least 10,000 Indians, of whom some 3,000 or 4,000 were warriors. They lived in a veritable forest of tepees and makeshift tents stretching three miles along the west bank of the Little Bighorn River. The Indians termed the camp the 'Valley of the Greasy Grass'. The whites knew the area as simply 'Little Bighorn'.

A GREAT POWER

Here were gathered the Hunkpapas, as well as Blackfoot Sioux, Arapahos, Sans Arcs, Brules, Minneconjous and Cheyenne. But the camp's leader was the Hunkpapa chief Sitting Bull, of whom a cavalry scout named Lewis Dewitt left us this description:

'Sitting Bull had a great power over the Sioux. He knew how to lead them. He told the Sioux many times that he was not made to be a reservation Indian. The Great Spirit had made him free to go wherever he wished, to hunt buffalo and to be a leader of his tribe.'

By June 1876, they all knew that a great battle was imminent. The Sioux feasted on buffalo meat, danced and chanted around their fires. Sitting Bull had 50 pieces of flesh cut from his body to prove his courage. Then he went into a trance. When he was revived, he told the tribe that he had seen a wonderful vision. He had seen white soldiers 'falling like grasshoppers' into his camp while a voice said: 'I give you these because they have no ears.'

On the night of 24 June 1876, while the Sioux held a holy sun dance to strengthen their resolve for battle and to ensure that the spirits of their dead would fly heavenward, General Custer arrived at the valley of the Little Bighorn. In his desperation for battle, he had outstripped his other units (he had made 60 miles in just two days) and turned up across the river from Sitting Bull's camp with 12 troops of US Cavalry – just 611 men.

Other detachments were on the way. Major-General John Gibbon had marched east from Fort Ellis, and General Alfred Terry had marched west from Fort Abraham Lincoln to meet up with him on the Yellowstone River. The two were now moving up the Little Bighorn with their combined force of 1,500 men.

Another 1,000 soldiers, led by General George Crook, straggled far to the south on the journey from Fort Fetterman. They were slightly less anxious for battle, already having encountered a war party of Oglalas, led by their fearsome chief Crazy Horse. The Oglalas had made a daring sortie to ambush Crook's men in the valley of the River Rosebud. Indeed, they almost succeeded in wiping out the force, such was the hopeless leadership of the general. He was saved, however, by the bravery of a party of Indian allies he had brought along as mercenaries: 250 Sioux-hating Crows and Shoshonis.

Custer was unaware that Crook was delayed and that his force was in total disarray. He knew that his other fellow generals were on their way, however, and was anxious that they should not share the glory of victory.

Now knowing the size of the Indian camp, Custer should have been concerned at his tactical disadvantage. He also should have reviewed his decision to turn down General Terry's offer of extra men and Gatling guns, which he believed would have held up his progress. And he certainly should have heeded his own Indian scouts, who begged him to hold back for two days until Terry and Gibbon caught up with them.

But General Custer was too arrogant to heed any such advice. He was too vainglorious to delay attacking Sitting Bull for one day longer …

At dawn on 25 June, Custer launched his attack. He advanced with three of his 12 troops, while another three moved forward under Captain Frederick Benteen and a further three under Major Marcus Reno. The remaining troops were left with the supply train.

Major Reno's modest force of 140 men crossed the Little Bighorn River and successfully attacked from the rear, taking by surprise the Hunkpapas, Blackfoot Sioux and Crazy Horse's Oglalas in their villages at the southern end of the camp. Women and children were cruelly shot down as they ventured from their tepees.

At the moment of Reno's attack, Custer and his much larger force of 225 men were scheduled to be attacking the Indians from the other side. But Custer was still four miles away – stumbling along the river bank looking for a suitable crossing. Likewise, the third column, under Captain Benteen, was still some miles from its target.

A GOOD DAY TO DIE

Reno could not sustain the attack alone. Sitting Bull's chief lieutenant, Gall, who had just seen his wife and children cut down by the troops, rallied his warriors for a counter-attack. Out-flanked,

> **TERRIFIED WOMEN AND CHILDREN WERE COLD-BLOODEDLY SHOT TO PIECES AS THEY SOUGHT SANCTUARY.**

Below: *Custer's last stand, from an engraving. Even though the defeat was brought about by his hasty pursuit of glory, he was still seen as a hero.*

CUSTER KILLED.

DISASTROUS DEFEAT OF THE AMERICAN TROOPS BY THE INDIANS.

SLAUGHTER OF OUR BEST AND BRAVEST.

GRANT'S INDIAN POLICY COME TO FRUIT.

A WHOLE FAMILY OF HEROES SWEPT AWAY.

THREE HUNDRED AND FIFTEEN AMERICAN SOLDIERS KILLED AND THIRTY-ONE WOUNDED.

SALT LAKE, U. T., July 5.—The correspondent of the Helena (Mon.) *Herald* writes from Still water, Mon., under date of July 2, as follows:

Muggins Taylor, a scout for General Gibbon, arrived here last night direct from Little Horn River and reports that General Custer found the Indian camp of 2,000 lodges on the Little Horn and immediately attacked it.

He charged the thickest portion of the camp with five companies. Nothing is k-n of the operations of this detachment, except their course as traced by the dead. Major Reno commanded the other seven companies and attacked the lower portion of the camp.

Above: New York World *told how the Indians had massacred 'hero' soldiers. The report appeared on 6 July 1876.*

outnumbered, and exhausted from their forced march, Reno's men retreated.

The vengeful Crazy Horse told his men: '*Hoka-hey!* It's a good day to fight. It's a good day to die. Strong hearts, brave hearts to the front, weak hearts and cowards to the rear.'

Now Sitting Bull, directing the battle from the high ground of his tepee, could vent his wrath against the hated *Pahuska* …

He ordered his chief lieutenant, the ferocious Gall, to ford the river to the rear of Custer's force and to take it from behind. The general was taken completely by surprise. In panic, he ordered his men to retreat to a nearby hill and take up defensive positions.

Struggling up this rise, with Gall's men screaming for blood at their heels, General George Custer must at last have lost his arrogant smirk. For there, atop the hill and staring down at him was Crazy Horse – with 1,000 mounted warriors. Custer was at a loss for words. He could not voice his next command. His troops were terrified. There was nowhere to run. Their leader, the 'Long-Haired One', was not invincible. He was suddenly proved to be one of history's biggest bunglers.

The force of 225 that Custer had led to war with the promise of victory and glory now stared death in the face. Crazy Horse's men delayed their revenge for a few moments as they stared down in disdain at the cowering cavalry. Then they charged.

The soldiers dismounted. Without a shred of cover, they grouped themselves in a broad circle and set about defending themselves with the resigned bravery of lost men. Whooping and shouting and screaming, the shrieking Sioux shot away at the cavalrymen. They fell by the score until a remaining few at the edge of the battle held up their hands in surrender. They were immediately hacked to death.

But where, Crazy Horse demanded, was *Pahuska*? Suddenly, Custer stood alone – in Sitting Bull's words, 'like a sheaf of corn with all the ears fallen around him'. He had been unrecognized at first because he had had his long hair cut short for the battle. But now they knew him, the Indians descended on him like flies to carrion.

Sitting Bull, Crazy Horse and their men celebrated their victory and mourned their dead. They had defended their people and their land with determination and valour. But in Washington Custer's Last Stand was labelled a savage massacre.

The body of the incompetent, arrogant, vanquished General Custer was recovered and given a hero's burial at West Point. Meanwhile, a series of punitive missions was launched against the victorious Indians, who quickly scattered.

Sitting Bull fled with 3,000 warriors to Canada, the 'Land of the Great Godmother', Queen Victoria. In 1881 he returned to the US and surrendered, spending two years in prison before being allowed to rejoin his tribe at Standing Rock reservation, North Dakota. Nine years later he was accused of once again inciting unrest among his people. Resisting arrest, he was shot in the back.

Crazy Horse also surrendered and moved to a reservation. But in 1877 he was taken to Fort Robinson where, while trying to escape, he was bayoneted to death. His last words were: 'Let me go, my friends. You have got me hurt enough.'

Custer, on the other hand, remained a hero. His phony legend of heroism took a century to dispel. The blindly blundering story of the man who by treachery and butchery helped wipe out entire nations has only recently been told.

Above: *Following the battle, Americans come to pay their respects at the graves of the men who died.*

Left: *Fearsome Oglala leader Crazy Horse. After Indian women and children were brutally murdered by the cavalry, he showed no mercy at Little Bighorn.*

CHRISTOPHER COLUMBUS Who really discovered America?

Columbus was determined to sail to the ends of the Earth in search of the riches of the Orient. Instead he stumbled across America, firmly believing that the West was really the East ...

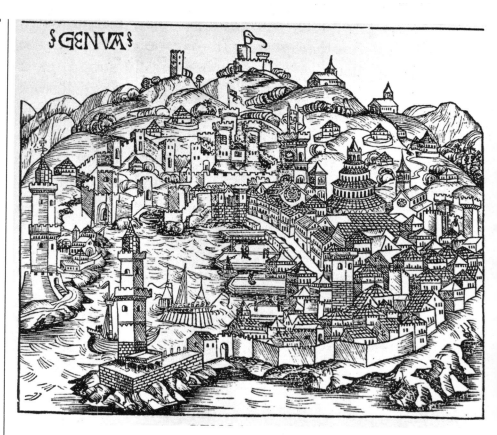

§ GENVA §

Ask any schoolchild: 'Who discovered America?' and the answer is likely to come straight back: 'Christopher Columbus'. But should the great navigator really get the credit for being the first man to open up the New World to the Old? Or did the Chinese, Phoenician, Irish, Viking or Ancient Greek sailors get there first? And, to rewrite history even further, did Columbus really mean to discover America? Was not his voyage one of the most enduring errors in history?

Christopher Columbus was without doubt the most pioneering voyager of his age, a brave and ambitious sailor who discovered America in 1492 when he traversed the unknown Atlantic from Spain to the West Indies. Generations of schoolchildren have grown up believing the great navigator opened up this Brave New World.

What they have not been taught is the astonishing catalogue of errors that led to his remarkable ocean voyages ...

Christopher Columbus was born Cristoforo Columbo, son of a clothmaker in Genoa, Italy, in about 1451. Little is known of his early life, but he went to sea as a youth and joined the Portuguese fleet after being shipwrecked off Lisbon in 1476.

A DREAM OF RICHES

A proud, stubborn, ambitious mariner, he was convinced the world was round – an unpopular theory in his day, but one that was gaining support among the scientific brains of Europe. He believed that the coast of spice-rich Asia and the gold-rich lands of the Orient lay west of Europe, and he dreamed of opening up a new sea route from Spain to the isles of the East Indies.

Ironically, many of the theories which were to lead Columbus to the New World were based on fallacy and wholly misinterpreted conclusions. He had read and reread in the *Apocrypha* that 'Upon the third day Thou didst command that the waters should be gathered in the seventh part of the Earth; six parts hath Thou dried up ...' And he had concluded that only one-seventh of the globe was therefore covered by sea. Columbus decided that, to make up the other six-sevenths, there must be a vast land mass to the west. The Atlantic Ocean could not be that big, after all!

For years, while sailing the shipping lanes around Portugal and Spain and down the coast of Africa to the Canary Islands, he had been planning an Atlantic crossing. The Italian captain first explained his dream in 1484 to King John II of Portugal. He sought the monarch's patronage for a voyage westward to discover a new route to the spice islands of Asia, which he described as being within easy sailing

Above: *Genoa at the end of the 15th century. Columbus was born here, but he accepted patronage from the Spanish royals to make his questing voyage.*

Opposite: *Explorer and adventurer Christopher Columbus believed a short sortie west from Portugal would lead him to the riches of the Orient.*

Right: *Columbus sets sail from Palos. He bids a fond farewell to his sponsors King Ferdinand and Queen Isabella of Spain.*

Below: *The three-masted* **Santa Maria,** *which bore Columbus and his crew across the Atlantic. It was later wrecked.*

distance. The disbelieving king turned him down.

Eight years later, he put his project to Spain's King Ferdinand and Queen Isabella – and it was accepted.

He assembled a humble fleet of three tiny, wooden-hulled ships in the bustling port of Palos, on Spain's southern coast. On Friday 3 August 1492 a gentle breeze carried Columbus and his 86 fellow seamen out of the harbour.

Led by his flagship, the 70-foot *Santa Maria*, and followed by her attendant vessels the *Pinta* and *Nina*, the small fleet headed for San Sebastian in the Canaries. Then on 6 September, eager not to miss the prevailing easterly winds, the ships turned westward into the open Atlantic.

MUTINY

The great navigator was at last on his way, heading for the greatest discovery – but also one of the biggest blunders – of any explorer.

The crew were more than a little fearful of what lay ahead. They were voyaging beyond the horizon of the known world. The mighty Atlantic Ocean seemed endless. And so it almost proved. The square-rigged ships at first made good progress in the following wind, but by mid-September, with land still not in sight, his men became worried. They feared they might never see Spain again.

The uneducated crew saw no glory in the mission, and they could not give a fig for its commercial aims – to bypass the Moslem-controlled trading routes to the Indies. All they were worried about was their safety and their comfort; few had bunks to sleep on and the inadequate food was already running low. There was even talk of mutiny.

For one man, however, the thought of sailing into the unknown held no terror. Christopher Columbus had no thought of turning back. Instead, perhaps to allay his crew's fears, perhaps doubting his own estimate of the distance to the Indies, he began to keep a false log. From 19 September, in a meticulous manner, he started underestimating the miles his ships were sailing each day.

The *Santa Maria*, the *Pinta* and the *Nina* were sometimes battered by high seas, at other times becalmed for days. They rode out the perils of the Sargasso Sea, and sailed ever west. Columbus was desperate for his expedition to succeed, but he was also mindful of the rewards that would be heaped on him by a grateful king and queen upon his return.

Hopes that the fleet was nearing land were often raised and dashed. More and more seagulls began to show ... then land birds. Sadly, the jubilant crewmen were probably deluding themselves that this meant a continent was just over the horizon. Most of the birds they saw were migratory.

On 11 October, however, the men of the *Santa Maria* spotted a green branch floating in the water. And at 2 o'clock the following morning, Rodrigo de Triana, a seaman on board the *Pinta*, raised the cry: 'Land!'

On 12 October, 37 days after leaving the Canaries, the fleet hove to off an island which Columbus named San Salvador (now believed to be Watlings Island in the Bahamas). Elated, he wrote in his log:

'There we soon saw naked natives ... A landscape was revealed to our eyes with lush green trees, many streams and fruits of various types.' The next day he wrote: 'I saw that some of the men had pierced their noses and had put a piece of gold through it ... By signs, I could understand that we had to go to the south to meet a king who had great vessels of gold.'

MONUMENTAL ERROR

On October 17 he noted: 'On all these days I have been in India it has rained more or less ...'

Columbus was referring to the new lands as 'India'. He still thought he had made his landfall on the eastern coast of Asia. And in the light of this monumental

error, he began his exploration of the New World – firmly believing that the West was the East.

Christopher Columbus sailed among the Caribbean islands until he reached the north coast of Cuba, thence on to Hispaniola (now Haiti and the Dominican Republic). Still believing that the Asian mainland was somewhere over the horizon, he wrote in his log on 28 October: 'I dare to suppose that the mighty ships of the Grand Khan come here and that from here to the mainland is a journey of only ten days.'

The fleet never attempted to reach the unseen 'Asian' mainland. Instead, after eight months at sea, they returned in

THE ROUGH CREW WHISPERED WORDS OF MUTINY – THEY FEARED THEY'D NEVER SEE THEIR HOMELAND AGAIN.

Above: *Columbus stopped long enough to raise the Spanish flag on Hispaniola before rushing back to Spain with news of his discovery.*

triumph to Spain, where Columbus was made 'Admiral of the ocean sea and governor of the islands newly discovered in the Indies'.

It was only later, after Spanish and Portuguese voyagers had explored and mapped the Americas, that Christopher Columbus received the posthumous accolade of discovering a new continent. But did this obsessive Italian émigré, hired by a foreign paymaster, really discover the New World?

UNCANNY RESEMBLANCE

Researchers suggest that it is possible that many other races, equipped with vessels far more primitive than his, could have reached it before him. People have been settled in America for 12,000 years – a fact ascertained using carbon dating, a process that accurately pinpoints the date of an artefact or other object to within 100 years.

The first settlers in America were probably descendants of Mongoloid tribesmen who reached the continent by crossing the land bridge across the Bering Strait from Siberia to Alaska. This much we know of the indigenous people, the first Americans. But who were the first people from other continents to reach America?

Some theoreticians claim that the Chinese, who were masters of technical and cultural affairs long before the Europeans, were the first outsiders to land in America. They point to the discovery of sculptures amongst the remains of ancient Central American nations and their uncanny resemblance to idols used in the Buddhist religion as proof that the Chinese arrived there in about 2000 BC. Another people who may have set foot in America before the time of Christ are the Phoenicians. Herodotus, the Ancient Greek historian, mentions the Phoenicians and wrote in 600 BC that sailors of Tyre and Sidon were hired by Pharaoh Necho of Egypt to sail around Africa. They accomplished this astonishing feat, and went on to sail the Atlantic in triremes – galleys with triple decks of oarsmen. It is thought that they reached the Azores, the site of the discovery in the 18th century of a hoard of gold Carthaginian coins.

However, the greatest backing for the claims arises from the discovery of an inscribed stone in a Brazilian coffee plantation in 1872. The translation reads: 'We are sons of Canaan from Sidon, the city of the king. Commerce has cast us on this distant shore, a land of mountains … We voyaged with ten ships. We were at sea together for two years … So we have come here, 12 men and three women on a new shore which I, the admiral, control. But auspiciously may the exalted gods and goddesses favour us.'

Is that proof that Phoenicians discovered the Americas long before the birth of Christ, and of course many centuries before Christopher Columbus? The argument rages to this day – against claims from many other lands and peoples.

CRYSTAL TOWERS

A 6th-century Latin manuscript which has survived contains evidence that the Irish may have been the first Europeans to cross the Atlantic. The *Navigatio Sancti Brendani* tells how St Brendan set sail in AD 540 with a crew of 14 monks. His mission was to 'find the land promised to the saints'. The *Navigatio* says that Brendan was an experienced sailor from Kerry in the west of Ireland and that his primitive boat was a 35-foot ketch, covered with the hides of oxen and greased with butter to keep it waterproof.

The document tells its story in colourful language that some sceptics believe makes it merely a fairy-tale. But, studied closely, it makes sense to many. The vessel took a northerly course, eventually coming across 'a floating tower of crystal' – probably an iceberg, thousands of which litter the northern approaches to America. They went through an area of dense mist – possibly the famous fog-shrouded Newfoundland Banks, where the warm Gulf Stream mixes with the violent Arctic currents. The manuscript does get fanciful, for Brendan claims they were guided by whales and angels disguised as birds before they reached land. The men landed on a tropical island surrounded by clear waters and inhabited by pygmies. This, say those who believe this theory, could have been one of the islands in the Bahamas group. Later he went on to find another land, which may have been Florida.

There is little hard evidence to confirm

HAD THE IRISH SAINT REALLY SAILED TO AMERICA FROM THE EMERALD ISLE IN A PRIMITIVE KETCH COVERED WITH THE HIDES OF OXEN AND GREASED WITH BUTTER TO KEEP IT WATERPROOF?

the claims of this ancient text, and it could be regarded as just fancy, were it not for the fact that the great Norse sailors testify in their sagas that the Irish were indeed the first to reach America. The Viking voyages, made in their famous longboats with imposing prows and shallow sides, are now established as historical fact. The Vikings made their journeys in short legs from Scandinavia, via Iceland and Greenland, establishing settlements en route. They were well supplied, developing a method of preserving their meats by trailing them in the salted water, and drinking water from cowhide pouches.

In the saga recounting the deeds of the great navigator Leif Ericsson, it is recorded that he reached the New World in AD 1000. He called it Vinland, describing it as a land of beauty and contrasting climates. The sagas, not written by him but based on his records, are believed to refer to the area now known as New England.

The discovery some years ago of eight houses, cooking pots, kitchen implements, boats and boatsheds at a site on the northern tip of Newfoundland offers, says Norwegian historian Dr Helge Ingstad, 'the first incontrovertible evidence that Europeans set foot in America centuries before Columbus's voyage of 1492'.

Another find, relating to the Norse adventurers is also the subject of controversy. In 1898 a farmer clearing land at Kensington, Minnesota, came across a stone covered in the characters of a strange language. The Kensington Rune, as it later became known, was said to tell the story of a 30-strong party of Norwegians and Goths who went west from Vinland in 1362, ending with a massacre in which ten of the party were killed. Again, experts are divided as to whether it is the genuine article or a clever fake. But those who believe in its authenticity say that its language is too complex for it to be a crude forgery.

Other finds may offer positive proof of the Vikings' first foothold on the continent. One such is the Newport Tower, in the centre of Newport, Rhode Island. The circular structure is supported on eight columns and could be old enough to have

Above: *Columbus returned to Spain, where he told Queen Isabella he had found a new route to Asia. He was rewarded with the governorship of the newly discovered province.*

**AT A DESOLATE HILL THEY
DISCOVERED AN EERIE
SACRIFICIAL TABLE
USED DURING MACABRE
CEREMONIES.**

*Right: The family man.
Columbus was father to two
sons, Diego and Ferdinand.*

*Below: A map of the four
great voyages charted by
Christopher Columbus, from
a book published in 1889.*

been constructed by the Vikings. But some say that the building is merely the remains of a church built by much later, Christian settlers.

SACRIFICIAL TABLE

Among this mass of Irish, Viking and Phoenician contenders for the discovery of America is one more – another Celtic expedition. A desolate place called Mystery Hill in North Salem, north of Boston, consists of a collection of ruins of a kind usually associated with the great megalithic sites of Europe. There are the remains of 22 huts, passageways and cooking pits, and an eerie sacrificial table with a speaking tube through which voices can be projected – presumably for use during macabre ceremonies.

The huge blocks of granite comprising the passageways are held in place by their own weight, and many thousands of artefacts from different periods have been

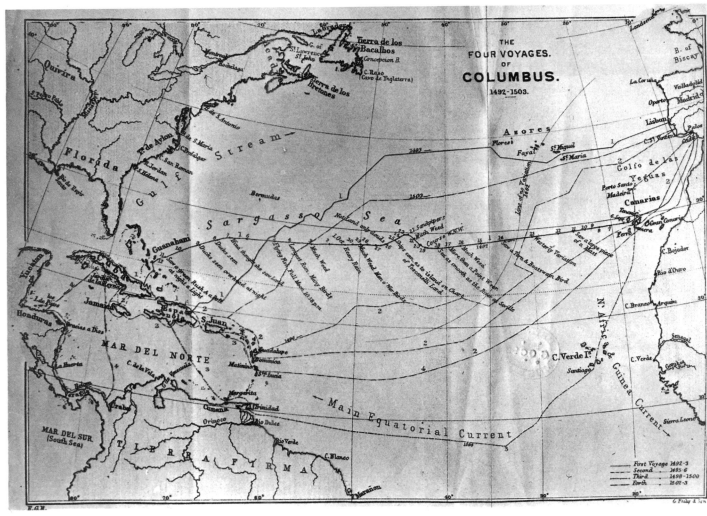

found there. Stones bearing chiselled inscriptions in the ancient Celtic form of rune writing called Ogham have been found too. Is this evidence of yet another race laying claim to America? Or is it perhaps not the work of the Celts, but of Ancient Greeks – perhaps even the great hero of Homer's legendary tale, Odysseus, arriving there on his voyage to the far frontiers of the world? The theories are endless.

What is now certain, however, is that it was not Christopher Columbus who first set foot in the Americas. For centuries, the crediting of the Italian navigator as the founder of the New World has been an astonishing mistake.

Even Columbus himself slowly began to realize that his earliest theories about the land to which he had sailed might be challenged by the evidence of history. In the ten years following his first crossing of the Atlantic, he made three further epic voyages, and only towards the end of his explorations did he begin to doubt whether he had in fact found the eastern coast of Asia.

On his third voyage in 1498 he began to wonder whether he had found a new continent. He had taken a more southerly course across the Atlantic and had made landfall on the island of Trinidad. While exploring in the nearby Gulf of Paria, he came to the place where the mighty Orinoco River of South America flows into the sea. In his log of 14 August 1498, he wrote: 'I believe that this is a very large continent which until now has remained unknown.'

AN IGNOMINIOUS END

In 1502 Columbus set out on his fourth voyage. For nine months, in gruelling weather, he explored the coasts of Honduras, Costa Rica and Panama. Then, in May 1503, he struck north in a desperate bid to reach the new Spanish settlement of Santo Domingo, on the island of Hispaniola. He failed. With his storm-battered ships – worm-eaten, leaking and altogether unseaworthy – he spent 12 months as a castaway on Jamaica before being rescued with his crew and taken back to Spain.

It was an ignominious end to the last

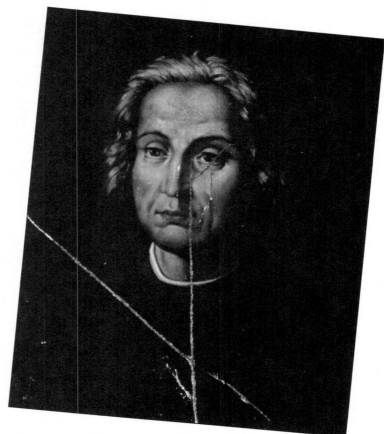

great voyage of the great navigator. He returned home still believing that the islands he had discovered on his first two voyages were off the eastern coast of Asia. He still believed that a passage through to Asia must exist between these islands and the great new land to the south.

Twice he had stumbled across the New World without really knowing it. He died on 20 May 1506, never to know that the land he had discovered was in fact the vast continent of America.

The result of his error was that the land that Christopher Columbus had risked his life four times to reach was named after one of his rivals. Fellow Italian adventurer Amerigo Vespucci explored much of Brazil's coastline – and it was the accounts of his discoveries that eventually won him the honour of having the great new continent named after him.

It is Christopher Columbus, though, who will probably continue to be credited as the man who discovered the New World. He may have made a giant error, but his discovery is part of the history of mankind and paved the way to the modern world. The tragedy for Columbus himself is that he died without ever knowing how stupendous his achievement was.

Above: *Columbus still gets all the credit for discovering the New World, even though there's evidence that ancient peoples made the journey there centuries before he set sail.*

TRAGICALLY HE DIED WITHOUT EVER KNOWING HE'D DISCOVERED ONE OF THE EARTH'S GREAT CONTINENTS.

SURVIVORS' VIVID STORIES OF AIRSHIP DISASTER

DAILY SKETCH, MONDAY, OCTOBER 6, 1930

DAILY SKETCH

INCORPORATING THE DAILY GRAPHIC

ONE PENNY.

MONDAY, OCTOBER 6, 1930.

No. 6,699. [Registered as a newspaper.]

R101 MEMORIAL NUMBER

THE LAST OF THE GIANT R101: WONDERFUL AIR PICTURE

...aster in which R101 crashed in flames near Beauvais, Northern France, within eight hours of ...iled, there being only eight survivors. Her commander, Flight-Lieut. H. C. ...another of the victims, initiated the construction of R101 and ...their air vessels.

THE R101
A flight to hell

Lord Thomson of Cardington thought that the world's mightiest airship would carry him to personal glory – blind ambition prevented him from seeing that the R101 would be his ticket to a blazing hell.

The R101 airship was a disaster long in the making. It was designed and built to satisfy the power and prestige of politicians. And it was flown in the face of all advice and protests in order to satisfy the whim of one man. The R101, this mightiest of British inflatables in the age of airships, was used to boost the already over-inflated ego of Lord Thomson of Cardington, the secretary of state for air. His arrogance cost the lives of all but six of its 54 passengers and crew in an inferno on a French hillside in 1930.

The most unnecessary disaster in the history of flying began seven years earlier, however, when in 1923 the Conservative government was persuaded by the Vickers aircraft and engineering firm that giant airships could be used for passenger services linking all major parts of the Empire. The government would commission them and Vickers, the most experienced builders of airships in Britain, would, of course, be paid to build them.

Vickers, greedy for the contract, were horrified when the Conservatives fell before a decision could be made, and in 1924 the first Labour parliament came to power on promises of nationalization and state control. Socialism was the order of the day and success for the fiercely capitalist firm of Vickers was not to its liking.

ASTONISHING DECISION

The new prime minister Ramsay MacDonald and his advisors then made the most astonishing decision. They decided to commission not one, but two airships to exactly the same specification: the R100, a capitalist airship, and the R101, a socialist airship. The R100 was to be built by Vickers and the R101 by the Air Ministry. By some extraordinary set of rules, the government would then decide which of the two would win its accolades and its orders.

No one was more astonished by this than Nevil Shute Norway – now better known as novelist Nevil Shute. At the time, he was Vickers' chief calculator, and he wrote: 'The controversy between capitalism and the state enterprise had been argued, tested and fought in many ways but the airship venture in Britain was the most curious of them all.'

Above: *Lord Thomson, the man who made the success of the R101 a life's ambition.*

Opposite: *Cover of the* **Daily Sketch***, which graphically illustrated the scale of the disaster.*

Below: *The R101 was visually stunning but it was plagued by design faults. It should never have left the ground.*

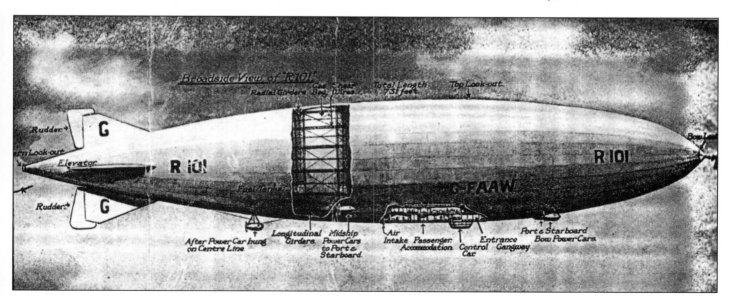

THE DESIGN WAS BEAUTIFUL
— AND LETHAL.

Lord Thomson, Labour's air minister, was responsible for the R101. So fanatical about the project was he that he adopted the name of the nationalized aircraft factory as part of his title. It was therefore as Lord Thomson of Cardington that he oversaw the building of the airship at Cardington, near Bedford. The first problem facing the design team was the ministry's decision that petrol engines would be unsafe for their airship. The Cardington team argued fiercely against deisel engines but were overruled. As a consequence, 8-cylinder diesel units were ordered – engines originally designed for railway locomotives. They weighed twice as much as the R100's petrol-power units, were far less efficient and vibrated alarmingly.

Such was the weight of the engines and other equipment built into the R101 that when the airship was first inflated and tested it was discovered that its lifting power was about half what it should have been. The team immediately began taking out of the craft all the gadgetry which they had confidently built into it. The effect was disastrous …

The gas valves were so sensitive that they leaked perpetually. The propellers broke when put into reverse, and a heavy backward-facing engine had to be fitted in order that the airship could manoeuvre when docking. The hydrogen bags which would keep it aloft rolled around inside the craft. The airship was unbalanced. It bucked up and down dangerously as soon as it was tethered at its mooring mast. The craft's outer casing split time and time again and ended up being covered with patches, and the fins, though beautifully streamlined, tended to stall.

Of course, many such problems were also encountered by the Vickers R100 team, led by designer Barnes Wallis, who was to become famous in World War 2 for his dam-busting bouncing bomb. But they were overcome – despite some less than salubrious conditions.

The R100 was being built in a leaky World War 1 airship hangar at Howden, Yorkshire. Writing much later about how untrained local labour was being used for much of the manual work, Nevil Shute complained: 'The local women were filthy in appearance and habits, and incredibly foul-mouthed. Promiscuous intercourse was going on merrily in every dark corner.'

Shute never gave an opinion as to whether this was the reason that the R101 was finished first! But, by hook or by crook, it was and a VIP crowd was invited to Cardington to watch it being floated out of its hangar.

DISASTER AVERTED

A few weeks later, on 28 June 1930, the largest airship in the world – 200 yards long and filled with 5 million cubic feet of hydrogen – was flown to Hendon to take part in an air display … and immediately

Below: *The Royal Airship Works, Cardington, where the ill-fated R101 was constructed.*

THE CROWD APPLAUDED THE AIRSHIP'S ACROBATICS, BLISSFULLY UNAWARE THAT DISASTER HAD NARROWLY BEEN AVERTED.

Left: *R100 flying over Farnborough. It took longer to build than its government-sponsored rival, but it flew beautifully.*

appeared to embark on a sequence of aerial stunts. It twisted and turned, then suddenly dipped its nose and dived spectacularly before pulling up sharply. The 100,000-strong crowd applauded, but they were even more impressed when moments later the aircraft, already too low for comfort, repeated the manoeuvre and pulled out of its dive just 500 feet above the ground.

The entire show had, of course, been entirely unplanned. The crowds were unaware that the craft's sweating coxswain had been struggling at the controls to avert disaster. Neither were they told that when the R101 was examined afterwards more than 60 holes were found in the hydrogen bags. The highly inflammable gas was pouring out everywhere.

The public was blissfully innocent of these problems. The Air Ministry technicians were frantic in their attempts to solve them. They had already cut their airship in two, inserted an extra gas tank in the middle, put the craft together again and once more hauled it to its mooring tower. Surely the extra lift would solve their problems. But within minutes, the whole skin of the airship began rippling in the wind, and a 90-foot gash opened up along its side. The next step was to begin disposing of every piece of non-essential equipment. Out went the expensive power steering and many of its more luxurious touches.

The R101's outer cover was a constant source of embarrassment. It rotted so quickly that a story went around that the culprits were construction workers who, too lazy to return to ground level, had habitually urinated from the topmost part of the airship. The chemical reaction of urine with the solution of dope on the outer skin was said to have been detrimental. It is known that as the airship emerged from its hangar one day in June 1930, a rip 50 yards long appeared in its side. It was repaired

but exactly the same thing occurred the following day.

At this time one courageous Air Ministry inspector reported: 'Until this matter is seriously taken in hand and remedied I cannot recommend the extension of the present permit-to-fly or the issue of any further permit or certificate.' His report was never published and was quietly pigeon-holed by the ministry mandarins.

Production of the rival R100 was meanwhile continuing apace. The Vickers airship lacked the beautiful lines of its sister craft but had one significant advantage: it could actually fly!

The Vickers team announced that their airship would embark on its flight to Canada in the summer of 1930. The Cardington team suggested a postponement both of the Canada trip and of their trip to India. Vickers, gleeful at their rivals' problems, refused to call off the R100's journey. On 29 July 1930, seven years after

Below: *R101 at its mooring tower. Wind constantly ripped its outer skin and hydrogen poured out of dozens of holes in the gas bags.*

Above: *Sir Sefton Brancker doubted that the R101 could survive a major voyage. He discovered, to his cost, that he was right.*

Below: *The luxurious lounge where passengers relaxed, in ignorance of the problems besetting the ship in flight.*

Vickers first proposed the giant airship project, the R100 set off for Canada. It completed the round-trip successfully and without fuss.

By now, Lord Thomson was beginning to fluster and bluster. He saw his pet project as a battle between capitalism and socialism, a battle that the socialists were losing. It did not help his case that the private-enterprise sister ship had so far cost the taxpayer somewhat less than his R101. The noble lord's airship must not be shown to be second-best. It had to fly – and soon.

Re-covered, lightened and lengthened, the R101 made its trial flight on 1 October 1930. The craft's oil-cooler having broken down, there was no opportunity for any speed trials. Poor-weather tests had not even been embarked on. The airship had not flown at full power. Neither had the R101 been issued with an airworthiness certificate … so the Air Ministry wrote one out for themselves.

HELPLESS!

The very day before the flight, a final conference about the trip was held at the Air Ministry. Lord Thomson piously warned: 'You must not allow my natural impatience or anxiety to influence you in any way.' No one believed his caution was sincere. After all, he had already announced: 'The R101 is as safe as a house – at least to the millionth chance.' And he had issued an official directive to everyone concerned in the project: 'I must insist on the programme for the Indian flight being adhered to, as I have made my plans accordingly.'

Nevil Shute wrote later: 'To us, watching helplessly on the sidelines, the decision to fly the R101 to India that autumn of 1930 appeared to be sheer midsummer madness.' He said of Thomson: 'He was the man primarily responsible for the organization which produced the disaster. Under his control, practically every principle of safety in the air was abandoned.'

But despite dissension among the designers, fears by Air Ministry inspectors and the alarm of the Cardington team itself, the great man would not be swayed. Lord Thomson had other reasons for pressing ahead with his personal flight to India. He wanted to make a magnificent impression when the airship arrived at Karachi. His ambition was to become Viceroy of India and he hoped that the spectacle would help him achieve that aim. And he had to fly straight away because he did not want to miss the Imperial Conference to be held in London in mid-October.

A fellow VIP booked on the flight was not so sanguine. Air Vice-Marshal Sir Sefton Brancker, the monocled director of civil aviation, was extremely sceptical, having been privy to reports on the R101's trials. He had learned that when the airship dived at Hendon it had virtually broken its back. He knew that hydrogen constantly poured from holes caused by the gas bags chafing against each other and the superstructure. But when he voiced his concerns, Thomson told him: 'If you are afraid to go, then don't.' Sadly, Sir Sefton accepted the challenge.

Lift-off from the Royal Airship Works, Cardington, was to be on the evening of 4 October. It was wet and miserable. At 6.30 pm Thomson and his valet stepped aboard. There were four other passengers, plus 48 crew.

STORM CONDITIONS

The leaky airship was so grossly overweight that it had to drop 4 tons of water-ballast to get away. At 8 pm, over London, it received a new weather forecast by radio, predicting a 40 mph headwind over northern France, with low cloud and driving rain. The senior crew member, Major G.H. Scott, grew alarmed. He had successfully captained the R100 to Canada and back, and he knew of the deficiencies of the R101. Yet he had decided to come along 'for the ride'. Knowing that the R101 had never flown in anything but good weather conditions, Scott discussed the radio report with Thomson. What the two men said will never be known, but the airship flew on.

As the rain lashed down on the 777-foot-long airship, the weight of tons of

water slowed it down and made it even more unstable. It rolled and pitched and was flying dangerously low, but inside the vast hull, crewmen went about their business while the passengers slept.

The twin-berth cabins formed the upper deck of a two-floor module sealed off from the roar of the engines and the beating of the weather. On the lower deck was the lounge, 60 feet long and more than 30 feet wide, with wicker settees, chairs and tables, and potted plants disguising the supporting pillars. Outside the lounge ran promenade decks with panoramic observation windows. Also on the lower deck were the ornate dining room, a smoking room and kitchens.

CRASH DIVE

Stairs led down to the control room, slung under the hull, which was the closest point to the ground. As the craft crossed the Channel, the watch noticed the surging seas perilously close beneath them. An officer grabbed the controls and brought the airship back to 1,000 feet.

The winds increased as the R101 crossed the French coast. Observers at Poix airfield estimated her height at only 300 feet. At 2 o'clock in the morning, the R101

Above: R101 dropping ballast as it struggles to rise. Without the stabilizing weight it rolled and tilted precariously.

INSIDE THE VAST HULL, CREWMEN WENT ABOUT THEIR BUSINESS WHILE THE PASSENGERS SLEPT.

was over Beauvais in northern France. It had travelled only 200 miles in more than seven hours.

Radio operator Arthur Disley had just turned in after tapping out this message back to Britain: 'After an excellent supper, our distinguished passengers smoked a final cigar and have now gone to rest after the excitement of their leave-taking.' Disley awoke later in his berth and realized something was wrong.

The nose of the R101 had suddenly dipped.

Engineers John Binks and Albert Bell were chatting in one of the gangways. Both fell with a bump. Foreman engineer Henry Leech, alone in the smoking room, slid off the settee. His glass and soda syphon clattered from the table. The R101 righted

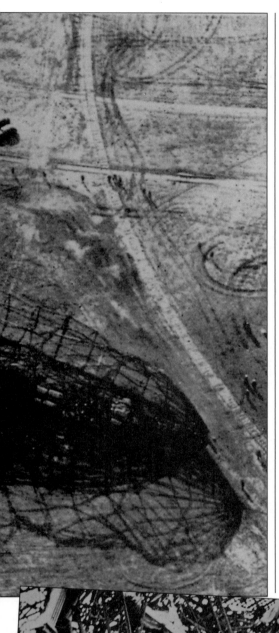

itself and again roared forward against the wind and rain. In the smoking room, Leech picked up the glasses and the soda syphon. They were unbroken. He replaced them on the table and lounged back on the settee.

Down below in Beauvais, several citizens were leaning out of their windows watching the strange airship sail by. It passed over the centre of the town, about 200 yards above the ground. It was rolling and dipping.

In the control car, the watch had just changed. The navigator looked at his altimeter – and was horrified to see that, although it recorded 1,000 feet above sea level, the airship was almost at ground level. The gentle hills around Beauvais were higher than he had thought. The engines were put at half speed and the release of water-ballast was ordered. Rigger Alf Church was walking to the crew area at the end of his term of duty when he heard an officer shout: 'Release emergency ballast.' Church ran back to his post and jettisoned half a ton of water from the nose.

The R101 was once again flying straight and level, but very low. Suddenly the nose dipped for the second time. As the airship's telegraph rang, coxswain Oughton wrestled with the controls. The elevators did not respond. The frail fabric at the nose of the ship had split. The wind was gusting in and the hydrogen was pouring out.

Below the doomed airship, on the edge of a wood, 56-year-old Alfred Roubaille was out poaching, hoping to bag a couple

COVERED IN PERSPIRATION THE COXSWAIN WRESTLED FRANTICALLY WITH THE CONTROLS – BUT THE R101 WAS PLUNGING TO ITS DOOM.

Left: *The charred remains of the death ship R101.*

Below left: *Every shred of fabric on the ship itself was burned, but the RAF flag survived the blaze to flutter forlornly on the wreckage.*

Below: *Air Marshal Salmond joined other dignitaries to survey the wreckage and wonder what had gone so catastrophically wrong.*

of rabbits for his family's Sunday lunch. He plodded across the sodden ground, stopping every now and then to lay his snares. Roubaille heard a roaring of engines above, looked up – and fled to the shelter of the trees. 'The airship started to sink towards the ground,' he later recounted. 'She was moving slowly forward and pointing her nose downwards. Just as the airship was nearing the ground, a strong gust of wind blew her down hard.'

Peering at the looming earth through the window of the control room, the first

Above: *Binks, Bell and Leech in the funeral procession leaving from Beauvais town hall en route to the railway station.*

officer, Lieutenant-Commander Atherstone, realized the airship was doomed. He ordered Chief Coxswain Hunt to race through the hull and alert everyone that the ship was about to crash. 'We're down, lads,' he screamed over and over.

Radio operator Disley heard the warning and swung his legs from his bunk. Leech leapt from the smoking room settee. In the engine-gondolas suspended beneath the

hull, engineers Cook, Bell, Binks and Savory watched horrified as the ground came up to meet them.

Thanks to the crewman in charge of the elevators, who died pulling at the wheel in a bid to make the craft climb, the R101 touched down lightly. One man leaped from a gondola and started running away as fast as his legs would carry him. He did not look back. Only Roubaille the poacher, from his sanctuary beneath the trees, witnessed the entire catastrophe which shook the world.

BLAZING INFERNO

The R101 was blown along the ground, then bounced 60 feet back into the air. Finally, it pancaked into the moist earth of a flat field no more than 100 yards from the poacher. For a moment, the only sound was the gush of escaping gas. Then a blinding flash lit the sky. Two further explosions quickly followed and a white-hot inferno engulfed the world's mightiest airship.

Engineer Henry Leech was still in the

Left: *The ill-fated R101 looked majestic in flight. But a close inspection revealed it wasn't fit to undertake a journey. One man's haste and obsession to win a race led to a series of faults and flaws which went unchecked.*

smoking room when the explosions started rocking the remains of R101. He had just got up from the settee when the blazing metal ceiling crashed down on it. Flattening himself to the floor, he crawled on all fours towards a hole that had opened in the wall and leapt through the flaming envelope of the airship. Once safely outside, he heard the cries of radio operator Arthur Disley still inside the blazing hull. He was clawing at the fabric, even attempting to bite an opening in it with his teeth. Leech ran back into the inferno to help him.

Both Leech and Disley seemed doomed. But then there was a miracle. Suddenly a fiery hole opened up in the hull and the two men flung themselves through it. They landed in wet bushes and raced to safety.

Another lucky crewman was engineer Victor Savory, who was blinded by the flash of flame that roared in through the open door of his gondola. Instead of cowering away from the heat, he bravely leapt for the opening and found himself lying on the soft soil of France.

Crewman Albert Cook also tried to get out of his gondola door but found it blocked by a girder, dripping with blazing cellulose from the hull. He dragged away the girder with his bare hands and hurled himself into the undergrowth below. He was pitifully burned. Recalling the horror later, he said: 'I lay down and gave up – but only for a moment.'

The gondola of engineers John Binks and Albert Bell also became engulfed in flames. They believed they were lost. But then came yet another miracle. A ballast tank above the gondola burst – and the water cascaded onto them, putting out the flames. They were the luckiest to be alive that dreadful night.

Poacher Roubaille could never forget his personal vision of hell: 'I heard people in the wreckage crying for help. I was a hundred yards away and the heat was awful. I ran as hard as I could away from that place.'

Of the 54 people, only six – Savory, Cook, Binks, Bell, Leech and Disley – survived. Lord Thomson of Cardington was among the 48 who died because of his blind ambition.

DRUG
TESTING

BEN JOHNSON
The fastest lie on Earth

As Ben Johnson raced to the finishing line and a gold medal on that hot September day he knew he was breaking a world record. The next day he broke a nation's heart.

A hush fell on the Olympic stadium as the world's top athletes lined up for the race of their lives, running for the title of the fastest man on Earth. The crack of a starting pistol shattered the silence. It sent the sprinters towards the finishing line 100 metres away at a breathtaking pelt, their muscles taut and glistening with perspiration, each face a mask of concentration. One man roared off the blocks faster than his rivals. His lightning reaction helped him to finish the race ahead of the field, almost before the echo of the pistol had died.

For Canadian Ben Johnson it was the moment he had dreamed of since childhood when he sped barefoot on a dusty tropical road. Now he was the record-smashing champion of the whole world, no messing. After years of toil and training, here at last was the glory he longed for. The strains of the Canadian national anthem being played in the Olympic stadium in Seoul, South Korea, that steamy Saturday afternoon in September 1988 sounded triumphantly for the athletes of a nation, heralding a future of hope. In reality it was a knell of doom for Johnson.

As he stood on the rostrum to have the coveted gold medallion draped around his neck, Johnson could barely disguise a look of anxiety. He knew he was a cheat.

AN ATHLETIC JUNKIE

Within just a few days, the world shared his shameful secret. A test for drugs used by athletes to enhance their performance proved positive. Johnson's fame turned to infamy and he was stripped of his honours,

humiliated in front of his country and the world.

The fair-play fans of field events across the globe might just have forgiven him the acutely public misdemeanour, believing him to be a pawn in the hands of unscrupulous and ambitious trainers and under pressure to be the best.

But the humbling experience of being unmasked as a fraud failed to teach him a lesson for life. Less than five years later he was snared for the same offence and he was banned from competing for life. Now Johnson's only claim to fame is as an athletic junkie who has dragged the reputation of his country and his sport through the mud.

Ben Johnson was born in Falmouth, Jamaica, at the close of 1961, one of five children. At the age of 14 he emigrated with his mum, brothers and sisters to Canada, leaving his dad in Jamaica. While his mum worked as a chambermaid in a Toronto hotel, Johnson discovered he was born to run. His pounding stride easily outstripped the other schoolboys he raced. Before long he was noticed by Charlie Francis, former world-class runner, gymnasium owner and athletics trainer, who realized the teenager possessed enough talent to take him to the top.

His first big league outing on the track, aged 16, was notable only for its singular lack of success. Johnson finished last in

Above: *Once Johnson could walk with his head held high as his country's finest athlete.*

HIS POUNDING STRIDE SOON OUTSTRIPPED THE OTHER SCHOOLBOYS – BEN HAD DISCOVERED THAT HE WAS BORN TO RUN.

Opposite: *Johnson leaves the drug control centre in Hamilton after being caught cheating by taking drugs to enhance his performance – not once, but twice.*

BURNING WITH ENVY AND FRUSTRATION, JOHNSON KNEW HE WOULD DO ANYTHING TO BEAT CARL LEWIS.

Below: *Johnson burned with ambition to beat athletic legend Carl Lewis,* **pictured below.**

Canada's Commonwealth Games 100-metres trial, but he continued his training with grim determination. Just a year later he won the nation's junior title as well as winning citizenship. By now he was running 100 metres in 10.79 seconds.

By 1980 he was fast enough to race in the Olympics, but Canada joined the USA in a boycott of the games brought about by the intervention of the host nation, the USSR, in Afghanistan. It left the way clear for Briton Allan Wells to win gold in the prestige 100-metres event.

But for the first time that year Johnson pitted his speed and strength against Carl Lewis, the American who had made history on the track with his astonishing times. Both competed in the Pan-American Junior Games. Lewis won the 100-metres event; Johnson trailed in sixth place. Lewis's cycle of success spawned a bitter rivalry

which bubbled under the surface every time they raced against each other. Lewis was determined to retain his title of undisputed speed king while Johnson was equally driven to snatch the top slot for himself.

Each day Johnson undertook gruelling training sessions in his bid to reach the top of his sport. Each year he edged closer to his goal. In 1981 he was the best runner in his country. The following year he was second to Allan Wells in the Commonwealth Games and by 1983 he made it into the semi-finals of the world championships.

In 1984, Johnson won the bronze medal in the Los Angeles Olympics in the 100-metres event.

The 1984 Games, troubled though they were by the boycott of Iron Curtain countries, had belonged to Carl Lewis, who scored gold in the 100 metres, 200 metres, relay and long jump. Lewis was heaped with accolades, having mimicked the success of the legendary Jesse Owens at the Berlin Olympics, where the affable star was repeatedly snubbed by Hitler because he was black.

Johnson burned with frustration at running once again in the shadow of the great man. He felt sure he could beat Lewis and yearned to prove himself right.

He didn't have long to wait. He claimed victory for the first time against Carl Lewis in the athletics World Cup. Already the bogey of drugs was looming large over the sport. Johnson brushed aside any doubts about his own stance on drug taking: 'I want to be the best on my own natural ability and no drugs will pass into my body.'

ROGUE COMPETITORS

It seemed the tough physical regime he was following had paid off: Johnson was no longer having to settle for second place. He won the Commonwealth and the World Championship titles in consecutive years before the fateful race at the Seoul Olympics. In the World Championships held in Rome in 1987 he not only beat Lewis but achieved a world record of 9.83 seconds. It was the year he won all his 21 races. Again, Johnson's name was linked with drug taking. His camp firmly denied

the suggestion. Coach Charlie Francis said: 'Ben's never taken drugs and never will. Some people do not know how to lose and all they can do is make excuses.' Francis insisted Johnson's astonishing strength came from four hours spent training each day, including 90 minutes devoted to throwing weights.

Olympic officials were increasingly aware of the menace posed by drug takers. The first track competitor to be disqualified after winning a medal was Finnish 10,000-metres runner Martti Vainio in 1984. There was no indication that the problem had been eradicated: if anything, gossip and speculation pointed to widespread use of steroid drugs to increase strength and endurance and cut down recovery time. To sidestep detection, junkie competitors stopped taking the drugs a month before competition. Officials were even thought to

be in cahoots with the rogue competitors taking drugs. There was known to be huge profits in it for those who sold the banned substances. Their trade was two-fold: the drug itself, and then an agent which would mask all traces of the illegal dope.

With the prospect of athletes across the board winning only with the aid of chemicals rather than by their efforts alone, the International Olympic Committee was concerned and made testing more rigorous than ever before, banning masking agents and diuretics which can inhibit the processes used to trace drugs. All medal winners and other competitors chosen at random have to give urine samples after their event. The sample is divided into two and stored in sealed containers. One bottle is analysed and if any indications of drugs misuse are found, the second sample is tested with the athlete and a medical representative present.

Before the Johnson scandal erupted, two Bulgarian weightlifters were stripped of their honours and sent home. In addition five other positive tests were taken.

MYSTIFIED

But without doubt the findings in the tests on Johnson were the most sensational. Commentators were still revelling in the excitement and thrill of the race when rumours emerged about Johnson's test result.

A substance called stanozolol was discovered in his urine. It is an anabolic steroid which is like the male hormone testosterone and boosts muscle size, strength and power.

There was outrage among his crew. While Johnson fled Seoul and the glare of publicity, his business manager Larry Heiderbrecht said: 'Ben is obviously sick at the news and will appeal. He is shattered.'

He went on to say that Johnson was probably the most tested sportsman in the world and did not take drugs anyway. There was talk of a blunder in the laboratories, a hoaxer meddling with the sample and the certainty of an appeal.

'It is obvious that something very strange has been happening. Nobody is that stupid to take drugs a few days before a big race. It would appear that the stuff has been in his system for a short period of time.

Above: *Charlie Francis, Johnson's coach, who once said: 'Ben's never taken drugs and never will.'*

Left: *Linford Christie, Britain's record-breaking runner, was horrified to learn his rival Johnson had been a cheat.*

Above: *Johnson bursts through the line in world-record time at Seoul. But his victory was a sham.*

Right: *At the Dubin enquiry in Canada in 1989, which probed the illicit use of drugs in sport, Johnson appeared to be a reformed character.*

THE PROTESTATIONS OF INNOCENCE WERE A SHAM — LIKE THE MAN WHO MADE THEM.

'Ben makes a lot of money from the sport and there is a lot of financial incentive for someone to do something. His training bag could have been left unattended and somebody could have interfered with it. The whole of Canada has been on his back but that would not make him take drugs.'

The people of Canada were mystified. Surely the local boy made good was innocent? After all, drugs testing which had taken place in Montreal before the country's athletes flew to Seoul had failed to pick up signs of abuse.

Even fellow athletes were incredulous at the turn of events. Britain's Linford Christie came third in the race, with Carl Lewis in second place. Although now in line for the silver medal instead of the bronze, he was far from pleased.

'It has been a sad day for athletics,' he said. 'I have never had any suspicion about Ben, he must have been tested over and over again.'

But any hopes of an error were dashed, as Johnson must have known they would be. His protestations of innocence were a sham. His silence was only broken by the

smashing of a glass bottle as he threw the illicit substance which had lost him the crown he so desired against the wall of his home.

Later, Carl Lewis claimed he had noticed the sure signs of steroid use before the start of that big race. Johnson's build was stockier than usual, his reactions faster and his eyes yellow. Lewis watched in amazement as Johnson produced some almost superhuman extra pace in the final spurt to victory.

THE FASTEST MAN IN THE WORLD?

Johnson was banned from competing for two years by the International Amateur Athletic Federation and stripped of the world record he clinched at the Olympics of covering 100 metres in 9.79 seconds. A row about whether or not he should ever race again ensued. The Canadian government, which had poured its dreams and cash into the promising career of the young runner, announced Johnson would never again wear its colours. But there was a groundswell of opinion which believed Johnson deserved a second chance. He had been a well-loved national hero who evoked pride and the public's sympathy. Many were convinced he was not only a patsy in the cut-throat world of international athletics, but was also capable of being the fastest man on Earth without using drugs. In fact, Johnson got letters of support not only from Canada but from across the world, along with token gold medals from those fans who felt he deserved the prestige award. His actions as an anti-drugs campaigner in schools and youth clubs around the country also won hearts and minds.

Less than a year later, Johnson talked publicly about the events which led to his disgrace. Speaking at a £3 million inquiry into drug-taking in sport he declared with his characteristic stammer: 'I know what it is like to cheat. I want kids not to take drugs. I also want to tell their parents and families.

'If I get the chance to run again then I will prove I am the best in the world. I will be back.'

He was asked by counsel Robert Armstrong if he thought he could be the fastest man in the world without taking anabolic steroids. He replied: 'I know I can be.' There was spontaneous applause from the public gallery.

Uncomfortably he admitted the statement of innocence made immediately after Seoul was a pack of lies. He said he didn't tell the truth because: 'I was ashamed for my family, other Canadian athletes and the kids who looked up to me. I did not want to tell what the truth was. I was just in a mess.'

His honesty furthered his support by the public, who believed him to be not weak but manipulated, and he was praised for his courage in coming clean. Olympic committee president Juan Antonio Samaranch pronounced that Johnson should not be dealt with any more severely than other competitors found guilty of drugs offences.

Even arch-rival Carl Lewis spoke out against a lifetime ban. There was talk of a multi-million dollar re-match between the two giants when the two-year-ban was ended.

Above: *Juan Antonio Samaranch, president of the International Olympic Committee, knew steroid abuse in sport was probably more widespread than the watching public had realized.*

Canadian TV producer Sheldon Reisler summed it up for many when he said: 'Hell, the only guy in the world who's clean is Eddie the Eagle Edwards [the British ski-jumper who came last in the Olympics]. The world is just saying "Thank God our guy didn't get caught."'

The prospect of him becoming a rich man in the wake of his immorality was hardly mentioned. No one was worried about the lack of an apology or display of repentance or that Johnson seemed to blame his coach, doctor and anyone else but himself.

The sport reeled from the exposé, then set about healing its wounds. Regulations about testing were tightened to ensure they were accurate and penalties against the cheats were increased.

Johnson started training again with a vengeance. He was no longer subsidized by the state but he had something to prove. Trainer Charlie Francis, whose name was so closely linked with the use of steroids in athletics and who was subsequently banned from national athletics, was off the scene. When the two-year ban expired, Johnson found himself a target for the drugs testers who descended on him five times in as many

months, each time producing a negative result. It seemed he had been redeemed.

His preparation for a comeback in January 1991 was accompanied with self-righteous comments such as: 'Steroids must be abolished. They must be treated by the law like heroin, and banned. I am damned glad that I was caught when I was. I didn't feel at ease with my medal anyway.'

Observers noted that he was sleeker, clear-eyed and far more relaxed than the Ben Johnson who was hooked on drugs. But rarely do sprinters surpass their best when they are in their late 20s or early 30s as Johnson by now was. He struggled to pack more power into his 5-foot-11-inch tall frame. When he returned to competition in the Copps Coliseum in Hamilton, Ontario, something vital was missing: the winning streak. Johnson appeared to have lost the stunning start from the blocks which gave him a devastating advantage over other runners. He came in second in a 50-metres race to America's Daron Council, ironically a former narcotics agent.

There was talk of Johnson spending too much time in bars instead of training on the track. But more worryingly, the message

JOHNSON BLAMED HIS COACH, HIS DOCTOR AND EVERYONE BUT HIMSELF.

Below: *Johnson yearned to be the best again following his ban – but he had disappointing results in his first races.*

the result appeared to broadcast was that the only way for Johnson to be the best was to take drugs.

Johnson struggled to regain winning form. It was crucial to a man who disliked coming second but still the raw edge of speed which he had once known – albeit through a chemical reaction – eluded him.

A PHONY

At the Barcelona Olympics in 1992 Johnson steered clear of the steroids scandal which this time shamed three British competitors, including Jason Livingston – nicknamed 'Baby Ben' after the fallen athletics idol. But if he thought he would leave Spain with a repaired image he was wrong. This time it wasn't steroids – it was a temper tantrum which let him down.

As the Games drew to a close Johnson wandered into the athletes' village without the mandatory security clearance. The young Spanish volunteers tried to explain they were only doing their job for the protection of all athletes at the Games. In the row which followed, Johnson was accused of punching one of the teenagers. Afterwards, he was sent home with new disgrace heaped on his muscular shoulders. His performance was as disappointing as his behaviour.

After a year of second-rate results, the winning formula was discovered again. Critics were quick to notice it coincided with the reappearance of Charlie Francis during his training sessions. Francis insisted he was only running into Johnson because his wife, hurdler Angie Coon, was working out at the same place.

Warning bells rang, however, when Johnson pulled out of Canada's national event in February 1993 as a result of injury and was not selected for the world indoor championships in March.

The storm clouds were gathering and finally burst open when a newspaper revealed Johnson had been tested positive for a second time. A urine sample taken after an indoor meeting in Montreal in January showed a high level of testosterone. It measured a ratio of 10.3 to one when six to one is considered a positive test.

Dr Arne Ljunqvist, head of a 5-strong

Above: *Johnson with Francis, the coach who oversaw his international disgrace.*

commission which dealt with the test, said: 'I can see no reason and no grounds on which the results can be contested. This is a clear-cut case of testosterone doping.'

Johnson remained behind the closed doors of his £400,000 detached house on the outskirts of Toronto, refusing to talk to reporters. His spokesman declared: 'Mr Johnson denies taking any prohibited substance or engaging in any improper practice since his return to competition.' But Johnson must have realized any denial from his own lips would have sounded hollow. He knew he was to be banned for life.

HUMILIATED BY HIS LACK OF SUCCESS, JOHNSON'S MONSTROUS DESIRE TO WIN SMOTHERED HIS BETTER JUDGEMENT.

Over page: Johnson remains haunted by his infamy.

Once again, he had been proved to be a phony: the faith put in him by the Canadian people was misguided, the forgiveness they showed him misplaced. British athletics coach Frank Dick said: 'This is very sad for the Canadian public who had forgiven Johnson once and are now having it thrown back in their faces. The man must be crazy.'

Canada's sports minister Jean Charest said Johnson had 'perverted the playing fields and hurt the sincerity of all the thousands of athletes who participate fairly'.

The only course left for the man whose glittering career was ended twice in the same shabby way was a silent withdrawal into obscurity, aged only 31. His international notoriety was now enough to shut any door in his face. Plans to blow the lid off the world of athletics where shiny syringes were as vital as clean socks collapsed like a damp squib. It was an undistinguished end to a fiasco.

The affair soured more than just one man's life and dream of being extra special. That vision was left in tatters, like the existence of the man himself. His actions caused wholesale damage to the integrity of a sport from which it may never recover.

Other athletes found themselves struggling to convince onlookers they were not only clean of drugs but worthy of the accolades they had won. Ben Johnson not only exposed the scourge of drugs in sport but illustrated how they were a positive benefit to anyone wishing strongly enough to win. He gave the lie to the old saying 'cheats never prosper'. Honest athletes are pushing for blood testing to eliminate cheats like Johnson, who can sometimes duck detection by using drugs which disguise illegal substances. Trying to make the best of it, Frank Dick remarked: 'Ben Johnson did a great service when he was caught in Seoul. It concentrated everybody on winning this war.'

But even now no one is convinced the sport is squeaky clean. It's been left to red-faced officials to limit the damage as best they can to ensure there is a future for athletics. Johnson, the man who wanted to bring honour to the sport, ended up bringing it to its knees.

MILITARY BLUNDERS

SCHWARZKOPF'S TACTICS WERE BRILLIANTLY SIMPLE: HE HAD LEARNT THE HARD WAY THAT AN ARMY WITHOUT AIR COVER WOULD SOON BE AN ARMY DEFEATED.

Safe in their positions of power, too often military leaders throw away the lives of their solders in their lust for victory. It is not their blood which stains the desert sands bright red and makes the seas and rivers bleed with anguish.

Right above: *Stormin' Norman Schwarzkopf, Commander-in-chief of Operation Desert Storm and a superb military tactician.*

Below: *Saddam in 1980 at the height of Iraq's war with Iran. In this address to his soldiers he assured them Iran would 'surrender or die'.*

Saddam Hussein's attack on Kuwait in 1990 was one gigantic blunder. How did he ever imagine that he could defy the world, especially once it became clear war was looming? Whatever Saddam's tortured reasoning, Iraq's doomed invasion has been quickly consigned to history as one of the most spectacular military failures of the 20th century.

And yet the Gulf War, which cost so few Allied lives, could have turned out so differently. True, the final result would certainly have been victory for the American-led coalition with its dazzling array of hi-tech weaponry. But had Saddam been a true, all-round tactician, Iraq would certainly have given a far better account of herself.

As the commander of Operation Desert Storm, General Norman Schwarzkopf, put it at the end of the war: 'Saddam is neither a strategist, nor is he schooled in the operational arts, nor is he a tactician, nor is he a general, nor is he a soldier. Other than that, he's a great military man.'

Saddam's problem was that he had learnt all his war-lore from the Soviets. He regarded battles as something to be fought on the ground and, ideally, from entrenched defensive positions. 'Let them come to us' could have been his motto. Had he had a more balanced military force, those tactics would undoubtedly have brought about the deaths of many more Allied soldiers. But Saddam Hussein didn't have balance. As it turned out, he didn't really have an air force.

And it was the air war, which began on 17 January 1991, that assured the Allies victory. Time and again during his meet-the-press sessions at Allied Command HQ in Riyadh, Saudi Arabia, Schwarzkopf would stress this. As a front-line Vietnam veteran he knew the effect day after day of bombing had on an enemy's morale and psyche. He had learned one of the great lessons which emerged from World War 2 strategy: an army without air cover would soon be an army defeated.

In his summing up of Allied tactics at the end of the conflict Schwarzkopf admitted that he was worried about the balance of ground forces. At the time US intelligence (wrongly, it turned out) had

predicted a defensive force of well over half a million. The Allies' fighting troops, as opposed to logistic support, was roughly half that. Schwarzkopf knew that in modern warfare an attacking army driving against heavily entrenched positions needed a five-to-one superiority of manpower. He explained how he redressed the balance.

'What we did, of course, was start an extensive air campaign ... one of the purposes was to isolate the Kuwaiti theatre of operations by taking out all the bridges and supply lines that ran between the north and the southern part of Iraq. That was to prevent reinforcement and supply coming into the southern part of Iraq and the Kuwaiti theatre.

'We also conducted a very heavy bombing campaign, and many people questioned why. This is the reason. It was necessary to reduce those [Iraqi] forces down to a strength that made them weaker, particularly along the front-line barrier that we had to go through.'

He went on: 'I think this is probably one of the most important parts of the entire briefing I can talk about. As you know, very early on we took out the Iraqi Air Force. We knew that he had very, very limited reconnaissance means. Therefore,

when we took out his air force, for all intents and purposes we took out his ability to see what we were doing down here in Saudi Arabia.'

AIR BOMBARDMENT

What Schwarzkopf did was move his main ground-attack forces as far west as possible to outflank the Iraqis and meet them where their defences were weakest. The 5-week air bombardment had left Saddam's troops in no real state to fight. The first attack alone, which lasted only three hours, dropped 18,000 tons of explosives on Iraq – twice the amount that razed Dresden and roughly equal to the power of the Hiroshima atomic bomb.

So how did the Iraqi High Command allow the Allies to take control of the skies almost unchallenged by their own warplanes? It wasn't that their aircraft were a poor match. Most experts agreed that Iraq's squadrons of Soviet-built MiG-29 fighters were technically superior – even to America's awesome F-15 Eagles. As for Britain's Tornado interceptors, it would, as one RAF man put it, 'have been like putting up a robin to fight a kestrel'.

Neither was it down to training. Most Iraqi airmen had been taught alongside the

Below: *Tracer fire lights up the night sky during the opening of the Allied air attack on Baghdad. But where was Saddam's air force?*

Above: *Aftermath of an air raid. With total control of the skies Allied bombers rained destruction on Baghdad.*

THE **RAF** TORNADOS HAD
THE HEAVIEST LOSSES –
BUT THEY WERE THE PILOTS
FORCED TO TAKE THE
GREATEST RISKS.

---

very people they were now being asked to shoot out of the sky. They were as competent and intelligent as their adversaries. There was just one important difference – they didn't have the will to fight. Instead of wreaking havoc among the incoming Allied fighters they rarely even engaged them in combat.

Part of the problem was that these airmen were never really trusted by Saddam and he had little interest in either the concept of air battles or the tactical importance of supremacy in the skies. He knew where he stood with ground troops, men who had lived their lives under his leadership, who readily bought the Ba'ath Party line and who had not been tainted with Western ideals. Fliers were a different breed. Their foreign training had given them a fresh outlook on life and they were not the type to obey orders blindly without thought for themselves. Sure enough, when the chance came, they were off.

Ten days into the war the first reports began filtering through of Iraqi planes landing in Iran. The Americans claimed 24 had gone, the Iranians said only seven. Whatever the truth, the trend had been set and more and more were soon fleeing across the border. By 29 January Israel's defence minister Moshe Arens said all 25 of Iraq's Soviet-designed Sukhoi-24 bombers were in Iran. And a few days later

it was claimed more than 150 of Saddam's most modern fixed-wing aircraft were parked up inside the territory of his detested neighbour.

The first wave were clearly defectors. Iran's UN ambassador talked of pilots arriving in his country 'to save their lives and their aircraft' and judging by the way four planes crashed before reaching the border, their fuel tanks empty, it seems Iraqi pilots were prepared to risk a great deal to avoid a scrap with the Allies. Later, Iraqi officials claimed Iran had offered Saddam the use of neutral airfields to protect his air force from total destruction.

The theory has never quite rung true. For a start Saddam is known to have placed airplanes in the centres of towns and villages, knowing the Allies would not risk civilian casualties. Why should he then entrust billions of pounds' worth of hardware to an old enemy he fought for eight long years? And when Iraqi deputy prime minister Sadoun Hammadi was sent to Tehran to make enquiries about the missing air force he was told bluntly that Saddam should have asked permission for his warplanes to enter Iranian air space. As he failed to do this, Iran had a duty to impound them.

Back in Iraq the night skies still echoed to the sound of incoming bombers. RAF Tornados took some of the heaviest losses – seven planes went down during the war – but this was partly connected to their very high-risk end of the operation. Their job was to come in low – at barely 80 feet – and pepper Iraqi airfields with a cocktail of bombs and delayed-action anti-personnel mines. Iraqi gunners may have got three of them; the other four went down because of various technical failures.

On the whole Saddam's anti-aircraft gunners put up a pretty feeble show. They didn't dare turn on their own radar because attacking planes picked up a 'lock-on' instantly and immediately fired off their own HARM missiles which travelled down the incoming radar beam to the AA battery which originated it. As a result many batteries switched off their radar-guidance systems and ended up firing blind into the night sky.

On 30 January, General Schwarzkopf confirmed that he had total control of the skies above Iraq. The operation had taken exactly two weeks and it had gone better than anyone could have dreamed possible. Senior Allied officers made great play of their so-called 'smart' bombs which could be guided onto their target through their own internal sensors. One piece of video tape showed an Iraqi lorry driver motoring across a bridge seconds before a massive bomb smashed it in two. The 'luckiest man in Iraq' was how the briefer described him to Western TV viewers.

If the Allies' public relations policy was going reasonably well, Iraq's was in tatters. Saddam might have hoped to try and lure at least some world opinion onto his side, but if that was his plan he had a funny way of going about it. Exhibiting captured Allied airmen on his national TV caused a wave of revulsion around the globe and merely stiffened the West's resolve to teach him a lesson. In strictly political terms it was a blunder to rival his half-hearted commitment to air defence.

The two British airmen who appeared on Iraqi TV were John Peters and Adrian Nichol, whose Tornado was shot down over the Kuwaiti border on the first day of the war. Peters's face was badly knocked about – he had been beaten by his captors – and he seemed to be contorted in his seat. He was able to answer few questions except to confirm he had been shot down by a missile. Nichol, a burly-looking man with the Union Jack flag clearly outlined on his bottle-green uniform, went a little further.

Questioner: What was your mission?
Nichol: To attack an Iraqi airfield.
Questioner: How were you shot down?
Nichol: I was shot down by an Iraqi system. I do not know what it was.
Questioner: What do you think about the war?
Nichol: I think this war should be stopped so we can go home. I do not agree with this war on Iraq.

Other pilots, among them Americans and Italians, were exhibited in a similar way. It did not go down well with the folks back home. Suddenly a huge weight of pressure was off the Allied political leadership as the pictures caused a massive swing of public opinion against Iraq. Now the voices crying for an end to the war in Britain and America were out on a limb. Saddam had attempted a high-risk gamble, presumably

to boost the morale of his own countrymen, and had ended by digging himself even deeper into the mire.

By early February, Iraq's much-vaunted tank battalions were being picked off in the manner of a duckshoot. Aircraft such as the A10 tankbuster found them easy meat while the Americans' Apache attack helicopters inspired such fear that even the sight of them in the sky caused some Iraqis to desert their posts. One story which found its way back to Allied ground troops, before the assault to liberate Kuwait, came from an Iraqi prisoner-of-war. He revealed how 12 tanks were drawn up together inside Kuwait when one commander spotted an incoming Apache on the horizon. He radioed to all his crews to stay put – intelligence reports showed the helicopter needed to be much closer before it was in range.

Seconds later six of the tanks were simultaneously blown to smithereens in the Apache's first withering salvo. The survivors in the other tanks didn't wait for an explanation from their commander. They fled their posts in time to watch the helicopter finish the job.

THE FINAL CASUALTY?

When the final 'Big Push' arrived – the launching of a ground attack on 24 February – General Schwarzkopf was again

Above: *Flight Lieutenant Adrian Nichol as he appeared on TV under interrogation. It was another blunder by Saddam, in that the British and American viewers saw their 'boys' being humiliated and demanded vengeance.*

IN THE FIRST WITHERING SALVO OF FIRE THE SIX TANKS WERE BLOWN TO SMITHEREENS — THE TERRIFIED SURVIVORS FLED FOR THEIR LIVES.

Above: *Saddam with his 'human shield' of European hostages. He believed sending these TV pictures to the West would help his public relations campaign. Nothing could have been further from the truth.*

able to turn the Iraqis' stubborn military dogma against them. Saddam had assumed from the outset that the assault on Kuwait would come from the sea. He stationed ten Iraqi divisions along the coast and planted thousands of mines along the length of the shore. When his generals reported in early February that the Allied fleet, headed by the vintage battleships *Wisconsin* and *Missouri*, was bombarding Iraqi positions he saw this as evidence that his early assumptions were right.

The dawn of 24 February seemed to confirm it. Egyptian, Saudi and Syrian troops, backed by the US marines, advanced into southern Kuwait while the US 1st Cavalry moved in from the south-west. The Iraqis' 3rd Corps assumed this was the main thrust and moved to intercept. They could not have been wider of the mark.

In fact the attack was coming from the west, spearheaded by heavily armoured American and British divisions. The Iraqis could never have known that such a vast body of men had moved into a totally new attack position within a few weeks. When last their air reconnaissance had checked, virtually the entire Allied camp was concentrated on Kuwait's southern flank.

After that, of course, they lost their air force. They had no eyes.

The ground war was won, comfortably, inside 72 hours. Many of the advancing Allied regiments found their outflanked enemy dug in and facing the wrong way. The Iraqi army, trumpeted weeks earlier by Saddam as the world's fourth biggest, was blown away like leaves before a hurricane.

In the years since the Gulf War many have argued that Schwarzkopf's campaign was a failure in that it failed to knock Saddam from power. Yet that was never the general's brief. His political masters were able to give him only one command and that was to free Kuwait. Any officially backed assassination attempt would have thrown the United Nations into total turmoil.

But if Saddam survived, it was a shaky survival. His two glaring blunders of the war – failing to mount an air defence and failing to guard his western flank properly – had humiliated him in front of his generals. Only the fear he managed to inspire in his High Command helped him avoid a coup.

There was a third blunder. Halfway through the conflict Saddam decided on a half-cocked attempt to drag in the rest of the Arab world. He fired a series of Scud missiles against Israel and succeeded in terrorizing the civilian population. It seemed certain that Israel would lose patience and strike back. Only enormous pressure from the Bush administration in America persuaded her not to.

But the Israelis have long memories. Their secret service, the Mossad, is regarded as the most effective and efficient in the world. There can be little doubt that Saddam Hussein remains high on their list of scores to be settled.

He could yet be the final casualty of the Gulf War.

THE FALL OF SINGAPORE

It was heralded as an island fortress which would never succumb to invading armies, but thanks to blundering British commanders, a tenacious foe and the epidemic of chaos and fear, Singapore fell into the hands of the Japanese with chilling speed.

The embarrassing defeat was a devastating blow to the Allies, who saw yet another prized jewel snatched from under their noses. More than that, there were horrendous casualties among the civilian and military populations. Seventy thousand British and Australian troops were forced to surrender. In February 1942 the city of Singapore was reduced to blazing rubble.

Churchill called it 'the worst disaster and largest capitulation in British history'.

But only afterwards was the extent of the military mismanagement of the campaign to keep Singapore revealed. The Japanese commander, General Tomoyuki Yamashita, declared: 'My attack on Singapore was a bluff. I had 30,000 men and was outnumbered more than three to one. I knew that if I had been made to fight longer for Singapore I would have been beaten. That was why the surrender had to be immediate. I was extremely frightened that the British would discover our numerical weakness and lack of supplies and force me into disastrous street fighting. But they never did. My bluff worked.'

Singapore lies at the south of the Malaysian peninsula and was acquired for the East India Company by Sir Stamford Raffles in 1819 from the Sultan of Johore. Although just 20 miles long and 10 miles wide, it went on to become a busy trading post and naval base for the British in southeast Asia.

It was two months after Pearl Harbor – when the might of the American navy was crippled in dock by a Japanese air onslaught – that the battle for Singapore got under way. A sizeable force of Allied troops had been chased down the Malay Peninsula and into Singapore by the beginning of February. Inexplicably, the island remained poorly defended, despite

> SINGAPORE DID NOT FALL BECAUSE OF JAPANESE MILITARY MIGHT; SINGAPORE FELL BECAUSE OF BRITISH MILITARY INCOMPETENCE.

Left: *Iraqi tanks roll through the streets of Kuwait. They were part of a huge army left defenceless by Saddam's pathetic air cover.*

FEARING THAT THE JAPANESE SOLDIERS WOULD GO ON A VICTORIOUS DRUNKEN RAMPAGE, THE GOVERNOR OF SINGAPORE ORDERED ALL THE ALCOHOL ON THE ISLAND TO BE DESTROYED.

the expansionist, imperial policies of the Japanese so forcefully advertised in Hawaii.

Only in January 1942 did British war leader Winston Churchill learn about the lamentable state of Singapore's defences. Immediately he ordered the island to be fortified to the hilt. 'Not only must the defence of Singapore Island be maintained by every means but the whole island must be fought for until every single unit and every single strongpoint has been separately destroyed. Finally, the city of Singapore must be converted into a citadel and defended to the death. No surrender can be contemplated,' he told war leaders. Wise words, but they came too late to change the destiny of the island.

Yamashita had his sights set on Australia and was keen to steamroller ahead before the morale of his men dipped or they ran short of supplies. He began with a wave of air strikes which devastated the weakening Allied forces on the ground. The British commanders, General Wavell and General Arthur Percival, were at odds through most of the brief campaign to keep the island secure. Wavell thought the attack would come from the north-west. Percival believed the invasion would be in the north-east and posted his best troops there. On 8 February Wavell was proved to have been the better tactician.

When the Japanese landed, the Australian defenders of the area could have surprised them with a blaze of spotlights and pinned them to the beach. But the order to switch on the lights never arrived after communication links were broken. As the enemy marched in, the Australians fell back and a counter-attack never came.

It was the first of many landings. Determined Japanese soldiers took to small boats and dinghies to cross the Johore Strait which divided their island goal from the conquered mainland. Some even swam the short, shallow distance. The defenders of Singapore were in disarray, hit by falling spirits, an active fifth column of Japanese residents on Singapore and the hopeless lines of communication.

It was the last, vital factor that spelled the inevitability of defeat for the Allies. For when the Australians were at last experiencing success in fending off the waves of Japanese soldiers on one shoreline, they were ordered to pull back. It allowed the enemy to flood in unopposed. Subsequent attempts at a counter-offensive by the Allies were bound to fail. By now the troops were utterly downhearted and beleaguered as much by the inadequacy of their own commanders as by the formidable warriors from the land of the rising sun.

In Singapore city there was mayhem. Streams of refugees had flooded in and sought shelter and food where they could. Buildings were still blazing from previous air attacks, dead bodies lay uncollected in the streets. Water supplies were falling fast and the risk of serious disease loomed. There was a frenzied scrabble to board boats leaving the besieged island. The governor of Singapore ordered all liquor to be destroyed so that Japanese soldiers could not go on a victorious drunken rampage when they arrived. Oil storage tanks were set on fire by the British themselves, anxious this valuable commodity should not fall into the hands of the advancing enemy. The intense furnace produced black rain which fell over the crumbling city.

By 15 February, seven short days after the island's defences were first breached, Singapore fell. A package was air-dropped to Percival's headquarters, falling to the ground in a flutter of red and white ribbon. Inside was a message from Yamashita advising him to surrender. It ended with the sinister sentence: 'If you continue resistance, it will be difficult to bear with patience from a humanitarian point of view.'

Percival felt he had no choice. He met the slight victor at the island's Ford assembly plant to sign away the vital outpost. The dream was shattered. Britain could no longer boast that she would successfully defend her colonies, no matter where they were in the world. The brutality of the Japanese invaders against captured British and Australian forces is well recorded, and bitterness about the slavery, torture and terrible conditions the men had to endure is still evident even today. Singapore stayed in the hands of the Japanese until their leader Emperor Hirohito was himself forced to surrender, in August 1945.

THE MASSACRE OF A GENERATION

World War 1 was littered with blunders, each costing countless thousands of lives. The conflict started with an assassination which led to miffed national leaders on both sides embarking on a course of protectionism and revenge. The commanders who held sway were old men with a theoretical rather than practical knowledge of warfare: it was the era when the military man judged most successful was the one who didn't lose his nerve in the face of mounting casualties. Any officer foolish enough to advocate withdrawal to save lives would risk the wrath of his political paymasters and would surely lose his job. So it came about that dogged men who prolonged the slaughter by staying put – even if that meant a mounting death toll and no advance – won the day.

In fact, there was comparatively little troop movement in World War 1. Across Europe, the sides met in head-on confrontation, found themselves equally matched and dug in defensively for a long, drawn-out war of attrition. Trench warfare was both demoralizing and degrading for fighting soldiers, who had to endure the most appalling conditions. The most they died for was a few feet of land.

Offensives in which men were sent over the top into no man's land were largely unsuccessful but were repeated time and again by the military leaders. Both British and German soldiers had the occasional triumph in breaking through the lines of defence, but once it was achieved there was no further plan in existence to capitalize on the gain. As men and officers hesitated, the enemy rallied and the gap was closed once more in their faces. Stalemate resumed. British officers were so incompetent that on at least one occasion they released gas when there was no wind and gassed their own men.

The terrible bloodshed of this military mismanagement left Flanders awash with the dead and wounded. Names like the Somme, Verdun, Passchendaele and Ypres will always be linked with aimless slaughter which claimed the flower of a generation. And for four years the killing went on, without a change in tactics to stem the flow of massacres. Nowhere was the pointless sacrifice of young men at the hands of their blundering leaders more starkly apparent than during the Gallipoli campaign of 1915.

Turkey came into the war specifically to take a swipe at its old imperial enemies, Great Britain and Russia. It lost about

FOR FOUR YEARS THE POINTLESS SLAUGHTER OF THE YOUTH OF TWO NATIONS CONTINUED, WITHOUT A CHANGE IN MILITARY TACTICS.

Above: *Churchill strides to his office at the outbreak of World War 1. He was then First Lord of the Admiralty.*

Left: *Australian troops march down the High Street at Freemantle to prepare for embarkation.*

70,000 out of a 100,000-strong army when it attacked Russian troops in the Caucasus, mainly through bitter weather conditions. Regardless of their victory, the Russians appealed to London for a diversion to relieve the pressure on its forces from the armies of the sprawling Ottoman Empire.

GALLIPOLI – A SEA OF BLOOD

The plan to strike at Turkey through the Dardanelle Straits – with an eventual goal of capital Constantinople – was inspired. The waterway which linked the Mediterranean with the Black Sea was clearly vital strategically. Gallipoli was the strand of land on one side of it. With comparative ease, the campaign should have opened up a second front for the German forces, a back door by which to tear into Kaiser Wilhelm II's troops. It was championed by the First Lord of the Admiralty, Winston Churchill.

There was a hopeful start for the British navy, who sailed into the Dardanelles in February 1915, blasted away at the outer fortifications and encountered little resistance. British marines even landed on the Gallipoli peninsula without difficulty.

But the British failed to capitalize on the element of surprise and withdrew the warships into the Aegean, having all but announced their intentions to the Turks. It gave the enemy six valuable weeks to re-arm and reinforce its scanty troops there. There was even the opportunity to mine the straits which had hitherto been a clear passage.

In March the attacking British ships sailed once again on Turkey, this time penetrating the narrow straits. Disastrously, two British battleships and one French were sunk by mines. Churchill was still determined to forge ahead with the operation despite the setback.

In the early hours of 25 April 1915 the largest amphibious force the world had ever known headed for the Gallipoli beaches. In charge was the gentlemanly Sir Ian Hamilton, without a proper map and with no information about the state of Turkish defences more recent than 1906.

Below: *Allied troops at Anzac Cove. A bloodbath lay ahead.*

tenths of the 2,000-strong invading force. The pilot of a spotter plane which flew over the beach that morning described the sea as 'a horrible sight, absolutely red with blood'.

Close by, a further 2,000 men landed on another beach without a shot being fired. They climbed the cliffs and explored the scrubland at the top as they awaited orders. Their officers asked permission to advance. They were poised to mount an attack on the forces pinning down their comrades just a short distance away. Permission was refused. They spent the day in limbo exposed in the open until Turkish troops pounced on them. The surprise engagement forced the British men back down the cliffs and to the water's edge where, in the absence of any direction from their commanders, they evacuated.

*Left: **General Sir Ian Hamilton**. He led the largest amphibious force the world had ever seen onto the beaches of Gallipoli, yet he had no intelligence regarding the Turkish defences that was less than nine years old – not even a proper map.*

His position throughout the bloody and lengthy battles to come was to cruise the sea nearby in a large, safe ship. None of his men was warned about the terrain he would be facing, or had landed on a hostile coast like this before.

There were to be various landing points and a further diversionary skirmish staged by the French at Kum Kale on the other side of the Dardanelles. This, it transpired, was to be the single success of the expedition. The 1,500 Australians and New Zealanders who before dawn tumbled out of small boats onto the beach in the first assault were no more than barely trained reservists. In the gloom they realized for the first time there were sheer cliffs ahead of them instead of sloping beaches. Even as they were landing, a hail of bullets rained down, killing many men before they even made it to the beach. Then the guts of the survivors won the day. In the face of an onslaught from enemy fire and then a wave of Turkish fighters who appeared on the beach, the colonial troops fixed bayonets and forced the Turks back up the hill from which they had come. The site of the landing was known thereafter as Anzac Cove, by way of tribute to their courage.

British troops then emerged at Cape Helles from the bowels of a workaday collier boat which appeared to Turkish eyes to run aground by accident, but when they saw the soldiers swarming out of the disabled craft, the Turkish fighters were quick to respond and wiped out about nine-

*Above: **Troops landing at Gallipoli**. They faced impossible terrain ahead and the Anzac commander begged Hamilton to pull the men out.*

Columns of troops did successfully breach the Turkish defences but lacked direction to make their gains effective. By midday on 26 April about 30,000 men had landed on the Gallipoli peninsula with little or no gain. General Sir William Birdwood, in charge of the Anzacs now besieged in hopeless conditions on the narrow shale beach beneath the Turkish-controlled heights, implored Hamilton to pull them out. But spurred on by the success of an

Above: British troops in camp on the Gallipoli peninsula.

AT THE END OF THE ATTACK **10,000 TURKS WERE DEAD OR DYING IN NO MAN'S LAND.**

Australian submarine in the Dardanelle Straits, Hamilton refused the plea with the advice: 'there is nothing for it but to dig yourselves right in and stick it out'.

Thus the now familiar trench warfare came to the Mediterranean with conditions every bit as foul as those in France and Belgium. There were few medical supplies and ammunition stocks were low. At Anzac Cove, the men were rationed to two bullets a day. Reinforcements were sent to the British and Australasian forces, just as they were to the Turkish side – now under the leadership of Mustapha Kemal, a future leader of the country.

On 18 May there took place the bloodiest conflict of the campaign with the Anzac Cove men being subjected to the most ferocious assault they had experienced. The Turks tried to overwhelm the Anzac trenches – to be met with volleys of bullets. At the end of the attack, 10,000 Turks were dead or dying in no man's land. It was more than the hardened fighters could bear. On 20 May they raised a Red Cross flag above the front line. It was shot into tatters. But moments later a young

Right: These men of the 2nd Royal Naval Brigade were among the few troops who got to practice their assault landings. Here they are shown emerging from a trench in a mock attack on the island of Imbros.

Turkish soldier emerged from the trenches, stumbled over to the Anzacs and, in faltering French, apologized for the killings. After he retreated, Red Crescent flags (the Eastern equivalent of the Red Cross) were raised by the Turks. It paved the way for an informal meeting of commanders who were later able to negotiate a cease-fire. On 24 May each side began the grim task of burying its dead in mass graves.

The truce was to end at 4.30 pm. Half an hour beforehand, the opposing soldiers met and exchanged gifts of cigarettes, fruit and mementoes. After some small talk, they shook hands, parted and returned to their respective trenches. Moments later the shooting started once more.

SCOT-FREE

Frustrated at the stalemate, politicians in London demanded another assault on Gallipoli. This time it was to come at Suvla Bay. Around 20,000 men overran the beach, making short work of the 1,000 Turks there to defend it. In charge, General Stopford, Lieutenant Governor of the Tower, was delighted. He congratulated his men before settling down for his afternoon

nap. The soldiers were allowed to swim and frolic in the sea. By the time Stopford was ready to advance the following day, the Turks had reassembled a strong army which stood in his way. Once more it was deadlock.

In October General Sir Charles Monro, who had replaced the ineffectual Hamilton, urged that the Gallipoli campaign be abandoned. Lord Kitchener, the British war figurehead, visited the scenes of suffering and reluctantly admitted there was no alternative but withdrawal. His influence and credibility were diminished in London, however, and still politicians wrangled. It was the appointment of Sir William Robertson which decided the matter. The general, who had risen through the ranks, was respected by war-time prime minister Herbert Henry Asquith; he favoured France as the theatre of war. He declared the government should end the sideshow in Gallipoli.

In December 1915 the bulk of the troops was evacuated, with complete success. Not a shot was fired.

In eight months the British and Australasian forces, some 500,000 strong, had notched up 252,000 casualties and gained nothing. For the Turks the dead and wounded numbered 251,000.

The fiasco reflected badly on Winston Churchill, innovator of the plan, who could scarcely believe how badly it had been executed. He resigned in fury and frustration. But the commanders responsible for the carnage throughout the war escaped without even a reprimand.

Above: *British troops in Gallipoli had little idea what they were fighting for. Only later did they discover the hopelessness of their cause.*

ROBERT MAXWELL
Robbing the poor to feed the rich

In World War 2 Robert Maxwell won the Military Cross for bravery and was honoured as a hero. After his death thousands of pensioners cursed him as a crook.

On Guy Fawkes Night 1991 Captain Gus Rankin, master of the luxury yacht *Lady Ghislaine*, radioed an emergency message that sent shockwaves through the world's corridors of power. The Publisher was missing, feared dead, off the Canary Islands. He had apparently slipped into the water while the vessel was cruising, and drowned.

Robert Maxwell had been best known as a self-important, publicity-seeking bully. Above all, he was obsessively vain. However, predictably, when any well-known figure dies the fulsome tributes come flooding in and Maxwell's passing proved no exception.

Former prime minister Margaret Thatcher spoke of the valuable information on Eastern Europe he would pass to her, her predecessor Edward Heath praised Maxwell's unstinting support for the European ideal, Neil Kinnock talked of his backing for the Labour Party in glowing terms, while John Major observed

that Maxwell would not want the world to grieve at his death but marvel at his extraordinary life. Even Mikhail Gorbachev chipped in with a piece of gibberish acknowledging Maxwell's enormous contribution to understanding between nations in mass-media management.

Gorbachev's words, as it turned out, could hardly have been further from the truth. For as the Maxwell family prepared for the great man's burial on the Mount of Olives in Israel, bankers, accountants and financiers quietly began to assess their exposure to Maxwell's business borrowings. They did not like what they saw. The bonfire of the vanities was about to begin.

A HOUSE OF CARDS

Within days the first hint of a monumental financial scandal was starting to creep out. Many in the City, together with most of the better-informed financial journalists, had known for years that the flagship company, Maxwell Communications Corporation, was heavily borrowed with comparatively few hard assets. It was a house of cards. Maxwell's death would bring it tumbling down.

Much of the empire was so complicated, with a worldwide web of interlinked companies and trusts, that no one except Maxwell himself understood how it worked. He had been careful to shelter much of his business away from prying eyes in discreet havens such as Liechtenstein and the Cayman Islands, where enquiries about financial matters – official or otherwise – tended to hit brick walls. Whenever he raided the coffers of his companies, cash left unspent would end up offshore.

Above: Family mourners await the funeral on Israel's Mount of Olives. Lifting the coffin was a feat in itself.

Opposite: Maxwell, a self-important, publicity-mad bully. Only he understood the complexities of his world-wide business empire.

Below left: With Margaret Thatcher. He passed her valuable information on Eastern European countries.

Below: Maxwell House, HQ of Maxwell Communications Corporation.

PENSIONERS WOKE UP TO DISCOVER THAT THE FUNDS THAT THEY HAD DEPENDED ON FOR THEIR OLD AGE HAD BEEN FRITTERED AWAY.

Below: Mirror *pensioners on the march after finding that their nest-eggs had been plundered.*

But one criminal fact already shone out like a warning beacon. Maxwell had clearly plundered millions from the pension fund of his favourite company, Mirror Group Newspapers. The estimates varied but the £400 million the experts calculated seemed about right. Word spread like lightning and politicians and the media turned on Maxwell with a vengeance. Even his own paper, the *Daily Mirror*, denounced him with righteous indignation as a fraud and a crook.

The vitriol was undeniably justified. Thousands of *Mirror* employees and pensioners literally woke up one morning to discover their pot of cash, which for some had taken 40 years to build up, had been frittered away by Maxwell in an attempt to keep his companies afloat during the cold recessionary years of the 1980s.

They guessed – and they were probably right – that the money went on a futile share support operation to try to prop up the London Stock Exchange price of MCC. The reason was simple: Maxwell used shares from his businesses as collateral to borrow more cash from the banks. The banks were happy as long as the businesses flourished but when share prices began plummeting so did the value of their security. In the months before his death they were getting more and more edgy and pressure mounted on Chairman Robert.

So why did those in the know stay silent? What happened to the great British tradition of a free, fearless press? Why wasn't the charlatan exposed?

Firstly, because he was notoriously litigious. Writs from Maxwell, it was said, could fly out faster than his presses could print. He seemed to relish the prospect of cowing his enemies in the courts and legal costs were irrelevant to him. In the knowledge that Britain's laws of libel were among the most oppressive in the world, and with the recession slicing into their profits, the newspapermen stayed ominously silent.

If the merest hint of a rumour defamatory of Maxwell came to his attention he would instruct his lawyers to send a curt note to every editor in Fleet Street. They would run the story at their peril.

But it wasn't only legal bluster that restrained the papers. Before his death and subsequent unmasking, Maxwell was seen as the Man Who Got Things Done. He was a World War 2 hero, champion of the world's starving, a former Labour MP and an entrepreneur who genuinely could count many of the world's monarchs, emperors, dictators, presidents and prime ministers as his close confidante. In short, he was hot on influence. His friends in high places could always oblige with a quiet word in the ear of a journalist who was sniffing a bit too close to a Maxwell scoop.

Below: *With Prince Charles and Prince William.*

AS THE YOUNG GERMAN BOY DROPPED THE GUN HE WAS HOLDING MAXWELL RAISED HIS.

Left: *Lieutenant Robert Maxwell MC leads his men during the Victory Parade through Berlin in September 1945.*

Opposite bottom right: *A youthful Maxwell in pensive mood as he waits to take his seat as MP for Buckingham.*

Below: *In happier times, Maxwell waves to his investors at a meeting of Pergamum shareholders.*

'THE BOUNCING CZECH'

And John Major was right about his extraordinary past. Almost from the day he was born, 10 June 1923, a Czechoslovakian of Jewish parents, his life was one long roller-coaster. Not for nothing was he nicknamed the 'Bouncing Czech'.

Maxwell was born Jan Ludwig Hoch in one of the poorest parts of Czechoslovakia. At 5 years old he assured his father, a farm labourer: 'When I'm older I will own a cow and a field and make my own living.' The peasants who had to mount a daily fight against starvation laughed out loud at such a ridiculous suggestion.

It seemed even less likely the following year when young Jan caught diphtheria – then an often fatal disease. There were fears that he would never fully recover; never become strong enough to earn a living on his own. As he would do so often in his life, he contemptuously swept aside the doubters and got on with fulfilling his dreams.

At 12 he walked an incredible 400 miles from his home village of Solotvino to the city of Bratislava to look for work. Later, he laughed off the achievement, saying: 'If I were a woman I would always be pregnant. I never can say no to a challenge.'

His war record bore out that claim. He started out as a Czech soldier in Central Europe where the Nazi atrocities he encountered left him with a burning hatred of Hitler. At one stage he tried to join the French Foreign Legion, lying about his age in order to qualify, but as Hitler's hordes swept across Europe, he found himself evacuated by the Royal Navy and ended up in Liverpool. From now on his determination to defeat the Nazis took a new edge. All his family, apart from two sisters, had become victims of the Holocaust.

Maxwell wangled his way into the British Army as Private J.L. Hoch, serial number 12079140. He fought with enormous skill and courage and was decorated with the Military Cross – one of the highest honours in the army – after leading his platoon against a German pillbox in Brussels in 1944. Later he would waste no opportunity to retell his war stories. One of his Mirror Group editors revealed: 'He told me of one time at the end of the war when he was in France. He went into a barn and found a German soldier who was about .15. He told Maxwell to put up his arms and surrender. Maxwell told him to drop his gun in German. The boy did. I asked Maxwell what he did then. "I shot him, of course, you bloody fool," he replied, smiling.'

The war over, he set about building a career in publishing. Wary of any lingering Jewish hatred in Europe, he adopted the very British-sounding name of Robert Maxwell. He spoke English superbly (he had mastered nine languages by his death) and used his British contacts, such as they were, to the full. But it was only after establishing a niche in scientific publishing and distribution in

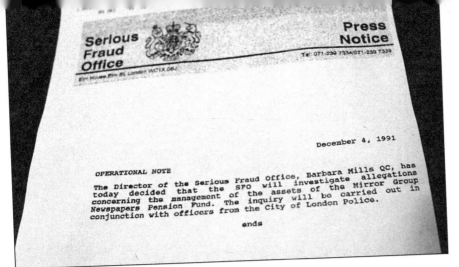

December 4, 1991

OPERATIONAL NOTE

The Director of the Serious Fraud Office, Barbara Mills QC, has today decided that the SFO will investigate allegations concerning the management of the assets of the Mirror Group Newspapers Pension Fund. The inquiry will be carried out in conjunction with officers from the City of London Police.

ends

Above: The Serious Fraud Office announces it is beginning a full investigation into Maxwell's various dealings.

HE TOLD THE STARVING PEOPLE THAT HE WOULD SAVE THEM. IT WAS JUST ANOTHER OF HIS LIES.

Germany that he spotted the hole in the market which would make his name.

Convinced that cheap scientific textbooks were in demand he used his £300 war gratuity to set up Pergamon Press. The company prospered into a £6 million multi-national enterprise and for most of the fifties and sixties Maxwell's wealth and reputation grew steadily higher. Then, in 1969, the bubble burst. Maxwell had agreed to sell Pergamon to a New York financier, who then tried to wriggle out of the deal by claiming there were irregularities in the accounts. The American was right. In a bloody internal battle Maxwell was sacked by his own board and vilified in a government investigation. The Department of Trade concluded he was not a fit person to run a public company.

Yet within five years he had bounced back. He regained control of Pergamon and began expanding his horizons with a vengeance. By the beginning of the eighties he controlled the British Printing Corporation and prepared to set up the single biggest European printing group. Cash for the deal came largely from the National Westminster, and with typical Maxwell nerve he called the bank's chairman with a plan to print all their cheque books. 'After all,' he boomed, 'you and I have a mutual interest in doing business together.'

In 1984 he seized control of Mirror Group Newspapers and immediately began restructuring an organization dogged by inept management practices. Because print unions then dictated their own manpower levels, MGN had been paying printers whether there was a job for them or not. As a result some 'inkies' would clock on for a shift under the name Mickey Mouse, or some equally absurd pseudonym. Then they'd trot off to do another job secure in the knowledge that no one at the newspaper would be checking to see where they were.

BONFIRE OF VANITIES

The print unions were then perhaps the most powerful in Britain. In Maxwell, though, they met their match. He modernized the presses and introduced new technology and full colour printing. Sackings were frequent but the paper slowly began to look better and better. The only embarrassing snag for its journalists was their chairman's desire to have stories constantly appearing about his own wonderful deeds.

The classic example was his decision to launch a mercy mission for the starving of Ethiopia in 1984. He persuaded British Airways' Lord King to lend him a Tristar to carry supplies, a readers' appeal fund was launched and the paper carried columns and columns of stories about the way Maxwell was opening doors which had long stayed closed through British government bureaucracy. One former employee recalled a typical early morning meeting at which Maxwell would issue orders in the manner of a general stalking his war room.

'Get me Lord Sainsbury on the phone at home. And the chairman of Boots. And those people who promised us the milk powder. I don't give a damn if this is Sunday morning. Tell them it's a matter of life and death.'

His arrival in Addis Ababa was like a scene from a Carry On film. Maxwell strode into the airport sweeping aside immigration officials and flashing withering stares at anyone in uniform who dared to enter into his presence. Behind him a so-called welcoming party trotted along meekly in a mixture of bafflement and excitement. Then he faced the assembled ranks of press, TV, and radio, sporting his blue John Lennon-style cap and wearing his best Churchillian demeanour.

'There have been complaints that Western aid to Ethiopia is too little, too late,' he boomed. 'Well, speaking on behalf of the British nation I dispute that.' No one ventured to ask how he obtained the authority to speak for Britain. Anyway, there wasn't time. Turning on his heels Maxwell was already heading for a group of Ethiopian government dignitaries. Grabbing the hand of the nearest minister he looked him straight in the eye and declared: 'Things are going to be very different for your country from now on. Kindly tell the president that Robert Maxwell is here.'

BULLYING

When not fighting battles abroad, Maxwell loved nothing better than a chance to torment his editors and senior executives. He would keep them waiting for hours outside his office in Maxwell House, London, while he chattered away to his subordinates around the world or called some nation's leader to offer the benefit of his advice. There were only a couple of seats and a cold water machine in the waiting room.

When they did get summoned into his lair the atmosphere would be electric. Maxwell would often pick out one individual for ritual humiliation in front of his colleagues. One personnel manager was torn to shreds because of a circular letter he had sent to all Pergamon employees. Maxwell claimed: 'My old grandmother, who could never speak a word of English, brought up in the mountains of Carpathia could write better English than this.' He then ordered the unfortunate executive to shuffle out into a side office and write down why he shouldn't be sacked. As he left Maxwell roared with glee at the effects of his bullying.

Maxwell employees were not the only ones who had to bow to his whims. He disliked going out of the office for anyone, preferring them to come to him. Visiting foreign dignitaries would find themselves transported to Maxwell House by Rolls or helicopter from Heathrow. And if a guest was particularly favoured Maxwell would send his Gulfstream jet anywhere in the world.

Occasionally such lavish entertaining turned to farce. Maxwell would simultaneously host dinner for a couple of Japanese businessmen, a buffet lunch for a US trade delegation, a reception for a party of Hungarian newspapermen and plan his own quiet lunch in his study. He would tour from room to room, engaging in conversation, charming any women present, espousing his views on the world but always making an excuse to move on. And, of course, none of his guests was ever aware of the existence of others.

His family (he and his wife Betty had seven children) learned to their cost that business was never separated from home life. The two sons with closest links to the business, Kevin and Ian, were expected to be at work for 7.30 am and could expect a huge

dressing down if they were late. They rarely escaped home before a full 12 hours at their desks.

John Pole, Maxwell's head of security since 1986, said: 'He would go home to celebrate Christmas and be bored by Boxing Day. The family would gather for what they thought was going to be a holiday only to find they were going to work, but in a different country. He treated them like employees. Gradually they needed to look to other things to maintain sanity and some family life of their own.'

Top: *Maxwell and his wife Betty, pictured in 1974.*

Above: *Sons Kevin and Ian found themselves embroiled in the SFO investigation.*

Above: *Maxwell in one of his definitive pompous poses. Editors at the Mirror Group hated his thirst for self-publicity.*

two weeks. Maxwell and the crimper would lock themselves away for two hours while the dyes were applied to both hair and eyebrows. Everything was done in secret. No one was supposed to know it happened.

It was the same with his powder puff. Maxwell convinced himself his nose was too shiny so he took powder everywhere with him to counter the effect. If he ever forgot his puff before an important meeting it would throw him into a minor panic. Everything and everyone would have to wait while he went to fetch it. One of his editors, the *Mirror*'s Mike Molloy, recalled: 'Maxwell was theatre, he was looking for an image.'

Only on the *Lady Ghislaine*, named after his favourite daughter, could Maxwell hope to unwind amid the trappings of absolute luxury and forget about crafting that image. He loved nothing better than to sunbathe on his private deck alone, smothering his bloated mass in suncream and sleeping. The yacht was his fortress, his haven, yet at the flick of a switch he could be talking to his minions anywhere in the world by fax or radiophone. The dummy pages of the *Mirror* would regularly be faxed to him for approval.

According to the paper's former foreign editor, Nicholas Davies, who became as close to Maxwell as any newspaperman, sailing on the *Lady Ghislaine* did nothing to quell his bullying habits. Davies recalls: 'On one occasion, after a very good lunch, he phoned his chief of staff, Peter Jay, in Holborn only to find he was out to lunch.

Vanity was one of Maxwell's biggest vices. He needed to impress – especially women – and he hated the thought that his good looks and once enviable build had gone. Such fears caused him to suffer from bizarre eating disorders. He would suffer from uncontrollable binges, stuffing sandwiches into his mouth at the rate of five or six a time, and then a week later attempt to sustain a hopeless diet of coffee and soup. It did little to affect his usual bulk of 310 lb.

His hair was another obsession. He used to employ a former Savoy Hotel hairdresser, George Wheeler, to colour it for him every

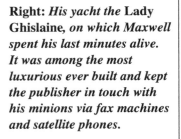

Right: *His yacht the* **Lady Ghislaine,** *on which Maxwell spent his last minutes alive. It was among the most luxurious ever built and kept the publisher in touch with his minions via fax machines and satellite phones.*

When Jay returned his call, Maxwell turned up the heat demanding to know why he had the temerity to leave the office without permission when the chairman was abroad.

'He demanded Jay write an explanation immediately giving reasons for his absence and fax it to him on the yacht. When he received Jay's long explanatory note Maxwell read it, roaring with laughter, at what he saw as a huge joke. Then he phoned Jay back and tore into him again, pretending to be furious.'

Jay, who eventually resigned to pursue a career as economics editor with the BBC, would later tell of the 'whirling chaos' that surrounded Maxwell's operations. It was this lack of structure that meant no one but Maxwell knew the whole truth about his affairs. At times he must have struggled himself.

Jay said: 'He was not just disorderly, he actively abhorred order. The key to the man was that he had the lowest threshold of boredom. He would come in and say: "What shall I do?" He'd get an idea and start ringing people. They would turn up and wait to be told what to do, by which time he would be on to something else … from grotesque schemes for transforming the world to fantastic rows about running newspapers.'

In a note to his successor Jay acidly observed: 'The job is essentially administration, a process of which the chairman is deeply suspicious and profoundly uncomprehending.'

PARANOID

Even when he was aboard the *Lady Ghislaine*, though, Maxwell could never truly relax. In his last years he became increasingly paranoid about the risk of attack, seeing himself as particularly vulnerable while on the yacht. He had one of his early captains, Englishman Mike Insull, buy an armoury equipped with guns for every member of crew. They were sent on courses to learn how to use them in the event of a boarding by raiders. But the guns were never referred to by name. Maxwell called them vegetables, and at the start of a voyage would sometimes sidle up to Insull and ask 'How many carrots and potatoes have you brought on this trip?'

Inevitably, after such a bizarre death, there was talk that Maxwell did not just slip into the sea by accident. Some remain convinced he committed suicide, broken by the knowledge that his entire business empire was only weeks away from crashing around his ears. Others talk of an Arab assassin hired to wipe out a man they considered an agent for the Mossad, the Israeli secret service. Another, even more outlandish, claim is that he was rubbed out by the Mafia for trying to break into their lucrative stranglehold on US newspapers. Finally, it is rumoured the remains of the Soviet KGB had decided to settle an old score.

Of the four, the suicide theory, argue old Maxwell acquaintances, is the hardest to accept. Nicholas Davies tells how only once in the years he knew Maxwell did he hear him refer directly to suicide. Davies had been summoned to his boss's London apartment to talk over the debut of the

European, his new weekly broadsheet paper. Maxwell appeared dispirited and had a heavy cold. He lounged on his bed in a white towelling robe making dismissive remarks about the paper. Then he walked to the window overlooking the city and began talking, half to himself.

'Sometimes I don't know why I go on. Everything I try, people turn against me … I've got no friends, no one I can talk to … no one to share my life with … Sometimes I think I should just end it all, throw myself out of the window. I sometimes feel I can't go on.'

It was one of the few occasions anyone ever heard Maxwell admit to the failure of

OUTLANDISH CLAIMS CIRCULATED AFTER HIS DEATH: ARAB ASSASSINS, THE KGB AND THE MAFIA WERE ACCUSED OF HIS MURDER.

Above: *Ever the extrovert, Maxwell cracks jokes with fellow party guests Liz Taylor and Malcolm Forbes. He loved nothing better than rubbing shoulders with world leaders or film stars.*

'IF YOU THINK YOU CAN PUSH US INTO AN AGREEMENT YOU'LL END UP IN THE EAST RIVER WITH YOUR THROATS SLIT.' HE WAS DEADLY SERIOUS.

his personal life. Perhaps he now knew his business empire was teetering on the edge of ruin as well. Had he stared into the abyss and realized what lay ahead? In his own mind, had he made a decision to end his life? If so, he picked the most theatrical way out possible. Disappearing from a yacht as it cruised the waters of the Canaries would, he

Above: The auction of fittings from Maxwell's London penthouse was billed as the sale of the century.

Below: Kevin Maxwell leaving court.

knew, guarantee even more column inches on the story of his demise.

The Arab attack theory is intriguing and if it sounds fanciful it should be taken in context with the rest of Maxwell's life. Everything that happened to him had the whiff of pure fiction. Just two weeks before

his death, the respected US Pulitzer Prize-winning author, Seymour Hersh, made extraordinary allegations in his book *The Samson Option*. Maxwell, he said, had for years been a Mossad agent who specialized in negotiating arms deals for Israel. But why should Maxwell bother with Mossad when he was on first-name terms with their own masters in the Israeli cabinet? And why, if Arab terrorists were responsible, did no credible organization claim responsibility?

The KGB conspiracy theory is neat and just about believable, but with Russia in a state of enormous upheaval at the time surely Red spy controllers had more important issues to tackle than killing a fat entrepreneur out on a sailing jaunt? It is said that for years Maxwell had been laundering US dollars for the Russians, taking a cut for his trouble and tucking away the proceeds in his Maxwell Foundation trust in Liechtenstein. He had also looked after the wealth of some senior Communist party figures who wanted to get their money out of the country in the face of an imminent counter-revolution.

With Russia on the brink of civil war, so the theory goes, KGB spymasters decided it was time to call in their debts. They reckoned Maxwell had made millions on the back of their cash, playing the foreign exchange markets with his natural gambler's instincts. The amounts were said to run into tens of millions of dollars and when Maxwell failed to take up the KGB's 'invitation' to pay their dividend there was talk of double-crossing. It was then that the KGB decided to show they could still flex their muscles and an agent somehow sneaked aboard the *Lady Ghislaine* to tip Maxwell over the side.

MURDER BY THE MOB?

Finally, of course, there's the mob theory. In February 1991 Maxwell had taken over the New York *Daily News* in a blaze of publicity. With a beaming face, and sporting a *Daily News* baseball cap, he gleefully held up the front page of his new baby bearing the headline: 'Roll 'em – hats off to Maxwell as News gets bigger & better than ever'.

Not everyone was happy. There were persistent rumours that for years the *News*'s distribution network had been in the hands of an organized crime syndicate. Maxwell, however, knew the Mafia men were on the run following a police crackdown. He reckoned the only barrier to introducing new technology and making the paper profitable was the intransigent unions.

Maxwell took one of his top aides into negotiations with the unions. Scotsman Ian Watson, then a senior executive with the *European*, was tasked with trying to persuade them to accept redundancies and economies. Watson later revealed: 'After seven of the ten print unions had agreed to the cutbacks, I went to see the leaders of the remaining three, who were holding out. I remember most vividly the conversation I had with one union official. He said to me, in a broad Brooklyn accent, "Are you a New Yorker? Do you know New Yorkers? Do you understand them? If you think you can push us into an agreement you'll end up in the East River with your throats slit. All of you."' Watson said later: 'He wasn't playacting. He was deadly serious.'

Maxwell took no chances. Firstly, he asked the Manhattan district attorney's office to conduct an inquiry into the organized crime allegations. Secondly, he decided he ought to get personal protection – those who met him whenever he was in New York said he seemed to be more and more preoccupied. So it was that only days before his death he held a meeting with the head of America's most respected private security firm, Jules Kroll of Kroll Associates.

Maxwell's full conversations with Kroll have never been made public, but those close to him, such as Nicholas Davies, believe Maxwell made it clear that people were out to kill him and destroy his businesses. He named names – business rivals, known enemies and political adversaries. At the end of their two-hour talk Kroll told him to set down a memo listing the bizarre events which had led him to draw this conclusion. He never did pen that memo for within a week he had drowned.

There is, of course, the other possibility, the theory that doesn't make headlines or attract TV documentary makers. This holds that Maxwell got drunk (as he often did, especially on the yacht where Dom Perignon was always available on ice) and took a walk round the decks in the early hours because he felt unwell. Certainly his crew recall him radioing through to complain about the air conditioning. Did he just slip over a low rail close to the waterline, as some have

suggested? If so, his cries for help would fall on deaf ears. None of the crew would have been on deck at the time and the speed of the yacht would have quickly carried her away from the drowning Maxwell's spluttering cries.

Whatever the truth, it matters little to the 30,000 *Mirror* pensioners who have endured agonies wondering how they will attain the retirement life-style they planned so carefully. Legal arguments about the Maxwell empire seem certain to rage on well into the next millennium. As for Maxwell himself, a hundred epitaphs could never tell his story of courage, meteoric rise, fraud and ultimate failure. All you can say is that he died as he lived … bizarrely, mysteriously … and with the newspapers chasing close behind.

Above: *A literary lunch at London's Dorchester Hotel in 1969. Already Maxwell is looking distinctly flabby – his weight became an obsession in later life.*

MAXWELL VOICED HIS FEARS TO THE HEAD OF A POWERFUL PRIVATE SECURITY FIRM; A WEEK LATER HE WAS DEAD.

THE RACE TO THE POLES

The quest for glory has driven men across frozen wastes to the very ends of the Earth, risking all on a gamble. Some win, and have riches and honours heaped upon them. And some lose ...

For years it had been the Holy Grail of seafarers: to find a shorter voyage from western Europe to the Orient, and to open a new trade link through the Arctic with all the profits that it entailed.

The search for a North West Passage had ended in failure many times, yet to explorers like Sir John Franklin that record served only as an added spur. If any nation was to find this elusive route it should, he felt, be his native Britain. Wasn't she the greatest naval power on Earth? Didn't her seamen have unrivalled experience? And, surely, her ships were the best?

On 19 May 1845 Sir John's expedition set sail with two ships, the *Erebus* and the *Terror*. Both had proved themselves more than capable of coping with icy seas (they had been used on an earlier jaunt by James Clark Ross to the South Pole) and they were stocked with enough carefully preserved provisions to last a good three years.

The Franklin party left in a fanfare of publicity with newspapers recording intimate details of the dangerous journey ahead. Nobody believed the voyage would be easy, but in the highest ranks of the Admiralty, and government itself, there was a quiet confidence that Sir John would somehow navigate his way through the labyrinth of straits, narrow channels and rocky gulfs known to lie in his way.

AN OMINOUS SILENCE

After two years, however, with no word from either *Erebus* or *Terror*, public opinion began to show signs of concern. Of

course, the crews couldn't yet be out of food or water but all the same it seemed an ominous silence. Throughout the bitter British winter of 1847–48 tension grew. The government had to be seen to be doing something in the face of mounting pressure, and after enlisting the help of the Hudson's Bay Company, who in turn alerted roaming bands of Eskimos out on the Arctic wastes, they offered a reward of £20,000 which they hoped would help track Franklin down.

It didn't. By the summer of 1848 plans for a full-scale British search and rescue mission were well under way. Two vessels would scour known North West Passage sea lanes around the Bering Strait, while a land party would head north from Canada. Another group, headed by the acclaimed explorer James Ross, would push into the Arctic region from the east.

That winter Ross and his crew landed on Somerset Island – thought to have been a

Above: *Sir John Franklin. His attempt to navigate the North West Passage turned into a disaster.*

THE SHIPS SET SAIL IN A FANFARE OF PUBLICITY, CONFIDENT OF SUCCESS, NEVER SUSPECTING THAT THEY WERE VOYAGING INTO THE ICY WATERS OF DEATH.

Opposite: *Robert Falcon Scott, a ruthless taskmaster and disciplinarian – yet he would hide when a sled dog had to be destroyed, leaving the job to his men.*

Above: *Franklin at Bear Lake. He believed passionately that British ships should be the first through the North West Passage.*

THE MUTILATED STATE OF THE BODIES INDICATED THAT THE DYING MEN HAD TRIED TO SURVIVE BY EATING HUMAN FLESH.

Right: *Austin's Expedition, one of the many ships sent to search for Franklin. The three largest from the left are* Assistance, Resolute *and* Pioneer. Intrepid *is slightly to the left of* Assistance.

possible staging post for Franklin – and covered 200 miles looking for him. They drew a blank and when they returned to England empty-handed it was seen by many as a certain sign of the Franklin party's death. Yet the Admiralty was nothing if not persistent and the following year a wave of 15 new search parties, carrying hundreds of would-be rescuers, set sail for the Arctic.

Among them was a nine-ship fleet commanded by Captain Horatio Austin with orders to search the Barrow Straits thoroughly. Austin came upon a god-forsaken, largely uninhabitable piece of land called Beechey Island and, true to his brief, decided to check it out. One of his officers, Captain Ommaney of HMS *Assistance*, took a search party ashore and with keen eyes carefully scanned the forbidding landscape.

Suddenly his eyes caught something odd: order amid the chaos, a symmetrical object in a sea of random rocks and scrub. When he got to it he found it was a primitive forge, a

store and what appeared to be a shooting gallery. There were hundreds of cans of meat stacked up ready to eat and, nearby, tombs bearing the names of three of Franklin's men. But what fate had befallen the others?

In 1853 Dr John Rae, an official with the Hudson's Bay Company, provided at least part of the answer. He had set out to cover the area around the Gulf of Boothia, an area where Eskimos were known to congregate as they waited to send hunting parties out onto the Arctic ice. Sure enough the Eskimos handed him a gigantic clue. Some other Eskimos, they said, had reported meeting a demoralized party of 40 white men who were travelling south to a point about 150 miles from where Rae now stood.

CANNIBALISM

The strangers had abandoned two large ships and claimed they were heading for the Back River. Many in their party appeared to be suffering from exhaustion and scurvy ... but at least Rae now knew there might be some survivors. Some Eskimos even claimed to have boarded the *Erebus* and the *Terror* off the coast of King William Island. Others offered grimmer news: they had stumbled upon the graves of some 30 men close to the Back River. Many of the bodies had lain huddled together in tents; others were found sheltering under a boat.

It must have been an appalling way to die, for as Rae noted after visiting the doomed camp: 'From the mutilated state of many of the bodies, and the contents of the kettles, it is evident

that our wretched countrymen had been driven to the last dread alternative as a means of sustaining life.' It was a wordy way to say that Franklin's dying men had become cannibals.

Rae's report to the British government cleared up at least part of the mystery, even though he freely admitted: 'None of the Eskimos with whom I had communication saw the white men either while living or after death, nor had they ever been at the place where the corpses were found, but had their information from natives who had been there.' Despite this the government handed over half the reward money in recognition of Rae's fearless investigations. It then declared the search over, mainly on the grounds that the cost of finding 100 men (possibly scattered widely across the Arctic) was impractical. Lady Franklin's plea for a new seafarer to take up the challenge was firmly rejected.

It made little difference to her. She was not a woman easily dissuaded by anyone and with the man she loved now missing for more than seven years she set herself on raising the money for a privately funded expedition. Influential friends rallied round and on 1 July 1857 a compact steamer called the *Fox* slipped her moorings at Aberdeen and under the command of one Leopold McClintock – a veteran of previous searches – headed for the Arctic.

After stopping to take on sledge dogs and an Eskimo interpreter in Greenland the *Fox* made for Lancaster Sound. The aim was to find a suitable mooring point from which to launch a land-based search. Unfortunately massive quantities of drift ice left the ship totally immobile and she was forced to drift aimlessly with the current for an agonizing 242 days … in the wrong direction. It was not until 1 March 1859 that McClintock unearthed his first

solid clue as to the fate of Franklin's men.

He was leading a small land party across the Boothia Peninsula when they met a group of Eskimo hunters. With help from his interpreter McClintock learned that years earlier a large ship had been crushed by ice off King William Island. All the crew had escaped, they believed, but then headed for a great river where they succumbed to the cold

It seemed to confirm Rae's discoveries and McClintock made haste back to his ship. His destination now was King William Island and the Back River and he divided his men into two with the intention of searching as thoroughly as possible.

On the island yet more hard clues emerged. Some Eskimos showed off items of silverware stamped with the crests of Franklin and his brother officers. Yet when McClintock at last reached the waters of the Back River he was disappointed. There were no signs of any crude settlement; no trace of white men whatsoever.

Above left: *The boat around which 30 of Franklin's men fought – and lost – their battle for survival. Some had resorted to cannibalism.*

Above: *An artist's impression of how Franklin's men would have struggled to cross the polar ice-fields.*

Above: *Lieutenant Hobson's party breaks open the cairn at Point Victory. Inside were records telling them how* Terror *and* Erebus *had been abandoned after two years locked in ice.*

Right: *Roald Amundsen. He walked away from a medical career to become an explorer.*

THE FINAL CLUES

The party crossed back to King William Island and headed up the west coast in an attempt to link up with the *Fox*'s other search party. Then, at last, they got the break they had been praying for. A weather-battered skeleton still dressed in the tatty remnants of European clothes was found lying on a snow-covered beach. On the body McClintock found a small pocket book containing a handful of letters – but still no formal record of the expedition's fate.

A little further on the searchers found two more skeletons, this time lying in a 28-foot-long boat which seemed to have once come from a ship. There were a couple of watches, two guns, spare clothing and tea and chocolate ... but still no paper records. In a further baffling twist, the boat faced north. Franklin's men could have been expected to flee south from the wrecks of their ships. Did the two unfortunates in the boat make a last desperate bid to turn back for the safety of the *Erebus* and *Terror*? If so, they had badly over-estimated their chances.

Instinct told McClintock to head north. His own log describes succinctly what happened next.

'A few miles beyond Cape Herschel the land becomes very low; many islets and shingle ridges lie far off the coast; and as we advanced we met hummocks of unusually heavy ice ... we were approaching a spot where a revelation of intense interest was awaiting.

'About 12 miles from Cape Herschel I found a small cairn built by Hobson's search party [Lieutenant Hobson was one of the *Fox*'s senior officers] and containing a note for me.'

Hobson it was who, on 6 May 1859, finally uncovered the secret of Franklin's doomed party. At Point Victory, on the north-west coast of King William Island, he found a large cairn surrounded by piles of equipment such as stoves, pickaxes, canvas shovels and instruments. There was also a rusty old cylinder which appeared to have been opened and then re-soldered. Inside they found two independently dated notices.

One log told how the *Terror* and *Erebus* had finally been abandoned on 22 April 1848 after more than two years trapped in the ice. Signed Captain F.R.M. Crozier, it ended with the postscript: 'start tomorrow, 26th, for Back's Great River'.

McClintock's men may have found the

last traces of the ill-fated Franklin expedition but they failed to answer the most important questions of all. Where did Franklin himself die? Why didn't his men join the Eskimos and learn their survival skills? And why had he been forced away from Back River? The answers remain largely conjecture.

The tragedy of Franklin's failure had, by now, been largely forgotten back home in Britain. It had certainly not dissuaded other explorers from pursuing the dream of conquering the elusive North West Passage.

A GLITTERING CHALLENGE

Foremost among them was a young Norwegian called Roald Amundsen. He was born in 1872, 13 years after the last hopes of finding Franklin had expired, yet throughout his boyhood he had nurtured an ambition to succeed where the Englishman had failed.

Although he had been channelled into a medical career the 21-year-old Amundsen decided to follow the instincts of his heart rather than his head. He threw up his studies to prepare for a career as an explorer, starting as a seaman aboard an Arctic merchantman and later serving as first mate aboard the *Belgica*, the first vessel to winter in the Antarctic.

On returning to Norway Amundsen decided to mount his own North West Passage expedition. He purchased a sturdy 72-foot ship called the *Gjoa* and during a series of voyages between 1903 and 1906 became the first man to navigate the route successfully. A glittering future now beckoned, with Amundsen a household name around the world and a hero at home. Instead of basking in the fame, the Norwegian immediately began planning his next challenge ... conquering the North Pole.

Amundsen's plans were to drift across it in a ship, a technique pioneered by his countryman Fridtjof Nansen in 1893. Nansen had noticed that wood used by Greenlanders was not from any indigenous tree population. Botanists reported that rough driftwood cast up on the shores originated from as far away as Siberia: it could only have travelled in a current which passed over the roof of the world.

Nansen's brave attempt to drift with the pack ice across the Pole had been technically

a failure, though he did get to within 272 miles of the Pole. His expedition lasted more than three years and he was given up for lost in Norway after setting out from his ship, the *Fram*, with one of his young officers, Hjalmar Johansen. In the summer of 1896 the exhausted pair stumbled onto a group of desolate islands called Frans Josef Land. Miraculously they there ran into an English explorer called Frederick Jackson, who at first refused to believe what he was seeing.

Finally Jackson ventured: 'Aren't you Nansen?' The man nodded, Jackson grabbed his hand and with typical British understatement told him: 'By Jove, I am glad to see you.'

Amundsen was convinced he could make Nansen's drift theory work but sadly never got the chance. Money was tight in his government's coffers and his expedition was still in the early stages of preparation when, in September 1909, news flashed around the globe that American naval officer Robert E. Peary had conquered the North Pole.

Cannily, Amundsen hid his disappointment and announced he would continue with plans for an Arctic 'drift'. In fact his motives were almost certainly very different. He was little over a year away from one of the greatest pieces of real-life drama in the history of man's exploration of the Earth.

Above: *Nansen meets Jackson after more than three years lost in the polar wastes.*

Below: *Admiral Peary. He beat Scott and Amundsen in the race to the North Pole.*

HE WAS AN UNLIKELY HERO, BEING UNASHAMEDLY LAZY, SOMEWHAT SLOVENLY AND PRONE TO BOUTS OF EXTRAORDINARY TEMPER.

Right: *Roald Amundsen. He was first to the South Pole, through meticulous planning, wide experience and sheer single-mindedness.*

Below: Terra Nova *at anchor near Cape Evans, Antarctica.*

SCOTT OF THE ANTARCTIC

That same year the Englishman Robert Scott, already a veteran of Antarctic campaigns, announced his ambition to conquer the South Pole. He chose an old whaling ship, the *Terra Nova*, and made plans to take a party of scientists with him. They would travel on sledges pulled by Manchurian ponies (Scott had been less than impressed with the efforts of dogs on his earlier expeditions).

Scott hardly seemed the ideal character to lead such a taxing adventure. When he was a naval cadet his lecturers regarded him as unashamedly lazy, somewhat slovenly and prone to bouts of extraordinary temper. Later in his career he was marked out as a ruthless taskmaster and stickler for discipline. Yet he inspired faith and respect among his men, perhaps because despite his weak chest and comparatively puny physique he drove himself far harder than he drove them.

Scott was also something of a romantic. His day-dreaming earned him the nickname 'old mooney' and he had a habit of crying when he heard certain hymns. He hated anything he regarded as cruel and hid himself away if it was ever necessary to put down a sled dog. Though he had the heart of a lion and unrivalled willpower, his failing was to lack Amundsen's more practical, direct approach to problems.

On 1 June 1910 the *Terra Nova* set sail from the Port of London bound for New Zealand. A couple of months later Amundsen, using Nansen's proven vessel the *Fram*, also headed south with the apparent intention of rounding Cape Horn to take the Pacific route up to the North Pole. His entire crew believed the Arctic was their destination.

On 9 September at Funchal in the Madeira Islands, Amundsen dropped his bombshell. Far from heading north, he said, they would press south. Their mission was to conquer the South Pole and anyone who didn't wish to proceed was free to leave. Unsurprisingly there were no takers. Scott had not yet reached Melbourne, Australia, but when he did there was a succinctly phrased cable waiting for him. It was from Madeira and read: 'BEG LEAVE TO INFORM YOU PROCEEDING ANTARCTICA STOP AMUNDSEN'.

The news was greeted first with incredulity, then indignation by members of the British team. They had been pitched into a race for which they had never been mentally prepared, but if that was the way Amundsen wanted it, so be it.

Scott made haste for his base camp on McMurdo Sound, on the far east of the Ross Ice Shelf, but found the going through pack ice extremely slow. While waiting for the camp to be resupplied he sailed further east to spy out the lie of the land. In the Bay of Whales his nagging suspicion proved correct. Amundsen's *Fram* already lay rocking gently at anchor. And the

single-mindedness. For a start, his only aim was to reach the Pole as quickly as possible and return safely. Scott would have to make regular stops to allow his scientists to carry out their observations.

Second, the Norwegian had learned from the Eskimos how to dress lightly and warmly in loose-fitting furs to survive polar conditions. His party were better insulated and drier than Scott's men could ever hope to be in their specially constructed suits that weighed almost twice as much and stayed perpetually sodden.

Third, Amundsen's Siberian huskies

Left: *Captain Scott sets out on his last journey. He wore a specially constructed man-made suit – but it quickly became heavy and sodden.*

Norwegian had started out 60 miles nearer the Pole than he would from his base in McMurdo.

Apart from that, Amundsen had won three main advantages through meticulous planning, wide experience and sheer

were excellent performers who had been transported from Greenland under the most carefully controlled conditions possible. All the animals were fit and in perfect shape for the torturous road ahead and they were working for men who knew how to get the best out of them. Each sledge had also been intelligently reduced in weight from the planned 165 lb to a much more manageable 48 lb. Scott, meanwhile, was about to discover that his Manchurian ponies, of whom so much had been made when his expedition left London, were hopeless in extreme snow conditions.

Above: *Manchurian ponies on Scott's expedition. They proved useless in extreme conditions.*

Left: *Amundsen taking a reading with a sextant. His Eskimo-style furs proved far more practical than his rival's gear.*

Above: *Once the ponies had gone, Scott had no choice but to man-haul his sled.*

Below: *Amundsen locating the exact position of the South Pole. He recalled how the Norwegian flag looked 'wonderfully well in the pure clear air'.*

THE RACE FOR GLORY

Amundsen left the Bay of Whales in October with four companions, four sledges, and 52 dogs. They covered 90 miles in the first four days and by 5 November had reached their southernmost supply point ready for the last push to the Pole. Amundsen was then able to strap on skis, attach a rope to a sledge, and have himself towed along. He later admitted: 'Yes, that was a pleasant surprise. We had never dreamed of driving on skis to the Pole.'

By this method the members of the Norwegian team found themselves only 270 miles from their target by the middle of November. Time was overwhelmingly on their side.

Scott, on the other hand, had left McMurdo Sound on 1 November and quickly ran into trouble on the Ross Ice Shelf. An Antarctic summer blizzard meant his ponies began sinking up to their necks in snow and had to be driven to their physical limits by the team. After camping for four days to wait out the storm Scott tried to push forward again. Within 15 hours his few remaining animals had to be shot and his party prepared to manhaul the sledges.

None the less the British kept going, in the clear knowledge that their duel was not only with Amundsen but also with the oncoming grip of winter. They got to their final supply point at the foot of the Beardmore Glacier well behind their planned schedule, but they still believed they could win the race. They now had the broad expanse of the glacier to move across. Amundsen, they reasoned, could not hope for such a straightforward passage.

Amundsen, indeed, had hit his first real snag. He had no choice but to negotiate a narrow ice spur he called the Axel Heiberg glacier and he found the snow so thick and crumbly that the dogs kept losing their footing. Time and again he was forced to retrace his steps to find another way up, and finally, with the way forward blocked by massive slabs of ice, he resigned himself to finding another route south. He still believed he had a good lead on Scott … and he was right.

Several hundred miles away across the unforgiving, icy wastes the British team was showing classic symptoms of fatigue.

They had just lugged their equipment 8,000 feet up the Beardmore Glacier and they remained less than half way to the South Pole.

By 7 December Amundsen had pressed ahead to latitude 88° 23' – 97 miles from the Pole – the farthest point that Irishman Sir Ernest Shackleton had reached the previous year. To commemorate the breaking of Shackleton's record Amundsen ordered the hoisting of the Norwegian national flag on one sledge. In his book *South Pole* he later recalled his thoughts.

'All the sledges had stopped and from the foremost of them the Norwegian flag was flying. It shook itself out, waved and flapped so that the silk rustled; it looked wonderfully well in the pure clear air and the shining, white surroundings … No other moment in the whole trip affected me like this. The tears forced their way to my eyes; by no effort of will could I keep them back. Luckily, I was some way in advance of the others so that I had time to pull myself together and master my feelings before reaching my comrades.'

A week later he was just 15 miles from his goal. Amundsen recalled that he 'had the same feeling that I can remember as a little boy of the night before Christmas Eve – an intense expectation of what was going to happen'.

At 3 pm the next day the magical figure of 90° south was confirmed by the team, though just to be sure they made a 12-mile circuit of the spot, taking further sightings as they went. By general agreement it was decided to leave a tent at the South Pole with the Norwegian flag fluttering from its roof. It would be a sight to chill the heart of Robert Scott.

As Amundsen headed home, Scott's men ploughed on – growing ever wearier from the weight of their sledges. Yet on New Year's Day 1912 their leader entered an optimistic note in his log: 'Only 170 miles to the Pole and plenty of food.' Perhaps it was a touch of over-confidence that caused him on 4 December to make perhaps the greatest mistake of the entire mission.

The last dash beckoned and it had always been agreed that the make-up of this final assault party should be Scott, Captain Oates, Dr Edward Wilson, and seaman Edgar Evans. Then, seemingly on a whim, Scott added the name of Lt Birdie Bowers. It was a crazy decision. The tent would be overcrowded, a carefully worked-out routine would be thrown into chaos and the food and equipment taken for four men

Above: *Scott's party finds Amundsen's tent at the South Pole. Inside was a letter addressed to Scott, who wrote in his log: 'Great God, this is an awful place.'*

'I HAD THE SAME FEELING … AS A LITTLE BOY ON THE NIGHT BEFORE CHRISTMAS EVE – AN INTENSE EXPECTATION OF WHAT WAS GOING TO HAPPEN.'

would now have to extend to five. Moreover, Bowers had left his skis at the bottom of the Beardmore Glacier. He would have to trudge while the others slid along.

They set out in more blizzards, which reduced the pace to just ten miles a day. At first Scott was upbeat, writing in his diary: 'It is wonderful to see that two long marches will land us at the Pole ... it ought to be a certain thing now and the only appalling possibility is the sight of the Norwegian flag forestalling ours.'

THE DEATH OF HOPE

But after 15 January his writings became gloomier. He noted: 'We started off in high spirits in the afternoon feeling that tomorrow would see us at our destination. About the second hour of that march Bowers' sharp eyes detected what he thought was a cairn ... half an hour later he

detected a black speck. We marched on and found that it was a black flag tied to a sledge bearer; nearby the remains of a camp ... this told us the whole story. The Norwegians have forestalled us and are first at the Pole. It is a terrible disappointment for me and I am very sorry for my loyal companions.'

Scott at last reached his goal on 18 January 1912. He found Amundsen's tent and a letter addressed to himself. Tired and devoid of morale, the British made camp and contemplated their shattered dreams. Scott himself wrote: 'Great God, this is an awful place. Now for the run home and a desperate struggle. I wonder if we can do it.' Maybe he already realized that time had run out. The bitter Antarctic winter would soon be closing in.

On 25 January his log states: 'Only 89 miles to the next depot but it is time we cleared off this plateau ... Oates suffers from a very cold foot; Evans' fingers and

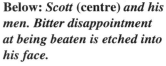

Below: *Scott* (centre) *and his men. Bitter disappointment at being beaten is etched into his face.*

nose are in a bad state and tonight Wilson is suffering tortures from his eyes … I fear a succession of blizzards at this time of year … not only stopping our marches but the cold, damp air takes it out of us.' As he wrote these words Amundsen was celebrating his own return to the Bay of Whales base camp. He'd gone there and back in 99 days – a journey of 1,860 miles across the most treacherous land in the world.

Despite their hardship, Scott's men found time to pursue their scientific objectives. On 7 February they arrived at the head of the Beardmore Glacier and immediately set about chipping off some of the rocks laid bare by the biting winds. They collected 35 lb before heading down to their base.

Now the problems began stacking up. First, they got lost and wasted vital rations trying to re-establish their route. Each man was down to his last meal when they stumbled upon the food depot they had been so desperately seeking. Then Edgar Evans fell and got himself concussed. He appeared dazed and rambling and, as Scott wrote, was 'absolutely changed from his normal self-reliant self'.

Later on, in the middle of a march, Evans dropped to his knees, uncovered hands bearing the ravages of frostbite, clothes dishevelled and 'a wild look in his eyes'. He died the same night. The survivors still had 430 miles to cover.

Captain Oates was the next to go. He no longer had the strength for sledge-hauling and could barely keep up because of his frostbitten feet. On 15 March he pleaded with the others to leave him behind so that they could improve their own chances. All three refused point-blank. But the following day a blizzard again swept in and the men were confined to their tent. In what was to become one of the most famous quotes in the history of exploration, the heroic Oates told his companions: 'I am going out and I may be some time'. He shuffled out into the driving snow where, somewhere, his body still lies.

Then came another setback. Oil had somehow managed to evaporate from the storage cans, which meant that the prospect of freezing to death became a distinct possibility. Two days after Oates vanished Scott, by now almost certainly in an exhausted mental state, wrote: 'We have the last half-fill of oil in our primus and a very small quantity of spirit – this alone between us and …'

On 21 March, while just 11 miles from their final supply depot, another blizzard confined them to their tent. Scott recorded: 'Had we lived, I should have had a tale to tell of the hardihood, endurance and courage of my companions that would have stirred the heart of every Englishman. These rough notes and our dead bodies must tell the tale but surely, surely, a great rich country such as ours will see that those who are dependent on us are properly provided for.'

At about the same time, Scott penned a letter to Wilson's wife. It read: 'If this letter reaches you, Bill and I will have gone out together. We are very near it now and I should like you to know how splendid he was at the end – everlastingly cheerful and ready to sacrifice himself for others, never a word of blame to me for leading him into this mess.

'I can do no more to comfort you than to tell you that he died as he lived, a brave, true man – the best of comrades and the staunchest of friends. My whole heart goes out to you in pity. Yours, R. Scott'

Then, at the end of March, came the final entry in the journal. 'Every day now we have been ready to start for our depot eleven miles away, but outside the door of the tent it remains a scene of whirling drift. I do not think we can hope for any better

Above: *Captain Oates' supreme sacrifice. He dragged himself out into the teeth of a snowstorm, hardly able to stand on his frostbitten feet. His final words to his friends have become enshrined in the history of exploration.*

Above: *Scott's grave in the ice that claimed his life.*

things now. We shall stick it out to the end but we are getting weaker of course and the end cannot be far. R. Scott. For God's sake look after our people.'

The bodies were not found for eight months. Wilson and Bowers had their sleeping bags closed, Scott's was open – one arm thrown across Wilson. Reports of the scene plunged the whole of Britain into mourning.

On two counts the expedition had been truly a spectacular failure. It had failed to reach the Pole first and five of its members had met their deaths in the most appalling circumstances.

But out of that failure came a breath of triumph. For all his faults, occasional muddle-headedness and temper tantrums, Robert Scott elevated the qualities of courage and determination to heights rarely seen. He died a hero. Few men have matched him.

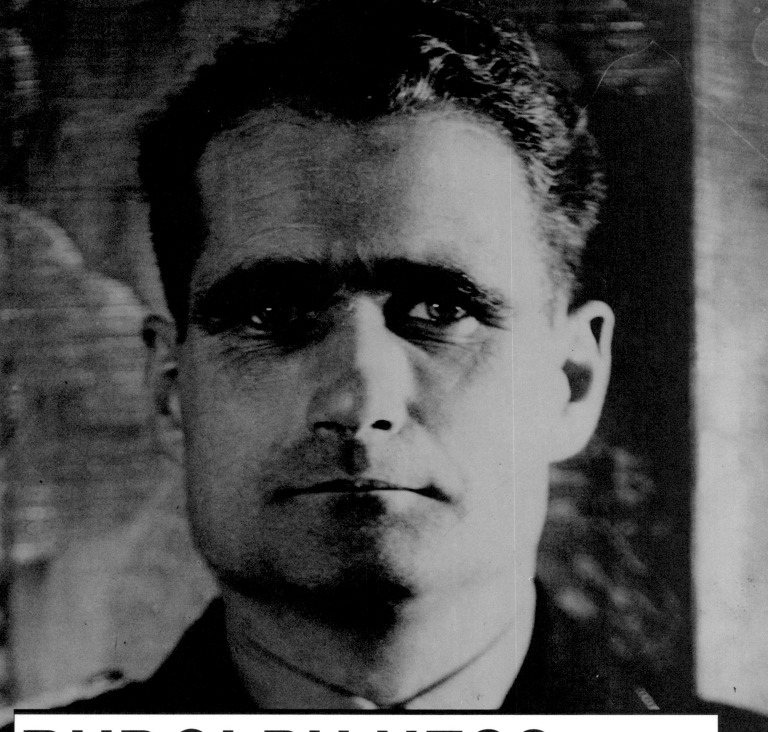

RUDOLPH HESS
A blunder of a peace mission

Rudolph Hess's desperate peace mission seemed too incredible to be true and the British politicians were wary. It was to be another 30 years before facts emerged that indicated that the real story might be even more amazing.

HE WAS BESOTTED BY HITLER AND DESCRIBED HIM AS 'FULL OF RARE DECENCY, FULL OF HEARTFELT GOODNESS ...'

Hitler never wanted to go to war with Chamberlain or Churchill. Despite his curt treatment of Britain's premiers, it is often recounted how he saw Russia as his main target, to provide an ample empire for the German race. The Führer would have preferred Britain as an ally rather than an enemy in his fight against the bogey of Bolshevism.

With this in mind, and with astonishing gall, his right-hand man Rudolph Hess decided to seek peace with Britain. He probably believed he had every chance of succeeding too. With the island fortress taking a heavy battering and thought to be staring into the jaws of defeat, he was guessing that the beleaguered British politicians would seize the chance an honourable end to hostilities.

In a covert expedition, Hess set off for enemy soil with the intention of seeing a Scottish duke he had previously met. This nobleman, he was confident, would introduce him to King George VI whom he felt sure shared the same repulsion as Hess himself suffered at the wholesale loss of life in the conflict.

But for a man of renowned intellect his decision was a blunder of enormous proportions. No one knows if he discussed the mad peace plan with Hitler. No one knows if he had lost his mind thanks to the grim reality of a world at war. In fact, no one even knows whether the real Rudolph Hess was incarcerated as a war criminal for 46 years in Spandau Prison, Berlin. What is sure, however, is that the night flight from Germany put an end to his glittering career and, in real terms, his life.

Walter Rudolph Richard Hess was born in Egypt on 26 April 1894, the son of a young German merchant forging a successful business in Alexandria. His abiding memories of the era spent in Egypt were of expeditions with his mother to witness nature in action in the desert beneath a scorching sun or by night under a star-lit canopy.

By 1908 he had left Africa for college at Godesberg on the Rhine and later went to a French-speaking school in Switzerland. He was being tutored in accounts and business studies in preparation for taking on his father's import and export business, not a role he relished.

ACE PILOT

So when World War 1 broke out in 1914 he volunteered to serve in the infantry, seeing action in some of the bloodiest and foulest of killing fields, including the Somme and Verdun. Despite two injuries, he fought on. It wasn't until a bullet pierced his left lung, almost killing him, that he was discharged and returned to friendly territory for convalescence. But it wasn't the end of his war. He emerged again as a fighter pilot a month before the war ended, and there was more fighting to be done in the chaos that consumed Germany after 1918. During this turbulent time he met the father-figure he yearned for, Dr Karl Haushofer, an academic who shared his views on politics and racial purity.

In 1920 he enrolled at university to study history and economics and that same year he first met and fell under the spell of Adolf Hitler. Struck by his tremendous oratory, Hess enrolled in the newly formed National Socialist Party on 1 July as member number 16.

In those early days Hess described Hitler as ' ... a character full of rare decency, full of heartfelt goodness, religious and a good Catholic. He has only one aim and for this he sacrifices himself quite unselfishly.'

Hess himself was a rather dour individual not given to laughter or joking. He did not smoke or drink and socialized only to broaden his mind by intense debate with other earnest young men looking for a new resurgence for their beloved homeland. He was certainly gullible and more than a little naïve, but stoically loyal.

When Hitler organized his uprising or *Putsch* in November 1923, Hess was at his side. They were consequently jailed for their insurrection and spent countless hours together during the 14 months they spent in a prison cell, exchanging ideas and discussing policies. Undoubtedly, Hess had a considerable input in Hitler's famous tome *Mein Kampf,* written at this time.

So the bond between Hitler and Hess was strengthening. In Hitler's subsequent climb to total power, Hess was in his shadow, working wholeheartedly for Nazism. There seemed a genuine affection between the two, shown when Hitler banned Hess from flying because he considered some of the stunts pulled off by the ace pilot too risky.

But Hess did have a distaste for wanton violence and mayhem even then. The brutality which emerged in bursts from Hitler, the leader he adored, were upsetting to him, to say the least. Most notable was the bloody purge Hitler carried out among his followers in the thirties after which Hess had to find words of explanation and comfort for distraught mothers and widows.

Hess had married his secretary Ilse Prohl but with little enthusiasm. Subsequently historians have questioned his sexuality, wondering whether or not he was gay. Some go as far as to list Albrecht Haushofer, son of the influential professor, the Duke of Hamilton and Hitler himself as Hess's partners.

It does appear the planned violent onslaught against Britain was causing Hess some anxiety. Previous peace offers to the British had fallen on deaf ears. In desperation, Hess turned to his old friend and confidant Haushofer who not only sympathized but passed on the name of a family friend in Lisbon, a Mrs Violet Roberts, who perhaps could help as an intermediary.

News that London was being pounded by the Luftwaffe and the sight of Berlin in flames convinced Hess that peace was preferable at any price. He authorized the letter to be sent to Lisbon, apparently unaware or uncaring that it might be intercepted by the British Secret Service, which it duly was.

When no reply came from Britain he sent his own letter, to which there was also no response. German morale was soaring so he knew any actions he took were unlikely to dent it. Also, he felt the Führer could easily extricate himself from the escapade which he admitted had little chance of success.

He then secured himself a plane from his flier friend Professor Willi Messerschmitt, ensuring it had sufficient capability to get him to Britain. It took some months of preparation and several abortive missions before the flight from which there would be no turning back took place. He wrote two letters to Hitler, several to his family and one to Heinrich Himmler, an adversary rather than comrade, protesting the innocence of all his men. In fact, only a couple of people did know about his plan, all of them among his staff. While others may have had their suspicions, Professor Haushofer, the man in whom he had confided many of his ambitions and woes during the previous 20 years, said he was ignorant of the peace bid. His wife Ilse, at home in bed because of illness on the day of his departure, knew nothing of his aims.

Above: *Hess with Hitler and others of the Nazi hierarchy. He was a valued confidante and advisor to the Führer, which made him an object of envy among other leading Nazis.*

Above: *Before the outbreak of World War 2, Hess helps Hitler to rally support.*

THE BLAZING PLANE CRASHED IN THE FIELD AND A LONE PARACHUTIST DRIFTED, BILLOWING DOWN TO EARTH IN THE MOONLIGHT.

TAKE-OFF

On 10 May 1941 the day dawned bright and sunny but the cloud cover Hess needed to breach Scotland's coast in safety was forecast and appeared. At last, this was the day he had waited for. Nobody thought twice about the Deputy Führer entering Augsberg airfield on an apparently workaday mission. After watching the tanks being filled and checking the guns were empty, Hess dropped into the cockpit and prepared for take-off. By 5.45 pm he was airborne, leaving Nazi Germany behind him for ever.

The circumstances of his arrival in Scotland are well documented. Shortly before 11 pm, a ploughman by the name of David McLean, of Floor's Farm, Eaglesham, near Glasgow, was deafened by a roar which shook his whole house. He rushed outside to see a plane crashed and blazing in a field and a lone parachutist billowing down to Earth in the moonlight.

At a distance, McLean called: 'Who are you? Are you German?' The reply stunned him. 'Yes, I am German. My name is Hauptmann Alfred Horn. I want to go to Dungavel House. I have an important message for the Duke of Hamilton.'

The plane had already been detected by radar as it crossed the Scottish coast. Either it was not intercepted or the weaponry used to shoot it down was defeated by the speed of the lone Messerschmitt. Royal Observer Corps staff were puzzled as to why a short range single German plane was traversing enemy airspace.

Nearby, the local home guard had also witnessed the spectacular descent of the aircraft and helped to take the pilot prisoner. Hess was unlikely to make an escape. He had badly sprained his ankle with his bumpy landing and was ensconced in McLean's comfy cottage when reinforcements arrived.

With an ancient revolver prodding his back, they left the farm for the home guard headquarters, a scout hut in Giffnock, a Glaswegian suburb. It took several hours for the wheels to grind into action. An interpreter, the Polish consul, was found. Two Royal Observer Corps officers arrived, one of whom immediately suspected the uninvited guest was Hess.

Maintaining his name was Horn and even brandishing an envelope bearing the name in a bid to convince his captors of the bogus identity, Hess asked once again to see the Duke of Hamilton.

A MISSION OF HUMANITY

Bizarrely, there was no response that night from RAF Turnhouse, under the command of the Duke of Hamilton, despite requests from the ROC men. It wasn't until 10 am the following day that the Duke turned up to interview the mystery prisoner. Hess requested a private audience with Hamilton during which he confessed for the first time that he was really Rudolph Hess and outlined the purpose of his flight. He was on a 'mission of humanity', he told Hamilton. 'The fact that I as a Reichs-minister have come to this country in person is proof of my sincerity and Germany's willingness for peace.' Further, he wanted a guarantee to be able to return to Germany, whether or not his mission succeeded.

Churchill was duly briefed about the airman still known as Horn, by now held in a military hospital in Buchanan Castle at Drymen, four miles outside Glasgow.

The cigar-sucking statesman was wary. Although Hamilton and the foreign secretary Anthony Eden professed the prisoner bore a striking resemblance to Hess whom they had both met before the war, the Duke was doubtful about the story. With a string of military mishaps behind him in the opening rounds of the war, could he really be lucky enough to capture a high-ranking Nazi with such ease? Of course, the possibility of an impostor claiming to be Hess was examined, but Churchill and his colleagues were at a loss to know what game Hitler was playing, with such odd tactics. They were still pondering when German radio broadcast that Hess had gone missing in a disturbed mental state.

Later the Nazi propaganda machine churned out bulletins describing how Hess, an angel of peace, had been lured into an evil British trap. It appeared the Germans, too, were having difficulty explaining away the bizarre actions of Hess. Hitler, by all accounts, was stunned at the letter he received from Hess detailing his plans, and decided the fate of his old friend was held

in the stars. Hess had promised he would not reveal the German plan to invade Russia in only a few weeks' time. Opening war on another front was a policy Hess believed to be madness, which was partly why he sought an accord with Britain. In the rambling explanation of his actions, Hess pointed out the Führer could simply deem his former deputy gone mad if any tricky questions arose. In turn, Hitler ordered that Hess be shot should he ever appear on German soil again.

Perhaps because the British military minds were so amazed at the German aviator's actions, they did not cash in on the capture of Hess in terms of morale-boosting publicity. They probably believed that the public, like themselves, would be unable to comprehend what had happened. Instead, they chose a whispering campaign designed to reach Germany only, alluding to Hess quitting Germany because he had lost confidence in the leadership and knew the war would be won by the British.

Hess was denied a piece of his aircraft as a memento, but allowed books, one of them being *Three Men in a Boat* by Jerome

Below: *Hess speaking publicly in 1937. He fervently believed in the Nazi policies of racial purity and national expansion, but disliked the party's lust for violence.*

K. Jerome. Later he requested a gun, probably planning to shoot himself, but was told the British government were short of guns at that time.

Lord Simon, the Lord Chancellor, posed as a psychiatrist in an interview with Hess in 1941. He reported that Hess had certainly come on the mission under his own steam and that Hitler knew nothing of the venture. He came to the conclusion, like many others, that Hess realized his own position in the hierarchy was being undermined despite unswerving, dog-like loyalty to his leader. It was his intention to pull off a coup with a negotiated peace that would ensure his position beside the Führer thereafter.

He also noted some worrying garbled comments from Hess which would have cast doubt on his sanity. Hess was convinced his food was being poisoned and that assassins lurked, waiting to finish him off. The British authorities were reluctant to declare Hess, codenamed Jonathan, insane because if they had there would have been various difficulties in holding him as a prisoner. He would most likely have been sent back to Germany under the rules of the Geneva Convention.

Hess was possibly expecting a grander reception and certainly better living quarters after his arrival in Britain, but the barbed wire and sentries which guarded him were in part to protect him from revenge plots. There was evidence that Polish servicemen planned to kidnap him and at the very least rough him up in retribution for the treatment their country had suffered at German hands.

He tried to commit suicide at least once during the war – he leaped over a stairwell at Mytchett Place, Surrey, where he was being held. The injuries he sustained were not life threatening. There were bouts of amnesia in which Hess claimed he could not answer any questions about himself.

JUDGEMENT AT NUREMBERG

When the war ended it was decided he was capable of standing trial at Nuremberg

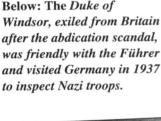

Below: The *Duke of Windsor, exiled from Britain after the abdication scandal, was friendly with the Führer and visited Germany in 1937 to inspect Nazi troops.*

alongside other notorious war criminals. At this time he set out his reasoning more concisely than ever before.

'The basis of my policy … must be an understanding with England. Even today, I have not yet given up this hope. I consider this war in which for a second time within a generation the people of a noble race are decimating each other and destroying their very substance as a terrible tragedy.

'The decision to go [from Germany] was the hardest I have ever made in my life. It was rendered easier, however, when I visualized the endless rows of coffins, both in Germany and in England, with mothers in dire distress following behind. I am convinced that mothers on both sides of the Channel will have understood my action.'

Along with Admiral Donitz, Admiral Raeder, Albert Speer and others, he was sentenced to life imprisonment at Spandau Prison in West Berlin. He was known as prisoner number 7. And here he spent year upon year in solitary confinement, held while other prisoners were allowed to go free. By 1967 he was the sole inmate in the complex, being guarded by a rota of British, American, French and Russian troops. It was the Russians who were most eager to see his imprisonment continue. Without Hess, they would have been banished from this legitimate foothold in West Berlin. Not only that, they were convinced he had helped draw up plans to obliterate Russia although it was claimed in London he knew nothing of Operation Barbarossa, Hitler's ill-fated invasion of the USSR.

Unaccountably, it was 23 years before Hess agreed to see his wife Ilse and son Wolf. By August 1987 the frail 93-year-old held in Spandau was ready to die. He committed suicide by strangling himself on the flex of a lamp. The bleak prison building was demolished soon afterwards but the controversy about Hess raged on.

Hess could have been the lone diplomat he always claimed, seeking to make peace, his brain becoming addled through pressure first exerted at home in Germany and later under interrogation.

There is also the suggestion that Hess was merely an expedient pawn, that peace negotiations were well under way and Hess was assigned for the most prominent and dangerous of roles by Hitler, to secure an

armistice. For whatever reason, the British side chose to abort the peace mission, if only to satisfy the masses who had pulled together for victory in a way no one imagined possible.

It is known Hess talked to the Duke of Windsor about an end to hostilities with Britain. The misguided Duke, who abdicated the throne for the love of American divorcee Wallis Simpson, was probably convinced the British would capitulate rather than face bloodshed. Any successfully negotiated peace would perhaps have removed King George VI from the throne and reinstated the banished Duke. The intervention of the incumbent King would have possibly been enough to scupper peace plans which certainly some members of the aristocracy favoured.

IMPOSTOR!

Then there is the storm caused by Dr Hugh Thomas, a consultant in Berlin's British Military Hospital, who became convinced the Hess held behind bars was an

Above: *Churchill in characteristic pose. He was perplexed by the bizarre actions of Hess and couldn't understand why the high-ranking German had taken flight from Germany.*

'I AM CONVINCED THAT MOTHERS ON BOTH SIDES OF THE CHANNEL WILL HAVE UNDERSTOOD MY ACTION.'

impersonator. He drew his amazing conclusions after witnessing the naked body of the ageing prisoner. In 1973 he was allowed to give Hess a complete medical check-up. The Russians were insistent that no comfort was shown to prisoner number 7. Their hardened attitude nearly resulted in the death of Hess in 1969 when they failed to call in help for several days after a duodenal ulcer perforated. On humanitarian grounds, Dr Thomas was anxious to see Hess accorded decent treatment. His discovery was electrifying.

History recorded how Hess as a young man had sustained a serious lung injury among others, but his body revealed no sign of a scar. On a subsequent examination, Dr Thomas asked: 'What happened to your war wounds?' According to the doctor, Hess blanched, trembled and uttered: 'Too late, too late.'

Convinced the real Hess was not the man who had been held for all these years by the Allies, Dr Thomas looked again at the flight from Germany. The plane used could not have covered the distance between Germany and Scotland without extra fuel tanks, yet a photograph taken by Hess's adjutant revealed no fuel tanks fixed to the wings of the aircraft.

There was the mystery of why he refused to see his wife and son – perhaps for fear of being revealed as an impostor. There were also lapses in his memory which no one could account for, when he failed to recognize people the real Hess had known well. The fastidious vegetarian Hess was known to be had also been replaced by a man greedy for food who would scoff meat, fish and anything else that came his way in a sloppy, unappealing manner.

Dr Thomas's theory is that Hess died in Germany before making his flight. News that he planned a hare-brained ploy for peace filtered through to other aspiring Nazi commanders – with up to five failed attempts at making the flight, it would not be surprising. Goering is known to have hated Hess and the intimate relationship he had with Hitler. Himmler, head of the SS, yearned to replace Hitler at the top. Both wanted Hess out of the way, but killing him would have offended his all-powerful long-time friend.

So they murdered the real Hess but had to make sure that a ringer arrived in Britain

> **THE DISCOVERY WAS ELECTRIFYING – AND EXPLAINED WHY HESS HAD REFUSED TO SEE HIS WIFE AND SON FOR OVER 20 YEARS.**

in his place to appease Hitler. Why would anyone take on such a thankless role? Many reluctant volunteers enlisted in fear of what might happen to their families if they wavered. After weeks or months of brainwashing, a lookalike might have been genuinely confused about fact and fantasy. He might accurately have guessed that any protestations at the Nuremberg trials would not have been believed.

There is even a theory that James Bond creator Ian Fleming entered into a ritual with satanist Aleister Crowley to lure Hess to Britain after the powerful deputy had been identified as a weak link in the chain of power. A biographer of Fleming says that in 1941 in Ashdown Forest, Sussex, Fleming joined Crowley and his son Amando in flowing robes chanting a spell which would woo Hess to British shores.

Official papers, however, concur with the notion that Hess worked alone and was indeed rather mentally disturbed at the time of his flight to Britain. Brigadier J. Rees, consultant psychiatrist from the army who tended Hess during his internment in Britain, wrote that he suffered from: 'periodic spells of depression and generalised nervousness ... he is suffering from insomnia and from attacks of abdominal discomfort'.

National archive material released in 1992 discounts the numerous conspiracy theories. No doubt is noted among the politicians of the day involved in the issue about the identity of the parachutist. Interviewers reported how he seemed resigned to his lonely future after deciding the mission for peace was his fate or destiny. Hess always denied Hitler had sent him. One government paper is being withheld for security reasons.

Whatever the truth, it is certain that when Hess hatched the plot to become unofficial emissary for peace, he was sealing his own miserable fate. Either he was killed in a hush-hush operation by his rivals in the Reich or he condemned himself to a life of bitter solitude lasting year upon interminable year, never to be shown mercy. While his prospects in Germany long term were perhaps less than shining, at least he would have escaped living in limbo and might have died with honour, something he would certainly have valued.

SUSPICIOUS CIRCUMSTANCES

MARILYN MONROE
The murder of a myth

Marilyn Monroe was an insatiable sex goddess whose only crime was the desire to make men happy. In the end, it seemed, that was at the cost of her own happiness ...

Left: *Baby Norma Jean Mortensen, who grew up to have the world's most famous face.*

Opposite: *A screen goddess and dream centrefold, Marilyn was adored by millions.*

Dr Ralph Greenson was first to inspect the body. He had broken a pane of glass to enter her bedroom but he knew she was dead even before he reached her side. She was lying face down, sprawled naked across her bed. In her right hand she still gripped her bedside telephone. 'I could see from many feet away that she was no longer living,' he said. 'It looked as if she was trying to make a phone call before she was overwhelmed.'

It was just before dawn on Sunday 5 August 1962, and Marilyn Monroe, the greatest sex goddess the world has ever known, was dead.

The years since have not dimmed her legend. Indeed, it has been fuelled, if not enhanced, by revelations of promiscuous exploits, scandalous affairs, marital infidelities and sinister intrigue.

The luscious, ripe peach of a girl with a walk that spoke volumes and lips that men lusted for had enjoyed countless lovers. Among them were stars and politicians – including US president Jack Kennedy and his brother Robert, the attorney general. She was beloved by millions. Yet she died alone. The question is: Did she die by her own hand? Or was she murdered?

Decades later, the life and death of Marilyn Monroe remains one of the most eerily fascinating mysteries, linking the murky worlds of crime, politics and Hollywood ...

UNLOVED AND UNWANTED

The girl the world came to know as Marilyn Monroe was born Norma Jean

Mortensen at Los Angeles General Hospital on 1 June 1926. Her mother Gladys, an emotionally disturbed film cutter, appeared on the birth certificate under her maiden name, Gladys Monroe. Her father was listed as Martin Edward

Below: *Initially Marilyn found success as a model with brunette hair. But she soon discovered 'gentlemen prefer blondes'.*

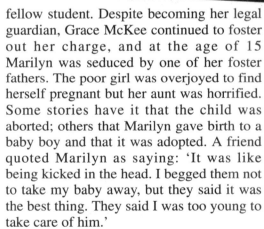

Above/above right: *As a bottle blonde, Marilyn was always cast as an empty-headed bimbo – when she yearned to be taken seriously.*

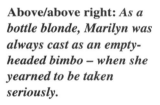

STARVED OF LOVE AND SEDUCED AT **15** BY HER FOSTER FATHER, THE POOR GIRL WAS OVERJOYED TO FIND HERSELF PREGNANT.

Mortensen. The young Marilyn, however, grew up never knowing who her real father was. Her mother's first husband, Jack Baker, had left her in 1923. She had then married Mortensen, a Danish baker, but the two parted before Norma Jean's birth. He was later killed in a motorcycle accident. The girl's most likely father was Charles Stanley Gifford, her mother's boss at the film cutting laboratory. After his brief fling with Gladys, Gifford left to start a dairy farm near Los Angeles. Remarried, he kept Marilyn's existence a secret from his new family until a deathbed confession in 1965.

Only two weeks after Marilyn's birth, her mother was committed to an asylum after trying to slit a friend's throat. Although Gladys continued to visit her daughter from time to time, Marilyn spent the next 15 years in children's homes and with a succession of foster parents. Shuttled from home to home, she became a shy, nervous girl who panicked easily.

At the age of 11 she went to live with her aunt, Grace McKee, and was enrolled at Van Nuys High School. It was here, she later said, that she first had sex, with a fellow student. Despite becoming her legal guardian, Grace McKee continued to foster out her charge, and at the age of 15 Marilyn was seduced by one of her foster fathers. The poor girl was overjoyed to find herself pregnant but her aunt was horrified. Some stories have it that the child was aborted; others that Marilyn gave birth to a baby boy and that it was adopted. A friend quoted Marilyn as saying: 'It was like being kicked in the head. I begged them not to take my baby away, but they said it was the best thing. They said I was too young to take care of him.'

Aunt Grace wanted Marilyn off her hands, and in 1942 she was pushed into her first marriage, to boy-next-door Jim Dougherty, a 21-year-old night shift worker at an aircraft factory. The life of a working-class housewife soon bored her, and escape came when Dougherty was conscripted in World War 2. They lived for a while on a base in California where she killed time in bars.

Marilyn soon discovered that she could make money by letting men take her back to their hotel rooms. As she told her maid Lena Pepitone many years later: 'I let my husband Jim do whatever he wanted with me even though I didn't really love him. So what was the difference?'

NUDE MODELLING

After Jim was posted abroad, Marilyn signed herself on at the Blue Book Model Agency and started posing for magazines and calendars. A natural brunette, she soon discovered that gentlemen preferred blondes. She went further than her famous bleached hairstyle, however. She also peroxided her pubic hair – a painful process but, she believed, essential if she was to wear sheer white dresses and no underwear!

As a model, Marilyn had no qualms about posing nude, but friends dismiss stories that she starred in pornographic films. Her famous calendar shot, lying naked on red velvet, was tame by today's standards. (Studio bosses were later so horrified by it that they ordered her to deny having posed for it at all. She refused and told everyone she had done it to pay the rent.)

Los Angeles was a city of dreams, and it was almost inevitable that Marilyn should meet an agent who would advise her to use her powers of seduction to become a movie star. With Dougherty now divorced and forgotten along with the rest of her tormented past, Marilyn sought invitations to Hollywood parties where she met the big studio moguls to whom she distributed her favours freely. Among them was Twentieth-Century Fox founder Joe Schenk, who was 70 and asked only that she sat with him in the nude while he fondled her breasts. Another of her lovers was Columbia boss Harry Cohn who, according to Marilyn, would indulge in no conversation apart from the simple instruction: 'Get into bed'.

In her desperate bid for fame, she later told Lena, she would have slept with almost anybody so long as they were 'nice'. She said: 'If I made them happy, why not? It didn't hurt. I like to see men smile.'

Her first steps up the ladder of stardom came with a string of minor parts in long-faded films like *Ladies of the Chorus*. But she came to the notice of the movie fans when she took the stereotyped role of a dumb blonde in the film *Asphalt Jungle*. The producer who gave her the role, Arthur Hornblow Junior, said: 'She arrived on the set scared to death and

dressed as a cheap tart. But she had a quality that touched the heart, evoked tenderness, made the blood race and stirred the senses. This can only be found in a juvenile delinquent!' Fellow producer Billy Wilder said: 'She had breasts like granite and a brain like cheese.'

Suddenly the poor girl from the wrong side of the tracks was sought after at smart cocktail parties – and at less salubrious Hollywood grope-and-groan shindigs. Being blonde, bosomy and deliciously beautiful, Marilyn was pigeon-holed into the dumb blonde category in real life as well as on set. Yet the actress was far from dumb and craved intelligent conversation.

She may even have sought an affair with the genius Einstein. Actress Shelley Winters recalled Marilyn telling her that she fancied him. When Shelley laughed at her notion of an affair with the most famous scientist and mathematician of the

> **'SHE HAD BREASTS LIKE GRANITE AND A BRAIN LIKE CHEESE.'**

Below: *Among her celebrated Hollywood co-stars was brooding idol Humphrey Bogart, who was even more sultry than she was.*

The movie star's next marriage was equally sensational. While still with diMaggio, she had been carrying a torch for playwright Arthur Miller. In June 1956, after Marilyn had divorced her second husband and Miller had divorced his first wife, the two were wed. By marrying the playwright, Marilyn was proving an important point to herself. She was no dumb blonde – she was the wife of one of America's most renowned intellectuals. She told the world: 'I've never loved anyone as much as I love Arthur.'

Her happiness was short-lived, however. Miller tried to provide for his wife a settled and ordered home life, but the attempt, in his words, to 'balance the two disjointed worlds' in which they lived became too difficult. Miller's work schedule prevented the couple wining, dining and partying in the manner Marilyn (and her studio bosses)

Above: *Taking a break from filming, Marilyn showed she was a girl who wanted to have fun.*

Right: *Loving and giving, Marilyn was every man's ideal girl. She enjoyed making men happy – and it showed.*

Below: *Baseball star Joe diMaggio hated his bride's sexy image and refused to take part in the Hollywood circus that dogged her every step.*

century, and an old man besides, Marilyn replied: 'That has nothing to do with it. Anyway, I hear he's very young for his age.' (After her death, a large framed photograph of Einstein was found among her possessions. On it was written: 'To Marilyn, with love and thanks, Albert Einstein.')

FRUSTRATED SEX SYMBOL

By the early fifties, Marilyn Monroe was stuck with the 'dumb blonde' image that coloured not only her locks but her life. She craved the care, affection and respect that no man had yet given her. At a party she met Joe diMaggio, the greatest baseball player the game had ever known, an authentic American hero. He was also a good man. They married in January 1954.

At 37, diMaggio was 12 years Marilyn's senior, and he put a protective shield around his new beautiful bride. He loathed her 'sex goddess' image, however, and reckoned the only place she should be sexy was at home with him. He refused to accompany her to showbusiness parties and shunned publicity shots with her. He was a homebird. Marilyn, now hooked on fame and under intense pressure from the studios, could not accept the role of a submissive housewife. They divorced only nine months after the wedding.

Marilyn was bitter. 'What good is being a sex symbol if it drives your man away?' she complained.

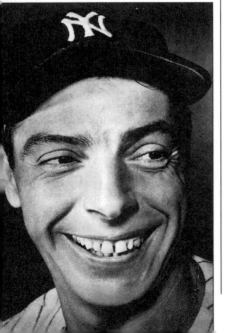

had come to expect. The writer was soon spending little time with his beautiful wife, shutting himself away in his study and working all day and late into the evening.

Often Marilyn would dress and make up ready for a dinner or a show, only to be disappointed when Miller would call off the date, claiming to be too busy. Sobbing with rage and disappointment, Marilyn would rip off her clothes and go to bed alone.

Marilyn's greatest disappointment, however, was in her attempts to have a longed-for child by Miller. Soon after her marriage she became pregnant but had a miscarriage after the sixth week. When her next pregnancy ended the same way she was beside herself with grief, sobbing: 'I can never have kids again.'

The star and the writer drifted further apart. Marilyn looked for love elsewhere, and fell for French actor Yves Montand, her co-star in the movie *Let's Make Love*. Their brief affair flourished during the filming, when Miller was away in Ireland and Montand's wife Simone Signoret was at home in Paris. Marilyn hoped their affair would lead to marriage but, filming over, Montand thanked her for a 'nice time' and flew straight back to his wife. Marilyn was left sobbing among the flowers and unopened champagne bottles in a hotel room she had booked for a romantic farewell.

Marilyn tried to drown her misery with booze, pills and a succession of affairs. Her marriage to Miller came to an end during the making of *The Misfits*, which he wrote.

Above: *Marilyn thought marriage to playwright Arthur Miller would bring her the credibility she craved. In fact it brought her only misery.*

Her blazing rows with him on set were blamed for the death of co-star Clarke Gable a day after filming ended. Monroe and Miller flew home on different planes and she announced to a New York columnist that she was divorcing.

The actress still clung blindly to the hope of a reconciliation with Yves Montand. A meeting was planned in New York at Christmas 1960, but just days before Simone Signoret telephoned Marilyn begging her to keep away from her husband. Montand cancelled the trip at the last minute.

At this desperate point in her life, with her marriage in ruins and rejected by her French lover, Marilyn turned back to Joe diMaggio for consolation. When he wasn't around, it was champagne, pills and a string of lovers, from politicians to a plumber working in her apartment block. Any available man was fair game for the insatiable love goddess. She hired a handsome masseur and seduced him at one of their afternoon sessions. She would invite her chauffeur to her room and lock the door for several hours.

She told one of her lovers, young screenwriter Hans Lembourne, who later became a Danish MP: 'I don't know whether I'm good or bad in bed. I can't sustain loving relationships. I drink, I lie. I often want to die – though I'm deadly scared of death. I

> ANY MAN WAS FAIR GAME FOR THE FRUSTRATED SEX SYMBOL: SHE SEDUCED POLITICIANS AND SHE SEDUCED HER PLUMBER.

Left: *In 1960 Marilyn starred in* Let's Make Love, *written by Miller, opposite Frenchman Yves Montand, one of her many amours. The film set was fraught with difficulties and marked the end of her marriage.*

believe in marriage and faithfulness, yet I go to bed with others when I'm married. God help me, what a mess.'

Significantly, she admitted to Lembourne that she was terrified of ending her days in an asylum, like her mother (and indeed her grandparents long before). 'I resemble my mother,' she confessed. 'I'm afraid I'll go mad like her.'

In her book *Marilyn Monroe Confidential*, Lena Pepitone recorded her impressions of the star when she was interviewed by her for the job as her maid. Although Lena grew extremely fond of her boss, she was horrified by her appearance at that first meeting.

The star was totally nude, as was often her habit as she wandered around her Los Angeles home. Said Lena: 'Her blonde hair looked unwashed, and was a mess. I was astonished by the way she smelled. She needed a bath, badly. Without make-up she was pale and tired looking. Her celebrated figure seemed more overweight than voluptuous. As she sprawled on a white couch she brought to mind a deluxe prostitute after a busy night in a plush brothel.'

However, Marilyn would go to extreme lengths to look good for special occasions. One such was a date with Frank Sinatra during a fling with the singer which she hoped would lead to marriage. Lena Pepitone realised the closeness of their relationship when she saw Sinatra 'clip two gorgeous emerald earrings on Marilyn's ears … they then kissed so passionately that I was embarrassed to be standing nearby.'

Frank Sinatra did not have marriage in mind, however. He was having affairs with other women and did not want any publicity. He even insisted Marilyn keep out of sight when she was staying at his home. One evening, slightly tipsy after drinking champagne while waiting for him

Right: Jack Kennedy, US president and philanderer, who bedded Marilyn before passing her on to his brother Robert.

Below: Marilyn adopted this hallmark pose in the 1955 film The Seven Year Itch.

in the bedroom, the actress wandered nude into the room where Sinatra and his friends were playing poker. Furious, he hissed: 'Get your fat ass upstairs!'

Sinatra eventually dropped Marilyn in favour of dancer Juliet Prowse, and the movie star sunk back into her heavy-drinking, pill-popping, sluttish ways at home in Los Angeles. Lena Pepitone recalled how the star would gnaw the meat off a bone, then drop it on the bedclothes, wiping her greasy hands on the sheets.

Left: *Marilyn and Montgomery Clift arrive for the preview of* The Misfits *in 1960. A month later she went into a psychiatric hospital for treatment after suffering serious bouts of depression.*

PRESIDENTIAL PHILANDERER

The date 20 January 1961 was an important one in the life of Marilyn Monroe. Her divorce from Arthur Miller was finalized and John F. Kennedy was inaugurated as president of the USA. Marilyn already knew the handsome young Democratic senator from Massachusetts very well indeed …

Jack Kennedy was an astonishing philanderer. It is amazing that word of his affairs did not leak to a wider audience during the president's lifetime. But the fierce loyalty of his entire White House staff meant that he would be alerted about his wife's movements and given due warning as to when there was need to break up a sex session or even a full-scale drug orgy. His philandering was also facilitated by his friendship with Peter Lawford. Actor Lawford was JFK's brother-in-law (he had married Jack's sister Pat) and he lived in Santa Monica, California, where his beachfront home was headquarters for both Jack and brother Bobby's West Coast expeditions.

It was here that the two were introduced to the world's most famous movie star, Marilyn Monroe. It is generally believed that both brothers had affairs with Marilyn and that they treated her cynically and dropped her harshly.

She was by this time dreadfully unstable, and even to have encouraged her into a clandestine friendship would have been cruel beyond belief. Yet they did just that – with tragic consequences.

Lawford, whom Marilyn had long known through his 'Rat Pack' fellowship with Frank Sinatra, arranged many meetings between JFK and Monroe. When Kennedy won the Democratic presidential nomination he made a barnstorming acceptance speech at the Los Angeles Coliseum, with Marilyn cheering him on. She then joined the young Kennedy for a skinny-dipping party at Lawford's beach house. Kennedy suddenly decided to stay on in California one extra day.

After JFK became president in January 1961, Marilyn sometimes travelled with him in disguise on the presidential jet Air Force One. At private parties Kennedy used to pinch and squeeze her and tell her dirty jokes. He was fond of putting his hand up her skirt at the dinner table. One night he kept going until he discovered she wasn't wearing panties. He took his hand away fast. 'He hadn't counted on going that far,' Marilyn joked.

In May 1962 Jack Kennedy held his 45th birthday party in Madison Square Garden. Marilyn was there at his side. She waddled onto the stage in a skin-tight dress and managed to blurt out a few lines of 'Happy Birthday'. She was scared and drunk. The crowd did not notice but JFK did. Marilyn Monroe could become an embarrassment. She would have to go.

In the last year of her life, the sex goddess was noticing the signs of her age – and she hated them. She said her breasts were getting flabby and she worried about stretch marks on her bust and bottom. 'I can't act,' she told Lena. 'When my face and body go I'll be finished.'

She even stuttered, an affliction the cause of which dated back to her childhood. She told a friend: 'When I was

Below: *Emerging from hospital, Marilyn was apparently cured of the drink and drugs addiction that caused her mood swings.*

Above: *Attorney General Robert Kennedy was supposed to be attending a dinner party on the night Marilyn died. He never showed up.*

Right: *The bed in which Marilyn died. Was it suicide, as the inquest decided, or murder?*

nine a man forced me to do something. I've never got over it and now I stutter when I'm angry or upset.'

Her film career was in tatters and she rarely turned up on the set on scheduled filming days. She fell into deep bouts of depression, possibly made a failed suicide bid and claimed that she had procured yet another abortion (that would make no fewer than 14).

Marilyn's last picture was called *Something's Got to Give* – and something did. Taking more pills than ever, she often did not arrive on the set until the afternoon. Sometimes she did not turn up at all. Her co-star Dean Martin quit and she was fired. The film was abandoned.

Poor Marilyn turned more and more to the Kennedy clan for support. She had shared her bed with the president and had then been passed on by him to his brother Robert. They had both enjoyed the sexual favours of the most lusted-after woman on Earth. Yet neither wanted anything more to do with her. Her life-style had become an acute embarrassment to them as, at the age of 36, with a long history of psychiatric problems, she turned more and more to drugs.

The Kennedys realized that, with her diaries and her knowledge of their Californian secret partying, the world's most popular blonde might be believed if she decided to break the presidential code of silence. It has been suggested that word was passed to Marilyn not to attempt to contact either Bobby or Jack ever again.

She was cut from the clan, and it was enough to send the unstable movie star over the edge.

A CONVENIENT DEATH

On the morning of 5 August 1962, Marilyn was found dead in bed at her newly acquired home on Fifth Helena Drive in Brentwood, Los Angeles. Tell-tale empty pill bottles were on the bedside table. Had she died by her own hand? Was it accident or suicide? Or murder?

The inquest verdict that she had killed herself by a barbiturate overdose was not seriously questioned for about nine months. But then, as the shock of her death receded, experts began to analyse the evidence more reasonably and to question the 'convenient' way in which Marilyn's life had been snuffed out.

Officially, the overdose that killed the star was more than 50 sleeping tablets. Marilyn, according to her aides, had great difficulty swallowing tablets without large quantities of water. Police who were called to the house found no glass in the bedroom. A post-mortem showed virtually no fluid in her stomach. And strangely, there was little trace of the drug in the victim's digestive tract.

All this evidence pointed to a frightening new theory: that Marilyn died not

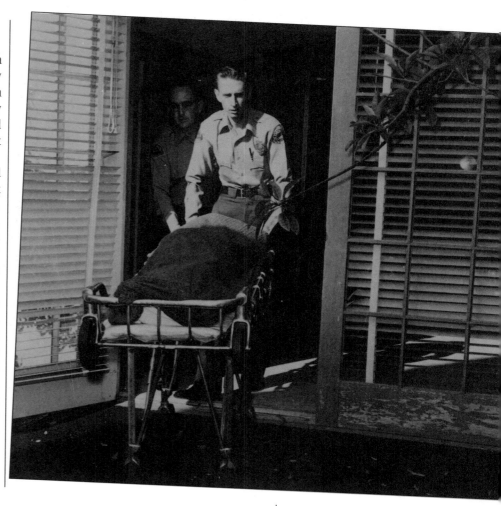

Above: *The glamour had gone when her body was wheeled out of the house she lived in so briefly, where the pangs of misery she had known grew acute.*

Left: *Actor Peter Lawford and his wife Pat Kennedy. They introduced J.F.K. to sex queen Marilyn, a meeting which had disastrous consequences for her emotionally.*

Above: *Jack and Robert Kennedy with FBI chief J. Edgar Hoover. After her death, there was speculation that all three were involved in the cover-up of Marilyn's killing.*

because she had swallowed an overdose of barbiturates but because drugs had been injected into her. Even top pathologists who investigated the case could come up with no other conclusion than that an intruder had injected the deadly barbiturate dose directly into her body.

But why? According to one of her closest friends, Robert Slatzer, Marilyn felt that the Kennedy brothers had used her then abandoned her. Her calls to the White House were no longer being returned and she was out for revenge.

Slatzer said that two important meetings had been planned for the day following her death. One was with her lawyer; the other was a press conference. At this conference, said Slatzer, Marilyn was going to reveal the truth about her love sessions with the president, or with the attorney general, or both.

The only thing that would have stopped her revelations would have been a phone call or a visit from Robert Kennedy on the night of 4 August – her last day on Earth.

On that night a dinner party had been planned at the home of Peter Lawford, down the road in Santa Monica. It was rumoured that Robert Kennedy was due to turn up. He never did. Nor did Marilyn,

who at about 8 pm received a phone call from Lawford inquiring if she was about to set out to join him and his wife Pat for the dinner. According to Lawford at the inquest, Marilyn told him she felt too tired and said: 'Say goodbye to Pat and say goodbye to the president, and say goodbye to yourself, because you're such a nice guy.'

'AN OBVIOUS CASE OF MURDER'

There were rumours at the time that Robert Kennedy, staying at the St Francis Hotel, San Francisco, had travelled south to Los Angeles on the night of 4 August for a meeting with Monroe. The story was denied but the theories that Marilyn had been silenced grew stronger.

It was said that her house had been bugged by Robert Kennedy, by the FBI, and even by Jimmy Hoffa, head of the Mafia-linked Teamsters' Union who was seeking incriminating evidence against his arch-enemy, the attorney general.

The theory that the FBI was involved in the star's death is not as far-fetched as it at first sounds. FBI chief J. Edgar Hoover made his agents collect for him every scrap of information about the private lives of leading politicians. It was one of the

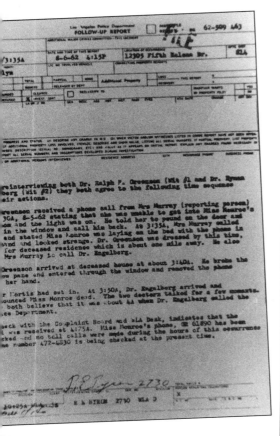

reasons Hoover's eccentric handling of the FBI had previously gone unchallenged. And in the Kennedys' case, the FBI's personal files bulged with scandal. Neither John nor his younger brother had been totally secretive in his extra-marital activities. In their relationships with Marilyn Monroe, it was thought that her state of depression and suspected nervous disorder might indeed cause her to spill the beans and irreparably damage the stature of the presidency.

Another sensational theory arose because of the belief that Monroe had an abortion about this time – and that the baby would have been Bobby Kennedy's. Marilyn had tried to contact him at the Justice Department in Washington on numerous occasions in the weeks before her death. Had an unborn child been the cause of Marilyn's death?

The horrifying storyline that secret agents killed Marilyn to protect the Kennedy brothers from worldwide disgrace was backed up by the research of dozens of authors, including the redoubtable Norman Mailer.

Even the first police officer to arrive on the scene, Sergeant Jack Clemmons, said:

'I was shocked to high heaven by the official verdict of suicide. It was obviously a case of murder.'

A further bizarre twist to the plot was advanced in 1981 by a reformed criminal, Ronald 'Sonny' Gibson. In his book *Mafia Kingpin*, he said that while working for the mobsters he had learned of a unique deal between the FBI and the Mafia. FBI chief J. Edgar Hoover had been furious with Marilyn over her embarrassing affairs with leading politicians and had agreed to turn a blind eye to her removal. The Mafia therefore ordered hitmen to bump off the star in order to repay old favours done for them by the FBI.

Weird theories indeed. But perhaps no more so than the established truth – that the most powerful man in the world and his brother had been having clandestine affairs with the most popular film star ever known.

The questions remain ... Who killed Marilyn Monroe? Did she die by her own hand, by accident or suicide? Or was she murdered?

When poor Marilyn's naked body was examined by her personal physician, Dr Ralph Greenson, she was clutching a telephone. Whom had she been trying to ring?

> **THE QUESTION WAS BEING ASKED: 'HAD THE PRESIDENT SILENCED THE SHOWGIRL?'**

Left: *A death report made by police detailing the 3.30 am call by housekeeper Mrs Murray to Dr Ralph Greenson when she failed to get a response from Marilyn through a locked bedroom door.*

Below: *Ex-husband Joe diMaggio made a twice-weekly order 'for ever' with a local florist for six red roses to adorn Marilyn's memorial.*

LOST CIVILIZATIONS

Wealth and wisdom beyond the wildest dreams – or mere fairy-tales? What is the truth about Atlantis, paradise lost; the fabulous El Dorado, a mythical city of gold; and, perhaps strangest of all, the extraordinary knowledge of the priests of an ancient tribe who still worship their guardians from a distant star?

It is the most fascinating exploration of all ... the search for a city, a land, even a civilization the existence of which no one can be certain. By word of mouth over hundreds of years, stories have tantalized the inquisitive. Tales of fabled countries, of idyllic landscapes, of sophisticated cultures – sometimes of unimaginable wealth.

Were these lost civilizations the result of a sudden flowering of the human spirit? Were they the result of visitations from another world? Why did they arise ... and why did they die?

Once upon a time the Sahara desert was green; rock paintings prove that a pastoral people dwelt there 5,000 years ago. A stone city stands testament to the lost civilization of Zimbabwe; centuries ago it was the heart of an African trading empire. Perfect geometrical patterns criss-cross the desolate plains of Peru; they were created by the Nazca Indians 1,500 years ago and could not be replicated even today.

Who were these peoples who came and went and left so little trace of their

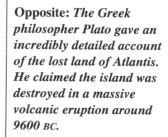

Above: *These marks in the desert suggest the Nazca Indians possessed some long-forgotten knowledge.*

Opposite: *The Greek philosopher Plato gave an incredibly detailed account of the lost land of Atlantis. He claimed the island was destroyed in a massive volcanic eruption around 9600 BC.*

Left: *An artist's impression of the idyllic Atlantean lifestyle.*

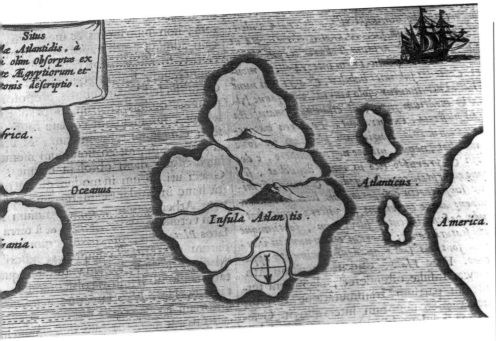

Above: *This 1665 engraving showing the position of Atlantis is based on Plato's assertion that it lies 'beyond the pillars of Hercules' – the Straits of Gibraltar.*

Below: *The Temple of Poseidon was said to be a shrine of breathtaking beauty.*

island paradise. Few great unanswered mysteries can have had as much energy, thought and words expended upon them as that surrounding Atlantis, supposedly blessed with lush vegetation, a cultured and civilized populace, a wealth of natural minerals including gold and silver, and food in abundance.

Did this paradise on Earth exist? Where was it? And what was the catastrophe that destroyed it?

The ancient Greek philosopher Plato was the source of legends about the great kingdom and city of Atlantis, which vanished from the face of the Earth centuries before the birth of Christ. In 347 BC he wrote an account of how, as a young man, he was listening to Socrates and Critias discussing philosophy with a group of friends. They described a kingdom 'derived from historical tradition' – a once-great nation whose people became corrupt and whose leaders led it into decline. According to the Egyptian priests quoted by Critias, it was destroyed by a violent volcanic eruption, followed by a tidal wave which plunged the tragic island beneath the waves forever.

According to Plato, the date of the destruction of Atlantis was around 9600 BC. It was sited, he says, 'beyond the Pillars of

existence so many centuries ago?

Here we examine three of the most enticing mysteries of all: at sea, on land and, strangest of all, in the skies …

AN EARTHLY PARADISE

Talk of a 'lost city' and the mystical name of Atlantis immediately springs to mind. According to legend, a people of great wealth, beauty and happiness inhabited this

Hercules' (or Straits of Gibraltar). He describes the magical land in incredible detail. He talks of its magnificent hot and cold springs, the elaborate temples, the luxurious accommodation afforded to visiting royalty. In all, he paints a splendid picture of a kingdom which enjoyed, before its decline and fall, the greatest benefits of civilization. He says:

'At the centre of the island, near the sea, was a plain, said to be the most beautiful and fertile of all plains, and near the middle of this plain … a hill of no great size. In the centre was a shrine sacred to Poseidon and Cleito, surrounded by a golden wall through which entry was forbidden.'

Because of Plato's account, Atlantis has become a holy grail for many adventurers, archeologists, historians and others fascinated with legends. But not one of them has been able to find the submerged remains of the ancient utopia.

Theories on the real identity and location of Atlantis have been endless, and the search to substantiate them fruitless. One eminent American politician, Congressman Ignatius Donnelly, sparked the modern-day interest in the lost kingdom when, in 1882, he published two works on the subject – *Atlantis the Antediluvian World*, and *Ragnarok, the Age of Fire*. His account put Atlantis, a huge continent which thrived and prospered for centuries before sinking beneath the waves for ever, in the middle of the Atlantic Ocean, .

But sadly for Atlantis enthusiasts, most of his theories have been debunked. The vast ridge in the Atlantic which runs from Iceland to Tristan da Cunha is not sinking – in fact, it is rising, and has been doing so for thousands of years.

Another theorist claimed that the eels which migrated to the Sargasso Sea had a memory of a freshwater source which once existed there, and that the 2.5 million square miles of weed that float on the sea off Florida hide the site of a submerged city. Both theories, unfortunately, are false.

Eel migration is now regarded as being no more mysterious than the migratory habits of birds, and the weed does not shroud a dead city; it is merely a perfectly natural phenomenon, carried by swirling currents off the Florida coastline.

Others have earmarked the Scilly Isles off Cornwall's coast as a possibility, and have raised the theory of a great land-bridge between Britain and America via Iceland and Greenland, or have speculated that the mysterious sunken island was even in the Pacific Ocean. All these theories have been scotched by the experts over the years.

An American photographer, Edgar Cayce, claimed to have seen into the past and mentally visited Atlantis between 1923 and his death in 1945. He said he had never read Plato but described the island in the way the Greek philosopher did. He said Atlantis had been destroyed by a great nuclear explosion when its gifted citizenry had learned how to split the atom. He further prophesied that 'a portion of the temples' would be discovered in 1969.

In that very year, archeologist Dr J. Manson Valentine was taken by a local fisherman known as Bonefish Sam to view curious rectangular stones lying in eight metres of water north of Paradise Point on the tiny Bahamian island of Bimini.

Valentine was ecstatic. He believed the two parallel lines of stones, about half a mile long and five yards square, to be the remnants of a great harbour wall. Divers and archeologists arrived in hordes, probing to see whether the stones were the work of Aztec, Toltec, Mayan, or any one of a number of other civilizations.

No one has yet been able to prove or

Above: *Congressman Donnelly's book started the modern-day Atlantis cult.*

THE PHOTOGRAPHER CLAIMED HE HAD 'VISITED' ATLANTIS AND PROPHESIED THAT THE ANCIENT CITY WOULD BE FOUND.

Below: *How Atlantis fitted onto the early maps.*

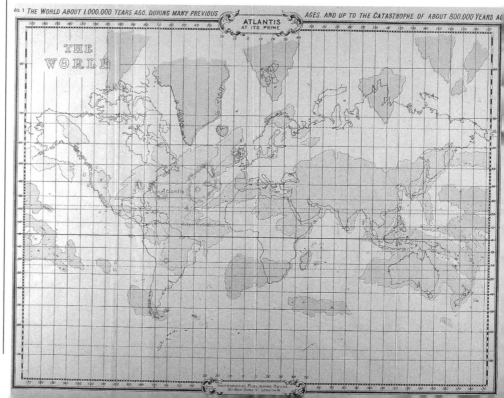

TRUE STORIES OF THE STRANGE AND THE UNKNOWN

July 1958 35¢

FATE

HAS ATLANTIS
BEEN FOUND?

TELEPATHY
IN PETS
MURDER
BY A GHOST

Above: *The cover of* Fate *magazine reports another false dawn for believers in the lost city.*

Above right: *Further interpretation of Plato's detailed description of Atlantis – a banqueting hall.*

Below: *The ruins of a Minoan town in the aftermath of the eruption.*

disprove that the stones were man-made, or whether they were indeed part of the ancient lost city of Atlantis. One eminent professor, Dr John Hall of Miami University, declared in 1970 that the wall was in fact a natural phenomenon called pleistocene beachrock, adding: 'Therefore, alas, for those who believe in the old legend, another Atlantis is dismissed'. However, two later expeditions to Bimini in 1975 and 1977 revealed a block of stone with a carved edge, something definitely crafted by a human hand. Its origins still remain a mystery.

A FIERY FURNACE

Many academics subscribe to the notion that, since the Atlantis described by Plato has never been found, the philosopher must have mistaken the location. The catastrophe he refers to, they believe, was in fact the mighty volcanic eruption which blasted the Minoan civilization off the face of the Earth.

Derek Ager, head of the Department of Geology at Bristol University, believes that this may be what happened: 'I have no doubt at all that there never was such a land mass beyond the Pillars of Hercules. The subject is just not worth discussing. On the other hand, I think it is quite possible, even probable, that the legend refers to the destruction of the Minoan civilization by the volcanic process.'

The centre of Minoan culture was the city of Knossos, on the island of Crete. From here the Minoans dominated the Aegean and the islands clustered in it. In 1967, the Greek archeologist Spyridon Marinatos began excavating on one of those islands, Kalliste. There he discovered the remains of a city which was to become known as the 'Pompeii of the Aegean' because, like its famous Roman companion in fate, it was destroyed by volcanic eruptions of such magnitude as to defy belief.

Kalliste, as the island was called in ancient times, is now termed Santorini or Thera, and is the southernmost of the Cyclades islands. There, buried beneath 100 feet of volcanic ash, Marinatos discovered the first sign of the tragedy which wiped out the inhabitants.

Scientists now believe that a volcanic

eruption four times greater than that which destroyed the Indonesian isle of Krakatoa in 1883 was responsible for the destruction of Kalliste. To give some idea of the scale of such an explosion, Krakatoa, when it erupted, produced the loudest bang in recorded history, spewing rocks, lava, ash and fire over a huge area. The volcanic ash cloud was carried as far away as Europe and the resulting tidal waves crossed the Pacific Ocean and damaged boats on the coast of South America. And this was only a quarter of the force of the explosion which ripped the ancient civilization on Kalliste asunder.

It is believed that when the Minoans were warned of their impending fate by minor earthquakes and eruptions, they took to the sea in boats and were probably no more than 70 miles away when the main eruptions occurred, raining down burning debris and choking ash upon their vessels. Whichever ships escaped the firestorm would have been smashed to matchsticks by the resultant tidal waves.

Some historians even suggest that the ash clouds could be the origin of the story of the Egyptian plagues described in the Old Testament, since they covered an area greater than 15,500 square miles and would easily have been visible as far away as Egypt.

So was the Atlantis described by Plato the Bronze Age Minoan culture which blossomed in the islands of the Aegean? We may never know. The golden age of Minoan civilization was utterly destroyed. All the human remains that have been found were blackened by ash or badly charred by fire, but it is known that the Minoans were a cultured people, civilized and refined; they enjoyed mains drainage and baths in their homes, unrivalled prosperity and command of the seas.

For 500 years the Minoans ruled supreme ... and then vanished. The mysterious island of Santorini or Kalliste is the most likely candidate for the site of ancient Atlantis. Plato's oft-retold story was probably no fairy-tale after all.

> **THE ANCIENT CIVILIZATION WAS BLOWN OFF THE FACE OF THE EARTH IN A SPECTACULAR EXPLOSION.**

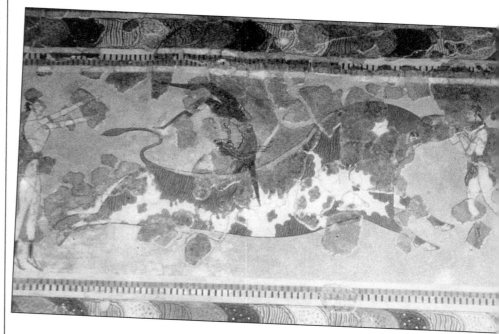

THE GOLDEN CITY OF EL DORADO

In many ways, the search for the lost city of El Dorado is even more tantalizing than that for Atlantis. The principal reason is the fabled wealth that lay within its walls. But the other reason is that whereas Atlantis was engulfed by the seas, El Dorado still exists in some form – and its golden age is much more recent.

The story of El Dorado begins with the Inca empire of Peru. When the Spaniards invaded the Incas in 1530, they discovered a civilized race, beautiful public buildings, an ordered society – and hoards of gold.

Capturing the city of Cuzco, the Spanish Conquistadors discovered plunder beyond their avaricious dreams. Golden art

Above: *This Minoan mosaic is typical of an art form which is still revered the world over.*

Left: *A Minoan snake goddess. Idols such as this were worshipped by the proud and wealthy islanders.*

Above: A *Conquistador* landing party. These greedy men were totally ruthless in their pursuit of gold.

treasures abounded: there was gold-plating on the temple walls and even the palace water pipes were made of gold.

But it was not enough for the invaders. The Spaniards captured the Inca emperor Atahuallpa and held him to ransom, demanding that a room 22 feet by 17 feet be filled to the ceiling with gold. The innocent Incas set about collecting this extraordinary ransom. With the room full of the precious metal, they waited patiently for the release of their emperor.

The ruthless conquerors, led by the illiterate but militarily brilliant Francisco Pizarro, reneged on the deal and cold-bloodedly killed their hostage. Then they embarked on a terrible reign of looting and pillaging, stripping the entire Inca empire of its age-old wealth. Still not content with their booty, the Spaniards began to look further afield for even greater treasure chests.

That is when they first heard the name El Dorado.

Myth and legend and fact all merge when El Dorado is mentioned. It was thus even in Pizarro's time. The conquerors were told that El Dorado was a mountain of solid gold lying to the north of Inca territory, so they marched to a treasure-filled temple hidden deep in the jungle.

Expeditions were sent into the jungle. The sole survivor of one of them, Juan Martin de Albujar, returned with stories of being held within a secret Inca capital and being freed with as much gold as he and his men could carry. All had been lost in the jungle, he said.

Another conquistador, Sebastian de Belalcazar who founded the Ecuador capital of Quito, heard the stories and coined the name El Dorado. But he failed to find it.

It was not only the Spanish who attempted to reach El Dorado. Between 1535 and 1540 several expeditions led by different colonial powers sought the 'lost city'. Georg Hohermuth, the German governor of Venezuela, followed the Indian salt trade routes, having learned from the natives that 'where the salt comes from, comes gold'. He set out with 400 men, searched for three years, encountered starvation and pestilence, and passed within 60 miles of the site of El Dorado. He returned empty handed, leaving 300 of his expedition dead in the jungle. Another German adventurer, Nicholaus Federmann, embarked on the same mission with as little success.

A hard-headed Spanish lawyer, Gonzalo Jimenez de Quesada, led the largest expedition to find the legendary golden hoard. In 1536 he headed inland from the Colombian coast with 900 men. Each step of the way had to be carved out with machetes. Disease and battles with the Chibcha Indians reduced their numbers to 200.

Quesada captured villages and tortured the inhabitants until they revealed the source of their precious metals and gems. He thought he had stumbled upon El Dorado when an Indian led him to the town of Hunsa, described as the 'place of gold'. Quesada looted gold plates and

large hoards of emeralds and bags of gold dust. The chief's house, lined with massive sheets of gold and containing a beautiful throne of gold and emeralds, was similarly sacked. The Spaniards slaughtered all before them, even stealing the gold rings from the ears and noses of the dead Indians.

THE LAKE OF GOLD

At last Quesada's expedition came to a lake 9,000 feet above sea level. And it was here that the legend of El Dorado had been born …

El Dorado, as the natives told them, was not a place but a person. El Dorado is Spanish for 'The Gilded One', probably the chief of the Muisca nation who lived in the

THE GREEDY SPANIARDS SLAUGHTERED THE BEWILDERED INDIANS AND RIPPED THE GOLD RINGS FROM THEIR EARS AND NOSES.

Left: *Pizarro. He kidnapped an Inca emperor and demanded a room 22 feet by 17 feet be filled with gold to pay the ransom.*

Below: *Conquistadors setting dogs on Aztecs. A more evil, heartless bunch of men would be hard to find.*

region which now surrounds the Colombian capital of Bogota.

The chief of the Muiscas was crowned in a unique ritual. His tribe would gather in a holy valley in the mountains for several days of prayer and celebrations. The climax of the festival was a boat trip onto Lake Guatavita. Incense was burned and flutes wafted their music across the waters until the boat reached the centre of the perfectly circular lake.

The new chief was then stripped naked while priests coated his entire body with gold dust. It must have been a hugely religious experience for the watching crowds as, with the sun glinting on his body, the king made his offerings to the gods by lifting up gold treasures and dropping them into the deep waters of Lake Guatavita. He would then bathe in the lake to wash off the gold dust covering his body. Apparently, this was a signal for the onlookers to take their golden tributes and throw them from the shore into the lake.

Right: *This gold disk with dancing figure was a primitive artform much sought after by the Conquistadors.*

Below: *One of the golden treasures which central American Indian tribes would offer up to their gods.*

Lake Guatavita thereby held the richest hoard of gold that even the Conquistadors of Spain could imagine. But they never found El Dorado – the man or the place or the gold.

In their ignorance, the poor Indians had neglected to tell their greedy tormentors of two vital facts. One was that El Dorado no longer existed; the last Muisca chief to be enthroned on the lake had been deposed a few years earlier.

The second vital fact was that El Dorado's people had no source of gold of their own; they gathered it by a combination of war and trading salt.

With the realization that the only way to find any of El Dorado's gold was to plumb the depths of Lake Guatavita, Quesada's brother Herman journeyed back to the site in 1545. He conscripted slave labour among the poor Muisca Indians and placed them in a human chain from the water's edge to the top of the mountains. Laboriously, they took water from the lake in buckets and passed it along the line to be tipped away. After three months of continuous toil, the level of the lake was lowered by 9 feet. Herman Quesada eventually abandoned the task, but he did recover several hundred gold artefacts from the receding waters.

Several more ambitious schemes followed. In 1585, another Spaniard whose name is now lost to history recruited 8,000 Indians to cut a deep channel to drain the lake. This time the level fell by 60 feet and many more golden objects were uncovered before landslips blocked the drainage channel.

A British company tried to drain the lake at the beginning of this century by

drilling a tunnel which lowered the water level, but the mud on the lake bed was at first too soft and deep to walk on – and once the sun had baked it, was too hard to dig through. Ludicrously, by the time fresh equipment could be transported to the site, mud had blocked the drainage channels and rains had filled the lake again!

Happily for the region, the Colombian government passed legislation protecting the site from treasure-hunters, but the fabled wealth of El Dorado still haunts explorers, adventurers and treasure seekers. For not all the gold ended up in the bottom of Lake Guatavita. There is no shortage of those who would still kill for the greedy dream of Andean gold. The mystery of El Dorado lives on …

SECRETS OF THE UNIVERSE

If the people of Atlantis had a civilization beyond belief, and the people of El Dorado had wealth beyond the dreams of avarice, what of the poor people of the Dogon tribe of Africa? They survive today, owning virtually nothing. Yet for centuries they have possessed the most astonishing scientific knowledge.

The Dogon tribe of West Africa live in a scattering of villages over a vast area of what is now the Republic of Mali. The terrain is rocky and arid, and their homes are built of mud and straw. Their life-style is primitive in the extreme by any Western standards. Yet extraordinarily, these primitive folk had detailed knowledge about stars and planets many hundreds of years before they were observed scientifically.

Have they and other primitive peoples gained their knowledge from other, greater, earlier civilizations? Or even from visitors from other planets?

The fascination with the Dogons comes because of a relatively recent scientific discovery. The glittering star Sirius, one of the brightest in the heavens, has a companion star which is so outshone by its near-neighbour that its very existence was not even suspected by astronomers until the 19th century. Invisible to the naked eye, this smaller star's nature was not revealed until the 1920s.

Yet the existence of Sirius B was known about hundreds, if not thousands, of years ago. It was recorded by a people whose primitive existence offers no outward clue to the extraordinary astronomical knowledge they have.

When French anthropologists Marcel Griaule and Germaine Dieterlen studied the Dogons, living amongst them and winning their confidence, they discovered a depth of knowledge of the Universe that astounded them. They found that when this race migrated to West Africa and settled on the Bandiagra Plateau some time between the 13th and 16th centuries, they brought with them secrets that they could not be expected to know today.

Not too surprisingly, they knew that the Earth was round and spun on its own north–south axis; they knew that the Earth and the other planets revolved around the Sun; they knew that our Moon was 'dry

Above: *A colourful portrayal of the Spanish treasure seekers. The llama needed to be strong. Apart from its rider, it was expected to carry bulky and heavy items of plunder.*

HOW COULD THE PRIMITIVE NATIVES HAVE KNOWN ABOUT THE GLITTERING STAR THOUSANDS OF YEARS AGO WHEN ASTRONOMERS DENIED ITS VERY EXISTENCE UNTIL RECENTLY?

Right: *An engraving of the ornamental representation of the Dog-star.*

Below: *A Dogon village in Mali. Primitive … yet these people had an incredible depth of knowledge of the Universe.*

and dead like dry dead blood'. For some reason, they knew that the Milky Way was shaped like a spiral – a fact impossible to detect without extremely expensive astronomical equipment.

Without access to powerful telescopes, they could not have been expected to know that Saturn was surrounded by its famous rings – yet they drew the planet with its halo in the dirt outside their huts. Even more incredible was that they knew that Jupiter had four main moons – impossible knowledge for any but the most sophisticated race.

Amazing as they were, the revelations about Jupiter's moons and other aspects of the Solar System paled into insignificance when compared with what the Dogons knew about more distant bodies.

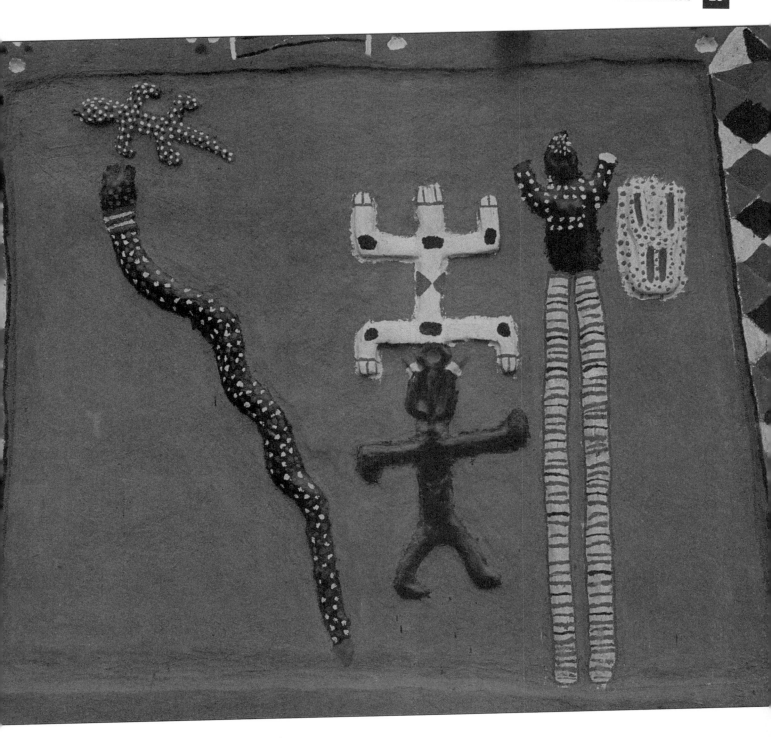

Lying at the heart of their beliefs about the Universe is the star Sirius, to them the brightest in the galaxy. The Dogons studied and charted all the various stars and planets that passed around and interacted with Sirius in the night sky – in particular, the path of Sirius B.

As author Francis Hitching reported in his *World Atlas of Mysteries*, Sirius B is 100,000 times less bright than Sirius itself. 'Yet,' said Hitching, 'the Dogon not only knew about this star but many of its characteristics.' He said they knew that it was white and although it was 'the smallest thing there is' it was also 'the heaviest star' made of a substance 'heavier than all the iron on Earth'. Hitching said this was a good description of Sirius B's density, which is so great that a single cubic metre weighs 20,000 tons.

Dogon drawings revealed the true orbit of Sirius B around Sirius – an elliptical path that accurately positioned the two stars over a timespan of 50 years, the

Above: *Wall coverings Dogon style. These decorations were used to adorn the walls of meeting houses. They often told the life story of one or more elders.*

Above: *These Dogon granaries are evidence of a remarkably advanced civilization.*

HE HOPED THE TRIBE'S HISTORY WOULD PROVIDE A VITAL CLUE TO ITS FANTASTIC KNOWLEDGE.

Opposite: *This Dogon dancer in his mud mask would have been a common sight at festival times.*

correct period for a complete orbit. As Griaule and Dieterlen wrote: 'The problem of knowing how, with no instruments at their disposal, men could know of the movements and certain characteristics of virtually invisible stars has not been settled.'

CREATURES FROM ANOTHER WORLD

In 1946 Marcel Griaule was allowed by the Dogon priests to share their innermost secrets. Any discoveries he had by then made counted almost as nought compared with what he now heard. For the Dogons told him that they had learned their extensive knowledge from visitors to Earth who came from a planet orbiting Sirius B.

The French anthropologist was astounded. And when he published his learned papers he was met with predictable scepticism. But there could be no doubt that Marcel Griaule had told the truth. He lived among the Dogons for 21 years and when he died in 1956 about 250,000 people attended his funeral in Mali.

His research was immediately taken up by other fascinated scientists and authors. American scholar Robert Temple set to work to trace more clearly the Dogons' movements before their arrival at the Bandiagara Plateau. Temple believed that the tribe's history might provide the vital clue to its fantastic knowledge.

The two million members of the Dogon and associated tribes arrived in an area about 250 miles south of Timbuktu between 400 and 700 years ago. They had migrated there from the north-east, probably having originated in North Africa, in what is now Libya. The tribe's closest neighbours at the time would have been Egyptian, but Temple found no key to the Dogon beliefs from that source. However, the mythology of ancient Greece and of Babylon did provide some clues.

In both Greek and Babylonian legend there are stories of creatures from another world who had supernatural powers and who passed on astronomical and astrological knowledge to the inhabitants of Earth. In both cases, these alien creatures were amphibian and they helped civilize this planet.

In his book, *The Sirius Mystery*, Robert Temple claims that the Dogons worshipped extra-terrestrial visitors who landed in the Persian Gulf in far distant times. The tribe called these creatures Nommos and have worshipped them ever since. Dogon drawings show a whirling, descending spacecraft or ark, peopled by the Nommos who are described as 'the monitor of the universe, the father of mankind, guardian of its spiritual principles, dispenser of rain and master of water'.

What further evidence supports the Dogon claims of a previous civilization brought to them by the heavens? Is it not all fantasy and mumbo-jumbo?

When Marcel Griaule first wrote his reports detailing the strange knowledge of the Dogons, they included one piece of information that seemed to make no sense whatsoever. The Dogons claimed that there was a *third* star in orbit around Sirius – a 'Sirius C'. This third star also influenced Sirius's movement in the heavens, despite the fact that it was four times lighter in weight than Sirius B.

At the time of the French reports, there was no evidence for a third star. The idea of a 'Sirius C' weakened rather than strengthened the case. But now, many years later, astronomers have detected such a star – possibly what they call a 'red dwarf'. Just as the Dogons have always believed. Just as they recorded when the Western world was young but their civilization was already old, many centuries ago.

THE WAR OF THE WORLDS

It started as an ordinary radio broadcast, but mounting panic and hysteria spread across America as the frightened voices of the announcers told their terrified listeners that the unbelievable had happened. Martians had invaded the Earth.

'Ladies and gentlemen, I have a grave announcement to make.'

That was the sentence that instantly concentrated the minds of millions of Americans as they tuned in to their radios on the night of Sunday, 30 October 1938. It also heralded the start of one of the most effective, and embarrassing, hoaxes the world has ever seen.

That night thousands upon thousands of people in the most powerful nation on Earth would flee their homes convinced that America had been invaded by men from Mars.

They paid the price for keeping only half an ear on the radio. For at 8 pm the CBS continuity announcer had faithfully informed his audience: 'The Columbia Broadcasting System and affiliated stations present Orson Welles and his Mercury Theatre of the Air in *The War of the Worlds* by H.G. Wells.'

Then came Welles's thunderous voice: 'We now know that in the early years of the 20th century, this world was being watched closely by intelligences greater than man's.' Clear enough surely: a live radio play with a script pretty close to the work of the original author. But at 24 Welles was already a master of building atmosphere, lulling an audience in readiness to shock them.

Before his opening lines were complete another actor took the microphone to interrupt with what sounded like a routine weather bulletin: 'Tonight's weather ... For

Opposite: Master of sci-fi H.G. Wells. His novel **The War of the Worlds** *was transformed by Orson Welles into a gripping – and believable – piece of radio drama.*

Below: *A poster advertising the film of the book. Thousands queued to watch it.*

H.G. WELLS' THE WAR OF THE WORLDS

Color by Technicolor

Cert X

A MIGHTY PANORAMA OF EARTH-SHAKING FURY!

Produced by GEORGE PAL WHO GAVE YOU 'DESTINATION MOON' & 'WHEN WORLDS COLLIDE'

the next 24 hours there will be not much change in temperature. A slight atmospheric disturbance of undetermined origin is reported over Nova Scotia, causing a low pressure area to move down rather rapidly over the north-eastern states, bringing a forecast of rain, accompanied by winds of light-gale force.

'Maximum temperature 66, minimum 48. This weather report comes to you from the Government Weather Bureau.

'We now take you to the Meridian Room at the Hotel Park Plaza in downtown New York where you will be entertained by the music of Ramon Raquello and his orchestra.'

So already many of the families who had tuned in from the start of the performance were receiving confused signals. Was this in fact a play? Perhaps not. Perhaps the Mercury Theatre was on another night. Or maybe father had got the time wrong. Either way the Raquello Orchestra sounded decent enough listening for the time being.

Welles had another, unforeseen advantage up his sleeve. He had come up with *The War of the Worlds* 'real life' scenario as a way to boost his show's pitiful ratings, grab a chunk of good publicity (if it worked) and persuade a sponsor to come in to offer a little security. Most important of all was to lure a few listeners from a rival station's popular Charlie McCarthy show, which went out at the same time.

The stakes were high. This was a last-ditch bid by Welles really to launch his Mercury Theatre. He'd been told on the quiet that unless there was some sign of an

Below: *The staff of Grover's Mill, New Jersey, talk over Welles's hoax the day after the 'war'. According to the radio play, the first aliens landed at the mill.*

improvement in the ratings the whole show was doomed.

AN INVASION FROM OUTER SPACE

That night, as it happened, Charlie McCarthy wasn't exactly hooking more fans. He had a new, totally unknown, crooner on and by around 10 past 8 people were getting bored. A few switched off but the majority began fiddling with their sets to see if there was anything a bit more interesting on CBS. They would not be disappointed.

Amid the crackles and high-pitched whines they suddenly realized that some kind of major news story was breaking along the country's east coast. CBS seemed to have a scoop – a scoop that was unfolding as they listened. Excitedly, families across the nation huddled around their radios to listen. None of the McCarthy defectors could have had the faintest clue that they were hearing a piece of drama.

'Ladies and gentlemen,' went the level voice, 'I have a grave announcement to make. The strange object which fell at Grover's Mill, New Jersey, earlier this evening was not a meteorite. Incredible as it seems it contained strange beings who are believed to be the vanguard of an army from the planet Mars.'

Then gentle, calming music – a masterpiece in terms of effect, for it gave the impression that the government had taken control of the media and was attempting to allay fears by playing familiar musical scores. Of course, the reaction was just the opposite – 'What's happening? Why won't someone tell us what's going on? Where's the president? Who's fighting who?'

This continued for several minutes, building up the stress levels of the audience almost to breaking point. Then the announcer again. This time the smooth statement had gone to be replaced by a whiff of panic. The voice had an edge to it as it told how the leathery-skinned Martians had started spreading out along New Jersey. Police were mobilizing to try and hold them back.

Then came more hurried announcements

Above: *A scene from Paramount's 1953 version of* **The War of the Worlds** *shows Martian spaceships hunting Earthmen.*

and ominous silences. By now listeners were calling in neighbours and phoning relatives in other states. It had taken only a few minutes to infect a large chunk of America with alien-fever.

When word finally came of terrifying battles along the eastern seaboard it was the last straw. Thousands did what came

Below: *Welles gets into his part. This picture was taken during the broadcast.*

naturally. They jumped in their cars and headed for the hills.

This, it must be said, was not exactly how Welles had planned it. Sure, he wanted to shock. Yes, he hoped this particular play would be a totally original piece of radio drama. And if a story found its way into the papers, well, who knew what spin-offs there might be from prospective sponsors.

Welles and his team – Paul Stewart and John Houseman – had been sweating blood on this particular play for seven days. It was to be the 17th in the current Mercury Theatre series but never before had they experienced such creative tension.

Resetting the play in America (the original work centred the action in London) was not so difficult. Neither was adapting it for what could easily be a family audience, though the scenes in which Martians drank the blood of their human victims were skimmed over.

No, Welles argued, it needed more shock value, more realism. It needed to sound a less than perfect production if it was to be a success.

On the Thursday before broadcast the three men gathered to hear the results of their labours to date. They heard a tape – the final product of countless script revisions and several rehearsals. They were not pleased with their achievement.

Welles, the lynchpin of the whole operation, was by now almost on his knees. He'd been rehearsing for another play in New York by day, switching to the Mercury team at night. Production assistants would recall later how he looked as depressed as anyone had ever seen him. He seemed like a poker player locked into a game where the stakes were increasing too fast. His pep talk to the team suggested he was ready to gamble his already considerable reputation on a one-off which might, or might not, work.

'Our only chance is to make it as realistic as possible,' he said. 'We'll have to throw in as many stunts as we can think of.'

BLOODCURDLING SCREAM

The production team burnt the midnight oil, adding real-life sound bites and clips from news reels onto the backing tapes. The next day Stewart perfected the sounds of a panicking crowd, screams and gunfire

Above: *Ain't takin' no chances. This veteran needed some persuading to put down his shotgun after Welles's broadcast.*

– the vital additions that would later fool the nation.

As the minutes ticked down to broadcast time the studio itself looked like it had hosted an inter-galactic war. Overflowing ashtrays, half-empty coffee cups and half-eaten sandwiches all bore tribute to the brain-storming sessions of the last 72 hours. But as Welles stepped towards the microphone, downing a cold bottle of pineapple juice in the process, the general feeling was of excitement – of producing a show which genuinely could break new ground.

The *coup de grâce* was delivered towards the end, at a time when the exodus of a terrified population was already well underway. The announcer crackled back onto air to reveal: 'We take you now to Washington for a special broadcast on the national emergency by the Secretary of the Interior.'

Welles got an actor to impersonate the politician in question. The official line was to urge people not to panic, though to make it clear that the Martian assault was now well underway. Not only New Jersey but the whole of the country was now experiencing the sight of spacecrafts landing by the dozen. Thousands of police, state troopers and civilians had already

AS THE NEWS CAME OF FEROCIOUS BATTLES ALONG THE EASTERN SEABOARD, THOUSANDS OF PEOPLE FLED FOR THE HILLS.

WHOLE FAMILIES BELIEVED THAT BRIGHTLY COLOURED WET TOWELS WRAPPED AROUND THEIR HEADS WOULD PROTECT THEM FROM THE NERVE GAS.

died horrible deaths under the wilting fire of ray guns.

There were the inevitable eyewitness accounts, many of them arriving courtesy of the superb actor Joseph Cotton. Of how fireballs which turned out to be spacecraft landed from nowhere. Of how terrifying beings emerged from them and started the killing. Then a step further. A voice sounding suspiciously like the president's came on warning people of the dangers of panic. The show ended with the strangled tones of the announcer shouting from the top of the CBS building that Manhattan was being occupied by a ruthless and hideous army. His last line was a blood-curdling scream, though by now most of the listeners were too busy trying to escape to take it in.

MASS PANIC

In New Jersey, site of the first landings, the roads were clogged solid with automobiles heading for the countryside. Whole families were seen emerging from their homes with brightly coloured wet towels wrapped around their heads – a recommended way of surviving the nerve gases they had been warned about. Valuables and prized possessions were being loaded into pickups and lorries ready for the trip out to the sticks. Evacuation had begun.

In New York City desperate wives tried in vain to call constantly engaged bars in search of their husbands. Crowds poured from restaurants and theatres as word spread like wildfire. Bus terminals and taxi ranks choked under the pressure of demand.

Even the US Navy was successfully conned. Sailors were ordered back to their ships in readiness to make a last stand against the invaders. Reports of meteor showers emerged from across the land. Some imaginative souls even tried to pretend they had had a close encounter with one of the aliens.

Troopers phoned their admin HQs to volunteer to defend America. Congregations spilled out of church services, some of the faithful predicting that this was, in fact, what had been promised all along – the coming of the Lord. In the South terrified women fell to their knees and prayed and according to later news reports there was even one attempted suicide.

Newspapers and radio stations fielded literally thousands of calls between them. Yet no one apparently stopped to wonder why all was sweetness and light over at CBS, where Welles was just bringing the show to a climax with threats of immediate martial law. He hadn't a clue what was going on outside.

The station did receive a lot of calls, which were all passed on to Welles and Cotton. Cotton dismissed them out of hand as 'just cranks' and although two policemen turned up at CBS with orders to find out what was happening those officers didn't mention the dramas being unveiled outside. Instead they just hung around, realizing the broadcast was make-believe, and enjoyed the final stages.

The first Welles found out about the effects of his legendary show came the following morning when he couldn't help but notice the wording on a huge advertising hoarding above the New York Times building.

It read: 'Orson Welles Causes Panic'.

He bought every paper he could find and revelled in headlines such as 'Attack from Mars in Radio Play Puts Thousands in Fear' or 'Radio Listeners in Panic – Many Flee Homes to Escape Gas Raids from Mars'.

Then came the backlash. A lot of egos had been bruised, macho icons demolished. Newspapers condemned the actor for being irresponsible and there followed a clutch of negligence writs against CBS amounting to a hefty $1.1 million. But later all the actions fizzled out and Orson Welles resumed his position as America's most lovable star.

CBS, meanwhile, congratulated itself for pulling off a superb and original stunt. The Mercury Theatre looked to be on the up and up and a long-awaited sponsor had at last come forward.

Radio's most influential show at last had a future.

In Britain there was a scathing response to the panic Welles had managed to induce. 'Only the Americans could get so worked up by a radio show,' was the typical reaction of the stiff-upper-lip brigade.

HOAXED!

Yet a sizeable section of Britain's TV viewing population is regularly hoaxed. One of the most convincing – too convincing, many argued later – was a TV drama called *Ghostwatch* which was broadcast on Halloween 1992. By the end of it the switchboards at BBC TV centre were jammed by thousands of worried callers and within hours one young man had killed himself in the apparent belief that he was about to become a victim of similar supernatural manifestations.

The *Ghostwatch* case is all the more remarkable because it had been clearly advertised in newspapers and trailed on TV as a drama, part of the BBC's Screen One series. But borrowing from the Welles school of spoofing, the producers quickly managed to persuade many people that what they were actually seeing was a serious, live TV investigation into spooky goings-on at a real haunted house.

The house in question was a totally fictitious council property in Northolt, Middlesex. The family who lived there, the Earlys, had apparently been plagued for years by a poltergeist whose specialities were lobbing plates and pouring out puddles into the middle of the carpet. This proved no problem for the BBC's special effects department.

There was also a belief that the two young Early sisters (the family roles were all played by actors) were exhibiting symptoms of possession.

In the same way Welles had used a weather report and big band recital to convince his audience that they were no longer listening to a drama, the BBC producers had to find a way of blurring the line between fact and fantasy. To do that

THE SWITCHBOARD WAS JAMMED AND ONE POOR BOY HANGED HIMSELF IN TERROR.

Below: *The aftermath. Orson Welles is 'doorstepped' by journalists eager for his version of events. His response: 'I had no idea the play would create such a furore.'*

Above: *Martin Denham, who killed himself. His girlfriend said: 'The programme affected him badly.'*

HER HUSBAND WATCHED,
POWERLESS AND
HORRIFIED, AS SHE
VANISHED INTO THIN AIR.

festations taking place around the country.

It looked for all the world like a live Halloween night special designed to fill a blank 90 minutes. Many among the millions of watchers must have been keeping only half an eye on the box, confidently expecting nothing would happen. They were wrong.

FIENDISH GHOUL

The plate smashing and puddle pouring was only the half of it. Clanking pipes, flying objects and flashing lights rammed home the impression that the BBC was filming a historic clip unique in the annals of broadcasting. Throughout it all analysis was provided by real-life experts in the paranormal – Maurice Gross, an authority on poltergeists, and Guy Lyon Playfair, author of a true account of the haunting of a house in Enfield, north London.

By the end many thousands were convinced that ghosts were, after all, real. And when Sarah Greene apparently vanished into thin air, the victim of some fiendish ghoul, the look of horror on her studio-bound husband's face set the first phones ringing on the BBC exchanges.

Perhaps the more impressionable viewers had read an interview with Sarah Greene in the newspapers earlier that week. In it she admitted she had already had a psychic experience on air and was rather nervous that the same thing could happen again.

She told one reporter: 'About ten years ago when making a documentary at the Royal Hospital in Chelsea I interviewed an old soldier who told me that the hospital had a regular ghostly visitor. He thought it was one of the original pensioners who seemed to hang around just to keep his eye on the old place.

'After the programme was transmitted I had dozens of calls from viewers who were sure that, while the old man was telling his story to me, they could see the ghost of the Chelsea Pensioner lingering near the staircase behind where we were sitting.

'We hadn't seen anything while we were filming, and we could see nothing out of the ordinary on the television monitor screen when we played back the interview.'

It was all good knockabout stuff. Interviewed afterwards, Michael Parkinson

they employed three well-known presenters who each had some background in 'serious' television – Michael Parkinson, Mike Smith and Sarah Greene (Smith's real-life wife).

Parkinson played the anchorman of the team, switching between the studio and Northolt. Greene was the roving reporter out with the Earlys as they prepared for the night's hauntings. And Smith manned the phone lines to gauge reaction from viewers and monitor any other ghostly mani-

made a direct comparison with Welles's *The War of the Worlds* and observed: 'You always get some viewers believing all they see on television is real. If it does for my career what it did for Orson Welles I shall be delighted.'

The critics were less enthusiastic. Stafford Hildred, writing in the *Daily Star,* described the scene in which Sarah Greene disappeared as 'the only enjoyable moment in 90 minutes of nonsense pretending to be a proper programme'.

The *Daily Express*'s Peter Tory, meanwhile, sounded a note of caution which proved tragically close to the mark. 'Most viewers,' he said, 'would have regarded it as nonsense, which it was. A minority – the elderly, the lonely, the nervous, the gullible, the young – were terrified out of their wits.

'Television with its formidable power should be very cautious when combining apparent reality with alarming fiction. The BBC proves once again that it is out of control.'

SCARED TO DEATH

For one family at least, those sentiments could not have been better put. Only hours after the programme went out 18-year-old Martin Denham, who had a mental age of 13, hanged himself from a tree near his home in Nottingham. His elder brother Carl told an inquest that after seeing *Ghostwatch* the teenager would not go to bed without a torch. The clanking central heating pipes had particularly worried him as it was a sound he heard regularly in his own house.

Carl said: 'He was so timid and the programme frightened him. He wanted to watch the programme so my mother sat up with him. She told him it was rubbish but he did not believe her. He was that scared by the clanging pipes of the central heating that he just went mad.'

Martin's girlfriend Rachel Young related how he had given her his most treasured possession – a crucifix – after the show went out. She was the last person to see him alive and she later told the coroner: 'He was very strange that night – the programme had affected him badly. He asked me to take his keepsake to remember him by.'

After the inquest at Nottingham in December 1992 the boy's stepfather Percy Denham made it clear he held the BBC responsible for the death. He went on: 'I think the balance of his mind was disturbed by this programme. He was a very nervous person and it upset him deeply. He became obsessed with ghosts.' Martin's mother April added: 'The BBC were totally irresponsible. Why did they say this programme was based on a real story when it was just a hoax?' Before he committed suicide Martin wrote one last note to his mum. It read: 'Mother do not be upset. If there is ghosts I will now be one and I will always be with you as one. Love, Martin.'

The BBC's solicitor Aideen Hanley, said at the time: 'Naturally the BBC and especially those connected with the making of the *Ghostwatch* programme have already expressed their sympathy in a letter sent last month by the executive producer.'

It was a grim reminder to all who work in broadcasting. As audiences go, nothing much has changed since 1938.

Above: *Parkinson, Smith and Greene pose for a publicity shot to promote* **Ghostwatch.** *Parkinson said later: 'If it does for my career what it did for Orson Welles I shall be delighted.'*

'IF THERE IS [*SIC*] GHOSTS I WILL NOW BE ONE AND I WILL ALWAYS BE WITH YOU AS ONE.'

COUNT ST GERMAIN
'A legend in his own lifetimes'

He fascinated the courts of 18th-century Europe, convincing kings and empresses that he was a healer, a mystic and over 150 years old. Even today there are those who claim that this enigmatic man still weaves his strange magic ...

Above: *The court of the French king Louis XV was marked by opulence and splendour. It was thought by socialites of the day to be the very hub of Europe.*

His epitaph reads: 'He who called himself the Comte de St Germain and Welldone, of whom there is no other information, has been buried in this church'.

The epitaph could equally have read: 'Alchemist, healer, sage, wit and dandy'. Or: 'The man who claimed to have discovered the secret of eternal life'. Or should it have been: 'Charlatan'? Or simply: 'Genius'?

There were those who he was all of these ... and more.

Count St Germain was the man from nowhere who captivated the courts of Europe. He first appeared on the social scene in Vienna in 1740. At first, no one inquired too deeply as to his past – his presence was enough. He set about making an instant impression by rebelling against the brightly coloured dress of the time and opting for austere, flowing black-and-white silk clothes. He set off his sombre appearance, however, with a dazzling array of diamonds – on his fingers, his shoe buckles and his snuff box. He never used money; his pockets were always filled with diamonds. He positively glittered.

The Count St Germain was indeed a dandy. But he was graceful, charming and quick-witted. He was also, if one were to believe him, notable for another strange attribute ...

He was 150 years old!

It was a claim he made with all seriousness. It made him one of history's most fascinating men. His allusions to his own immortality drew to him the attention of Europe's intellectual and social elite. To the great French poet and dramatist Voltaire, he was 'a man who knows everything and never dies'.

But there were many other reasons why this fascinating eccentric has gone down as one of history's most puzzling men. Even now, the story of the man who called himself Count St Germain remains an unexplained enigma, perhaps because the stories he told of himself may have actually been true ...

Count St Germain was described in the scant historical records of 1740 as being a mature man, somewhere between 45 and 50 years old. He was taken under the wing of two leading socialites and dictators of fashion, Counts Zabor and Lobkowitz, the first of many to fall under the spell woven by St Germain. They installed him in a modish apartment, and through them he became well known in the social world of Vienna.

They also introduced him to a sick army general, the Marshal de Belle Isle. The nature of the general's ailment was not recorded, but it seems that after a visit from the mysterious count he was completely cured. As a token of his gratitude, Belle Isle took St Germain to Paris, then the very

THE GREAT FRENCH POET AND PHILOSOPHER VOLTAIRE SINCERELY BELIEVED THAT THE COUNT WAS 'A MAN WHO KNOWS EVERYTHING AND NEVER DIES'.

Opposite: *Count St Germain looked young and athletic when he revealed his true age was in fact beyond 100 years. Had he really found the secret of eternal life? Or was he merely a smart fraudster?*

Above: *After ailing Marshal de Belle Isle was miraculously cured by the count, the military man gave glowing references to him which paved his way into the highest echelons of French society.*

Astonished, the countess studied the charming stranger who looked not a day over 50. Then she calculated the age to which he was now laying claim: more than 120 years old!

It was but the first of the many astounding claims he was to make. He became the talk of Paris, and rumours circulating pronounced him both a genius and a devil. But in the opulent court of the Bourbon King Louis XV, the arrival of this alchemist, sage and amusing fellow caused the greatest interest.

In 1743 Count St Germain was summoned to Versailles to meet the king, whom he greatly charmed, together with the king's mistress, Madame de Pompadour. The count told them he had studied the mysteries of the Great Pyramid

epicentre of cultured European life. There, he equipped himself with a laboratory, where he set to work on his alchemical studies.

In fact, the count had two pursuits. One, as old as time itself, was to discover the secret of turning base metals into gold. The other was to discover the elixir of life – 'the secrets of eternal wealth and eternal beauty', as he once described it.

A MAN OF SECRETS

It was in Paris that the strange legend of Count St Germain really began to grow. One of the first to hear of his claims that he was much older than he looked was a countess, who remarked that as a young woman in Venice in 1670, she had heard the name 'St Germain' announced by a footman. The aged countess asked St Germain if by any chance the man was his father. 'No, Madame, that was me,' he replied calmly. 'Madame, I am very old,' he told her, and said he remembered her beauty from their meeting in Venice all those years ago.

in Egypt, and the secrets of Himalayan mystics and Italian occultists. Louis, completely spellbound, commissioned him to carry out secret missions for the Crown.

This may well explain how Count St Germain found himself under arrest in England. Spy fever gripped the British nation after the Young Pretender, Prince Charles Stuart, had staged the Jacobite rebellion in order to regain the Crown for his father. The Jacobites had rallied the Highland forces, taken Edinburgh and invaded England. The prince's army reached as far south as Derby but turned back, pursued by the Duke of Cumberland and his forces.

The Jacobites suffered a crushing defeat at the Battle of Culloden in 1746 and the English troops, fearful that any foreigners could be Jacobite sympathizers, started making wholesale arrests. One of the foreigners arrested was the count.

St Germain was said to have been found with pro-Stuart letters on him – reinforcing the theories of historians that he was indeed on some kind of mission for Louis. However, the unlikely explanation that they were planted on him seemed to satisfy the authorities, and he was released.

While in custody, the count had caught the attention of several prominent people, not least of them Horace Walpole, who wrote in a letter to a friend: 'The other day they seized an odd man who goes by the name of Count St Germain. He has been here these two years and will not tell who he is or whence, but professes that he does not go by his right name. He sings and

HE JOURNEYED TO INDIA TO STEAL THE SECRETS OF THE INDIAN MYSTICS.

Below: *The palace of Versailles, grand residence of the French king. At their first meeting there, the king found the mysterious count fascinating and charming.*

Above: *Louis XV of France gave cash backing to the count in his bid to make gold from metal and gems.*

Right: *Madame de Pompadour, the king's mistress, was equally beguiled by the smooth-talking count.*

plays on the violin wonderfully, is mad and not very sensible.'

Later that year, St Germain moved back to the city of Vienna, where he enjoyed the same adulation as in Paris. He set up another laboratory, and was feted by the Viennese court.

Between 1747 and 1756, he paid two visits to India, a land which fascinated him. From there he wrote to Louis of France that he had perfected his alchemy skills and could now 'melt jewels'. He said that the secret had been gained from Indian mystics and was guaranteed to cause a sensation on his return to Europe.

Louis had by now become so fascinated by St Germain that, upon the count's return to France in 1756, he was given another laboratory, paid for by the monarch, to enable him to carry on with his promising experiments in alchemy.

The relationship forged between the mysterious count and the king evaporated, however, after Louis sent him on a mission to Holland in 1760. Ostensibly, he was in Holland to drum up financial support for France's war effort against Britain in the conflict which became known as the Seven Years War. At The Hague, the count made an enemy of the Duc de Choiseul, Louis's foreign minister, who told his master that St Germain had taken upon himself the mantle of peacemaker and had made representations to English diplomats with a view to ending the war. The count was forced to flee from his erstwhile patron's wrath and he went briefly back to London, returning to Holland in 1764 to establish more alchemy laboratories.

AN AMAZING ODYSSEY

He stayed for two years, eventually fleeing the country with a fortune of 100,000 Dutch guilders he had amassed from manufacturing not gold but paint and dyes. He next turned up in Belgium, sporting the name Marquis de Monferrat. He remained there for only a year.

Then began an amazing odyssey across Europe and into the court of the Russian empress Catherine the Great. Such was the spell he held over Catherine, weaving tales of science and travel, that he was given special status. In 1768, when Russia had just embarked on a war with Turkey, this extraordinary man found himself advising the head of the nation's forces. And in recognition of his advice, he was given a title; the name he chose for himself was 'General Welldone'.

In 1774 Count St Germain arrived in the gracious German city of Nuremberg, raising more funds to set up yet another of

Below: *An alchemist at work using a rich variety of symbols in his quest to find wealth beyond his wildest dreams by making gold.*

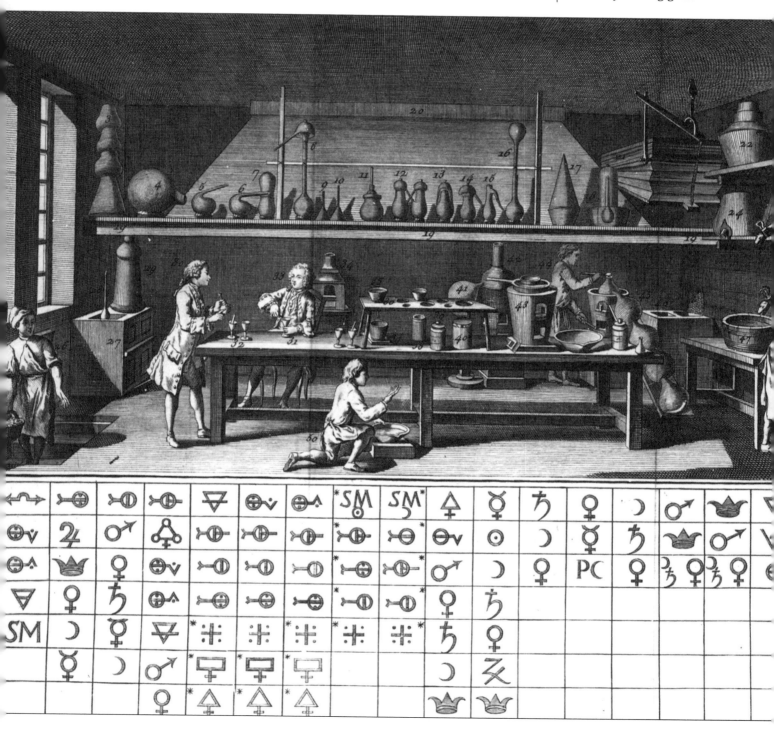

THE COUNT WARNED THE KING AND QUEEN OF THEIR IMPENDING DOOM; THEIR REFUSAL TO HEED HIM COST THEM THEIR LIVES.

Below: *The Duc de Choiseul, who wrecked the special relationship between king and count by casting doubts on the loyalty of the latter.*

his beloved laboratories so he could continue to experiment in alchemy. From here he tried lamely to curry favour once again with the very same French court from which he had had to flee.

He seemed to have remarkable foresight, for he warned Louis XVI, the old king's successor, and his wife Marie Antoinette of a 'gigantic conspiracy' which would engulf them and sweep away the old order of things. With hindsight, it is easy to recognize that this could only have been a reference to the impending French Revolution which in 1789 did indeed engulf them, and cost them their lives. They were both guillotined in the Place de la Revolution, the king on 21 January 1793 and his queen on 16 October.

During this time the count dabbled widely in the occult, freemasonry and dark arts. He approached Prince Frederick Augustus of Brunswick, claiming to be a mason. But, unbeknown to St Germain, the prince was Grand Master of the Prussian Masonic lodges and knew the claim was false. Prince Frederick became one of the few people to dismiss St Germain as a phony.

The last records of him show that he travelled to Berlin, Frankfurt and Dresden, finally arriving at what is believed to be his last resting place. He was taken under the wing of Prince Charles of Hesse-Cassel, in Schleswig, Germany, where he dazzled the prince with his worldly knowledge. His showmanship was fading, however. He was too old to play the charmer or the dandy.

DEAD AND BURIED?

The count was by now well into his 60s, although still claiming to be many decades older. He died in 1784 and was buried in the local churchyard near his benefactor Prince Charles's home in Eckenforde. Hence the tombstone erected to his memory: 'He who called himself the Comte de St Germain and Welldone, of whom there is no other information, has been buried in this church.'

So was this to be the end of the story? Buried in a quiet corner of a country churchyard? The last resting place of a gifted adventurer, diplomat, socialite, healer and alchemist? Many think not.

Reports of sightings of the mysterious count continued to come in for another 40 years. In 1785 a group of occultists staging a conference at Wilhemsbad reported that he had appeared before them; in 1788 he was said to be back in France warning the nobility of the revolt of the peasants set for the following year. And in 1789 he was reported to have turned up at the court of King Gustavus III of Sweden. He told a friend, Madame d'Adhemar, that he would see her five more times – and she said he was true to his word. The last time she saw him, she reported, was in 1820.

What explanation can there be for this strange figure? Was he merely a charlatan, or was he indeed a genius?

Certainly there are records in existence which say he used his charm and guile merely to make people he met part with their money. But he also had a private fund of wealth and never failed to delight in showing off the diamonds which lined his pockets. He had an excellent knowledge of chemistry, and gained great status as a healer after attending to the French Marshal de Belle Isle.

He was master of more than six foreign languages and boasted of having studied jewellery and art design at the court of the shah of Persia, as well as having learned the mysteries of the occult in faraway places. Certainly, when his knowledge was thoroughly tested by sceptics, it seemed to stand up to close scrutiny.

Emperor Louis Napoleon III was so obsessed by the legend of St Germain that he instituted a special commission to study his life and background. Ironically the findings of the inquiry board were destroyed in a fire in 1871 – something the followers of St Germain say is too uncanny to be an accident. It was an act which they considered to be the work of the count himself.

One account of the count's life says that he was born in 1710, the son of a tax collector in Italy; another that he was born in Bohemia (now part of Czechoslovakia), the son of an occultist. That, say his followers, could account for his strong bent towards the dark forces and mysticism.

A 19th-century mystic, theosophist and occultist, Madame Blavatsky, claimed that St Germain was indeed an immortal, and could be ranked alongside Buddha, Christ and others, because he enriched the world with his presence and knowledge.

In 1972 a Parisian named Richard Chanfray claimed to be Count St Germain. He went on television and, in a clever experiment involving the use of a camping stove, apparently managed to turn lead into gold. He failed to prove that he was the celebrated count. But then no one could prove that he was not!

Even today, Count St Germain attracts a dedicated, cult following. Many people believe he is still alive and will visit them again before the turn of the century. However, as to his past, where he came from, how he supported himself, and where he gained his strange powers – the mystery remains and continues to fascinate people in this modern age.

Above: *Marie Antoinette, once the first lady of France, reduced to penury before she died at the hands of French revolutionaries. Could she have been saved if only she had listened to Count St Germain?*

ELVIS PRESLEY
Is the King dead?

'The King is dead. Long live the King!' The age-old saying is charged with sinister significance with regard to Elvis Presley, the king of rock 'n' roll, whose sexy snarl inflamed teenagers and infuriated parents. For there are those who remain convinced that Elvis never died …

Sunlight was peeping through the windows of Graceland when former beauty queen Ginger Alden awoke. Instantly she noticed the bed beside her was empty.

Calling out for her missing lover, she pushed open the bathroom door and found him curled up on the carpeted floor, his face contorted in a death mask, still clutching a book about the Turin Shroud which he had been reading. Elvis, the King, was dead.

The first person she telephoned was his tour manager Joe Esposito. There followed a 7-minute ride to Baptist Memorial Hospital where the body was attended by Elvis's personal doctor, George Nichopoulos, who kept urging the rock 'n' roll idol to breathe. But to no avail. Elvis was pronounced dead in the hospital at 3.30 pm. A subsequent postmortem revealed he died from a heart attack.

That's what happened on the day Elvis died, 16 August 1977. Or is it? Niggling

Opposite: *In his prime Elvis Presley was an all-American boy with clean-cut good looks and greased hips. Did he pay the ultimate price for superstardom, by dying a fat-faced junkie?*

Below: *News of Elvis's death stunned the world. British newspapers reported how his body was discovered following a heart attack.*

doubts were suppressed as the news sent shock waves around the world. Millions mourned for the man they worshipped. His family, especially dad Vernon and daughter Lisa Marie, were inconsolable.

SINISTER RUMOURS

But soon the rumours were abounding, some credible, some frankly astonishing. There were many who knew the King to be a bloated, drug-dependent monster who almost certainly died of an accidental overdose. Others claimed he killed himself, either in a fit of guilt about a fling with his stepbrother's wife or in order to escape a long, lingering death from cancer which had been diagnosed. Yet the official report on his death failed to mention drugs of any kind.

More sinister, there is one school of thought which claims that Elvis was murdered, most probably by vindictive Mafia men. They struck after Elvis the FBI agent helped put some of their bigwigs behind bars. Finally and most fantastically, there is the theory that Elvis didn't die at all. An actor lay in state at Graceland for

Above: *At 13, Elvis Aaron Presley had already mastered the smouldering star look which would generate his fortune.*

Right: *Colonel Tom Parker puts the finishing touches to a deal which would take Elvis to Pearl Harbor for a blockbusting benefit concert.*

the queues of fans to mourn, an imposter is buried in the coffin that purports to be encasing the star, and Elvis is alive, well and lurking incognito, possibly at Graceland itself. A survey carried out in 1993 discovered that as many as one in ten people believed the King was still alive.

THE HEARTACHE BEGINS

Elvis Aaron Presley was born on 8 January 1935 in East Tupelo, Mississippi, the only son of Vernon and Gladys Presley. A twin named Jesse was delivered still-born as Elvis's first cries were echoing around the room.

Mum Gladys was enchanted with the cute baby who grew up to be a handsome, happy child. So much so, she cossetted the youngster throughout his early years, the protective cloak she flung around him even extending to fetching him from school long after his friends were allowed to go-it-alone. In the end he insisted she walked behind him, ducking behind bushes and trees to cause him minimum embar-

rassment. Bursting with pride for her fine, charming son, she told him daily that he was as good as everybody else, despite their poverty.

His first taste of music was at the Assembly Church of God which he attended with his parents, enjoying the rhythm and melody of the gospel songs.

To celebrate his tenth birthday he went with Gladys to a local hardware store, his heart set on buying a gun. A guitar on display also caught his eye. He couldn't afford either of them but Gladys knew which she would prefer her darling boy to own. She settled the matter by offering to make up his savings with her own cash if he wanted the guitar. It was a deal. The instrument, costing less than $8, put him on the road to mega-stardom.

He began to perform gigs when he was still at school, attracting an eager following of girls even at that early age. He achieved only moderate academic success at school and as soon as he left, landed a job driving a truck paying $41 a week.

Elvis paid to make his first disc. On

Above: *On stage, Elvis swivelled his hips and snarled with his lips, and sent hordes of female fans into a frenzy. The shock waves of his performances vibrated through America and left him bemused.*

HIS MOTHER DOMINATED HIS LIFE — SHE WAS OBSESSED WITH HER DARLING BOY AND WOULD HIDE BEHIND BUSHES TO WATCH OVER HIS SAFETY.

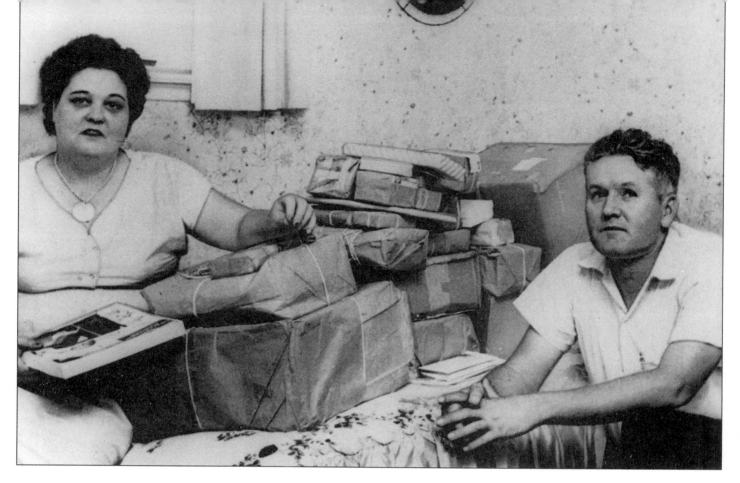

Above: *By 1956 Elvis was established as the King of rock 'n' roll. His parents, Gladys and Vernon, were on hand to help sift through the piles of fan mail and gifts sent to him.*

Far right: *The bond between mother and son was powerful. After her death, his personal life spiralled into shabby disarray.*

Opposite: *Elvis bought Graceland, a lavish former church, with his new-found wealth as a home for himself and his immediate family. Now it is a mecca for loyal fans.*

one summer Saturday afternoon in 1953 he turned up at the Memphis Recording Studios which offered the facility to cut a record for the sum of $4, intending the tunes as a gift for his mother. There he met the woman who helped launch his career.

Assistant Marion Keisker liked what she heard when Elvis crooned 'My Happiness' and 'That's When Your Heartache Begins', two numbers originally by the Inkspots. For weeks and months afterwards she pestered her boss Sam Phillips to hear the talented teenager. It wasn't until 1954, though, that Phillips recorded 'That's All Right Mama' with Elvis on his Sun Record label. Within two days a local disc jockey had played the record 14 times in a row. It shot to number 3 in the Memphis Country and Western charts and secured a firm following of fans.

With him Elvis had a backing group, the Starlight Wranglers – later called the Blue Moon Boys – and their popularity was such that it attracted the attention of one Colonel Tom Parker. A middle-man in show business, with enough experience to spot a sure-fire winner, he cut a deal there and then which would earn him half of Elvis's cash throughout his career. In

1955 Elvis signed with RCA records and could afford to buy his mother a pink Cadillac.

The first TV appearances on the Tommy and Jimmy Dorsey Show in January and February 1956, spread Elvis's reputation nationwide. He became a sensation.

He was a curious mix. On the one hand he had sideburns – then considered to be daring – wore vivid coloured clothes and exuded the same kind of animal magnetism as his own idol James Dean, already dead in a car crash. Yet also he was unashamedly religious, a church-goer who loved his country. It was the devil in him, however, which had the greatest appeal.

Colonel Parker takes credit for the hip-swivelling style and alluring lip-curl which set hearts a-fluttering and parents blazing across middle America in the fifties. The sexy snarl earned him as many enemies as it did fainting fans. He was denounced by church leaders, town dignitaries, on television and radio and in the home. But it did nothing to dent his mushrooming popularity and only served to enhance his fame.

Chat-show host Ed Sullivan even banned him from the show because he deemed Elvis was 'unfit for a family audience', but finally the phenomenon of Elvis was enough to make him change his mind. Sullivan insisted, however, that he was only filmed from the waist up. Viewing figures rocketed to 54 million, higher than those for President Eisenhower.

Police in Florida even forced the star to sing without moving. Elvis was bemused by the fuss. He told his mother: 'I don't feel sexy when I'm singing. If that was true I'd be in some kind of institution as some kind of sex maniac.'

When 'Heartbreak Hotel' was released in 1956, it confirmed his place at the top. In the same year he released a further eight singles which all stormed into the charts, among them 'Blue Suede Shoes', 'Hound Dog' and 'Love Me Tender'. Aged only 21, he had the world at his mercy.

Flexing his new-found spending power, he splashed out on Graceland, a former Christian church, in Memphis, Tennessee, painted it blue and gold and installed his parents and grandmother.

But the rock 'n' roll years had to go on ice when Uncle Sam demanded Elvis did his duty on the draft for two years. Elvis didn't mind. Standing up to 'do his share'

Right: *Elvis enlisted for military service just like other young men of his age. But the meagre army pay packet which his fellow soldiers survived on was only a fraction of his earnings.*

Below: *Elvis and his father mourn together after the death of their beloved Gladys. Later, Vernon could do little to curb his son's extraordinary excesses.*

like every other US boy was wonderful publicity. And it wasn't as if he was like all his fellow soldiers. He hardly needed his 478 per month army pay.

Elvis made sure his parents were close by during his basic training in Texas. He rented them a home and it was wile staying there that Gladys fell ill. She returned to Memphis where doctors discovered she had acute hepatitis and severe liver damage.

Elvis battled to win leave and rushed to her bedside, but all his fame and wealth could do nothing to save her. She died, aged 46, with her husband by her side. Vernon phoned Elvis at Graceland and he rushed to mourn over her lifeless body. The inconsolable cries of father and son cut through the night.

At her funeral Elvis collapsed three times, weeping uncontrollably and wailing: 'Oh God, everything I have is gone.'

SEXUAL EXPERIMENTATION

The loss of his beloved mother was to prove a blow which Elvis never overcame. Her devotion to him had cemented a rock-solid bond but equally had stifled any emotional maturity he might have achieved too. Many blame the apron-strings tie for the sexual confusion Elvis found himself in as an adult. Certainly, on her death he seemed to lose a respect for life.

Still in the army, he was stationed in Germany and began experimenting with sex. One biographer, Albert Goldman, says that when he ate at the Lido nightclub in Paris in 1959 he ended up taking the entire chorus line of Bluebell Girls back to his hotel. This then apparently happened every night for two weeks.

Not surprisingly, he was exhausted by living life in the fast lane and was looking for a prop. He started popping pills.

Even while Elvis was in uniform, he was still churning out hit after hit, thanks to the efforts of Colonel Parker. With the army eventually behind him, he was free to pursue the career in films for which he yearned. For seven years he made an average of three films a year, none of which

became known as modern classics but all of which were well supported by the fans.

As the demands made on him intensified, so did his dependency on drugs. He swallowed uppers and downers and took painkillers in pill form or by syringe: Elvis had no intention of missing out on the partying that surrounded him and his entourage, no matter how busy his schedule. He stayed with the Memphis Mafia (as his personal staff were known) in a plush Bel Air mansion which once belonged to Aly Khan and Rita Hayworth. There he hosted licentious parties night after night with scores of eager, hopeful girls outnumbering the men at the party to the tune of six to one.

Elvis took his pick; his trusted men had the best of the rest. He wasn't known for his gentlemanly behaviour towards the women he had chosen. If they upset him he was likely to throw an object at them or even toss them out of the door into the street.

Such parties became key to his very existence. He lived by night and slept all day. He had long since given up hope of shopping or eating out like other people because he would have been mobbed in the attempt.

At home in Graceland two-way mirrors were installed so he could watch other couples having sex without them realizing. Camera equipment was also moved in so the King could produce and direct his own blue movies. There was a succession of one-night stands. Elvis could pick any girl and he knew it, but soon the lure of a gorgeous, willing girl wasn't enough. Often he would pay two prostitutes to make love as lesbians to excite him sufficiently before seducing the girl he had chosen. In addition he wooed his film co-stars, beauties like Ann Margret, Tuesday Weld and Ursula Andress. From Hollywood he also dated Natalie Wood, one of the few girlfriends to be taken back to Graceland.

Outside the bedroom, his actions were increasingly bizarre too. He brandished pistols around and would shoot out a television screen if the programme he was watching annoyed him. He thought nothing of flying himself and his team 1,000 miles for a peanut butter and jelly sandwich if the mood took him. Elvis totally lost touch with reality.

His other interest was football and he ran a club called Elvis Presley Enterprises. Along with everyone else in the team, he would take two uppers before going on the pitch. The pills gave them enough energy and stamina to play five games in a row.

TRUE LOVE?

Much of the cavorting happened even while he lived with Priscilla Ann Beaulieu, the woman he was later to marry. He first met her in 1959 in Bad Neuheim, Germany, when he was a GI and she a 14-year-old convent girl, daughter of a US army officer, clad in a crisp sailor suit.

Elvis liked his women petite, feminine and above all, young. His preference was for shapely legs and bottoms and virginal dress. Priscilla – or Cilla as he called her – was all of these things and more.

He asked her to spend Christmas with him in 1960 which she did. Her gift to him was a musical cigarette case which played 'Love Me Tender'; he gave her a puppy. But, of course, she had to return to her mother and stepfather in Germany.

Elvis missed her and pleaded with her

Above: *Priscilla was only 14 when she met Elvis for the first time. He soon decided he wanted to marry her and he wooed her in a transatlantic romance after seeking her stepdad's blessing.*

NIGHT AFTER NIGHT, HE WOULD TAKE THE ENTIRE CHORUS LINE OF GIRLS BACK TO HIS HOTEL BEDROOM.

Above: It seemed like a fairy-tale marriage when pretty Priscilla wed idol Elvis. In fact, she was sucked right into his twilight world of self-indulgence and infidelity and remained miserable for most of the years they spent together.

HE WENT TO BED WITH OVER A THOUSAND WOMEN, AND FELL IN LOVE WITH A 14-YEAR-OLD CONVENT SCHOOLGIRL.

---

stepdad to allow her to finish her schooling in Memphis. A year later he agreed and in October 1962 Priscilla started living at Graceland and enrolled at the Catholic High School nearby. When she graduated he presented her with a Corvair.

Before her arrival, Presley had shown his stepmother a snap of Priscilla and said: 'I've been to bed with no less than 1,000 women. This is the one, right here.'

But whatever his feelings for Priscilla, he was unable to stop himself leching, both at home and in Hollywood. The couple finally married in 1967 when she reached 21, in the Aladdin Hotel, Las Vegas, followed by a honeymoon in Palm Springs, California. Nine months later Priscilla gave birth to their daughter, Lisa Marie.

Life with Elvis was no easy ride. For a start, she rarely saw him as he still lived by night and she by day. They were never alone as when they did see each other, members of the Memphis Mafia were always in evidence. And Elvis only made a modest effort to hide his series of flings from her.

'I was always on guard, always dressing to please him, always fighting for territory and fighting for what I believed in.

'I wasn't brought up to believe in divorce and when I married I thought it would be for ever.

'Everywhere I went I had women wanting him. Not just wanting him, right in front of me there were things going on. It was a shock to be confronted with this at such a young age. All the time I was desperate to please,' says Priscilla now.

She believes her devotion to wifely duties almost put their child at risk. 'To Elvis I was like his kid he had raised. He used to refer to himself as Daddy.

'I gained only 9 pounds during that pregnancy and the baby was 6 pounds. I had a husband I wanted to keep. I didn't want him to look at other women, that was my motive. I don't pride myself on it and I don't recommend it. I almost starved myself. I ate only eggs during the day, apples at night, maybe one meal. I didn't drink milk and that wasn't good for the baby.'

After five years of marriage Priscilla told Elvis she had fallen in love with another and was leaving Graceland. The man in question was Mike Stone, Elvis's friend and karate instructor.

The news devastated the King. The pain was in losing one of his prized possessions to another man. He toyed with the idea of having Stone assassinated but pulled out at the last moment.

Somehow the domestic disaster gave him a new career spur and he began live performances again after a break of some seven years. The excesses with drugs, drink and women continued unabated.

Once he bought 14 Cadillacs in one night and gave them all away to friends. He spent $13,000 on handguns in one spree. His spontaneous purchases and generous gestures were without rhyme or reason.

A 20-year-old beauty queen, Linda Thompson, became his girlfriend and was showered with costly gifts, including cars and houses. But his philandering continued and she too quit the relationship. For some nine months before he died Ginger Alden was his regular girlfriend. She claimed they were engaged and had an enormous diamond to show for it.

A NEEDLE HEAD

Stepbrother and former bodyguard Rick Stanley said afterwards: 'He didn't show moderation. Not just with drugs but with anything he did. There were no half-

Left: *Baby Lisa Marie was the child they longed for and adored. But even she wasn't enough to keep the handsome couple together.*

Below: *Ginger Alden, who found Elvis's body, had been dating the King for nine months before his alleged death and claimed they were engaged.*

THE FANS WHO FLOCKED TO HIS CONCERTS NEVER REALIZED THAT THEIR OVERWEIGHT IDOL WAS REDUCED TO WEARING A NAPPY.

Below: *Elvis in action in one of his last shows. On a diet of junk food and drink, his weight had soared. But dutiful fans still flocked to scream their appreciation.*

measures. In 1972 and 1973 he started getting into needles. That's when I really started to worry, when he became a needle head. His body began to look like a pin-cushion.'

Despite his blatant misuse of drugs, there was no shortage of doctors willing to cash in on his addiction and provide a ready supply. Elvis lived on liberal helpings of drugs, junk food like hamburgers, ice cream and milk shakes washed down with whisky. Not surprisingly, his weight ballooned and he became cumbersomely large. He was so fuddled he lost control of his bodily functions. The legions of fans who still flocked to concerts never realized their idol was reduced to wearing a nappy.

In his final 24 hours it is known he visited a dentist at 10.30 pm where he had two fillings, played two hours of racquet-

ball at 2.30 am and retired to bed at 6.30 am.

At 9 am Ginger awoke to find him still sleepless. She reported that he told her he was going into the bathroom to read a book, *The Scientific Search for the Face of Jesus*. It was there that she found him in gold pyjamas just over five hours later.

Dr Jerry Francisco, the Memphis state medical examiner, decided death was due to an erratic heartbeat, adding there were signs of advanced heart disease.

Warning bells started to ring when Elvis was buried with haste, just two days after his death. Graceland was scrupulously cleaned within hours of Elvis's death, it was later discovered, eliminating any forensic evidence. Police continually refuse to probe the death.

And Dr Francisco's claim that there was no evidence of drug abuse caused many who knew Elvis to wonder. It was an open secret that he used drugs regularly – even the audiences at his concerts could detect he was under the influence. The autopsy report was declared secret for 50 years. Altogether, it smacked of a cover-up.

Later it was discovered that 2,372 uppers, 2,680 downers and 1,095 other narcotics had been prescribed to Elvis in Tennessee alone. It was surely within the bounds of possibility that he took an overdose.

Years later Elvis's doctor, George Nichopoulos, told British author John Parkes that he believed the singer was killed by the Mafia. Death was due to a fatal karate chop to the back of the head, he insists.

Why was the Mafia interested in Elvis? It is claimed he was the victim of a $900,000 fraud pulled off by an arm of the mob and helped the FBI track down the top-ranking villains. The hearings against the men involved and were due to go ahead within days of his death. Elvis's involvement in the affair had been covered up in case the Mafia sought reprisals.

In addition, Elvis was, in name at least, an FBI agent. In 1970 he visited President Richard Nixon in the White House to voice his concern about the declining moral fibre of America's youth. He dreamed of becoming an undercover cop who would help save the country from chaos and injustice. Secretly, he used the meeting to stoke up the obsession held by American

politicians that the Beatles were responsible in no small part for this, probably because the super group had decimated his popularity.

In any event, he considered himself as a top cop, absurd as it may seem when his record with drugs is taken into consideration.

A SWEATING CORPSE

Revelations that Elvis lived were made in 1989 by journalist Gail Brewer Giorgio in a book which she called *The Most Incredible Elvis Presley Story Ever Told*. Touched by Elvis's death, she wrote a fictional book about a pop star who faked his death. But when the title was suppressed after being published in 1979 she began to get suspicious. Was her made-up plot really a mirror of what had happened at Graceland?

She started some exhaustive research which she claims produced firm evidence that Elvis was alive. Hundreds of thousands of fans filed reverentially passed the coffin bearing Elvis's body in the short time before it was buried, but many left debating the unusual hairstyle and cut of the nose. Bizarrely, some even mentioned the corpse was apparently sweating. The weight of the body in the coffin was around 7 stones lighter than the bloated Elvis was when he had died, she claims.

Personal belongings like photographs and jewellery, even a plane, went missing after Elvis's death. Two days before his collapse he was heard saying goodbyes to all his most trusted members of staff. Some people believe the writing on the death certificate was actually done by Elvis himself.

There were two life insurance policies cashed in before the death. Yet a third, valuable policy has never been claimed. Fans cite this as evidence that while Elvis might fake his own death, the thoroughly upright side of his character would not allow fraud to take place in his name.

Gail Giorgio was astonished to find a man called Elvis Aaron Presley with 75 million dollars worth of stocks and shares in receipt of a security number issued by the FBI and a classified tax record.

If that wasn't enough, it is known that Elvis used the pseudonym Jon Burrows. And Gail Giorgio found a man of the same name living in Kalamazoo who not only looked like Elvis but shared the same flourishes of the pen – his handwriting was virtually identical. She also discovered Graceland was paying off credit card bills run up by a Jon Burrows as recently as 1991.

Friends recounted how Elvis was not only depressed about his advancing years and expanding figure but also at how he felt trapped by his fame. He longed to stroll down a street or around a shop like other people. A faked death would give him the new beginning he craved. Was it hard fact, mere coincidence or the product of a fertile imagination? The arguments raged on.

LONG LIVE THE KING!

Since his demise, there have been three photos produced as evidence that the King is alive, one of which was taken at Graceland. It shows a figure watching the fans trooping past the burial plot. The

Above: *Dr George Nichopoulos, who tried frantically to revive Elvis, later said he believed the star was killed by a fatal karate chop to the back of the head.*

HAD HE ENDED HIS LIFE WITH A COCKTAIL OF DRUGS BECAUSE HE KNEW HE WAS SUFFERING FROM AN INCURABLE DISEASE?

quality of the snap is not sufficiently sharp to decide whether or not it is Elvis.

There is also the strange case of the telephone calls made sporadically in the last 15 years purporting to be from Elvis. Miss Giorgio has even received one herself. Experts believe the voice matches tapes of the King made while he was alive.

The claims have been denounced by those close to Elvis, among them Priscilla Presley who said: 'Elvis is dead and it is ludicrous to say otherwise.

'To say he is alive is a hurtful and ridiculous lie and deeply upsetting to his family, friends and fans.'

His stepmum Dee Presley agrees. She tells how he ended his life with a cocktail of drugs because he knew he was suffering from bone marrow cancer. She says her husband Vernon, Elvis's dad, found a note signed by the star detailing why he was going to commit suicide. Vernon even revealed that on the night he died he was actually reading a pornographic magazine, not a religious book as was claimed. The secrecy surrounding Elvis's death was maintained to spare Lisa Marie from

knowing the truth about her degenerating dad and to keep the clean-cut image intact.

Meanwhile Elvis's stepbrother David, son of Dee by a previous marriage, revealed how Elvis was tortured with guilt after bedding the wife of another stepbrother, Billy. It was that terrible guilt which led to further drug abuse, he said.

'It haunted Elvis to the grave. He mentioned it often and it was one of the things that helped to kill him. Elvis regretted the affair from the moment he did it.

'He was worried that Billy would find out. In a short time, he cut Billy out of his life completely.

'He was plagued with paranoia and desperately lonely because he didn't know who to trust. Finally, by his own hand, he found the peace he craved for.'

Cynics simply point out that his fortunes revived dramatically on his death and have boomed ever since. Whatever the truth, it is certain that the official secrecy thrown up around the death – with files about it still under wraps for another 35 years – will continue speculation for years to come.

In 1992 Dr Vasco Smith, a political

Below: *Fans file past the grave. Yet many question whether the real Elvis lies interred here or simply a lookalike.*

Left: *Presley's stepmum Dee claims the King killed himself rather than face the agony of death from bone marrow cancer.*

Below: *Thousands pay tribute to the elaborate shrine at Graceland. Is Elvis lurking in the main house observing death rites from a window?*

leader from Memphis, pledged to cut through that grey shroud of confusion and half-truths with a far-reaching investigation.

'There has been a cover up at high level and it's time the whole scandal was dragged into the open and exposed' he said

He points to how Elvis was a known drug user who had been in hospital four times in the previous two years for treatment after overdoses.

'With an intake like that, no one can ignore the possibility that Presley took a fatal overdose. It could have been accidental in his confusion or it could have been deliberate, depending on his state of mind.

'Or, as some people say, the overdose could have been administered deliberately by his enemies.

'But it is impossible to believe he wasn't full of drugs when he died. Even if it means digging Elvis out of the ground to get at the truth we have the power to do it and we certainly have the determination to do it.'

So the body of Elvis may yet be exhumed to silence the nagging doubters once and for all.

Dr Francisco continues to stand by his verdict, claiming he doesn't have the power to release the records of the post-mortem.

With the conspiracy theorists and rumour mongers still at work, Elvis, the rock 'n' roll genius of a generation, will never be able to rest in peace. dead or alive.

CLOSE
ENCOUNTERS

With mounting evidence from impeccable sources, it seems absurd to deny the possibility of life in outer space. Some have risked ridicule in order to describe their ordeals; others have been cold-bloodedly silenced ...

' **N**o one would have believed in the last years of the 19th century that this world was being watched keenly and closely by intelligences greater than man's and yet as mortal as his own; that as men busied themselves about their various concerns, they were scrutinised and studied ... '

So began H.G. Wells's *The War of the Worlds,* a novel which has long had a niche as a definitive piece of sci-fi. Yet, for a select few, those lines mean much more than mere fiction. They are a chilling reminder of ordeals that defy earthbound logic and reason. Of close encounters with alien life forms.

Strange objects in the sky have mystified human beings since prehistoric times. Every generation has been fascinated by them and as our knowledge of the Universe increases, so surely should our acceptance of the prospect of life on other planets. With more than 100,000 million stars in our galaxy alone, it seems statistically incredible to suggest the Sun is the only one which has managed to spawn life. But reports of contact with inter-planetary craft are still treated scathingly by officialdom. UFOs are for the batty, the weird, the charlatans and the dreamers.

Except that they're not. Many of the worldwide files on UFO sightings contain evidence from impeccable sources such as police officers, doctors, firemen, pilots and other trained observers. Some have risked ridicule to tell what they saw. Others have

even dared to claim the ultimate in culture shock – actual contact with an alien.

FIRE IN THE SKY

One of the most fascinating cases is that of Travis Walton, an American forester, who claims he was kidnapped by aliens on 5 November 1975 and held for five days. His story is unusual because it was witnessed by six colleagues who were subsequently put under intense police interrogation on suspicion of concocting the UFO story to cover a murder conspiracy.

The gang of forestry workers had no reason to fear anyone or anything as their pick-up truck bounced down a lonely mountain track in the Apache-Sitgreave

Opposite: *This picture, based on an eye-witness description, shows 'alien' life forms leaving their spaceship after it landed in a French lavender field.*

Below: *This gigantic UFO was spotted over Papua New Guinea in June 1959.*

HIS 'MATES' DESERTED HIM, FLEEING THE SCENE LIKE BATS OUT OF HELL; WHEN THEY RETURNED, ASHAMED OF THEIR COWARDICE, IT WAS TOO LATE.

Below: A UFO, or a strange cloud formation? This bizarre photograph was taken near the dormant volcano Mount Rainier in the US.

National Forest near Snowflake, Arizona. None could have anticipated that danger was approaching their high-spirited group. Only when it was too late would they begin to comprehend the amazing nature of the bizarre experience waiting for them around the next corner.

Walton's best friend, Mike Rogers, was at the wheel of the truck. As it rounded a corner all of the men saw a glowing, yellowish object hovering 15 feet above a clearing. Walton jumped from the truck and ran towards it to get a better view. Later he was to vividly recall the moment.

'The guys were calling me saying "get away from there, get back in the truck",' said Walton. 'I guess that egged me on. I was scared but I was showing off a bit too.' He was struck by a beam of blue light which pitched him backwards 'like a limp rag doll'. His mates in the truck fled the

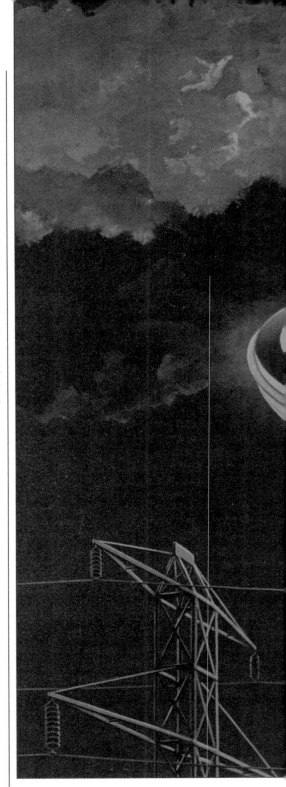

scene like bats out of hell but later, ashamed at abandoning their colleague, they returned. The strange craft had vanished – along with Travis Walton.

During the next five days, with Walton still missing, the six became suspected of killing him and dreaming up a cock-and-bull story to cover their tracks. Police launched a massive manhunt but found no trace of the missing man. Then, on 10 November, Walton's sister answered a

call from a public phone in a neighbouring town. It was Travis. He was badly shaken and had no idea of where he had been for the last five days. Under hypnosis he revealed: 'I know people won't believe me but I was in their spaceship and I met those creatures. We all saw the saucer that night. I was excited and just ran towards the glow. I felt no fear.

'Then something hit me. It was like an electric blow to my jaw, and everything went black. When I woke up I thought I was in hospital. I was on a table on my back and as I focused I saw three figures. It was weird. They looked like foetuses to me, about 5 feet tall, and they wore tight-fitting tan brown robes. Their skin was white like a mushroom but they had no clear features.

'I guess I panicked. I grabbed a transparent tube and tried to smash it to use it as a weapon, but it wouldn't break. I was

Above: *An artist put together this drawing from the reports of several eye-witnesses who saw a UFO over Exeter, New Hampshire, in 1965.*

Above: *This object was captured on film by a Mr Barney Wayne, manager of a photographic studio in Bulawayo, Southern Rhodesia, as he drove through the north of the city. Numerous experts and press photographers pronounced it genuine.*

THE CREATURE'S BENT CLAWS AIMED THE WEAPON AT HIM AND INFLICTED TERRIBLE INJURIES.

petrified. I wanted to attack them but they just scampered away. I knew we were in a spaceship and I felt we were moving. Then things went black again.'

He also saw what he described as a very 'human-like' figure just before blacking out again. Walton continued: 'When I woke again I was shaky. I was on the highway. It was black but all the trees were lit up because just a few feet away was the flying saucer. I was in my working clothes. I just ran and recognized a village a few miles from my home.'

The experience affected all the men badly. Three refused to go back into the woods to help the search for Walton, and Rogers lost his contract with the US Forest Service. Walton himself suffered at the hands of malicious gossips but he never changed his version of events. And 18 years later the whole, amazing story was made into a major film, *Fire in the Sky*, starring James Garner. 'If I hadn't believed Walton after talking to him for several hours I wouldn't have touched it with a barge pole,' Garner insisted later.

KIDNAPPED BY ALIENS

Walton's trials were mirrored in France in 1979 when a young married man, Frank Fontaine, went missing for a whole week. At 4 am on 26 November he was helping two friends load a van with clothes for Gisors market near Paris when they all spotted a 'bright and twirling light' descending nearby. Fontaine drove towards where it seemed likely the light would land. It was the last anyone saw of him for a week.

One of Fontaine's friends described his disappearance in these words: 'When we came out Frank's van was 200 metres away. It was covered in a bright light, like a halo surrounding it. Three other bright lights were nearby. Then they all converged on the van.' As the frightening halo lifted into the night sky, the friend and a companion rushed forward to find the van empty. The engine was still running and the headlights were on.

When Fontaine turned up, at exactly 4 am the following week, he claimed he had blacked out in the bright lights and had awoken at the same spot, assuming the van had been stolen. He had no idea that a whole week had passed.

The victims in most recorded UFO abduction cases are returned unharmed, apart from the psychological scars and an inevitable amount of ridicule. However, there are exceptions and of the few documented cases that exist it seems one danger of a close encounter is a large dose of radiation. The symptoms are usually clear cut … and difficult for UFO sceptics to easily explain away.

TOO CLOSE FOR COMFORT

One such case occurred in Finland on 7 January 1970 when two friends out on a skiing trip spied a UFO which left them suffering from appalling physical side-effects for around two months. Aaron Heinonen and Esko Viljo had stopped to admire a few stars pinpricking out of a cold sunset when they suddenly spotted a much brighter light emerging quickly out of the dusk towards them. Surrounded by a thin cloud of smoke was a circular saucer-shaped object with a dome above.

Abruptly, a beam of light fired down from the spaceship to the ground. Heinonen later recalled: 'Suddenly I felt as if someone had seized me from the waist and I took a step backwards. Then I saw the creature, standing in a beam of light, with a black box in its hands. From an opening in the box there was a yellow, pulsating light. The creature was about 35 inches high with very thin arms and legs. Its ears were small and close in to the head and the face was like wax. Its fingers were like bent claws around the box.'

Heinonen was hit by a blast of light from the mysterious box and the pair were covered in a strange red-grey mist. Then, as suddenly as it had arrived, the beam of light and the spaceship were gone.

Heinonen was paralysed down his right side and his friend had to virtually carry him two miles to their home. 'For two months afterwards I felt ill,' he said later. 'My back was aching and all my joints were painful. My head ached and I had to vomit. When I went to pee, the urine was nearly black – it was like pouring coffee onto the snow.'

Viljo suffered a reddened and swollen face. He became incoherent and absent-minded. Paul Kajanoja, one of the doctors who examined the two men, commented: 'The symptoms are like those after being exposed to radioactivity. Both men seemed sincere. I don't think they made the thing up. I am sure they were in a state of shock when they came to me.

Above: *A scene from the most famous UFO movie of all –* **Close Encounters of the Third Kind** *– shows investigator Dr J. Allen Hynek trying to solve the puzzle.*

Something terrible must have frightened them.'

A DIAMOND ON FIRE

Three other victims of 'UFO radiation' caused enormous headaches for the US government during the early eighties. Their account has an extraordinary ring of truth about it, partly because of the sheer detail it contained and partly because of the inexplicable, and indisputable, side effects the three suffered. No doctor has ever been able to explain what caused the conditions which later dogged their lives.

Vickie Landrum, her grandson Colby Landrum and their friend Betty Cash were driving towards Dayton, Texas, on 29 December 1980 when young Colby saw a huge glowing object at tree-top height above the lonely forest road in front of them. Frightened, but curious, they stepped out of the car to get a closer look.

At that time the object was still some

Above: *The US military gets very edgy when unidentified intruders such as this fly into American airspace. This photo was snapped by nurse Ella Louise Fortune near the Hollman USAF base, New Mexico, in October 1957.*

THE DOCTORS WERE BAFFLED AND WORRIED: MEDICAL TEXTBOOKS ARE LIGHT ON ADVICE FOR TREATING CONDITIONS CAUSED BY ALIEN BEINGS.

three miles away although as they drove cautiously towards it they realized it was heading their way. Verging on panic now, they accelerated, but the UFO – many times bigger than their automobile – stopped directly in front of them, hovering above the road. They glimpsed a conical burst of flame from beneath the craft and Vickie recalls screaming: 'Stop the car or we will be burned alive.' Every time the flames belched out the object would rise up several metres, only to gradually fall again when the blast petered out. For all the world it looked like a sci-fi scene of an alien craft in trouble or, as Vickie would assert later, 'like a diamond on fire'.

The UFO seemed to be made of an aluminium-type metal and was lit so brightly it turned night (it was around 9 pm) into day. Its diamond shape had blunted points and hazy blue lights ringed its centre. Occasionally it made a beeping sound and Cash and the Landrums recall worrying that it would set the trees alight if it moved off the road.

The three of them got out of the car to get a better look, but after a couple of minutes Vickie bowed to her grandson's plea to return inside. Betty, however, stayed put. Her eyes were captivated by the amazing machine in front of her and her senses were somehow dulled to the burning heat.

It was only when she became conscious of one of her rings burning into her skin that she snapped out of the reverie. Vickie's frantic calls for her to get back in the car were heeded. Even then there was a moment's hesitation. The handle of the door was too hot to touch by hand. Betty had to use her leather coat for protection before she could grip it.

By now the UFO was heading away … but almost immediately a new puzzle emerged. The sky suddenly filled with the sound of helicopters – 23 in all – which, as Betty put it later, 'seemed to rush in from all directions … it seemed like they were trying to encircle the thing'.

The three of them reached a larger road which enabled them to keep track of the chase. Later their descriptions helped experts identify the choppers as Chinooks (which have distinctive double rotor blades) and small, fast-attack helicopters similar to a Bell Huey. The pilots appeared to be in an erratic trail formation, though one group had managed to shadow the UFO fairly closely and was clearly illuminated in its light.

After a close encounter lasting 20 minutes Betty turned onto another highway and headed home to Dayton. She dropped off Vickie and Colby and returned to her own house, where a friend and her children were waiting. She didn't mention the UFO. Probably she was in shock. She was certainly feeling very, very ill.

Of the three witnesses Betty had easily the longest exposure to the craft's energy source. As the night wore on her skin turned red, as though she had a bad dose of sunburn. Her neck puffed up, blisters burst onto her scalp, face and eyelids. She was violently sick throughout the night and by morning was close to a comatose state. Vickie and Colby later presented themselves to doctors with similar symptoms, though less severe.

The local hospital began treating all three for burns. No one had told them about a possible UFO involvement and even if they had, the medical textbooks are light on advice for treating conditions caused by alien beings. The doctors were both baffled and worried. Betty's swollen appearance, together with the bald patches spreading across her scalp, had changed her features so drastically that visitors failed to even recognize her. All the doctors could suggest was that she had suffered a massive dose of some kind of electromagnetic radiation.

OFFICIAL COVER-UP?

The interrogation of all three witnesses, in which each was questioned separately, showed their recollections to be remarkably consistent. Not only did they notice the same features on the UFO, they also provided similar sketches identifying the choppers as Chinook CH-47s. Yet this caused a new problem. Of the 400 or so helicopters running commercial flights in the Houston area, none was twin-rotor. And the nearest army base, Fort Hood near Killeen, Texas, said it had no aircraft anywhere near Houston on the night of 29 December.

Hood's spokesman Major Tony Geishauser observed: 'I don't know of any other place around here that would have had that number of helicopters. I don't know what it [the UFO] could be, unless there's a super-secret thing going on and I wouldn't necessarily know about it.' Other air bases, further away, were contacted by the media. All denied knowledge of any large-scale helicopter movements on 29 December.

Interestingly, on the previous day at least one helicopter had been sent to investigate UFO activity above Ohio county, Kentucky. Dozens of residents reported seeing strange lights in the sky and several witnessed the services helicopter flying above them. Yet, once more, the military denied having any choppers flying that evening.

It was not as if Betty, Vickie and Colby's story lacked corroboration. An off-duty cop and his wife driving near Huffman, Texas – close to the point the UFO first appeared – reported seeing a major movement of CH-47s. And oilman Jerry McDonald told of seeing a UFO from his back garden. 'It was kind of diamond-shaped and had two twin torches that were shooting brilliant blue flames out the back,' he said.

Investigations into the Huffman incident continue to this day. One group specializing in the probing of unusual phenomena, the Houston-based Vehicle Internal Systems Investigative Team (VISIT), offered two mind-boggling theories.

The first is that the craft was a UFO that had got into trouble. It was flying on some kind of emergency energy system which resulted in the belching of blue flames. It

Below: *The clearer the photo, argue the sceptics, the more likely it is to be faked. This picture, taken on 16 June 1963 at Peralta, New Mexico, is among the clearest of any UFO snaps on record.*

had been tracked on radar and the military guessed it could crashland. The CH-47s were therefore ordered in as troop carriers to cordon off the area from inquisitive eyes while the single rotor choppers were attack craft ready to offer such protection as they could give. When the UFO solved its propulsion problem it headed for the coast and was escorted along the way.

One factor in support of this theory is that those experiencing close encounters with UFOs rarely suffer any personal injury. The suggestion is that if there is anyone out there they are friendly beings. They intended no harm to befall Vickie, Betty and Colby but could not control their radiation emissions.

The second theory holds that on the night of 29 December the military had 'road tested' a top-secret new invention. The 'alien craft' could in fact have been some kind of weapons system, an electronic jamming device or a revolutionary power plant. It could have been slung below the belly of one of the helicopters and all personnel involved would have donned protective clothing. The injuries Betty received could have been the result of a mega-strong microwave power pack or exposure to tiny droplets of some revolutionary fuel.

The US government, however, has always adamantly refused to admit it owns the helicopters, even though they were seen by six, separate, reliable witnesses. In view of the fact that no one will admit to authorizing the chopper excursion, the obvious conclusion is that a highly classified operation was going on that night.

Vickie and Betty later sued the American government for $20 million but the case was dismissed on the grounds that the military had no such object in its possession. The dilemma for the authorities was: if the flying craft was American, then the case should proceed. If it was not, and the court ruled it was not, then exactly who was transporting a dazzling, diamond-shaped, flame-belching machine across the night skies of Texas?

The whole bizarre affair has one tantalizing postscript. In April 1981 Colby Landrum saw a CH-47 landing in Dayton. The sight brought back memories of the Huffman incident and he became increasingly distressed. To try and get him to face up to his fears, Vickie took him to the site of the landing and introduced herself to the pilot. Without prompting, he told her he had been to the area previously to check out a UFO reported to be in trouble. When Vicki explained her interest he suddenly became nervous and refused to talk further. They were politely invited to leave the CH-47.

The VISIT group later tracked down this pilot and questioned him. He confessed to knowing about the Huffman incident but emphatically denied he had ever been in the region on that fateful December night. To date, none of the helicopter pilots involved has ever broken ranks and told what he knows.

SOMETHING VERY ODD

Although what happened at Huffman was exceptional, even by the standards of the most ardent ufologist, it is by no means unusual for UFOs to have a physical effect on everyday objects. Stories of cars malfunctioning close to strange flying lights in the sky are legion and many witnesses will tell of engine failure, bizarre static noise on the radio, rough running, impossible readings on their instruments and light failure. Occasionally a vehicle's internal wiring is completely blown out.

Drivers often report inexplicable heat or vibration or the feeling that they have driven into a field of static electricity. Some even talk of smells that are, quite literally, alien to them. Yet in most cases once the UFO concerned has passed on everything returns to normal.

One of the best documented examples of this phenomenon again happened in Texas. (It should be noted that Mexico appears to have more than its fair share of UFO activity and perhaps some of this occasionally spills across the border.) On the night of 2 November 1957 Patrolman A.J. Fowler was on the night shift at Levelland police headquarters. Up until 11 pm it was the usual routine of investigating break-ins, pulling in drunks and calming down the odd wild party. Suddenly everything changed. Patrolman Fowler would remember that shift for the rest of his life.

Soon after 11 pm he took a call from a

Above: *A UFO over Milan in 1962? Or an over-productive imagination at work? This drawing was artist Gaspare de Lama's portrayal of his sighting.*

motorist called Pedro Saucedo who had been out driving four miles west of the city with a friend. Pedro sounded excited, panicky even, as he relayed how a brilliant yellow and white cigar-shaped object passed above his truck at very high speed. As the UFO crossed the road Pedro's headlights died and his engine failed. He had clambered out for a better look but was immediately crushed by a searing heat and found himself flat on the ground.

Seconds later the headlights flickered back into action and the engine started without any problem. Pedro had never seen anything like it. Was it a flying saucer? What were the police going to do about it? Had anyone else reported seeing something similar? Officer Fowler made what he judged to be the right calming noises and rang off. He didn't feel inclined to call out the National Guard. Probably the guy had had a few too many, seen a meteor and let his imagination take over. Either that or he was just a good old-fashioned nut. There were always plenty of those for the night roster to handle.

Then another call came an hour later. This time a motorist travelling around eight miles east of Pedro – on the UFO's apparent flight path – reported coming across a bright, 200-foot-long egg-shaped device which had touched down right in the middle of the road. As the car drew near its engine had stalled and the headlights failed. But this driver could see the surrounding countryside clearly in the light of the craft.

UNTIL 11 PM IT WAS THE USUAL ROUTINE OF INVESTIGATING BREAK-INS, PULLING IN DRUNKS AND CALMING DOWN THE ODD WILD PARTY. SUDDENLY EVERYTHING CHANGED.

When he opened his door it took off, quickly toned down the illumination and merged into the night sky.

Now Fowler was curious. Was this some kind of stunt? Were some colleagues playing him up? If so they were playing with fire. The cops took a dim view of juvenile behaviour like that. He was just convincing himself that practical jokers or unusual weather phenomena were to blame when a third call came in. Neville Wright was heading towards Levelland when his car's ammeter began flickering, the lights cut out and the engine spluttered to a halt. He'd checked under the hood but could find nothing wrong. Then he'd spotted the brilliant stationary light on the road ahead.

Within the space of the next hour four more positive sightings came in, all from good witnesses. A fire chief told of a red light that passed close to him and temporarily seemed to drain his car's battery. A sheriff and his deputy radioed that they had seen an extremely unusual red flying object. Patrolman Fowler was by now convinced something very odd was happening in the skies above Texas that November night.

To this day no scientist has been able to explain the string of vehicle electrical failures, let alone the UFO itself. Unproven theories have it that a super-powerful electromagnetic field was generated by the saucer, that its microwaves heated up the engine's vital electrical components or that refined ultra-violet light caused current to short and stray. One suggestion is that microwave radiation can interfere with tungsten headlamps to impose a massive and sudden drain on the battery. None of these ideas has ever been put to the test, at least not publicly. If the US government knows more, it is staying silent.

The role of governments in the UFO debate is itself fascinating. Exactly what do the major powers know? If alien cultures have indeed reached planet Earth, why the big cover-up? Are our politicians really worried that we're all going to throw ourselves off the nearest bridge? Or is it that privately, at least, many in government accept that some kind of UFO activity has been going on for years? To admit it would be a political minefield. Once you admit something you have to explain it to the voters.

SOVIET SKULDUGGERY

Thankfully, some governments do take a less secretive attitude. In June 1952 six Norwegian army jets on training flights over the remote Spitzbergen islands reported debris across a mountainous area close to the Hinlopen Straits. Hours later a team of investigators was on site and allied powers in the West were alerted. Was this Soviet skulduggery at work? Perhaps a missile on test or some kind of revolutionary aircraft?

The wreckage was certainly an eye-opener. There were 46 holes in the object's rim which could have been linked to its propulsion methods. Of occupants there was no sign. The press jumped on the story but most editors tended to follow the official line that the crashed craft was a failed piece of Soviet hardware. It was not until 1955 that a senior Norwegian army officer revealed the truth.

Colonel Gernod Darnbyl, of the Norwegian General Staff, said: 'The crashing of the Spitzbergen disk was highly important. Although our present scientific

Below: Police probe the remnants of a 'crashed UFO'. Civil engineer Barney Barnett's discovery in the New Mexico desert remains one of the world's great mysteries.

knowledge does not permit us to solve all the riddles I am confident that these remains from Spitzbergen will be of utmost importance. Some time ago a misunderstanding was caused by saying that this disk probably was of Soviet origin. We wish to state categorically that it was not built by any country on Earth. The materials used in its construction are completely unknown to the experts that took part in the investigation.' He revealed that US and British scientists had been given access to the remains. To this day their reports have never been released.

Another government which takes the open-book approach is that of France, which has some of the world's most sophisticated defence technology. In 1974 the French defence minister Robert Galley made an astonishing statement in which he seemed to suggest that UFO sightings had become of enormous concern to his government. He told a radio interviewer: 'It is irrefutable that there are things today that are inexplicable, or poorly explained ... I must say that if your listeners could see for themselves the mass of reports coming in from aircraft pilots, from patrol police and from those charged with the job of conducting investigations ... then they would see that it is all pretty disturbing.'

Certainly officialdom has started to slacken the chains of secrecy around UFO documentation. Spain released its files in 1976, Americans were given access to the so-called Blue Book project in 1977, France set up a government-backed UFO study group in the late seventies, while Australia went public on its records in 1981. Even Britain, which still has one of the most secrecy-obsessed governments in the world, has relaxed its guard a little. In the early seventies the UK agreed to keep a permanent record of UFO sightings (prior to then all reports were destroyed after five years) and in 1982 it was decided that questions from the public about specific incidents could be answered.

The problem here, of course, is in the phrasing of the question. Asking a Whitehall mandarin whether a UFO which crashed in hills above Bala, north Wales, in the mid-seventies contained any evidence of alien life forms will make you none the wiser. The civil servant will, truthfully, reply that there was no such evidence –

even if there were characteristics about the wreckage which could not be explained by conventional science. Similarly, too vague a question will elicit too vague an answer.

Some hard evidence of UFOs, though, does seem to exist. On 2 July 1947, at about 9.50 pm, a Mr and Mrs Wilmot of Roswell, New Mexico, were enjoying the evening dusk when they suddenly saw a glowing object travelling quickly northeast towards the neigbouring town of Corona. The next day civil engineer Barney Barnett, of Socorro, New Mexico, was working out in the desert 250 miles west of Roswell. A metallic object glinting in the sun caught his eye and he drove over to check it out. He thought it might be a crashed aircraft. What he found was a metallic craft 30 feet in diameter ... but it

seemed no earthly hand had fashioned it. Around it lay dead bodies, bodies with very small eyes and very large heads and bereft of hair. They were wearing grey body suits.

Minutes later a group of archeological students working nearby arrived to take a look. They were equally astonished and, like Barnett, concluded that this was perhaps the first hard evidence of alien life. At least, this is how the story goes.

Apparently the army then turned up and cordoned off the entire area. Barney and the students were told it was their patriotic

THE IMPOSSIBLE HAD HAPPENED: AT LAST THERE WAS HARD EVIDENCE OF ALIEN LIFE.

Above: *Phone home! A scene from Spielberg's* E.T. *Public fascination with UFOs helped it become one of the biggest Hollywood blockbusters of all time.*

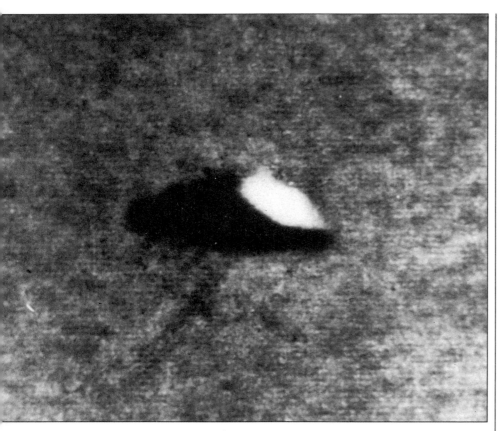

Above: *A trick of the light or an alien spaceship? This photo was taken by a postman on his rounds in 1955.*

THE SCEPTICAL BRITISH CORONER WAS FORCED TO CONCEDE THE POSSIBILITY OF ALIEN FORCES AT WORK.

---

duty to reveal nothing of what they had seen. In 1947, with the Cold War looming fast, orders like that from the military certainly carried weight with the American public.

But before he died Barney did talk – to a close group of friends. Gradually the story leaked out and several journalists took a keen interest. They could find no reason for Barney's friends to lie, neither could they unearth anything about his past character which suggested he'd be the kind of man who enjoyed hoaxing others. Was he hoaxed himself? Were the students pranksters who just liked to be as elaborate as possible? If so, they were truly convincing. Barney's account suggested a great deal of military hardware was brought onto the crash site together with the soldiers to operate it. The students, sadly, were never traced.

SEXUAL FANTASY

The Roswell incident does have some factors in common with close encounters elsewhere. Grey body suits and small eyes, for instance, formed part of the description of aliens given by a Brazilian farmer called Antonio Villas Boas. He encountered them

when they landed in his field. His account remains the most incredible and far-fetched of all … because he claims to have had sex with one of the extra-terrestrials.

One night in 1957, Boas had been ploughing the fields with his brother when he noticed a ball of red light in the sky above. The following night the red ball was still there and, as he was alone this time, he grew scared and decided to drive his tractor away. Boas claims the red ball then landed in front of him and he was captured by five entities wearing grey, tight-fitting suits and helmets which revealed only their small blue eyes.

He says he was led onto the spaceship where he was forcibly stripped and a thick, transparent liquid was spread over his skin. Then he was marched into a small room where a blood sample was taken leaving a small scar (the scar was later verified by those investigating Boas's claims). Half an hour later a beautiful female alien walked in completely naked. 'Her body was more beautiful than any I had ever seen before,' said Boas. The alien then embraced him and forced him to copulate with her. Sex took place a second and then a third time, though Boas was vague about the intervals between each. The alien then seemed to suggest his seed was wanted for breeding stock – she pointed at her belly and then the sky.

Later, after Boas was returned to his field, he consulted a doctor. Burns seemingly caused by radiation were found on parts of his skin. However most of the locals contended his account was pure fantasy.

THE MOST MYSTERIOUS DEATH

Quite often incidents such as this are dismissed purely on the grounds that all information relating to them has been gleaned by journalists: reporters after a good story are not, it is argued, going to worry too much about over-egging the pudding. Yet some investigations into UFO activity are carried out openly by responsible, naturally cautious authorities, and they don't come much more sceptical or cautious than your average British coroner.

One such coroner is James Turnbull, of Yorkshire, England. In the mid-eighties he

took charge of an inquest touching the death of a quiet Polish exile, Zygmunt Adamski, who vanished one night while en route to buy potatoes from his local shop in Leeds, Yorkshire. He didn't drink and he had no known enemies. But he was found dead five days later on top of a coal tip 30 miles away near the railway station at Todmorden. Adamski was half-naked but his body was spotlessly clean as though he had just stepped out of a shower. The smooth sides of the coal tip indicated nobody had tried to climb it.

Parts of the body were burned with corrosive substances which scientists were unable to identify. Tests showed the deceased had succumbed to a heart attack eight or ten hours before his body was dumped. The local rumour-mongers had no doubts: Adamski had been scared to death by a flying saucer.

If such talk was dismissed as nonsense by the authorities they quickly changed their tune. One policeman first called to the scene of the 'crime' told how he had seen what looked like a flying saucer only hours before the body was discovered. PC Alan Godfrey, a down-to-earth father of two children, said he had been on night duty when he encountered the UFO on a lonely road. It was the size of a bus and floated about 5 feet from the ground. The bottom half was spinning and he could see rows of windows around a dome. But when he tried to alert his station to what he was seeing he couldn't. His walkie-talkie wouldn't work.

Such facts as these were laid before Coroner James Turnbull. His comments at the inquest speak volumes because he was a neutral and expert assessor of evidence.

'This is quite the most mysterious death I have ever investigated,' he said. 'As a coroner I cannot speculate. But I must admit that if I was walking over Ilkley Moor tomorrow and a UFO came down I would not be surprised.

'I might be terrified ... but not surprised.'

Above: *We are not alone. Jillian Guiler (played by Melinda Dillan) and son Barry (Cary Cuffey) are transfixed by the bright lights of a UFO above their home. Scenes like this from* **Close Encounters** *gave the UFO debate a new edge.*

JIMMY HOFFA
'A tainted folk hero'

Jimmy Hoffa was a small man with a gigantic lust for power. Rough and tough, he fought his way up from the bottom of the heap and didn't care who he trampled on or how many enemies he made ...

The day that Jimmy Hoffa vanished, a nation held its breath. Was this just another wild stunt by the charismatic champion of the American working man? Or had the 'little guy' breathed his last?

Jimmy Hoffa left his home on the outskirts of Detroit on 30 July 1975 and was never seen again, alive or dead. Ever since in the minds of the ordinary people who had followed his amazing exploits – sometimes with admiration, sometimes with awe, but often with horror – there has been a huge fascination as to his fate.

For Hoffa's firebrand exploits were the stuff of legend, lovingly reported by the media. He was that curiously American animal: a tainted folk hero.

He had fought the Kennedys, courted the Mafia, stolen workers' millions, been imprisoned, courted Richard Nixon, done battle with the Mafia, won back the workers and split the unions. And then he was suddenly gone.

Ironically, James R. Hoffa was christened with the middle name 'Riddle'. And the riddle of his disappearance has intrigued America and confounded the authorities. The FBI is still actively investigating the Hoffa disappearance, still conducting the biggest manhunt in its history. The US Justice Department still has a 'live' casefile on him.

But the authorities never did make a single arrest in the case nor did they turn up any evidence of Jimmy's body. So what happened? Was he turned into glue? Ground up in a mincer? Compacted in a garbage plant? Cemented into a bridge? Squashed inside a junked car? Fed to Florida's alligators? Or could he perhaps still be alive?

HOOKED ON POWER

Born 14 February 1913, from his humble beginnings Hoffa rose to the top with the help of the underworld. He made little pretence of being a nice guy. In the rough-and-ready Depression era, he fought his way from a job as a loading dockworker to become president in 1957 of America's largest and most powerful trades union.

His power turned the disorganized International Brotherhood of Teamsters into a major force. Anything that involved cartage was operated by the Teamsters, descendants of the stagecoach drivers, pony expressmen and muleteers of pioneer days. Even the Michigan State Police joined Hoffa's union.

When he was attorney general, Robert Kennedy grilled Hoffa mercilessly about

Opposite: Cunning, controversial, conniving. Yet nevertheless Hoffa, seen here giving evidence at a rackets' hearing, was a hero to thousands and mourned by many as America's mouthpiece for the working man.

Below: Teamsters pickets demonstrate solidarity outside a trucking firm in dispute with its drivers.

Above: *There was no love lost between Hoffa and Robert Kennedy. Hoffa even threatened to sue Kennedy after being branded a communist.*

IN JAIL HE BOASTED HE'D NEVER READ BOOKS – JUST THE CONTRACTS HE'D TAKEN OUT ON OTHER PEOPLE'S LIVES.

---

and he had never been to jail. That changed on 4 March 1964 when he was sentenced to eight years on two out of three counts of jury tampering. Seven weeks later he was back in court for a 3-month trial that ended with him being given an additional 5-year sentence for mail fraud, milking the Teamsters' principal pension fund of $2 million.

He went to prison in 1967 after his appeals had all been lost. Even behind bars, however, he was still a hero with a loyal, almost fanatical, trade union following. America has always rooted for the little guy, and Hoffa was tiny. Five foot 5, never weighing more than 13 stone, he did daily push-ups in prison. He boasted that he had never read a book ('I read contracts, not books') but behind bars he read ten books a month.

Before going down, Hoffa had arranged for a weak caretaker deputy, his cohort from the local Detroit branch, to become the union's titular head. Frank Fitzsimmons turned out to be more tenacious once he became president.

Hoffa served only 58 months of his 13-year sentence. Then, in December 1971 when the Federal Parole Board had turned down his third parole appeal, President Nixon suddenly commuted his sentence. He was free. But there was a catch in the Nixon deal: Hoffa was barred from union activities until 1980 – which just happened to coincide with the end of Fitzsimmons's term of office.

Hoffa cried loudly that the president had betrayed him; he claimed Nixon and Fitzsimmons had conspired against him in secret. Why would the president of the USA get involved at all? For money, said the Phoenix-based *Arizona Republic* newspaper, which obtained an incriminating document from law enforcement officials in 1979. The newspaper said that Nixon got half a million dollars out of Mafia funds.

An alleged 19-page mob diary threw new light on the links between criminals, unions and politicians. The diary was handed to the FBI by convicted hitman Gerald Denono, who said he stole it from another mobster, bagman Edward 'Marty' Buccieri, who was murdered in 1975. The document, which covered a 15-month period from 1972 to 1973, itemized $28

his strongarm tactics. Employers bought union peace and stability, plus a share of the pension fund rip-off, and all it cost them was their integrity.

He liked to boss other people about. At Lake Orion, neighbours didn't like to stop and chat with Jimmy for long because they would get a rake shoved in their hand with instructions to work!

Hoffa was a devoted family man with a puritanical streak. But he still went in for diamond cufflinks, convertible cars, top-line hotels and furnishings – as long as the Teamsters picked up the tab.

How much of a crook was Hoffa? He boasted he had 'a record as long as your arm': 23 arrests dating back to 1937, the year he married Josephine Pozywak. However, he had been fined only twice (the first time for $10, the second for $1,000)

million in illegal financial transactions. The diary named Nixon aides Bob Haldeman, Charles Colson and John Ehrlichman.

Hoffa allegedly promised Nixon endorsement by the Teamsters and other unions in the 1972 election. Nixon needed this backing since he had already angered the unions in 1971 with his price control measures.

Once he was out of prison, Hoffa's mission was therefore to wrest control of the Teamsters away from his one-time protégé Fitzsimmons, who was now firmly entrenched and obstinate.

Hoffa would tell people: 'I know the union business upside-down around and over. The members are interested in how many bucks they can make. I get them for them.'

There was a split in the trade union ranks and the ensuing feud was violent. Detroit Teamsters official Dave Johnson was beaten up, his office was machine-gunned and his boat was blown apart. Union organizer Eugene Paige's house was blown up. Another official, George Foxburgh, was hit by a shotgun blast and lost an eye. Fitzsimmons's son Dickie, a local branch official, was drinking in a bar when his Teamsters-owned car exploded in a ball of flame outside. This was on 10 July 1975 – exactly three weeks before Hoffa vanished.

It was trade union civil war.

Hoffa was interested purely in power, not riches. He already had a $1.7 million pension pay-off that he'd taken in a cash lump sum, and he had other business interests. He had, of course, served time for theft of an enormous sum from the

Above: *More than 10,000 truckers, warehousemen and taxi drivers crammed into Madison Square Gardens in 1960 to hear Hoffa crusading against a new labour reform law.*

Teamsters' pension fund, Yet he still enjoyed the personal loyalty of 2.2 million members of America's most powerful union.

Then he disappeared.

AN UNDERWORLD RUBOUT

Late in the afternoon of 30 July 1975, 62-year-old Hoffa left his ritzy suburban home in Lake Orion, 45 miles north of Detroit.

He was wearing a blue sports shirt and dark trousers. He was going to the Machus Red Fox restaurant in Bloomfield township.

Hoffa is believed to have been abducted from outside the restaurant – the victim of an underworld rubout. But by whom? And why?

Hoffa had told his wife that he had a dinner date at the restaurant with two men: Anthony Giacolone, a Detroit hoodlum, and Anthony Provenzano, known as Tony Pro, a soldier in the influential Mafia crime family of Vito Genovese. Giacolone was a simple hood, but Provenzano, a former amateur boxer, was more than just a Genovese soldier. He was a local leader of the Teamsters in Union City, New Jersey.

Tony Pro and Hoffa bore a fierce hatred for one another. They had been friends and allies, but after a joint spell in the Federal Penitentiary at Lewisburg, Pennsylvania, something happened to change their comradeship to loathing.

Justice Department lawyer Phil Fox says: 'They had a real thing about each other – bad blood. But it's unlikely we'll ever know what happened to Hoffa.'

Phil Roemer, a former FBI agent who investigated the case, says: 'There doesn't seem to be much doubt that Tony Pro was one of the organizers.'

Says Mafia author Howard Abadinsky: 'Tony Pro knew Hoffa's fate, but the decision must have come from a much higher authority than him. He was just a soldier.'

Everybody knew that Jimmy Hoffa's disappearance was a Mafia hit but nobody could prove anything. Tony Pro continued to deny any involvement right to the end. Two years later he was convicted and given a life sentence for the murder of another Teamsters official. In 1988 he died in

THEY'D BEEN ALLIES – AND THEN SOMETHING HAPPENED TO TURN THEIR FRIENDSHIP INTO BITTER HATRED.

prison aged 71 – still denying any knowledge of Hoffa's 'hit'.

Mafia bigwig Russell Bufalino is reputed to have ordered Hoffa's death. The accepted theory is that the Cosa Nostra had such a good business siphoning off Teamsters' pension money and shaking down employers that they didn't want hardheaded Hoffa coming back and running it all. Fitzsimmons was far more accommodating.

A FAMILY AFFAIR?

Another name linked to Hoffa's disappearance was his own foster son ...

An independent and reputable witness said he pulled up beside a brand-new 1975 maroon Mercury and for a few seconds saw what everyone believes was the abduction. He recognized Hoffa as one of four passengers. He was leaning forward shouting at the driver, and he had his hands behind his back, perhaps tied.

The witness identified the driver as heavy-set and swarthy, and picked him out of the mugshot book as Hoffa's own foster son, Charles L. 'Chuckie' O'Brien. Raised as a son by Hoffa, Chuckie had become his bodyguard and personal assistant. Now the key figure in the disappearance, he fiercely proclaimed his innocence.

The FBI did find the maroon Mercury, and sniffer dogs picked up Hoffa's scent on the back seat and in the trunk.

So who abducted Jimmy Hoffa? And was he indeed murdered?

Just before he vanished, Hoffa had drawn a million dollars in cash, the FBI revealed. Also, twice in the year before his death he had sent emissaries to the Justice Department offering evidence that would criminally implicate his arch-rival Fitzsimmons. The department wasn't interested.

Fitzsimmons, his successor as boss of the Teamsters, was obviously a prime suspect, as the man who had most to gain by ordering Hoffa's liquidation. But lung cancer killed Fitzsimmons in the summer of 1981, thereby terminating his presidency and an enduring line of inquiry.

Or was the culprit the CIA? Through Hoffa, the agency had recruited Mafiosi Sam Giancana and John Roselli to assassinate Cuba's Fidel Castro. Both Roselli and Giancana were later murdered and their killers never found.

Roselli had hinted in 1976 that he knew who had assassinated John F. Kennedy 13 years earlier. Soon after, his body (or more accurately, several pieces of it) were found floating off the Florida coast in a 55-gallon drum.

As memories faded, the investigation into the disappearance of James Hoffa seemed to be going cold. His wife died in 1980 after a long illness. His children, James P. Hoffa and Barbara Ann Crancer, continued their fight to force the FBI to release all information files.

In Hollywood's version of the affair, with Jack Nicholson in the title role of Hoffa, actor/director Danny DeVito gave a collection of possible explanations, yet chose none. The movie shed no new light on the Hoffa case and deliberately avoided making a definitive statement about his death.

THE END OF THE LINE

Then in August 1992, a hitman who claimed to have carried out nearly 100 murders came forward to say: 'I killed Jimmy Hoffa.'

The man appeared on nationwide TV in America, claiming to be dying from emphysema, and said he wanted to set the record straight. He took a lie detector test and explained how he took the contract to rub out Jimmy Hoffa. He told viewers:

'I was in Federal Prison in Atlanta, about to be paroled. A person from a known southern family contacted me and told me the contract would pay $25,000. This was too much money. Normal work was ten grand, that was the going rate, sometimes 15.

'I was flown to Detroit and taken to a junkyard. In the office there I met three men, one of them was known to me as Sally Bugs. As soon as I saw Jimmy Hoffa I knew who he was. He wasn't a tall man but he was well-built.

'Five of us including Jimmy got into a panelled truck. Sal drove and we took off. I didn't know where we were going because we were never told anything.

'We drove all the way from Detroit to

Chicago's Lake Michigan. Jimmy was gagged with tape and they drugged him with a hypodermic to keep him quiet.'

Apparently, during the trip Hoffa recognized Sally Bugs as Salvatore Briguglio, a hood who would be killed a year later in New York's Little Italy while working for no less a character than 'Tony Pro' Provenzano.

The hitman continued: 'I've clipped people who'd beg and plead and say "take pity on my family" – that kinda thing. Not Jimmy Hoffa. He was a man's man. Tough as nails.

'Jimmy refused a shot of whisky, cursed at Sally Bugs and offered half a

Above: *Hoffa helped to recruit Mafia gunmen to assassinate Cuban leader Fidel Castro, another shady link in the chain which bound him to his fate.*

SEVERAL PIECES OF THE BODY WERE FOUND FLOATING OFF THE COAST OF FLORIDA IN A 55-GALLON DRUM.

THEY DUMPED HIM OVER THE SIDE WITH LEAD WEIGHTS TAPED TO HIS LEGS. WHEN THE BUBBLES STOPPED COMING UP, THEY KNEW HOFFA WAS FINISHED.

Below: *Pickets from the Teamsters union demonstrate their loyalty to Hoffa, the man who pilfered their pension fund and plotted, even killed, in pursuit of power.*

million dollars to call off the hit. It was refused of course. At that point I think he realized that this was the end of the line.

'As darkness came, we got into a yacht and motored to what looked like a Navy pier. Sal ordered us to strip Jimmy down naked. He never asked for mercy. I had to admire the guy for that.

'He wasn't afraid. He copped no pleas. He didn't beg for anything from us. Under the seat were these pigs of lead somewhat like what are used in a Linotype. They were taped with two-inch tape to each of his legs, to be used as weights, and he was dropped over the side.

'When the bubbles stopped coming up, we pulled up the anchor, started the motor and headed back to shore.'

Couldn't they just have shot him? The hitman told television viewers: 'One of the things a mechanic does is give the customer what he wants. That was the way the customer wanted it and this was the way it was done.'

Is that how Hoffa ended his days? The tiny man of gigantic presence had fought against the Mafia and for the Mafia. As leader of America's most powerful union, he ended up doing its bidding – and cheating on his millions of members. Yet the American people still find his story fascinating. This man who was a thorn in the side of authority remains in some quarters as much of a popular hero as he was in his heyday.

Meanwhile, the umpteen conflicting theories as to his fate are added to year by year. But there is still nothing concrete – not even a 'cement overcoat'.

BIZARRE
BUT TRUE

JIM JONES AND DAVID KORESH
Mad messiahs

Every few years a new 'messiah' appears on the scene, seducing the desperate and the gullible with promises of a new life on Earth and heavenly salvation. Too often their faith is rewarded only with destruction and the most hideous deaths.

In their minds, his disciples believed the Rev Jim Jones was a saviour who would lead them to harmony and happiness.

In reality, Jones was a power-crazed zealot with scant regard for the well-being of his followers. When his earthly empire started to crumble he led almost 1,000 people to their deaths in an astonishing mass suicide rather than face disgrace and condemnation from the rest of the world.

On his orders, the people he had united at a jungle settlement in Guyana willingly slurped arsenic poisoning. His triumphal cries were ringing in their ears. 'We were too good for this world. Now come with me and I will take you to a better place.'

Jim Jones was the only, lonely child of a World War 1 veteran and a Cherokee Indian woman. His father, suffering a lung disease as a result of his service, was unable to work and survived on a paltry pension. He searched for a scapegoat for his woes and found it in the form of the country's black population. To young Jim's horror, he backed the racist Ku Klux Klan.

PULPIT POWER

To escape the shame he felt at his father's extremism, Jim immersed himself in religion. His first taste of 'pulpit power' was when he stood on the step outside his suburban home and preached the gospel to passers-by. He was 12 years old.

Jones was already deeply involved in religion and was intent on making it his life's work. He took a Bible studies course at Indiana University, working as a hospital porter to finance the extra learning. It was here he met his future wife Marceline Baldwin, a nurse four years his senior, with whom he adopted seven children from various ethnic backgrounds.

His next step was to become a pastor in an Indianapolis church, which meant first-hand experience of crossing the race divide. He was gratified to discover the faith and support he commanded among his congregation when he clashed with the bigots who wanted to keep blacks out of the church.

Above: *Masked and robed, the Ku Klux Klan sought to cow and kill black people living in America. To his horror, Jim Jones found his father was an active supporter of the menacing and sinister movement.*

Opposite: *Hundreds of devotees of Jim Jones drank poisoned cordial from a trough to die alongside their leader. Waverers were persuaded to down the spiked potion at the point of a gun.*

Above: *Pictured in 1976, the Rev Jim Jones looked clean cut and dapper. Neighbours were impressed with the charitable works carried out by Jones and his supporters. There was little to indicate that he was a budding sex maniac and sadist who would bed women, girls and even men to satisfy his enormous appetite. No one suspected he would start torturing children with electric cattle prods and administer savage beatings.*

He cautiously gauged the feelings of this new-found flock. Would they help him build his dream, a church for all races and creeds?

He discovered that he could exact money from them with relative ease. The People's Temple was duly built on the wrong side of the tracks in Indianapolis.

It was a mainly black congregation and Jones quickly assumed the style of the flamboyant coloured preachers who ranted, sang, whispered and bellowed with enormous dramatic effect.

Jones had already learned how people would unite behind him in the face of adversity. With this in mind, he publicized how he was the victim of a race hate campaign which included dynamite being thrown in his garden and a bottle being smashed in his face. As he expected, the people who sat enthralled through his compelling sermons drew together in fierce support of the man they considered their leader.

He had a dream, a vision of a socialist community where people would work for the good of others, seeking not to better their bank balance but improve their souls. He sincerely yearned to lead a peaceful colony in which brotherhood and humanity were paramount. Sadly, his ideas became warped along the way.

Once again, toying with the strength of his followers' beliefs, he branched out into faith healing. It was accompanied with all his usual flourish and showmanship but for the first time, he ventured into the realms of deceit. Among the sick and crippled people who queued up to see him were decoys from his most trusted disciples. While the genuinely sick people remained unmoved by his theatrical hands-on healing, the frauds would rise and claim they had been miraculously cured. Cruelly, he claimed he could cure cancer. In reality, the hapless victims were taken into the toilet by his wife Marceline who produced a mouldy chicken's liver in a piece of tissue claiming it was the obnoxious tumour. Jones also claimed he could raise the dead. It was a tempting lure for the old and the sick.

AN IDEAL COMMUNITY?

However, it was a dangerous ruse and Jones knew it. Before too long the state authorities and probing newspapers would be ready to expose his antics as phony. In a bold move, Jones planned the departure of himself and his trusting band to California's Redwood Valley where they could live in peace among other hippy drop-outs of the age.

On the face of it, the People's Temple was everything a community could wish for. Members were always ready to lend a hand, be it on local farms or as foster parents or in charity work. Jones himself worked tirelessly to secure local positions of political power, including the foreman of the county grand jury and a director of free legal aid services. Local police forces received donations for the widow and orphans' fund, while newspapers won cash awards for printing 'outstanding journalistic contributions to peace and public enlightenment'. By 1976 Jones was the picture of respectability when he was photographed rubbing shoulders with Rosalynn Carter, the campaigning wife of presidential hopeful Jimmy. He even received an invitation to the subsequent inauguration ceremony in Washington. With the opening of a new Temple in San Francisco, thousands more were recruited to his cause. Soon there was another Temple opened in Los Angeles. Jones decided the big city was a better hunting ground and based his whole operation there.

But behind the scenes there were sinister undertones. By now Jones, with his dyed black hair and sunglasses which never left his nose, had perverted most of his lauded principles to satisfy an egoistical mania. Disciples were told to hand over their earnings and savings and this meant the coffers of his degenerating organization were overflowing.

More worryingly, Jones appeared to have embarked on a licentious campaign, using his position of authority to bed any woman or girl he chose. Marriages were broken up and Jones appointed himself as the arbitrator for future matches. He chose the most desirable women as wives for his trusted church elders. Equally, he enjoyed intimate relations with men. All the men who joined the church were publicly humiliated for their own sexual mores. Adults judged by large assemblies to need punishment were pitted in a boxing match against one or more stronger, fitter opponents to take a beating.

Children were thrashed and tortured with an electric cattle prod. Inevitably, there were those whom Jones could not control who were shocked and disillusioned by the excesses of Jones and his cohorts. Gradually word began to spread that the People's Temple was not the golden haven it appeared to be. Officials were reluctant to believe the man who did so much work for the community was a crook and a pervert, but the dribble of bad publicity grew into a flood and was hard to ignore.

When the cracks in his American operation started to show, Jones once again took the actions of a desperado. He uprooted the movement he had moulded, this time to the struggling republic of Guyana.

> **HE CLAIMED HE COULD REMOVE CANCEROUS TUMOURS — THE 'PROOF' WAS A MOULDY CHICKEN'S LIVER WRAPPED IN TOILET PAPER.**

Below: *Supporters flocked to the People's Temples launched by Jones in America. His sermons held their rapt attention. They were astonished at his ability to heal the sick. Little did they know as they handed over the cash they had that Jones was a faker who used actors in the audience when performing 'miracles'. Once they were in the clutches of the eerie Jones it was hard to escape. This picture was taken by Greg Robinson, one of three pressmen to be killed by Jones's henchmen at Jonestown.*

IN THE NEW, 'JUST' SOCIETY THE BRAINWASHED DISCIPLES WERE FORCED TO SLAVE FROM DAWN TO DUSK, AND ANY PROTESTS WERE SWIFTLY SILENCED BY ARMED GUARDS.

BRAINWASHED

He was, he told his people, setting up 'a new, just socialist society'. A thousand of his followers, by now brainwashed and unquestioning, went with him, handing over their passports 'for safe keeping' after they arrived. Their new home, called 'Jonestown', was patrolled by armed guards, apparently to defend the residents from bandits. But it was not the Shangri-la they were led to expect. They had to work from dawn until nightfall on a diet of rice and onions. Those deemed to be slacking in their work or doubting the wisdom of the leader were put in a tiny box where they would have to stay for days at a time. Children were led through the dark corridors of the jungle to a well where they would be dunked in time after time, shrieking in terror.

Cult devotees might have lived out their days in a twisted Utopia if the growing scandal about their activities hadn't pursued them to the jungle. US Congress-man Leo Ryan was concerned enough about what he had heard from anxious constituents to investigate the sect himself.

Taking with him a TV crew, Congressman Ryan flew down to Jonestown. Once there, he told stunned disciples: 'If any of you want to leave, you can come with me under my personal guarantee of protection.'

Incredibly, despite the picture of Jones glowering over the assembly, one person plucked up enough courage to choose escape from the tyranny, then another. It was late, there would be no return home to the US that night. Suspicious of what might happen during darkness to those who wanted to leave, Ryan offered to stay at Jonestown while the TV crew spent the night in the nearest town some six miles away. Away from Jonestown, one of the TV reporters discovered a note in his pocket signed by four people which read: 'Please, please get us out of here before Jones kills us.'

But the full story of why devotees

Popular Congressman Leo Ryan (above) *was known for his forthright approach and no-nonsense attitude. He vowed to investigate claims of abuse at Jonestown. Ryan begged cult member Brian Bouquette* (right) *to speak to his mother – but in vain. The next day, he was among 911 people who took poison rather than face the condemnation of the outside world.*

Left: *Father, mother and son lie in a last loving embrace. If the children were too small to drink from a cup, their parents used syringes to squirt the deadly squash into their mouths.*

Below: *Larry Layton, 32, was one of Jones's trusted lieutenants. He asked to 'escape' Jonestown with Congressman Ryan. When a group of cult members tried to flee, he was among them and fired a hidden gun. He even tried to shoot the pilot of the rescue plane sent in. Later he was charged on five counts of murder and three of attempted murder in Jonestown.*

suddenly sought escape from the master would never be known. The extent of the power-mad frenzy displayed by Jones to those who once loved him will remain a secret for ever.

For when the journalists returned to collect Ryan and the 20 people who by then had decided to leave, a violent carnage began. One loyal follower lunged at Ryan with a knife, slashing himself in the process.

The journalists hauled Ryan onto the truck which was waiting to take them to the aircraft. But as they fled a tractor with armed assassins aboard trundled towards them. In a blast of gunfire, Ryan, a TV reporter and cameraman, a newspaper photographer and a fleeing cult member were all horribly killed. The survivors huddled together and tended each others' terrible wounds, receiving help from terrified locals who revealed aid was hours away.

Jones knew the end had come for him also. He gathered his people around him for the last time and urged them to drink the cordial he offered that had already been laced with poison. Gun-toting church elders were on hand to make sure his will was done.

Even babes in arms were to die: their parents administered the noxious squash with a syringe. Amid failing choruses of gospel songs, the scores of faithful collapsed and died. Finally, a gunshot rang out. The Rev Jim Jones, 47, fell dead with a bullet in his head. The next day, 19 November 1978, Guyanese troops found the macabre scene of death and discovered whole families cold in a last, loving embrace.

Above: *An inferno engulfed the compound at Waco after a 51-day seige, killing 87 followers of self-professed messiah David Koresh. Small children were among the dead. America watched in horror as the flames ripped through the Branch Davidian headquarters, fanned by the wind. Controversy still rages about what sparked the deadly blaze.*

THE WACO TRAGEDY

In the eighties, Vernon Howell was known to few outside his family and friends.

But by 1993 his name and face were splashed across every newspaper in the world. For Vernon Howell became David Koresh, the crazed leader of a sinister sect who died with 86 disciples in a fireball following a seven-week siege. Only nine people escaped when his headquarters at Waco, Texas, was set ablaze. Children and their mothers were among the dead.

The tragedy of such a senseless loss of life sent shock waves around the globe. There was horror that another quasi-messiah had taken control of the lives of so many; and anger that an early attempt to end the siege degenerated into a bloody shoot out. Finally, the watching world was sickened by the slaughter captured on TV cameras as the FBI moved in.

Vernon Wayne Howell was born in 1959 in Houston, Texas. His mum was just 15. Bonnie Clark, who worked in a nursing home, never married his 20-year-old carpenter father, Bobby Howell. The couple split up when Vernon was 2 years old.

Bonnie married Roy Haldeman and moved to a suburb of Dallas, but there was friction at home when young Vernon clashed with his stepfather. His hobby was reading the Bible and by the time he was 12, he had memorized the New Testament. His mother recalled how he would pray daily for long periods. 'I've seen him sitting by his bed on his knees for hours, crying and praying,' she said. 'Vernon was always a good boy.'

Despite his fervour for religious studies,

he dropped out of high school in 1977. He wanted to be a rock musician. If only he had succeeded, all those people who perished on 19 April 1993 when Waco burned might still be alive today.

When the dream of fame from guitar-strumming faded Howell looked for a new way to achieve fame for himself. Whether he planned for the infamy and notoriety now inextricably linked to his name, no one knows.

He became a member of the Seventh Day Adventist Church, being formally baptized into the faith when he was 20. The religious movement was founded in the last century on the firm belief in the Second Coming as described in the Bible's Revelation of St John. Its preaching also includes dire warnings of earthly disasters before the Son of God returns. It is particularly strong in America and the Caribbean.

But the peace-loving movement was not feisty enough for Howell. He was expelled by the time he was 22 when church elders realized his interpretation of the Bible was both radical and dubious. He was, they considered, a bad influence on the young.

By 1981 he alighted on the Branch Davidians, a group of disaffected Seventh Day Adventists who were based in Mount Carmel, in the farming heartland of Waco, Texas. It divided from the Seventh Day Adventists in the 1930s under the leadership of Victor Houteff, a Bulgarian born Adventist and, ironically, a confirmed pacifist. At the time Howell joined, it was led by Lois Roden, who was in her sixties.

THE BRUTAL MESSIAH

There followed a bizarre sequence of events which gives an early indication of Howell's disturbed state of mind. Although a humble handyman when he joined, his influence and power over the Branch Davidians mushroomed. He was showered with money taken out of the savings and pay packets of loyal followers living in San Bernadino, California. Some say he became Roden's lover. What is certain is that he and her son George fell out in spectacular style.

Howell was already calling himself a messiah, much to George's fury. In a macabre episode, George dug up a corpse from the local cemetery and challenged

Above: *Americans were shocked that a cult leader had once again taken control of the lives of so many – and once again led those misguided followers to their doom. In sight of the charred remains of the Koresh stronghold, Rhiannon Gardner of California and Linda Caliva of San Diego put up crosses in memory of those cult members slaughtered in the fire and the four ATF agents who died in the original raid.*

Left: *David Koresh, pictured here with his mother Bonnie and younger brother, was just like any other fresh-faced American boy. But after falling out with his stepfather, Vernon Howell – as he was known then – threw himself into religious studies. By the time he was 12 he had learned the entire New Testament off by heart.*

HE DUG UP THE ROTTING CORPSE AND CHALLENGED HIS MOTHER'S LOVER TO BRING IT BACK TO LIFE.

Below: *Ambitious David Koresh had the looks of a rock star. When he failed to make the big time as a musician he set his sights on religion. After being thrown out of the Seventh Day Adventist Church, he swiftly worked his way up the ranks of the Branch Davidians until he was undisputed leader.*

Howell to breathe life back into it. In reply, Howell reported the grave-robbing escapade to the police. In order to prove his claim, Howell and his supporters embarked on a raid under the cover of darkness to snatch the body. George Rodin was equally determined he would not be exposed to the sheriff. There followed a shootout which ended in arrest for Howell and his friends. They were charged with attempted murder but never convicted. Instead, George Rodin found himself behind bars on a different charge.

The squabble between the two factions in 1987 ultimately spelled the start of absolute power for Howell in the Branch Davidians. He changed his name to David Koresh and ruled with an increasing

brutality. With all charges against him dropped, the local lawmen had to return an arsenal of weapons they had seized during the troubles.

Koresh married a 14-year-old girl called Rachel Jones in Hollywood. She became mother to his son Cyrus and daughter Star.

How could a man hold so much sway over the lives of so many, for so long?

For a start, Koresh knew the workings of the Seventh Day Adventist Church well. He knew the emphasis laid on the content of the scriptures – and became an expert himself. It meant he was in a prime position to convert existing church members to his way of thinking.

Also, he knew church worshippers were told to expect the Second Coming at any

Left: *At meetings, disciples were bombarded for hours with the word according to Koresh. Koresh knew the Bible better than anyone else in the room – and he was clever enough to pervert the message to his own ends. For many his words had the ring of truth and they abandoned their loved ones and their homes to be with him at Waco.*

Below: *It was known that Koresh had a stockpile of weapons at his Waco compound. After four men were killed in a shootout, the FBI was taking no chances. They moved heavyweight equipment like this M-1 tank into position during the 51-day siege. When the FBI got the go-ahead to move in, its men were fully protected. Bullets fired by the cultists bounced off the armoury.*

time. If he presented himself as that Second Coming, he knew he would win a core of dedicated followers.

To prepare the ground for manipulation, Koresh would cage his quarries in a marathon Bible class lasting for 10 hours or more. During that time he would rant endlessly about his beliefs, brooking no opposition from his audience. Here he could plant the seeds that would flourish into a dedicated belief.

There was also an element of fear which threaded through his teachings. He was, he insisted, the Keeper of the Seven Seals, and could trigger the end of the world. Those who accepted the word that he was the Lamb of God were warmly welcomed. There were kisses, hugs, flattery and a sense of belonging. Those who refuted the claims were cast out, insulted and frequently cursed.

Like all cult leaders, he found the easiest prey were people who had lost their jobs, were recently divorced or had suffered some other setback in their lives. They were looking for fulfilment and Koresh would pose as the answer to their prayers.

He spread his net worldwide, coming to Britain in 1988 to poach more supporters from the traditional Adventists. In advance of his visit came Steve Schneider, a trusted lieutenant who had once studied at Newbold College, the Adventists' centre near Bracknell, Berkshire.

The church turned down Schneider's request to use the church and college for a series of 'Bible meetings' featuring Koresh. Undeterred, he secured a house near the college campus which still lent it some established church authority. When Koresh arrived, he would hold meetings starting at 9 am and still in full swing after midnight. Weary and befuddled, his audience were massaged into his way of thinking.

Livingstone Fagan was there. He

listened and readily believed all he heard about Koresh. Ordained as a pastor in the Seventh Day Adventist Church, he was defrocked after only three weeks after using his post to spread the word according to Koresh.

But he remained a firm believer and set about recruiting family and friends to the cause. The aim was to entice as many people as possible on a fact-finding mission to Waco to capture their imagination. In fact, many never returned home again. Once on Branch Davidian territory they were bombarded with the message morning noon and night. They were in turns humiliated and lauded by Koresh, who methodically worked away at destroying their egos and individuality.

From 5.30 am each day, the place was run like a military camp with extensive Bible study sessions. Koresh sought complete control, cutting his followers off from outsiders who would challenge his authority. At first, there was never any easy moment at which to leave. After a few weeks, most were too scared to up and go. They were told their name would go on a hit list and they would never be safe.

Australia and Hawaii were targeted as well by Koresh, greedy for increased power by boosting the size of his flock.

Above: *A wounded agent is comforted on his way to hospital. In all 20 agents were injured in the raid.*

Right: *ATF agents in full riot gear were determined to probe Koresh's spreading arsenal. But the cultists had been given a fair warning of their arrival. They were armed and ready when the agents appeared. The army of agents backed up by tanks did little to shake their determination to protect Koresh.*

Far right: *Flags flew at half mast as investigators searched for the bodies of those who died.*

The clapboard farm was fortified and the number of arms on the property increased.

Meanwhile, Koresh was running amok inside. While men were told that celibacy was the road to heaven, women were seduced and enslaved by him. It was his Biblical destiny to sleep with 144,000 virgins, he preached.

But it didn't stop there. Soon he was indulging in three-in-a-bed romps and, worse, abusing young girls. In addition to sex, they faced beatings for imagined felonies. Koresh sired numerous children and bragged about his harem. No one questioned his right to rule. For protection he was surrounded by armed guards known as the 'mighty men'.

Worried families could only guess what was going on behind closed doors. On the face of it, the Koresh community appeared relaxed and contented. One British father, whose wife and 11-year-old daughter had joined Koresh, went to Waco to see for himself what was going on. He was impressed by the specially built play area and range of schooling facilities and returned reassured, saying: 'Everyone seemed normal to me. Everyone seemed happy.'

A DEATH PROPHECY

Among his teaching, Koresh prophesied he would appear on TV in 1993 – and then die

by fire. But no one could guess at the truth of his vision until March of that year when the peace of everyday life at the compound was shattered forever.

There was deep concern at the number of weapons held at the enclave. Agents from the Bureau of Alcohol, Tobacco and

Above: *Jean Holub during a news conference on 18 March. She had taped a message to Koresh, her grandson, pleading with him to end the siege of Mount Carmel peacefully.*

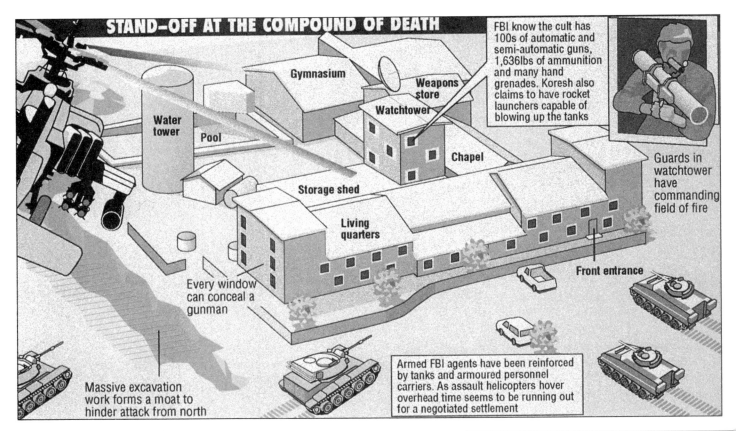

STAND-OFF AT THE COMPOUND OF DEATH

FBI know the cult has 100s of automatic and semi-automatic guns, 1,636lbs of ammunition and many hand grenades. Koresh also claims to have rocket launchers capable of blowing up the tanks

Guards in watchtower have commanding field of fire

Gymnasium

Weapons store

Watchtower

Water tower

Pool

Chapel

Storage shed

Living quarters

Front entrance

Every window can conceal a gunman

Massive excavation work forms a moat to hinder attack from north

Armed FBI agents have been reinforced by tanks and armoured personnel carriers. As assault helicopters hover overhead time seems to be running out for a negotiated settlement

Above: *A plan revealing how the FBI proposed an assault on Mount Carmel. Negotiators used high-tech gadgets to discover what was going on behind closed doors at the compound. Tiny cables could relay pictures of whole rooms while sophisticated bugging devices monitored even the most private conversation Koresh had.*

THE TRAUMATIZED CHILDREN ACTED LIKE ZOMBIES.

Right: *Three of the surviving cultists on their way to a court hearing to face charges relating to the seige. Jaime Castillo, Derek Lovelock and David Thibodeau claimed the blaze was caused by heavy-handed government tactics. Koresh, they insisted, was on the verge of surrendering, ready to lead his people to safety.*

Firearms were determined that Koresh and his followers would be investigated.

An army of them, backed by tanks, circled the sect HQ and moved in to arrest Koresh. But as they advanced they were met with a volley of gunfire from an array of automatic weapons. There was even a blast from a 50 mm howitzer. Within seconds, 20 agents were hit, four of them fatally. In the ensuing gun battle, two sect members died: Briton Winston Blake and Koresh's own daughter, Star, aged 2.

The agents withdrew, dazed and bloodied but still determined to get their man. There was nothing for it but to sit and wait. It was the start of a 51-day siege. Negotiations followed deadlock. With enough food inside to last a year and sufficient arms to hold the agents at bay, it was clear Koresh was in no mood to cave in quickly.

While diplomats tried to coax and cajole Koresh from his lair, a more scientific approach was silently set in operation. Using an armoury of high-tech gadgets and bugs, the authorities were able to spy on cult members and their leader.

Fibre-optic cables like those used in hospital surgeries were placed in walls, air vents and chimneys and used to relay

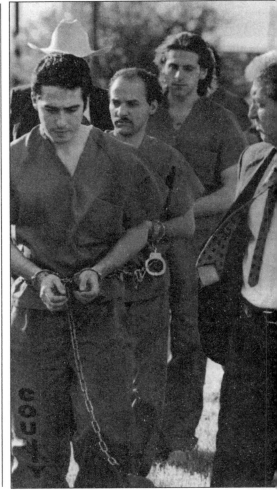

colour pictures of entire rooms. Aircraft flying overhead could monitor conversations inside and pinpoint people. Thermal imagers also helped to identify the whereabouts of those behind the walls.

As the days went past, agents began to draw a picture of life inside the compound – and learned Koresh had no plans to surrender.

In response to pleas, he did release a group of children. Shocked social workers caring for them afterwards declared they were like 'zombies'. They had been subject to the same indoctrination as their parents and now thought their adopted father had rejected them by casting them out. They were so deeply disturbed by their life-style and ordeal, they could barely communicate.

Finally, the Bureau decide charm diplomacy had run its course. It wanted Koresh and his crowd out of their hideaway – and quickly.

Koresh was talking more like a desperado than a saviour and by now the listening agents knew the extent to which he was abusing young children. They were unconvinced by promises from his lawyer that he would surrender his arms.

M-60 tanks trundled towards the compound firing harmless but disabling CS gas inside. The tanks would advance, shoot off some gas and then withdraw again to give those inside ample time to surrender. The only response was a blast of gunfire.

The disciples donned gas masks and retired to a prepared bunker at the heart of the complex. It was only when this last refuge was pierced by a tank that Koresh gave the order to die.

Agents insist fires were lit at three or more points around the site simultaneously after Koresh made his wishes known. Gunfire was also heard before agents penetrated the compound, giving rise to the theory that Koresh and his men shot those trying to escape.

Experts – who were concerned that tried and trusted methods to end the siege peaceably were ignored – have confirmed that Koresh would have probably chosen to die in a scorched earth sensation. It was unlikely he would have confided a mass suicide plan to anyone until moments before it occurred, they concur.

But the nine survivors are certain that there was no master plan for everyone to

die, that David himself wanted to walk out alive and even that a date had been set for surrender.

It was a tank breaking into the compound knocking over a kerosene lamp that torched the place, not cult followers, they maintained. The tanks also collapsed inner stairways, leaving children trapped in a room upstairs.

The final truth may never be known. Few secrets were imparted from the badly charred remains of those who died. The only certainty is that an evil ruler of bodies and minds refused to die alone.

Above: *Janet Reno had only become attorney general a matter of weeks before the Waco seige. After studying reports and analysis for a week, she sought permission from President Bill Clinton to move in on Mount Carmel and break the deadlock. She told him her concern was for the children inside at risk from poor sanitation and appalling disease.*

los q nacim a qny o hñ
a & hombre Ricos

ANCIENT RITUALS

Bizarre, erotic, or simply cruel and bloodthirsty, the significance of many ancient rituals is shrouded in mystery. What is clear is that the ancient peoples never doubted that it was worth risking their lives for their strange beliefs.

A line of young men gathers on a remote, rocky beach. Ahead of them is a half-mile swim across waters teeming with sharks. Then a perilous race up a bare rock face, vying with their rivals for the best route.

Their goal? To be first to find a rare egg and return with it intact to their 'sponsor'.

It sounds like some weird and wonderful TV game show (with the man-eating sharks thrown in to boost ratings). In fact, this old religious ritual was regarded with enormous solemnity on Easter Island, that wild and craggy volcanic outcrop that has spawned one of the world's most mysterious civilizations.

The 'Bird Man' ritual was first noted in the 15th century, though its origins may date back much further. It is probably a unique ceremony and was devised to mark out great warriors who, for a year, would become the personal earthly envoys of the god Makemake. The seabird link stems from local legend – it was believed Makemake appeared on Earth in gull form.

So, in September of every year, the athletes would gather at the island's southern village of Orongo to make the hazardous swim across the straits to the island of Moto Nui.

Each contestant would be sponsored by a tribe warrior and the training and selection programme was worthy of any modern-day Olympic swimmer. But the contestants also had to be expert climbers capable of ascending the cliffs of Moto Nui at speed. Their task would then be to track down a nest of the Manutara (or Frigate) bird and bring back an egg to Easter Island.

Opposite: *An Aztec eagle and serpent gods. Animals and birds had cherished places in Aztec culture and were credited with mystic powers – both good and evil. Eagles and seabirds were among the most revered.*

Below: *These stone figures on Easter Island remain the subject of endless fascination for archaelogists. Were they simply sculptures or do the stones hold the secrets of some long-ago lost ritual?*

el Grande Templo de Mexico

Above: *The grand temple of ancient Mexico. Human sacrifice was a regular part of the Central American religions and this etching shows victims being hurled down the steps.*

The successful swimmer's sponsor would immediately be ordained Bird Man for the year and could look forward to a key role in many other important nature rituals.

It seems the Bird Man cult never really spread to other Polynesian islands, which worshipped their own deities. But its characteristics and themes are mirrored in dozens of other ancient rites around the globe.

Most seem to follow a similar thread: namely that the Nature gods, of whatever description, must be appeased to ensure sufficient food and guard against natural disasters such as drought or flooding. Often fertility ceremonies were interwoven, again to ensure productive farms and the birth of a new, healthy generation of future workers.

Where the rituals involved some kind of test, or act of courage, this helped reinforce the religion as a doctrine worth dying for.

A GAME OF SLAUGHTER

The Bird Men of Easter Island were therefore by no means unusual in harnessing athletic skills to religious ritual. In Central America Olmec priests invented a sport called 'The Ball Game', a cross between Spanish pelota, volleyball and soccer.

By 400 BC it was spreading to the Toltecs, Aztecs and Maya, who each adapted it to local rules.

Teams would play on H-shaped courts laid out north to south or east to west. A line was drawn between two high side walls and the aim was to nudge a large rubber ball into your opponent's half, using only hips, knees and elbows, under rules very close to volleyball.

A team could also score an outright victory by guiding the ball through either of a pair of stone rings which jutted out from each wall about 20 feet above the ground.

Such marksmanship was rare. The rings were only a little larger than the ball. But, bizarrely, if a player did succeed he was allowed to take the clothes and worldly goods of any spectators he and his team could catch.

It was not a poor man's pastime and in fact only noblemen were allowed to play. They kitted themselves out in protective padding, leather jerkins – even facemasks and gloves. Yet despite these safeguards serious injuries, even death, were accepted as part of the game.

Such intense action gave it a popular following, but it was the ritual significance that was the real hook.

The court was supposed to represent the

Universe. The stone rings were sunset and sunrise and the route of the ball portrayed the paths of the Sun and Moon.

Aztecs would study the course of a game intensely to see what it predicted for the future. In one case the Aztec ruler Montezuma played against a neighbouring chief to test the merit of a seer's claim that strangers would overthrow him.

Montezuma won the first few games but lost the match and, legend has it, it was not long afterwards that the assault on Mexico was started by Hernando Cortez.

The implications for teams which lost were immense. Their side bets could leave them so broke that they were forced into slavery to ensure they got food and board. The idea was that they could buy their freedom back for the same price if they ran into money.

For the Maya people the stakes were even higher. Some matches ended with the losing team ritually slaughtered.

If sport quickly became absorbed into ancient rites, dances and acting soon took on even more significance as a connecting link between mankind and Mother Nature.

FERTILITY RITES

Sometimes these took the form of a morale-boosting attempt to highlight people's mastery of the forces around them. One classic example of this is the bull-leaping dance of the Minoans, a culture which ruled Crete for 500 years from 1920 BC.

This dance required young men to somersault over a bull's horns, proving that man was indeed the dominant power on Earth. The animal, itself feted as an example of male fertility at its finest, was never harmed. Many historians believe the later Greek legend of the Minotaur is rooted in the bull-leaping ceremony.

The emphasis on man's dominance was, however, less common in rituals than the desire to appease the wild powers of

IF THEY LOST THE MATCH PLAYERS WERE IN DANGER OF LOSING THEIR FREEDOM — OR EVEN THEIR LIVES.

Below: *The mythical Minotaur is one of many half-man-half-beast creatures that feature in the old religions. Here the Minotaur is about to be slain by the Greek, Theseus.*

Above: *Pumpkins cut into the faces of monsters are a traditional part of Halloween today. The Celts called the festival Samain Eve. It was a night when the forces of magic poured from their boltholes in woods, caves and burial mounds.*

nature. Who wanted to spend time heralding the glory of humanity when the summer's harvest had just been wiped out by flooding?

In parts of Europe and Asia it is still the custom to build a straw figure, representing the Nature Spirit, which is then carried through the village accompanied by dozens of wailing, mourning women. Depending on local custom the straw man is then either buried, tossed into water (considered a useful rain charm) or brought back to life and carried among the rejoicing women back to the village.

Occasionally the straw doll is given a phallus – a plea to the fertility gods – and enclosed in a coffin.

Other forms of the ritual centre on dressing the doll in a man's shirt and carrying it to the boundary of a neighbouring village. Women then tear the figure to bits and hang its shirt on a sapling.

The tree is cut down soon afterwards and borne home amid much celebration. Folklore suggests it is the symbol of rebirth for humanity, which is itself portrayed in the form of the destroyed doll.

In some parts the effigy is replaced by a young man called the 'King of the May' (many nature rituals were and are performed around this month because it was an important pagan festival before Christianity) who is swathed in bark and bouquets of flowers.

At the end of the ceremony his attendants give him a head start before chasing after him. If he escapes them he holds office for a year. If they catch him he is subjected to a mock beheading, his crown is struck off and his 'corpse' carried on a bier to the nearest neighbouring village.

The idea behind this, seemingly, is to inflict the spirit of a useless king on the neighbours in the hope that it won't dog your own chances of future prosperity.

Other forms of nature worship include sword dancing or, more commonly in England, Morris dancing. Both are tributes intended to ensure that the seasons continue in their ordered manner, that the soil stays fertile and the crops arrive in abundance.

The Morris men and women, with their fussy white pleated shirts, white trousers or skirts with bells at the knee and hats covered with flowers, are still a common enough sight on English village greens.

Traditionally the leader bears a sword which has a piece of cake spiked on the point. As the dance progresses, slices are handed out to the audience who in turn are expected to cough-up some money to the 'Treasury', a money chest slung round the shoulders of a Morrisman called the Squire or Clown.

He will generally carry his symbol of office – a stick with a bladder tied to one end and a cow's tail at the other.

The dancers bear maces or wands, which they clash together during the course of the dance. Cups and lances also figure prominently and it is thought these are key symbols of what remains essentially a fertility rite steeped in mystery and legend.

Many old civilizations saved their reverence for the forces of nature – Sun and Moon, night and day, wind and sea and thunder and lightning. But sometimes tribal leaders have also found themselves elevated to the status of gods. This could mean their subjects regarded their well-being as crucial to the survival of the entire community.

It followed that if the leader got sick, the omen was bad. If he showed great courage, vigour or wisdom, the portents would be rosy.

This kind of adulation could, of course, cut both ways. There were established rules laid down to discover when a leader was past his best and needed replacing. If he stayed on, and wasn't up to the job, the god he represented could wreak a terrible revenge.

The methods used were both sneaky ... and ruthless.

Earlier this century an old African tribe called the Shilluk, which lived close to the White Nile, would worship its king as a reincarnation of its legendary founder Nyakang. Nyakang was the rain-giver, on whom all life and prosperity depended. He had to be appeased at all costs.

A ROYAL EXECUTION

The problem for a king was that he could not be allowed to get old or decrepit. If he did, legend had it that men would die young, cattle would sicken and crops fail.

The tribe elders would therefore keep a close eye on their king as he advanced in years and one of the main tests of his health rested on how well he satisfied the sexual desires of his wives, of whom he had many.

If he failed to come up to their expectations they would report his performance to the chiefs who would then immediately condemn the king to death (there was no right of appeal in this court).

Often the first an unfortunate monarch would glean from such plottings would be on awakening from his mid-morning nap to find a long white cloth had been laid over his entire body. This indicated the grim news that sentence had been passed. The king would then be taken prisoner and starved to death, with a young maiden of the tribe assigned to tend his needs over his last days.

This method of execution was later abandoned as cruel after one, unknown, king suffered too long. It was replaced with a quicker – though equally horrific – end with the king strangled in a specially built execution hut.

A similar religious system existed in Nigeria until recent times. Here the Ju-Ju, or priest-king, was elected for seven years during which time he had the riches of his people heaped upon him. However, at the end of that time he was expected to kill himself, always assuming a usurper had not already succeeded in despatching him.

Despite the obvious drawbacks in running for priest-king it seems the exotic 7-year life-style attracted plenty of

candidates who saw death afterwards as a price well worth paying.

In Ancient Britain the Celts had a similar system in which every king had his *geasa*, a nature spirit who ensured farming and prosperity would flourish. If crops failed or cattle died the king would take the rap for somehow displeasing his *geasa*. It is unclear whether he would suffer summary execution as a result.

The problem of choosing a new king was particularly tricky for the old religions.

IF THE KING FAILED TO SATISFY THE VORACIOUS SEXUAL APPETITES OF HIS MANY WIVES, HE PAID THE ULTIMATE PRICE.

Above: *The Cerne Abbas giant. Childless women still sit on the tip of the figure's penis in the hope that it will help them conceive.*

CHILDLESS WOMEN RESORTED TO THE GIANT'S ENORMOUS PHALLUS IN A DESPERATE ATTEMPT TO CONCEIVE A CHILD.

Above: *Julius Caesar saw the Druids as a dangerous and well-organized resistance movement. But he failed to stamp them out completely.*

Right: *Druids worship at Stonehenge in 1974. Though many identify the religion with the monument, Stonehenge is at least 1,000 years older than the first Druids.*

A ruler might have had dozens of children, some born at almost the same time to different wives. Sorting out heirs was nigh on impossible and rather than hold an election Celtic Druid priests persuaded the people that they could identify the rightful heir by going into a 'bull dream' or trance.

This involved slaughtering a bull and allowing the chief Druid to gorge himself on the meat. He would then fall into a trance while others of his religion recited incantations over him.

Once the sated priest had recovered he would recount his dreams and deduce from them the identity of the new king.

THE OLD MAGIC

The Celts were particularly attached to ritual, to the point where it governed almost everything they did. It took on a supreme importance during the celebration of their two main seasons (warm and cold).

In Ireland all four main seasons were marked with festivals, the most important being Samain, a date we now call Halloween.

It marked the end of one year and the beginning of another and was a time when cattle would be herded in and slaughtered for winter meat supplies. Only those beasts needed for breeding would be spared.

Samain Eve was also the night when the world was deemed to be assaulted by the forces of magic pouring from old caves and burial mounds. It was thought that mortals could pass the other way into the kingdoms of fairies and hobgoblins.

Folk legends linked to Samain refer to the god Dagda, always portrayed as a figure of immense strength and appetite and carrying a mighty club. He was considered a god of fertility, rejuvenation and endurance and among the many Celtic tributes to him is the massive chalk-cut figure in Dorset – the Cerne Abbas giant – whose most striking features are an enormous phallus and serrated club.

To this day childless women sometimes sit on the tip of the figure's penis in the hope mystical forces will help them to conceive.

The other main Celtic festival, Beltane, was celebrated at the beginning of May. It was a time when cattle could be driven back to graze on open grassland and was marked by the burning of beacons across the land.

Often terrified animals would be driven between two blazing bonfires, a rite thought to protect them from disease.

Perhaps more than any other ancient British Isles religion, the Druids are remembered as a people who made human

sacrifice a way of life. The most usual method would be by knife, spear or sword, with the blood of the chosen one poured on to sacred objects such as stones or old trees. But there are also recorded instances of burnings, drownings and hangings.

Caesar described in his writings how Gaulish Celts would build massive wicker baskets, pack them with living victims (preferably, though not necessarily criminals) and set the frame alight. This sacrifice was supposed to ensure the well-being of the tribe.

Drownings would be performed under strict ceremonial rules, the hapless victim forced headfirst into a barrel of water and held under until all struggling ceased.

Life may have seemed cheap, but to the Celts death was never considered an end. So obsessed were Celtish warriors with the fate of their victims that they would decapitate them and suspend a gruesome array of trophies on the bridles of their horses. The aim, it appears, was to bring the ghosts of the vanquished under the power of the victor.

For years Stonehenge, one of the world's greatest prehistoric sites, was thought to be a temple for Druidic rites. Some evidence has been advanced suggesting that the Druids did, at one time, use it for their rituals.

But in fact Stonehenge is at least 1,000 years older than the Druid religion, built with surprising skill by the ancient Britons as either a temple or some kind of astronomical observatory.

Many elaborate theories have been advanced as to its true purpose but none have produced solid proof.

THE EGYPTIAN WAY OF DEATH

If Stonehenge was a wonder of ancient architecture, the great pyramids of Egypt are close to a miracle. Their purpose as burial chambers is clear, but the extraordinarily precise design, and elaborate death rituals, gives glimpses of an intelligence and civilization which modern people still find difficult to fathom.

The kings of Ancient Egypt were considered to need to have all their worldly goods entombed with them when they died. Food, weapons, clothes, money and jewels were seen as necessities of death upon

which the fragile new spirit would rely as he or she wandered through the afterlife.

This was also why the Egyptians developed the art of mummification, or embalming, a ritual elevated almost to an art form in its aim to preserve the body for the convenience of the soul.

First, all internal organs would be carefully removed from the corpse (on the grounds that they would decay quickest). Then the body would be dried out with salt water, dusted with a type of bicarbonate of soda, wrapped in bandages, soaked in oils and finally placed in a painted coffin.

Throughout the rite, magical spells

Above: *Stonehenge. Anyone who has visited the strange forbidding stones can only marvel at the atmosphere they generate. The reason for the construction is still questionable – was it a site for ritual ceremony or some giant astronomical computer?*

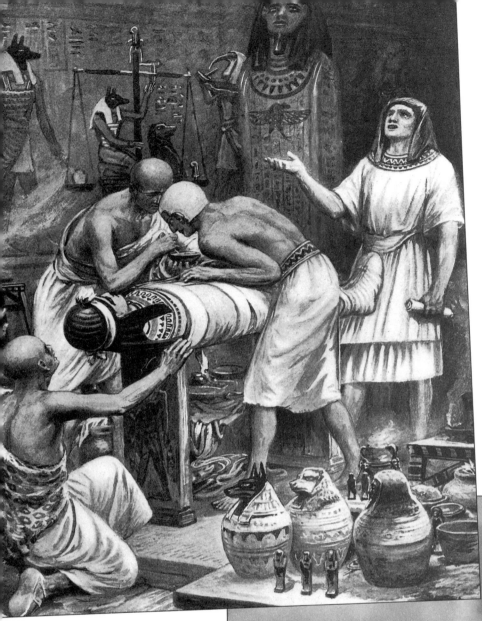

would be chanted to ensure the spirit could look forward to everlasting life in the underworld.

Some of the richest Egyptians would even set up a trust fund to pay a priest's salary after their death.

His main job would be to replenish the grave regularly with food and water, removing the rotting morsels left on previous visits.

In recent years followers of the so-called pyramidology cult – founded by those who believe that mystical forces flow through the pyramids – have used these customs to construct their own incredible theories.

Some claim that a tomato placed under a precisely constructed and sited pyramid model will take longer to rot than one left next to it in an ordinary cardboard box. The same strange forces are said to sharpen razor blades mysteriously.

No conclusive scientific proof has ever been produced to support this claim.

Whatever their hidden qualities, the pyramids were marvels of early

Above: *Embalmers at work on the body of a wealthy Egyptian. All internal organs would have been removed in a process interwoven with magical rites.*

Right: *The Cheops pyramid and the Sphinx. The pyramid contains around 6 million tons of stonework covering an area of 15 acres. It is the only one of the original seven wonders of the ancient world still surviving.*

engineering. One, the tomb of the King-God Cheops, is the only one of the original seven wonders of the ancient world still surviving.

Like most pyramids it was the focal point of a meticulously constructed complex of funeral buildings, all designed under strict ritualistic rules to safeguard the royal journey into the spirit world.

The pyramid of Cheops covers 15 acres, is 450 feet tall and contains an estimated six million tons of stonework. At least two 'emergency' tombs were crafted in case the king died suddenly before the masterpiece was complete.

The actual tomb chamber, measuring 16 feet by 34 feet, was positioned high above ground level. The king's stone coffin was laid on a tiled floor and on the face of the mummy was laid a gold mask dripping with jewels. Around it were arranged the inevitable weaponry and vitals, and even Cheops's favourite furniture found its way inside.

As the death rite ended the coffin, and all exits from the chamber, were sealed. On their way out labourers pulled away the props that held up three massive blocks. These slid over the burial chamber entrance with such precision that it was impossible to tell from outside where the door lay.

When Cheops's grave was eventually raided in the 9th century by the Caliph al-Mamum, he could find no way in and was reduced to boring straight through the stone itself.

Even the narrow ascending passage used by priests as an escape tunnel after administering last prayers was plugged by huge pieces of granite.

Just for good measure word was spread that terrible curses had been laid ready to descend upon the head of anyone who dared to attempt a break-in.

Around the pyramid lay many monuments and the funeral temple where priests carried out the 'survival rites' which it was hoped would ensure the king's safe transit to the other world. Excavations in nearby rock have uncovered small boats, though their purpose has never been explained.

THE UNIQUE POWERS OF THE PYRAMIDS ARE STILL UNDER INVESTIGATION TODAY.

Below: *A model boat from the Tutankhamun exhibition at the British Museum. The Egyptians believed their kings would need all worldly goods with them in their tombs for use in paradise.*

THEY MADE THEIR ENEMIES'
SKULLS INTO DRINKING
GOBLETS AND DELIGHTED IN
DRINKING WINE FROM THEM.

Right: *Papyrus from the Ancient Egyptians' 'Book of the Dead' shows departed souls in their lives on the 'other side'.*

Below: *Tutankhamun's gold death mask. No wonder the tomb robbers of ancient Egypt risked their lives to plunder the world's wealthiest tombs.*

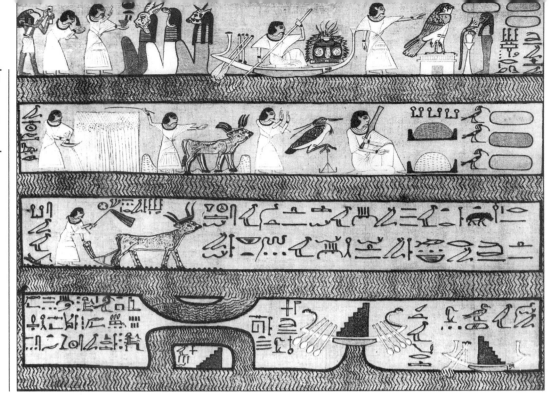

RITUAL ATROCITIES

If death rituals were important to the Egyptians, they were a way of life to the Scythians, perhaps the single most powerful tribe ever to roam the Steppelands of Russia.

Almost every important occurrence would be marked by ritual atrocities and even the simple act of having guests to dinner was bound by long-established ground rules.

It was the custom to make drinking goblets out of the skulls of enemies and any visitor sipping his wine from one would be regaled with colourful – and rather too detailed – accounts of the passing of its original owner.

Warriors were expected to drink the blood of the first opponent they killed, a ritual linked to enslaving the fallen man's ghost. And once a year Scythian fighters would gather for a festival to drink from skull cups and tot up the number of slayings each had achieved over the previous 12 months.

Any warrior whose tally was nil was treated with contempt by his brothers and forced to endure incessant jeering and teasing at the hands of the women and children.

For the Scythian kings who reigned 2,000 years ago, the expectation of a glorious afterlife was a view cherished from early childhood.

And when the grim reaper called on them he could count on a great many more souls into the bargain.

It was accepted that a king would need his loyal servants in death just as much as in life. If he died, they would have to die too.

According to the 5th-century Greek historian Herodotus, the death rituals of the Scythians – centred on tombs called *kurgans* – were among the most elaborate and complicated ever devised.

He wrote: 'When a king dies they dig a great square pit and, when it is ready, they take up the corpse which has been previously prepared in the following manner.

'The belly is slit open, cleaned out, and filled with aromatic substances, crushed galingale [a sweet-smelling plant] parsley seed and anise. It is then sewn up once more and the whole body coated with wax.

'The corpse is laid in the tomb on a mattress with spears fixed in the ground on either side to support a roof of brush laid on wooden poles. In other parts of the great square pit various members of the king's household are buried beside him: one of his concubines, his butler, cook, groom, steward and chamberlain – all of them strangled.

'Horses are buried too – and gold cups – and a selection of his other treasures.

'This ceremony over, everybody with great enthusiasm sets about raising a mound of earth, each competing with his neighbour to make it as big as possible. At the end of a year another ceremony takes place: they take 50 of the best of the king's remaining servants, strangle and gut them, stuff the bodies with chaff and sew them up again.

'These servants are native Scythians, for the king has bought no slaves, but chooses people to serve him from amongst his subjects.'

Some 2,000 years later it is easy to dismiss the Scythians and Druids as bloodthirsty heathens meting out pointless deaths.

Yet it seems they had none of the doubts of the modern age as to the promise of an afterlife. To them, rituals were the link to an unknown world – visible evidence of the life cycle.

Bizarre and brutal … but never pointless.

Above: *These scenes from Scythian life were found on 3rd- or 4th-century vases found north of the Black Sea. Scythian kings would often take their entire household with them to the grave. They reasoned that they would need servants just as much in death as in life.*

SHIPWRECKS
Riches of the sea

Billions of pounds' worth of treasure lies abandoned in wrecked ships, waiting to be snatched from the clutch of the jealous sea. For those daredevils prepared to risk their lives the rewards are obvious: a fortune in gold and silver, or an agonizing death.

There are few places in the world that can match the Isles of Scilly's record for disaster at sea. For centuries mariners on the Western Approaches to England learned the hard way how this ten-square-mile stretch of treacherous rocks and reefs could destroy any ship whose master was foolish enough to stray too close.

Many thousands lost their lives through poor navigation or were dragged to their deaths in lethal currents amid some fierce Atlantic storm. Not for nothing is one stretch of this unforgiving coast called 'Hell Bay'.

The Scillies are truly a ships' graveyard and in these shallow waters beneath ever-shifting sands hoards of treasure still lie untouched. So far the islands have produced two outstanding successes for the marine archeologists.

The first was the wreck of the *Colossus*, the second that of HMS *Association*. Both finds owed much to the bravery and skill of the late Cornishman Roland Morris, a man who fashioned the art of modern-day treasure-hunting.

For as long as he could remember the story of the *Association* had fascinated Morris. The events of the wild night she went down with the pride of her fleet

Opposite: *Admiral Sir Clowdisley Shovell. Hours before the HMS* Association *disaster he had feared his fleet was off course. Yet a conference among his captains did little to improve matters. The navigational position of the ships was estimated too far south and in the dead of night they blundered onto a lethal Scilly reef.*

Below: *The* Association *and other ships on the rocks – 1,648 lives were lost that night and the sea around Scilly heaved with the bodies of young men.*

Above: *Islanders find the body of Sir Clowdisley washed up on beach. They buried him just above the high-water mark at Porth Hellick, St Mary's Island. The body was later recovered and given a full state funeral at Westminster Abbey.*

THE BRITISH FLEET SAILED PROUDLY ONWARDS, MERE HOURS FROM HOME – AND DISASTER; BEFORE DAWN THE SEA WOULD HEAVE WITH CORPSES.

remain probably the greatest Royal Navy loss in home waters. It was a night the waters around Scilly heaved with the corpses of young men.

AN ERROR OF JUDGEMENT

The 90-gun *Association* was the flagship of Admiral of the White Sir Clowdisley Shovell, one of the most experienced seamen of his day. On 29 September 1707 he set sail from Gibraltar after taking part in the siege of Toulon. English sea power was at its height and Sir Clowdisley's men o' war, which totalled 12 ships of the line, would have been an awe-inspiring sight as they headed for home waters.

The vessels included the 100-gun *Royal Anne*, flagship of Sir George Byng (Vice-Admiral of the Blue), the 96-gun *St George*, captained by James Lord Dursley, the 70-gun *Eagle*, under Captain Robert Hancock, and the 48-gun *Romney* under Captain William Coney. There were also four fireships, among them HMS *Firebrand* and her master Captain Francis Piercy.

On the morning of Wednesday 22 October the fleet was approaching the mouth of the English Channel. Sir

Clowdisley ordered three vessels to be detached from the main body to Falmouth, enabling advance preparations to be made for the reception of the entire fleet. Around midday *Lennox*, *Valeur* and *Phoenix* steered ahead on an easterly course. By nightfall it was clear they had fallen victim to a serious navigational error.

All three ships fell among the Scilly rocks and it was only the skill of the captains which prevented serious loss of life. *Lennox* and *Valeur* managed to keep clear and later anchored off the main island, St Mary's, but *Phoenix* was holed and had to be beached close to the island of Tresco to stop her sinking. The repairs later forced her to convert to a sixth-rate warship.

Back at the main fleet Sir Clowdisley was himself in trouble. He now suspected he was off-course and ordered his ships to heave to while soundings were taken. There followed a brief counsel of all the sailing masters and a consensus was reached. They were almost certainly around the latitude of Ushant, it was agreed, which meant a due easterly course would take them safely into the open waters of the English Channel.

Only one master dissented – Captain

Henry Hobart of the *Panther*. He argued strongly that they were much closer to the Scillies than was being suggested and risked being blown on to some of the outlying reefs. It was a brave speech, and his estimated position was, in fact, extremely close to the mark. But Sir Clowdisley overruled him and ordered the fleet to steer due east.

Why the seamanship of him and most of his captains was so sadly lacking will always be a mystery. Perhaps it was an eagerness to get home, over-confidence in their instincts or simply a blind determination not to lose an argument. Whatever the reason, they were now only hours from disaster.

By 6 pm the ships were underway again and the die leading them to certain doom was cast. As the fleet edged forward Hobart had a growing sense of dread. He could not ignore his admiral but he had a duty to save the lives of his crew if possible. Quietly, almost without being noticed, the *Panther* glided slowly down to the southern flank of the fleet where she remained one of the few ships which didn't have to change course.

THE WRATH OF THE SCILLIES

By now the weather was muggy and stormy and the watch on HMS *Association* – the ship leading the vanguard – was having understandable difficulty spying through the gloom. At around 8 pm she struck on the deadly Gilstone reef and sank with all hands. *Eagle* and *Romney* quickly followed her to their doom and *St George* also ran on, only to be lifted off minutes later by a gigantic wave.

Firebrand was lost, though 25 of her crew were saved, but the most remarkable escape was engineered by the *Royal Anne*, whose officers thought fast enough to set the topsails and weather the storm only a few yards away from the teeth of more rocks.

When Navy men later checked the muster lists for the wrecked ships the appalling carnage was finally laid bare. At least 1,648 lives were lost in the space of a few hours, among them Sir Clowdisley's. His body floated ashore at Porth Hellick, a sheltered cove on St Mary's, and the local folk buried him just above the high tide

mark. According to one (unlikely) legend he was still alive on the beach but was murdered by an old crone hunting booty from the wrecks who had spotted his expensive rings. It is said the woman confessed on her deathbed, but no record was ever kept of her name.

Sir Clowdisley's body was later recovered by the Navy and taken to Plymouth aboard the *Salisbury*. From there it was brought to Westminster Abbey for a state funeral with full military honours.

Three years later the first treasure-hunters had moved on to the site of the *Association* wreck, though it seems with only limited success. A letter to the *London Letter*, an old Scottish newspaper, of 9 July 1710 read: 'We hear from Scilly that the gentlemen concerned in the wreck where Sir Clowdisley Shovell was cast away have taken several iron guns and seven brass guns, with a cable, and have found the *Association* in four fathom at low water, the hull of the ship being whole, wherein there is a vast treasure – the Queen's Plate, several chests of money, beside ten chests of Sir Clowdisley's own, with great riches of the Grandees of Spain. 'The divers go down

HOBART'S SENSE OF IMPENDING DOOM GREW STRONGER AS HE TRIED TO EDGE HIS SHIP INTO A SAFER POSITION.

Below: *Lady Hamilton, mistress of Lord Nelson and wife of Sir William Hamilton. At least Sir William managed to come to terms with her infidelity. He never quite got over the loss of his priceless cargo.*

Above: *Turner's* **St Michael's Mount.** *Scenes such as this fire dreams of long-lost treasure in every amateur scuba diver.*

in a copper engine and continue two hours under water.'

But the report goes on to hint that high winds and 'boisterous' seas had already scattered much of the sunken hoard. A fortune in pieces of eight and pieces of four still lay waiting to be found.

Some 91 years after the *Association* foundered it was the turn of HMS *Colossus* to suffer the wrath of the Scillies. She was

another of the Navy's front-line ships, a 74-gun man o' war of about 1,700 tons.

At least her skipper, George Murray, could hardly be blamed for losing her. He'd hove to just off St Mary's and, seeing the signs of a vicious Atlantic storm brewing, secured her with three cables. Within minutes of the full fury of the storm sweeping in, one cable had parted and two others dragged. At dark she was on the rocks and her priceless cargo, a collection of ancient vases from the Mediterranean, was lost.

The vases – more than 1,000 of them – belonged to Sir William Hamilton (whose wife Emma was Nelson's mistress), and had been amassed during his time as British government minister in charge of Sicily. That terrible night he also lost large marble friezes, terracotta, bronzes and some fabulous Greek and Italian jewellery.

It would have been limited consolation to him to learn that most of the crew saved themselves in the rigging and only one man, quartermaster Richard King, died.

TREASURE TROVE

So it was that the fate of these ships would become intertwined, thanks to the tenacity of Roland Morris. He'd studied their history for most of his life and knew the waters well. During the war he'd worked tirelessly off the Cornish coast as a salvage

Right: *Turner's* **The Shipwreck.** *This would have been a tragically familiar scene to seamen of the 18th and 19th centuries.*

THE TREASURE-HUNTER WAS DETERMINED TO COMMIT MARINE SUICIDE IN A HOME-MADE DIVING BELL.

Left: *Faulkner's* **The Shipwreck,** *1827. The sight of any vessel on the rocks was enough to bring locals running to the nearest shoreline in their scores, in search of wrecked cargo.*

diver, building up a massive personal dossier on the most likely locations of known wrecks. But it wasn't until 1967 that he was able to put that knowledge to the test.

Throughout the early sixties interest had been growing in the fate of Sir Clowdisley's fleet. However, confusing marks and entries on old maps meant the precise location was far from certain.

Between 1965 and 1967 the Naval Air Command Sub Aqua Club used inshore minesweepers manned by the Royal Navy Reserve to search for the *Association*. They found it right at the end of their allotted time, on 4 July 1967, resting in sand beneath the Gilstone Ledge.

It was left to Morris to confirm what the team suspected. He'd obtained a salvage licence from the Ministry of Defence for the *Association* and had already guessed, from his knowledge of currents and seabed movements, that she lay on the Gilstone. Within days of his operation commencing he'd located three bronze cannons and Sir Clowdisley's personal plate.

At first Morris used explosives to free the cannon but was forced to stop amid furious objections from the National Maritime Museum and the Institute of Archaeology. Eventually sheer persistence was rewarded and the team recovered a huge cache of coins, including Spanish pieces of eight, silver crowns and golden guineas and Portuguese 4,000 *reis* pieces.

The find sparked the marine equivalent of the Californian gold rush as dozens of unauthorized treasure-hunters converged on the spot. In the excitement two of the enthusiastic amateur boats capsized and one die-hard fortune seeker even attempted to launch himself on the *Association* in a copper diving-bell he'd made himself. Fortunately, Morris was able to talk him round.

Eight years later, armed with a British government licence, Morris achieved his second major triumph. He led a four-man team onto the ship he believed to be the *Colossus* and quickly gained confirmation in the form of a Greek potsherd. The treasure trove that followed set the world of marine archeology alight.

The team divided its seabed search area

Below: *1829 shipwreck engraving. Treasure ships such as this could scatter cargo for miles. The combination of shifting sands and unpredictable currents made the treasure-hunter's task enormously difficult.*

*Above: **Scenes of panic aboard the wreck of the Deutschland, 1875. Survivors scramble to reach the safety of a tug.***

*Below: **Wrecked and saved. How the Boy's Own Paper depicted the drama of a shipwreck.***

into square metres with a man assigned to search each square four times. By the end of the salvage operation they had brought up more than 7,400 fragments dating back to the 4th century. Handles, rims, bases, bowls and cups were painstakingly logged and reassembled under the watchful eye of the British Museum.

After the *Colossus*, Morris entered semi-retirement, concentrating his energies on his Penzance restaurant, the Admiral Benbow. He would later take his greatest secret to his grave.

A GRISLY END

If Roland Morris drew on instinct and perseverance for results, Herbo Humphreys is the man who has turned the art of treasure-hunting into a science.

His hunting ground is the eastern Atlantic – especially the Little Bahama Bank – a sea area where many a Spanish merchantman met a grisly end. Just as the *Association* and *Colossus* fascinated and tantalized Morris, so the 'Floating Fort Knox', that is the *Maravillas*, has been an abiding challenge for Humphreys.

The *Maravillas* lies on Little Bahama, her fabulous cargo spread over a massive debris field. Her official manifest shows that around £600 million (at today's prices) of bullion, coins and jewels went down with her. However, historians estimate she could have had up to 11 times as much in contraband aboard. They believe around 90 chests of gold and silver lie somewhere on the seabed.

Humphreys, a former pilot, ship's captain, parachutist and Vietnam veteran, had only two interests as a boy – boats and business. He made his fortune in his teens,

Left: *A picture that sums up the romance, drama and danger of a storm at sea in 1896. It shows Captain Nutman of the wrecked vessel* **Aidar** *refusing to leave an injured crewman as a lifeboat approaches.*

Below: *Wreck of the* **Cromdale**, *1913. She broke up inside two hours during a ferocious south-westerly storm in British waters.*

staking the £5,500 he won in a horse-riding competition on Philippines Gold at 25 cents a share. He later sold the stock at $30.

From there it was a tour of Vietnam, a property and travel business and a hotel investment on the Cayman Islands. An avowed anti-communist, he worked through peaceful means to undermine the Sandanistas in Nicaragua and later took the crusade against extremism on to Guatemala, Laos and the Philippines.

Above: *The* Campania *sinking after a collision in 1918 with HMS* Revenge. Campania *had been converted into one of the world's first aircraft carriers.*

Below: *A pair of schooners on the rocks in Bigbury Bay, south Devon, England, in 1925.*

On the way he logged the possible sites of a lot of interesting shipwrecks. When the communist threat died down, and with his business empire in sound shape, he began to devote more time to his hobby of finding sunken treasure. More especially, finding the *Maravillas*.

The ship – full title *Nuestra Señora de las Maravillas* – was heading home to Cadiz, in Spain, from Havana when disaster struck. On the night of 4 January 1656 her crow's nest watch had clearly

been in a mellow and relaxed mood amid the beautifully calm seas, but his mood changed in an instant when he spotted white water churning almost underneath the ship's bows.

The *Maravillas* had somehow drifted on to Little Bahama's western edge … and the rest of her fleet were close behind. The captain ordered cannon fire to warn the other masters away, but it was too late. His vessel was rammed by another ship and began to founder.

As she went down many of the 650 people aboard pleaded with priests such as Don Diego Portichelo de Ribadenevra, of the Holy Metropolitan Church, Lima, for absolution. In a colourful and emotional account of the mayhem, he later told a Spanish marine investigation at Castile: 'The confusion of the people was so great that they did not realize the importance of the sails to get them out of danger and instead occupied themselves in trying to stem the flow of the water pouring into the ship.

'With the sails idle, the currents rapidly drove the ships towards the banks. She bumped against the rocks so forcefully that her seams began to crack. Though the people were bailing with four pumps and pails the water rose as high as the second deck.

Above: *A floating coffin. The wreck of the* **Morro Castle** *attracted huge crowds of sightseers at Asbury Park, New Jersey, on 9 September 1934.*

'Up to that time I had heard confessions from many people, among them Admiral Don Matias de Orellana who told me that we would surely die and that I should grant absolution to everyone … they took me to the poop deck with many people following us who wanted to confess. They told me I should confess them in general and that they did not want to die without it. Noticing their determination and given the short time that remained for us I wasted no words and abbreviated as much as possible.'

All around him men were diving into the seas to find certain death. With their pockets still crammed with gold they sank to the bottom like stones. Portichelo de Ribadenevra told the inquiry how he prepared to swim for it, tearing off his shirt to reduce his weight in the water. He said: 'There I was, left in my underwear, the crucifix that I had brought with me in my hand.

'At that time I heard a voice saying "Is there some priest who can absolve me for I have been the greatest sinner in the world?" I stood up on the hatch cover with some difficulty. My companions held me by the belt of my underpants. I don't know how, I suddenly found myself forgetting about the danger I was in. I raised my voice and told

them: "Here is a priest. Say now: I sinned, my Lord God, and I shall absolve you."'

So it carried on through that grim night. Some two score souls survived clinging to the wreckage but more than 600 were doomed. By the time dawn arrived and another ship of the fleet came to their rescue all that could be heard was the sound of a quiet hymn floating across the water on the breeze.

The passage of the years has not lessened the scale of the tragedy. However, it has ensured that nothing about Humphreys's task is easy. Neither is it cheap.

The payroll includes marine archivists in Spain, restorers and marketing experts to turn artefacts raised into hard cash and the staggering £180,000 per month cost of operating on the 160-mile patch of seabed for which the Bahamian Government has granted salvage rights.

Humphreys has brought in the most advanced gear in the world, such as satellite-linked global navigation aids, able to pinpoint the user on the Earth's surface to 200 yards, sonar, magnometers and a highly skilled crew of divers and engineers. He has ploughed £3 million of his personal wealth into the project and has so far pulled out about the same in finds. But with up to

THE MEN JUMPED OVERBOARD BUT THE STOLEN GOLD IN THEIR POCKETS SENT THEM PLUMMETTING TO THE BOTTOM OF THE OCEAN.

Above: *English fire-ships amongst the Spanish Armada. The Armada vessels, wrecked in 1588, are the richest known to be lying on the ocean bed.*

70 outside investors wanting a slice of the action, the pressure to find the *Maravillas*'s treasures never lets up.

THE RICHEST WRECKS

Herbo, of course, is not the only treasure-hunter in the game. And because there are so many rich wrecks around the globe there's plenty of room for others to play … provided they have the cash.

Listing the richest wrecks of the seas is an impossible task. However, the 12 that follow all figure high in every treasure-hunter's dreams.

The Spanish Armada: sunk in 1588 at various locations between France and Iceland, but mostly concentrated around south-west Ireland and the Hebrides. The ships' cargoes of gold ducats, jewel-studded artefacts and personal jewellery is, literally, priceless.

The *Flor de la Mar*: this Portuguese vessel foundered in 1512 off the Straits of Malacca between Indonesia and Malaya, close to Diamond Point. She carried diamonds, rubies, Chinese and Arabic coins and gold and bejewelled statues of animals. Some historians estimate the value at an incredible £5.5 billion, and not surprisingly Portugal, Indonesia and Malaysia have all claimed a share if and when the wrecked booty is ever raised.

Until then, the seas around are regularly patrolled by gunboats.

Sixteen unidentified Spanish galleons: they were part of a 20-strong fleet wrecked en route from Veracruz to Spain in 1553. The hulls are thought to lie off Padre Island, Texas, and the estimated value of the gold and silver bullion aboard is put at £1.2 billion.

The Mendoza fleet: Spanish ships sunk in 1614 somewhere off Cape Catoche, Yucatan. Treasure is valued at around £600 million. Mystery surrounds the fate of this fleet, commanded by Admiral Juan de la Cueva y Mendoza, which simply vanished during passage between Mexico and Cuba.

La Madelena: another Spanish ship, which went down off Cape Canaveral, Florida, in 1563. She carried more than 50 tons of silver ingots, a ton of gold, jewellery and 1.25 million *pesos*. The victim of a hurricane, only 16 of her 300 passengers and crew survived.

The *SS Merida*: an American ship, she was carrying £350 million worth of Mexican gold ingots when she collided with a steamship while sailing from Veracruz to New York. The wreck site, off Virginia Capes, is known but in 1933 an attempt to recover the gold failed.

The *Santissima Trinidad*: sunk in 1711, 15 miles west of Havana, she carried assorted treasure today worth about £300 million. Unlike her four sister ships, which were also lost in a ferocious storm, her remains have never been traced. Ironically, hers was by far the richest manifest.

Jamaican Merchant: a pirate ship which had enjoyed rich pickings off the Haitian coast. She is believed to have gone down east of the Ile de Vache together with her £270 million booty.

The *John Barry*: an American vessel lost off Oman on 28 August 1944. She carried 1,800 tons of silver worth a conservative £142 million.

La Lutine: one of the most famous wrecks in the world, her bell still hangs in the Lloyd's of London marine insurance house. Traditionally it is rung once for bad news, twice for good. Most of the *Lutine*, however, still lies beneath the waves of Terschelling Island in the Zuider Zee, Holland. Originally a French frigate, she was captured by the British and was being used to deliver pay to a British garrison at Texel Island before sailing on to Hamburg to deliver £130 million worth of gold and silver bars to German merchants. Her bullion is now protected by some of the deadliest fast currents in the world.

Rommel's treasure: this was reputed to have been cast overboard in strongboxes in the Gulf of Bastia, east Corsica. The treasure included gems, art treasures and precious stones looted by the Germans and worth around £80 million. The six chests were cast away on 18 September 1943 to keep them from the Allies. They have never been seen since.

Above: *Wreck in Hope Cove, Salcombe, Devon, 1936. Salvagers were – and are – always in hot competition to get to ships like this first.*

Left: The wreck of **Silvia Onarato** *on Goodwin Sands in 1948. The Italian ship broke her back within eight weeks of the sinking in 1948.*

A SNAGGED AIR PIPE — AND A DIVER AND HIS DREAMS OF TREASURE ARE CONSIGNED TO OBLIVION.

The *Santa Cruz*: this Spanish treasure ship was sucked onto rocks in Cardigan Bay, just off the Pembrokeshire coast, in January 1679. The gold and silver cargo, contained in 220 chests, is worth around £40 million.

A DANGEROUS CHALLENGE

Treasure in terms of bullion and jewels is, however, not the only lure of shipwrecks. In many cases items of historic interest are just as valuable – and just as big a draw, especially if the task of recovering them is dangerous. Humphreys, for instance, has a burning ambition to recover artefacts from the *Titanic*. His plan has been to target the liner's debris field to locate, among other items, a jewel-studded copy of the *Rubaiyat of Omar Khayyam*. The project has already been swamped in legal niceties and protracted courtroom arguments.

For many wreck hunters the thrill of the dive itself is often what matters. Many rotting hulls present a dangerous challenge to those who would explore them. An air pipe can easily be snagged or pulled loose and powerful and unpredictable currents

can sweep divers into oblivion before they know it. And then there's always the sharks and stingrays …

But of all the thousands of wrecks scattered around the globe few can match one lying in the mouth of the River Thames for risk factor. Quite simply the *Richard Montgomery* carries enough high explosives to flatten the nearby town of Sheerness and shatter windows ten miles away. If she blew, her 3,172 tons of TNT would be the largest non-nuclear explosion in the history of mankind.

The *Richard Montgomery* is the only officially listed 'dangerous wreck' in British waters. Divers are banned from reaching her – though that doesn't stop them trying – and Department of Trade inspectors check the cargo every couple of years to see how stable it is.

The argument has always been that the risk involved in getting the explosives out is greater than the risk of letting them be. Over the years, though, the TNT in its waterproof casings is likely to have grown increasingly unstable.

This ship's fate was sealed on the night of 20 August 1944 as she sought a Thames

Below: *The most famous shipwreck of them all. The magnificent* Titanic *slips beneath the waves under the gaze of her shocked survivors.*

berth en route to Cherbourg. Her draught was 31 feet and her allocated berth 24 feet at low tide. When the tide went out the *Richard Montgomery* was dumped firmly on the same sandbank where she remains to this day.

To locals the hull became something of a landmark. They sailed tourists out to it, clambered across the hull and even stripped what copper they could find. Fishermen would use it as a mooring point and a dumping ground for stray bombs pulled up in their nets. There was a nasty rumour that it had bombs on board but it wasn't until years later that the British government confirmed the truth and sealed it off.

Today the most common visitors to the hull are daredevil divers who just want to tell their friends they've brushed alongside. Government officials would rather everyone just forgot about her. No one, it seems, wants to make a decision.

Would it have been the same if she'd had bullion aboard? Would the Admiralty, the Port of London and the secretary of state for defence all have passed the buck, leaving the Department of Trade to inherit the headache?

The spectacle of landlubbers dithering and meddling in the wreck and treasure business infuriated old Roland Morris. He couldn't bear the thought of the authorities grabbing the limelight (and often the cargo as well) when they'd done nothing to advance the cause of the search itself. Unlike most of his ilk, Morris found himself in 1978 in a position to hit back.

For years he'd been hunting a wreck known in Cornwall as the *Dollar Mine*. It was thought to have been carrying 19 tons of silver coins when it sank in 1798, a hoard now worth millions. Morris found the ship somewhere off Gunwalloe, near Helston, Cornwall, but the National Trust, owner of the shoreline, immediately slapped in a claim for half of anything recovered. A livid Morris accused the Trust of seeking something for nothing and in a fit of pique abandoned his project. He swore he would take the secret of its location to the grave ... and he kept his word.

Today only one man – a Scillonian who was one of Morris's helpers on the *Dollar Mine* hunt – is reputed to know the site of the wreck. To date he has kept his mouth shut.

Morris would have approved.

Above: *The wreck of* **Zeebrugge ferry,** **Herald of Free Enterprise.** *She sunk with incredible speed after a crewman left the ship's car entrance doors open by mistake.*

FURIOUS, MORRIS SWORE HE WOULD NEVER REVEAL THE LOCATION OF THE TREASURE, AND THE GRAVE HAS KEPT HIS SECRET.

PHINEAS TAYLOR BARNUM The philosophy of humbug

With his weird and wonderful collection of freaks, his fantastic stories and his opportunistic ability to make money out of every potential disaster, Phineas Taylor Barnum really was the greatest conman on Earth.

'**R**oll up, roll up! See the Greatest Show on Earth. Ladies and gentlemen, I can assure you you won't be disappointed.' So the self-proclaimed 'Prince of Humbug' would pull in the crowds to gawp and stare at his circus of oddities.

Phineas T. Barnum takes a place in history as perhaps the greatest showman ever as he awed Victorian audiences with his collection of strange and wonderful freaks. The son of a storekeeper, he must have been one of the first people to recognize that any publicity is good publicity. Carefully planned campaigns ensured massive coverage of everything he did.

THE SCIENCE OF MONEY MAKING

The penny showman was known for his glib one-liners such as 'There's a sucker born every minute' and the immortal 'You can fool some of the people some of the time but you can't fool all of the people all of the time.' He even gave lectures on his ability to con the public; on a trip to England in 1858, he delivered a speech in St James's Hall, Regent Street, entitled: 'The science of money making and the philosophy of humbug.'

Barnum maintained that people wanted to have the wool pulled over their eyes, and he was more than happy to do so – for a price.

His entry into the dubious world of peepshows and freakshows happened quite by chance. Until the age of 25, Barnum tinkered about with a number of different jobs, never settling on any chosen career. He ran a newspaper, tended a bar and kept a store in his home town of Bethel, Connecticut. It was when he started

Above: *The man-bombshell. Barnum signed this acrobat as a certain crowd puller. The man was fired out of his cannon by a spring – the explosion followed a second later.*

Opposite: *Barnum was a natural self-publicist but even he occasionally had to resort to advertising to pull in the crowds.*

Left: *Barnum described his elephant exhibits as 'a stupendous assemblage of titan tuskers and mammoths'.*

WHEN HIS GOLD-MINE DIED
ON HIM AND WAS THEN
PROVED FALSE, BARNUM
LOUDLY PROCLAIMED THAT
HE HAD BEEN THE VICTIM OF
A HOAX.

Below: A press release extolling the wonderful world of Barnum.

to sell theatre tickets that he was bitten by the showbiz bug.

Barnum had learned of the existence of a wizened old negress by the name of Joice Heth, who, it was claimed, was the oldest living woman on Earth and nurse to former President George Washington. He found her being exhibited in Philadelphia and hurried to buy the rights in her as a curio. She came with ancient papers which included an original bill of sale that showed George's father Augustine Washington had bought her as a slave on 5 February 1727.

As part of her act, she rambled on about the days when she was George's nurse

delving into details which included the famous cherry-tree incident. But she always baffled audiences when she referred to the tree as a peach tree. Phineas exhibited her first in Niblo's Garden in New York on 10 August 1835.

As befitted the master of hype, his entrée into the world of freakshows was accompanied by a fanfare of publicity that was to become synonymous with everything he did. He took out a series of adverts in which he claimed the old crone had been 'a member of the Baptist church for upwards of one hundred years'. The press wrote reams on the phenomenon.

Alas for poor Phineas, his new-found 'crock of gold' did not last long: the old lady died. Worse was to come when the authorities carried out an autopsy on the body and declared publicly that Joice Heth was in fact 80 years old. Quick-thinking Barnum buried her in his family plot and capitalized on her again by defending his good faith in her authenticity and claiming that HE had been the victim of a hoax! He told anyone who wanted to listen that he had been duped by both Joice Heth and her original owner, having bought her in good faith.

For the next few years following her death, Barnum was pushed to find a profitable replacement. He struggled to make ends meet with a few wild animals and acrobatic troupes. However, his fortunes took a turn for the better when he decided to go into the museum business.

In 1841 he bought Sadder's American Museum, New York, and shortly afterwards purchased its arch-rival, Peales Museum. He then merged the two.

Renamed simply the American Museum, his new venture opened early in 1842, to the delight of the curious New Yorkers who filed through its doors. It was the perfect vehicle for Barnum's ingenious hoaxes. He entertained the public with rare specimens that he claimed were true freaks of nature. There were 'Niagara Falls', a woolly horse, the bearded lady, the 'Egress' and his renowned 'Feejee Mermaid' (in reality, the upper torso of a monkey sewn onto the body of a fish).

The Museum also became one of New York's entertainment hotspots, filled with genuine museum exhibits: minerals, fossils and natural history specimens, as well as an

P. T. Barnum's New & Greatest Show on Earth!

My great Traveling Centennial Academy of Object Teaching cost a million and a half of dollars, employs 1,100 persons, 600 horses and ponies, and will be transported East to Maine and West to Missouri on 100 solid steel railroad cars. It by far surpasses all my former efforts; consists of sixty cages of rare wild animals and amphibia, including Barnum's $25,000 *Behemoth*, the only HIPPOPOTAMUS in America; vast Centennial Museum of living Mechanical Automata and other curiosities; a CENTENNIAL PORTRAIT GALLERY; BEST CIRCUS IN THE WORLD. A JUBILEE of Patriotic Song and Splendor; superb Historical Tableaux; National Anthems by several hundred trained voices, accompanied by music and roar of cannon; *the whole audience to rise and join in singing the national hymn, "America."* I carry my own park of Cannon and a large Church Bell, fire a national salute of 13 guns each morning, accompanied by the public bells, and give the most extensive and gorgeous STREET PAGEANT ever witnessed, glittering with patriotic features, and attended by three bands of music. Each night a grand display of Patriotic Fireworks, showing WASHINGTON, American Flags, etc., in national colors of fine red, white and blue, fine Balloons, etc. You will never see the like again. Admission to all, 50 cents. Children under nine, Half Price.   P. T. BARNUM.

aquarium. Barnum built a theatre he dubbed the 'lecture room' for which over the years he sold a staggering 41 million tickets. He even brought the famous Swedish singer Jenny Lind to the USA on a concert tour in 1850.

The American Museum burned down twice but Barnum rebuilt it and carried on his strange trade until 1868, when he returned to his childhood home town of Bethel, Connecticut. There, suitably skilled in the art of humbug, he embraced the world of politics, sat in the state legislature and even ran for Congress.

THE GREATEST SHOW ON EARTH

It was while in Connecticut that he came up with his greatest idea. Teaming up with two partners, he put together the grandly titled, 'P.T. Barnum's Great Travelling Museum, Menagerie, Caravan and Hippodrome'. He called it 'The Greatest Show on Earth' and it catapulted him into the limelight he so desperately courted.

The show opened on 10 April 1871 in Brooklyn, with such sensational attractions as Siamese twins, midgets, three-legged wonders, strongmen, the Giant, the Fat Lady, the Thin Man, the Armless Wonder as well as the usual fire-eaters, sword swallowers, magicians and snake charmers.

For the next 20 years, his circus heralded the start of spring in America by kicking off its tour in Madison Square Garden.

Again his highly hyped exploits ate up acres of newspaper space. When it was remarked that he had no giraffe in his circus, he issued a press statement claiming that tragically he had been forced to feed it to the lions to keep them alive on a tough sea voyage across the Atlantic.

On one visit to England he fell in love with the Brighton Pavilion and its palatial Indian design. It perfectly reflected his own style, with its showy columns and arches, so he had a close copy built, calling it 'Iranistan'. To add to the Eastern flavour, he even arranged for an elephant to plod around in a nearby field and perform for passing train passengers by pulling a plough.

Barnum was also kept in the news by the fires that seemed to dog his business. Apart from two at the American Museum, one in

Above: *Programmes like this helped launch Barnum's showbusiness career.*

BARNUM'S CAREER WAS DOGGED BY MYSTERIOUS — AND CONVENIENT — FIRES.

1865 and another in 1868, he also lost a menagerie of animals in a blaze in 1872, the winter quarters of his zoo in 1877 and even his Connecticut home.

Ten years after the launch of his circus, Barnum joined forces with James Bailey to form 'The Barnum and Bailey Greatest Show on Earth'. This piece of theatre was transported around America on four trains made up of 107 railroad cars, each 70 feet long.

THE DIMINUTIVE QUEEN VICTORIA ADORED THE TINY MIDGET AND MADE HIM HER PET.

Right: *Circus acts were all very well, but what the punters really wanted was freaks and plenty of 'em. Barnum never failed to impress with motley assortments such as these, and he spared no thought for the feelings of his employees. If they didn't like being dubbed 'living monstrosities' they could always seek employment elsewhere!*

Opposite below: *P.T. Barnum with perhaps his best-known performer, 'General' Tom Thumb.*

A REAL-LIFE TOM THUMB

Yet while Barnum was an amazing self-publicist and entrepreneur, he would have been nothing without the men and women whose freakish looks helped to fill his coffers. These 'performers' became overnight stars as they fed the voracious Victorian appetite for sensation.

General Tom Thumb was the most celebrated of them all. As his name suggests, he was a man of tiny proportions yet perfectly formed. A rare find, and one Phineas Barnum put to good use.

Tom Thumb was not his real name. He was born Charles Sherwood Stratton on 4 January 1838. A healthy 9lb when he entered the world, he astonishingly remained at that weight until he was 5 years of age. He then measured a tiny 2 feet 1 inch. What made Stratton extremely unusual was that he was a true midget and not a dwarf. His body was perfectly proportioned.

His parents quickly realized the earning potential of such a Lilliputian miracle and put the lad on display, something that was seen as the norm in mawkish Victorian times. It wasn't long before Barnum got to hear of the minuscule boy on show in Bridgeport, Connecticut. He raced to sign him up and tempted him to join his circus for the princely sum of $3 a week.

Phineas immediately re-christened him General Tom Thumb and set about training the toddler in the art of showmanship. He spent days and nights schooling him in the strange ways of the peepshow world, teaching the boy to act 'regal, impudent and autocratic'.

Tom Thumb's first public appearance brought the house down when he recited a pun-littered speech written by Barnum. American audiences took to the little person Barnum hyped as a 'dwarf of 11 years of age, just arrived from England'.

The general revelled in his image as an arrogant, barking bombast. He also acted out roles such as Cupid, Yankee Doodle Dandy, Napoleon and a scantily clad gladiator.

The master showman stormed Europe. Queen Victoria, herself rather lacking in height at only 4 feet 11 inches, identified with the midget. She loved Tom Thumb and summoned him to give three Royal Command Performances at Buckingham Palace. He became known as the 'Pet of the Palace'.

Tom also proved highly popular at the Parisian court, with Barnum being allowed to exhibit his profitable protégé in a minuscule carriage in the imperial enclosure at Longchamps.

Tom Thumb's statistics were amazing enough, but Phineas Barnum, always keen to take things one step further, exaggerated Tom's age by 6 years and advertised his height at 30 1/2 inches. In fact, by the time the 'general' had reached maturity, he had attained a 'towering' 3 feet 4 inches and sported a dashing military-style set of whiskers.

Tom's marriage to midget Lavinia

Warren, who stood at almost the same height as the man himself, was a showbiz affair. Barnum, ever a shrewd businessman, saw the opportunity to make an extra buck

Above: *The train that carried Barnum and Bailey on their yearly tours.*

> **DESPITE THE FACT THAT HE WAS BORN WITH THREE LEGS HE MARRIED AND FATHERED FOUR NORMAL CHILDREN.**

Below: *Another of Barnum's personal favourites – Johanna, the intelligent gorilla. He described her as 'a stumbling block to doubters of the Darwinian theory' in an attempt to convince his public that he was truly a man of science.*

and the public went wild for his photographs of the couple's happy day.

Tom and Lavinia eventually settled down to live off the amassed fortune the couple made together – a staggering three-quarters of a million dollars. But tragically Tom fell ill and died of apoplexy back in Bridgeport at the age of 45.

A VICTORIAN FREAK SHOW

Madam Fortune, the Bearded Lady, joined Barnum and in the first nine months drew a massive 3 ½ million paying customers. When she married and had two children her own son also became an exhibit. Given the showname 'Infant Esau', the child was born thoroughly covered in hair, with full fair-coloured whiskers. Curiously, Barnum dressed the boy in girl's clothes until he was 14 years old in the hope of hoaxing the public into believing the child was in fact a girl.

The Three-Legged Wonder, Francesco Lentini, spent time at many circuses including Barnum and Bailey's. Born in 1889 into a large family of 12 children in Rosolini, Sicily, he found it hard to cope mentally with the extra leg that grew from the right side of his body.

A visit to an institution for the severely handicapped and deformed children at the age of 7 helped him to snap out of the depression that had reached chronic levels as he became more aware of being an oddity.

Surgeons had advised his distraught parents that to try to remove it could spell instant death or paralysis. They believed that the third leg was part of an undeveloped Siamese twin. Instead of the egg dividing in two, it only partly divided, leaving Francesco with just a leg of the brother he never had, attached forever to the base of his spine.

Francesco was highly intelligent and mastered four languages. However, the only career path he could take was that of the freakshow circuit. He joined the Ringling Brothers' Circus before touring with Barnum and Bailey. Fascinated audiences gasped in wonder as he ran, jumped, rode a bicycle and horse, drove a car and even skated on ice. He became known as the 'Three-Legged Wonder', and had people in gales of laughter when he played football, having trained himself to use the middle leg to kick the ball around.

He made fun of his own disfigurement by telling people he was the only man he knew who brought his own stool everywhere with him. His sense of humour helped him through life. Once when asked how he fitted himself with shoes, he said he bought two pairs and gave the extra one to a one-legged friend.

The Three-Legged Wonder even married and had four normal children. He retired to Florida and died in 1966 at the grand old age of 77.

Barnum was famous for his frauds, but he seemed to be able to carry them off because a tolerant public found them so entertaining and elaborate. The master

JOHANNA, THE FAMOUS GIANTESS GORILLA AND MOST INTELLIGENT ANIMAL ALIVE.
THE ONLY ADULT GORILLA OF HER SPECIES
A VERITABLE GIANTESS OF THE FOREST
A MOST REMARKABLE ANIMAL
MORE NEARLY APPROACHING MANKIND
HER ACTIONS WHEN EATING ARE TRULY ASTONISHING
SHE SMOKES CIGARETTES WITH THE GRACE OF A LADY
SHE IS ON EXHIBITION IN THE MENAGERIE PAVILION
ALL WITHOUT EXTRA CHARGE.
JOHANNA'S VIEW OF THE GREAT BARNUM-BAILEY SHOW.

showman and trickster once presented what he claimed to be the 'Wild Men of Borneo' as proof of the missing link between man and ape.

They were a fierce-looking pair, short and squat. In fact, they were actually American-born midget brothers who had never seen a jungle in their lives. Christened Hiram and Barney Davis, they changed their names to the more showy Plutano and Waino.

Barnum did not stop there. He also showed 'Zip the Man Monkey', supposedly a savage Neanderthal creature. Although he looked like a monster from a far-flung land, with a shaven head topped with a matted knot of hair, the creature was really a poor negro simpleton child encouraged to emit growling noises to earn a few pennies.

Scotsman Angus Macaskill was born in the Outer Hebrides in 1825, where he grew to a staggering 7 feet 9 inches in his bare feet. Billed as the 'strongest man the world has ever seen', his amazing feats stood testimony to his power.

Angus started out his working life as a docker and a fisherman before going on to fame in Barnum's Greatest Ever Show. Barnum got his money's worth out of the huge man. Not only did he display his freakish strength in the circus ring, he also used him to help to erect the big top tents. The mild-mannered giant hammered thick tent-pegs into the ground using not one but two 14lb hammers – one in each hand.

Angus knew that he could kill a man with his awesome power. As he gripped one wrestling opponent's hand in a friendly gesture, the man was horrified to see blood oozing from under his fingernails.

Like General Tom Thumb, Angus Macaskill came to the attention of freakshow enthusiast Queen Victoria. In response to yet another Royal summons, Barnum took his prize 'Hercules' to Windsor Castle.

GRIPPED BY THE COLOSSAL HAND, THE MAN WATCHED HORRIFIED AS THE BLOOD OOZED FROM UNDER HIS FINGERNAILS.

Below: *Jumbo the 'monster elephant' on his journey through New York to Madison Square Gardens for a Barnum extravaganza. The showman bought him from London Zoo but later claimed he was the only living 'mastodon'.*

LAST SIX WEEKS.
BARNUM & BAILEY
GREATEST SHOW ON EARTH.

CHANGE OF PROGRAMME. CLOSING EXHIBITIONS OF THE GRANDEST & MOST SUCCESSFUL SEASON EVER KNOWN IN OLYMPIA.

FINAL PERFORMANCES in LONDON of the BARNUM & BAILEY Greatest Show on Earth.
Positively Closing the Glorious and Triumphant Sojourn
ON SATURDAY, APRIL 2.

THE ENORMOUS HORSE FAIR SHOWING THE VAST CAVALCADE OF HIGH-CLASS STOCK OWNED & EXHIBITED BY THE GREAT BARNUM & BAILEY SHOW AN ACTUAL SCENE ON THE GREAT HIPPODROME TRACK. OVER 400 CHOICE THOROUGHBREDS FROM ALL PARTS OF THE WORLD

AND THEN TOURING THE WHOLE OF GREAT BRITAIN.
Travelling the Entire, Mighty, Undivided Show UNDER A DAILY EXPENSE of £1500, with New Acts and New Features introduced into the already Magnificent and Stupendously large Programme of
THRILLING PERFORMANCES AND GRAND DISPLAYS.
Visiting the Provinces upon its own specially constructed 70 Railway Cars, every car nearly 60 feet long.
NEARLY A FULL MILE OF RAILWAY CARS,
And exhibiting all the myriad wonders under TWELVE ENORMOUS CANVAS PAVILIONS,
One alone of which is double the capacity of Olympia.
LAST SIX WEEKS
Of the Grandest Show ever devised by man.
Last chances of witnessing the Most Magnificent Exhibition, the ingenuity, ability, wealth, and wonderful resources of the
KING OF THE AMUSEMENT WORLD, as set before the bewildered eyes of London.
CHANGE OF PROGRAMME.
NEW ACTS INTRODUCED. NEW FEATURES PRESENTED. NEW ATTRACTIONS ADDED.
New Races, new Clown Capers, new Animal Tricks. Ending the London Engagement in a blaze of glory. Eye-Feasts of
Splendour and Thrilling Interest. First presentation of the Mammoth
FOUR HUNDRED BLUE RIBBON HORSE FAIR,
And numerous other remarkable features.
A VERITABLE TORNADO OF WONDERS. BEWILDERING ARRAY OF NOVELTIES.
And a very Vesuvius of Brilliant Attractions never seen here or anywhere else.
A PROGRAMME OF AMAZING EXTENT
Of startling Struggles, hotly contested Races, and Aerial and Equestrian Rivalries, carrying the spectators by storm, and wildly and
enthusiastically applauded by everybody.
STUPENDOUS STRUGGLES BETWEEN CHAMPIONS.
Daring Deeds by Intrepid Gladiators. Tournaments, Games, Combats, Sports, Feats, Displays.
A Perfect Avalanche of Startling Events.
Races that enchanted Roman Senators.
Furious Two and Four-Horse Roman Chariot Races.
Bareback Equestrian, High School, Classic, Athletic, Acrobatic, Gymnastic, and Aerial Contests of all kinds, together with
TRIALS OF SKILL, ENDURANCE, AND BRAVERY,
In Three Rings, upon Two Stages, on the Race Track, in the Grand Aerial Enclave, and upon the 450-feet Spectacular Stage.
Pageants Exhausting Art and Luxury.
The whole vast space of the many Arenas a BEWILDERING SCENE OF KALEIDOSCOPIC SPLENDOUR.
REALLY THE WORLD'S SPECTACULAR SENSATION. THE MIGHTY METROPOLIS OF WONDERLAND.
The United Universal Press a Unit in its praise. Enlightenment and Science its greatest aids.
A Stupendous Place, where Wonder itself is lost in Wonder.
Volumes could not enumerate its myriad Treasures, to all of which are added the Double
MENAGERIES OF WILD AND TRAINED BEASTS.
THREE HERDS OF PERFORMING ELEPHANTS, Grand Horse Fair, Droves of Camels, Shetland Ponies, Zebras, Llamas,
Alpacas, Guanacos, Tiny Zebras.
THE FAMOUS COLLECTION OF WONDERFUL FREAKS.
Armless and Legless Men, Bearded Lady, Tattooed People, Dog-Faced Boy, Moss-Haired Girl, Expansionists, Sword Swallower, Fire
King, Musical Phenomena, Egyptian Juggler, Giant, Midget, Giantess, Fat Woman, Skeleton Dude, Laloo and Lala, Whirling Dervishes,
Head Swinging Soudanese, and Others.
A PERFECT PANDEMONIUM OF ORIGINALITY AND HUMOUR
By the CLEVEREST CLOWNS IN THE WORLD.
And in wondrous addition thereto the GRAND SPECTACULAR MILITARY DRAMA of
THE MAHDI: Or, for the Victoria Cross,
With 1200 Men, Women, Soldiers, Sailors, Soudanese, Horses, Camels, &c., depicting with truth and accuracy
actual events in the War in the Soudan.
AND ONE TICKET ADMITS TO ALL. TWO GRAND EXHIBITIONS DAILY at 2 and 8 p.m. Doors open at 12.30 and 6.30.
Early Gates open (Hammersmith Road) at 12 noon and 6 p.m., for 3s. seats and upwards. Early entrance fee, 6d. extra. Owing to the
stupendously large show and the general magnitude of the exhibitions necessitating great preparations, the Menageries, Freak, and Horse
Fair Departments can only be open from 12 to 4.15 p.m., and from 6 to 10.30 p.m. No promenade tickets sold. Every ticket entitling
holder to a reserved numbered seat, and admitting to all advertised departments without extra charge.
PRICES.—Amphitheatre, 1s. and 2s.; Arena seats, 2s., 3s., and 4s.; Balcony seats, 3s.; Stalls, 5s., 7s. 6d.; Private Boxes (five and six seats),
£3 3s.; Single Box seats, 10s. 6d. Special prices for Royal Box when not engaged. Children between 4 and 10 years of age half-price to
all except 1s. and 2s. seats. Box-Office open from 9 a.m. to 9.30 p.m. 1s. and 2s. seats on sale only after doors open. All other seats
may be booked in advance at Box-Office and at usual Libraries.

BURNED ALIVE

On his many trips to England, the master showman was a regular visitor to the London Zoological Gardens. It was on one such visit that he came to hear about an elephant for which the curators needed to find a new home. The flamboyant Barnum stepped in and bought Jumbo.

It was a decision that the zoo would live to regret. The public loved the African elephant and there were howls of outrage as the British press declared the sale an act of vandalism.

Barnum revelled in the limelight. He shipped Jumbo to the USA, avoiding taxes by saying he was going to breed from the animal. He urged the public to come and see 'The Only Mastodon on Earth'. The mastodon, a creature related to the elephant, was long extinct but Barnum never let scientific facts get in the way of a good scam.

Four years later Jumbo died in a tragic accident. The facts were straightforward enough – the animal was hit by a train – but Barnum callously manipulated the story, claiming Jumbo had died gallantly, saving a baby elephant by sacrificing himself.

Barnum needed a replacement and once again he turned to the Royal Zoological Society in London. Surprisingly, they fulfilled his order and a female, Alice, was sent to take Jumbo's place. The ambling giant was presented as the male elephant's 'widow'.

She was often displayed beside Jumbo's gruesome remains, his stuffed hide on one side and his gleaming skeleton on the other. Sadly, Alice also met a grisly end when she was burned alive in a fire in 1887.

Never the shrinking violet type, Barnum was thrilled when London's waxwork museum Madam Tussaud's asked him if he would like to be immortalized as an exhibition. The impudent entertainer sent them a complete outfit, even down to his socks. Fittingly it was in London (where he had an enormous following) that he climaxed his long career. The 'Greatest Show on Earth' went on display in the huge Olympia exhibition halls and Londoners packed in to get a glimpse of the man who was as famous as any one of his living freaks.

The egoistical Barnum had an open carriage made for him to ride around the ring before the start of the show. Once again he had royal patronage: young Prince George sat enthralled through the entire show, joyfully joining in the National Anthem which he dubbed: 'God Save Grandmother'.

Besides being a showman, Phineas became a real estate speculator. He also gave numerous lectures around the world. And as a politician he served four terms in the Connecticut state legislature before going on to become mayor of his home town, Bridgeport. Today the small town's Barnum Museum stands testimony to the greatest showman on Earth.

Although Barnum was married twice – to Charity Hallett in 1829 and a year after her death in 1873 to Nancy Fish – he never fathered any children. His showmanship went to the grave with him in 1891 at the grand old age of 81.

Ironically, the *New York Evening Post* had printed the old man's obituary days before his death and Barnum had read it. Was it his last attempt to 'plant' a story in the press? No doubt he got a great kick out of it.

ALICE MET A GRISLY END WHEN SHE WAS BURNED ALIVE IN A FIRE.

Opposite: *A handbill from a Barnum season at Olympia. By now the master showman was as well known as any of his freaks and he revelled in the applause of an adoring public. He even had an open carriage specially made for him to ride around the ring before the start of the show.*

Left: *The twopenny programme for Barnum at Olympia. He chose the exhibition halls to stage the climax of his career and milked every ounce of publicity from the fact that the young Prince George would be present.*

THE BARNUM AND BAILEY

PROGRAMME PRICE 2ᵈ

P. T. BARNUM.

J. A. BAILEY.

GREATEST SHOW ON EARTH AT OLYMPIA

DREAM OF FLIGHT

Since time immemorial human beings have dreamed of flying like a bird, but over the centuries only lunatics and geniuses dared to attempt the impossible. Some crashed to their bloody deaths, some flew too high and were punished for their foolhardiness, and a few – a brilliant few – learned to master the last untamed element.

Like all the best dreams, this one began as an impossibility. A person to fly like a bird? Madness. The stuff of doddery inventors or good-for-nothings with little else to do.

True, the story of flight is littered with its fair share of eccentrics, optimists, conmen, opportunists and, inevitably, the downright bonkers. Yet amid all the dross that goes with any great scientific advance, there were a few jewels. Two such were the Montgolfier brothers of Avignon in France.

The Montgolfiers came into the race to get airborne on the back of a pretty grim record. Even in make-believe stories it nearly always ended in tears for the would-be flyers. The classic example is the attempt by Icarus to escape from King Minos of Crete. He glued feathers to his arms with wax and took off for home. As almost every school child knows, he flew too near the Sun, the wax melted and – whoops! – no more Icarus.

A LEAP INTO THE UNKNOWN

History is littered with the stories of men who thought this unfortunate Greek was on the right lines. They all ended up in the drink as well. There was King Bladud of London who in 852 BC became the first of the so-called tower jumpers. He jumped, he crashed, he died – but he didn't deter others from having a try as well. Across the world for nigh on a thousand years (and even today) there have been people prepared to chuck themselves off high buildings in the name of scientific progress.

There were one or two who took care to improve their chances of survival. The 'flying tailor' of Ulm, Germany, for instance, made sure he landed in the town's river. Luckily his wings kept him afloat until his derisive fellow-citizens fished him out. Then there was the intrepid Sieur Bernier, who started out by jumping off a stool and worked up, via a table and window, to the second storey of a house. There is no believable record of how his career ended.

Some of the most colourful early attempts to fly were made by monarchs, who doubtless convinced themselves God was on their side. According to the 10th-century tome *Shah-Nameh* (*King's Name Book*) of Persia, King Kai Koos had a pretty good stab with one of the most bizarre flying contraptions ever conceived.

The book records: 'To the king it became a matter of great concern how he might be enabled to ascend the heavens, without wings; and for that purpose he consulted the astrologers who presently suggested a way in which his desires might be successfully accomplished.

HE JUMPED OFF A STOOL; AND THEN OFF A TABLE; AND THEN OUT OF A SECOND-STOREY WINDOW …

Opposite: *The Montgolfiers' moment of triumph. This engraving shows last-minute preparations for the first free flight with the Marquis d'Arlandes and Dr Pilatre de Rozier acting as test pilots.*

Below: *This plan for a flying machine, dated around 1883, was drawn by inventor Professor Boronowski. It was powered by steam and far too unwieldy to be any use.*

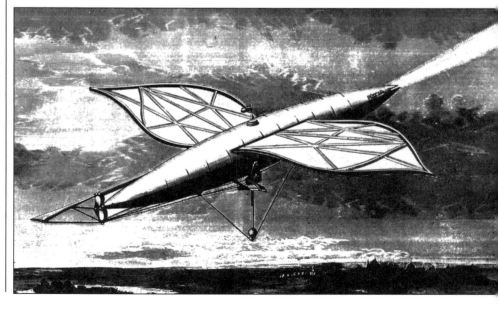

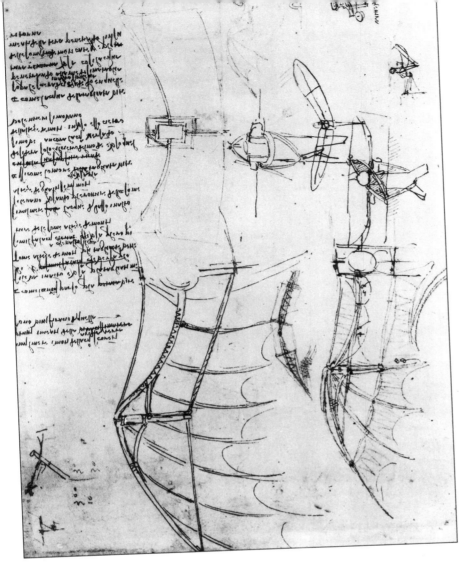

Above: *Leonardo da Vinci's design for a fixed-wing aircraft was years ahead of its time. Whether it would actually have flown is quite another matter.*

'They contrived to rob an eagle's nest of its young, which they reared with great care, supplying them with invigorating food. A frame of aloes wood was then prepared and at each of the four corners was fixed perpendicularly a javelin, surmounted on the point with the flesh of a goat. At each corner again one of the eagles was bound, and in the middle the king was seated with a goblet of wine before him.

'As soon as the eagles became hungry they endeavoured to get at the goat's flesh upon the javelins and by flapping their wings and flying upwards they quickly raised the throne from the ground. Hunger still pressing on them, and still being distant from their prey, they ascended higher and higher in the clouds, conveying the astonished king far beyond his own country. But after a long and fruitless exertion their strength failed them and unable to keep their way the whole fabric came tumbling down from the sky and fell upon a dreary solitude in the Kingdom of Chin – where Kai Koos was left a prey to hunger, alone, and in utter despair.'

Cutting through the journalistic licence of the day, we can safely conclude that Koos bombed out.

By the 17th century the weird science mob were still in charge. Jesuit maths lecturer Francesco de Lana conceived a lighter-than-air machine hoisted aloft by four balloons and propelled by oars and a large sail. Forty years later, in 1709, another Jesuit, Father Laurenco de Gusmao of Portugal, built a flying craft he called the Passarola. It had a kind of parachute contraption above a dove-shaped hull and two large flapping wings. Neither invention could be described as successful.

Then in 1742 the Marquis de Bacqueville flew for France (almost) when he leapt out of his town house on the River Seine with huge paddles attached to his arms and legs. If he'd landed in the river the paddles might at least have been a useful buoyancy aide. As it was he plopped onto a barge and broke his leg.

A BAG OF HOT AIR?

So what of the Montgolfiers, Joseph and Etienne? In 1782, so the story goes, they were at home watching the fire when they noticed how fragments of ash swirled up the chimney. Observing correctly that warm air rises, they later launched the first, experimental hot air balloon by igniting a paper fire under an open silk bag.

A year later, in the autumn of 1783, the first documented manned flight took place with a doctor called Pilatre de Rozier in the basket. But, for safety's sake, his balloon remained tethered to the ground.

The Montgolfiers' next move was a free flight and they dutifully asked the permission of Louis XVI. He replied: 'Take two criminals who are under a death sentence and tie them to the balloon basket. That will be a novel way of disposing of worthless men.'

As it turned out the king's suggestion was shelved. A nobleman, the Marquis d'Arlandes, cajoled him into accepting it would be wrong for such a historic moment to be handed to a couple of scumbag killers. The king gave way and it was d'Arlandes and de Rozier who on 21 November 1783 made the world's first independent flight across most of Paris.

Flushed with success, de Rozier sought to break new ground. An argument was developing among prospective aeronauts over which was the more effective flier: a balloon filled with hot air or one that used the new lighter-than-air gas hydrogen, discovered in 1766 by the English chemist Henry Cavendish. The Frenchman thought the obvious solution was to combine the two. In 1785 he rigged up a 10-foot hot air balloon beneath a 40-foot hydrogen one. In doing so he also created the world's first flying bomb and doomed himself to becoming the first victim of an air crash. Science discovered hydrogen and fire don't mix.

This appalling device disintegrated in flames a quarter of an hour out on its flight path across the English Channel. The mangled bodies of de Rozier and his co-pilot were found near the seashore, about four miles from Boulogne.

In spite of numerous accidents like these, the next century saw the golden age of ballooning, while by 1794 the world's first air force unit was seen in battle as France's General Morlot directed his forces against the Austrians and Dutch at Fleurus. The first air raid followed 55 years later when the Austrian 'air force' bombed Venice with 30-pounders. And, naturally, there were some classic *Boys' Own* tales as adventurers queued up to outdo each other in the world's most fashionable form of transport.

Not least among this band were James Glaisher and Henry Coxwell of Wolverhampton, England, who took off in 1862 to see how high they could go. Without oxygen they managed the almost unbelievable altitude of 30,000 feet (nearly six miles). By then Glaisher was unconscious and Coxwell's limbs had frozen to the point of uselessness. Yet he somehow managed to grip the safety valve cord with his teeth and returned safely to Earth.

THE BATTLE FOR THE SKIES

By now science had switched its attentions to gliders as a possible way forward for powered flight, and once the petrol engine appeared in 1885 whole new avenues began to open up.

In 1900 bicyclemakers Wilbur and Orville Wright of Dayton, Ohio, produced a biplane glider which they tested in the

form of a gigantic kite over the sands at Kitty Hawk, North Carolina. Three years (and much experimentation) later they finally strapped a homemade 12 hp motor on it and on 17 December Wilbur flew the contraption for 59 seconds over 300 yards. Within two years they'd redesigned the aircraft to the point where it could manage 24 miles in 38 minutes.

The age of powered, manned flight had arrived … and with it a whole new band of enthusiastic fruitcakes set on getting their names in the history books. Incredibly dozens got their batty ideas commissioned – very often by the paranoid military hierarchies of Britain and Germany who in 1914 were busy squaring up for the first test to decide which of them was master of Europe.

On the German side Villehad Forssman (he was in fact a Swede but he was happy to work with anyone mad enough to pay him) was one of the great optimists of the story of flight. As a designer he was so bad the British should have decorated him for the trouble he caused their enemy.

Forssman's only qualification, it seems, was that he once built a monoplane called the Bulldog for Prince Friedrich Sigismund. On the strength of this, and some earlier tinkering with dodgy airships in Russia, he was taken on by the German aircraft company Siemens.

Above: *The Chanute multiple-wing glider is put through its paces in 1896. By now scientists had realized that fixed wings were the way forward to powered flight and the arrival of the internal combustion engine had opened up undreamt-of opportunities.*

> **TO** PROVE HIS ARGUMENT HE TESTED HIS THEORY — AND CREATED THE WORLD'S FIRST FLYING BOMB.

Any entrepreneur will tell you it is very hard to lose money making much-in-demand military hardware in times of war. Yet Siemens managed it (certainly in the early stages of hostilities), largely because Forssman talked them into building Bulldogs. The German generals were desperate for planes ... but not that desperate.

Above: A classic in the ranks of weird and wonderful aeroplanes that never stood a chance. This is the Avion Ader built in 1890. Amazingly, there was no shortage of test pilots volunteering to try it out.

Forssman then turned his attention to producing the world's first seriously efficient bombers and came up with a giant flying pig of a plane that was too heavy in some parts, too weak in others, and carried engines that were hopelessly underpowered. He solved the problem of the tail section's excess weight by bunging a gunner's turret on the nose of the thing. Unsurprisingly, it was completely unfit to fly.

Siemens dumped the Swede and employed an engineer called Harold Wolff to salvage something from the wreckage. He failed – even though he had an ace pre-war test pilot, Walter Hohndorf, at the controls – and in 1915 the whole unwieldy mishmash crashed during a brief hop off

the ground. Unfortunately it wasn't quite a write-off. Siemens, by now getting desperate for a return on their Deutschmarks, vowed they would get the thing accepted by the military somehow.

A deal was struck. The generals would take the plane into service (at a reduced purchase price) if it managed to achieve a height of 6,000 feet in under half an hour and could carry a 1,000 kg payload for four hours. Siemens wheeled out another pilot, Bruno Steffen, and promised him a 10 per cent cut if he could coax the monster through its paces.

Steffen agreed and asked for five volunteers to make up his load. There were no takers. Undeterred, and packed up with ballast, he took off to quickly find the plane was so heavy it flew under constant risk of either stalling, spinning or rearing up on its tail like some bellyflopping whale. He managed to make 6,000 feet with little over 100 seconds to spare but on the way down all four engines failed. Steffen, clearly a brilliant airman, glided the machine down for a textbook landing.

The military engineers moved in, checked instruments, pronounced the test successful and sentenced a whole new intake of fresh-faced recruits to use the flying coffin for 'training purposes'. Thankfully fate intervened in time.

Shortly after Steffen's epic performance the bomber was being tested by ground crew with its engines running when the fuselage suddenly snapped in two just behind the wings. It was the last straw and the plane was junked for good.

Not so its creator Forssman. Although little is known of him after his Siemens fiasco it appears he did find some other monumentally clueless backer who allowed him to mash together yet another winged nightmare. Soon after the Armistice an Allied Control Commission team discovered purely by chance in a dusty old hangar a partly-constructed triplane of incredible dimensions.

It had a wingspan of 165 feet, a length of 150 feet, and landing wheels 8 feet in diameter. There were to have been ten engines and it could supposedly carry enough fuel to keep it airborne for three days, during which time it would have flown to New York to drop propaganda leaflets.

The designer's name was noted as Forstman – almost certainly a misspelling. No other aircraft maker would dared have build something so huge with a structure so ludicrously weak. Thankfully it never even got out of its hangar, let alone taxied down a runway.

TARRANT'S FOLLY

Lest for a moment it be thought the British were above such foolhardy ventures, there is one outstanding case which easily rivals Forssman's fudges. Step forward W.G. Tarrant of Byfleet, Surrey, a man whose dalliance with aeroplanes proved a predictable triumph of natural law over unnatural optimism.

Tarrant's background was in building, particularly wooden buildings. In the early days of World War 1 a lot of business came his way from the War Office (in common

THE FLYING COFFIN WAS PRONOUNCED A SUCCESS AND ANOTHER INTAKE OF FRESH-FACED RECRUITS WAS FED TO IT.

Below: *Now we're getting somewhere. This picture shows the Wright brothers' first powered flight on 17 December 1903. They managed to travel a mere 300 yards in 59 seconds. Two years later the plane notched up one flight of 24 miles in 38 minutes.*

THE PLANE WAS NOSE HEAVY AND HAD A TENDENCY FOR THE TAIL TO SHOOT UP IN THE AIR, BUT THE TEST PILOT HAD NO CHOICE.

with just about every other carpenter in the land able to wield a chisel). So it was that when the government sent out a clarion call for anyone able to design a really monstrous bomber he decided to have a go. There were only two designers in the running: Fred Handley-Page, who had built thousands of planes in his time, and Tarrant, who hadn't. Not even one.

Sure enough, bearing in mind the cock-up theory of war, the government's own Royal Aircraft Establishment at Farnborough came down on Tarrant's side. He was invited to build a 'bloody paralyser', a craft that could pack such a payload as to rain havoc on Berlin. It would be sweet revenge for the German bombing of London with Zeppelin airships.

As it turned out, Tarrant's Tabor was never ready to fly in anger, but by the end of the war the RAE had become so involved in the project they had almost adopted it. The decision was made: the Tabor would be finished and even if there were years of peace ahead it could always be turned into a passenger plane.

In early spring 1919 it was wheeled out for the attentions of the press and got some rave reviews. But many were puzzled by the engine set-up of the triplane – four between the bottom and middle wings and two between the middle and top. Far from being a startling innovation of design this crackpot arrangement had been the result of necessity. The 600 hp Siddeley Tiger engines hadn't produced the goods expected of them. Where originally the plane should have carried four, it now had to have six. There was only one place to put them ... so onto the top wings they went.

When questioned about this Tarrant's team had an instant answer. Yes, you would normally expect engines in that position to bring the tail of the plane up and send the entire machine out of control. But they had worked out all the figures and the downdraught from the top wing would be sure to keep the tail firmly in place. They probably had a point, and if the plane had ever managed to take off they might even have proved it. But while their theory no doubt worked for a Tabor in flight, no one seems to have checked what problems taxiing at low speed might bring.

On 26 May the Tabor, more than 37 feet high with an incredible wingspan of 131 feet, was towed out for its first test flight. As the world prepared to quake at this latest display of awesome military power from the British, there were behind the scenes rows going on at Farnborough. Tarrant was worried about the balance, the RAE wasn't. Tarrant took the initiative and ordered half-a-ton of lead to be packed into the nose. Now he had a plane which was nose heavy, with a tendency for the tail to shoot up in the air.

As the last of the six engines was finally coaxed into action, test pilot Captain F. Dunn took over for the inaugural flight. He taxied about for a while to get the feel of the controls and then turned into the wind for take-off. He opened up the lower engines – no problem there. Then he throttled the two top ones. Immediately the Tabor toppled nose forward, her propellors ripping up the earth and tearing the hull to pieces. All three captains on board died, though three RAE engineers were saved.

Tarrant's folly never left the ground. He went back to building houses.

At least the Tabor never got accepted as a front-line plane. Unfortunately, military history is littered with anecdotes of undeniably bad aircraft that did.

BLOODBATH

One of these is the Brewster Buffalo, used extensively by the Americans in World War 2 against the far superior Japanese Zero fighters. Stories of its inadequacies are legion. On one occasion it was claimed Brewsters were sent up to escort a squadron of fully loaded Blenheim bombers. Embarrassingly, the Brewsters couldn't keep up.

Then there was the story of a US pilot who was visiting an RAF base in Rangoon. Among its aircraft the RAF had two of the US fighters. The American casually asked what the procedure was for warning of a Japanese air raid. 'Long before the RAF gets around to announcing an alert,' he was told 'you will see two Brewsters taking off in a westerly direction regardless of the windsock. That's the signal. The Japanese always fly in from the east.'

The Brewster's problem was that it was heavy on armour plate, light on firepower. As a result US pilots got planes that were easily out-manoeuvred by the Japanese and

rarely able to get a shot on target. In one of the worst bloodbaths, during the Midway Battle of 4 June 1942, a US Marine squadron put up 25 fighters (including 19 Brewsters) against 36 Zeros escorting a fleet of bombers.

Inside half an hour, 13 of the Brewsters were shot down and the rest were so badly damaged they were never used again. A Captain Philip White, who did get his plane home, observed later: 'It is my belief that any commander who orders pilots out for combat in a Brewster should consider the pilot as lost before leaving the ground.' Australian airmen would no doubt agree. They were given 154 Brewsters to help defend Malaya. Inside three months every one was destroyed.

Even when this hapless fighter chanced upon sitting targets – a so-called duck shoot – it couldn't perform. One flight log showed that three Brewsters managed to

intercept an unprotected flight of Japanese bombers. Then the crews found that out of a combined total of 12 guns, only one actually worked.

A SUICIDE MACHINE

If the Brewster was too slow, the German ME-163 Komet proved too fast. In 1941 this tiny rocket-powered interceptor achieved a test speed of 600 mph, an unimaginable speed by the standards of the day. Intelligence reports of its existence had been one of the biggest headaches for Allied air commanders. In fact, it is likely the Komet accounted for more German casualties than it inflicted upon the enemy.

The Komet worked using a highly unstable rocket fuel mixture of C-Stoff (a solution of hydrazine hydrate in methanol) and T-Stoff (hydrogen peroxide with a few – laughingly named – stabilizers). No

Above: *The* **Hindenburg** *disaster, on 6 May 1937. This terrifying photograph showing the scenes that day in New Jersey sums up the spirit of the early aviators. For all their bravado, many knew in their hearts that they were dealing with technology still in its infancy.*

Above: *Another of the early gliders takes off with its brave test pilot hanging on for dear life. For the men who did manage to get themselves airborne, there was the obvious problem of how and where to land. Without controls, they quite literally flew on a wing and a prayer.*

ignition was needed. As soon as the two fuels met, they transformed into an explosive hot gas, a feature that accounted for more than one unfortunate ground crew member who slopped one of the fuels into a bucket containing dregs of the other.

Its only chance of operating effectively was for everything to be kept as simple as possible. And it was. The pilot had only five engine controls: off, idle, and thrusts 1, 2 and 3. Recruits were prepared for the terrifying G-forces it created by being locked into a pressure chamber and exposed to the agonies of rising to 24,000 feet in a minute and back down to sea-level in half that time.

One would-be Komet pilot wrote later: 'Our bowels felt as though they were expanding like balloons, forcing us to scream with agony, while if we happened to be suffering with a slight head cold and a blocked sinus these sudden pressure changes resulted in such searing head pains that the agony was indescribable.'

Only volunteers were accepted for 163 Squadron and it's easy to understand why. The engine could explode, at any time, without any warning or any apparent reason. Death was then guaranteed instantaneous. You took off on a wheeled trolley but often as not this gave the motor such a jolt that it would cut out on the point of take-off. Landing was even more haphazard because the plane landed like a glider on a single undercarriage skid. The main difference was that a glider can come down as slow as 30 mph: a Komet was supposed to do it at 100 mph.

Crash landings on both take-off and landing were, therefore, an everyday occurrence, as was steam spurting into the cockpit to obscure vision completely. The only advice if anything, however minor, went wrong was to bale out and hope you didn't get sliced in half by the tail fin on the way. The pilots who knew they were about to crash probably prayed for an explosion. On occasions a Komet would come down with just one ruptured fuel tank and the pilot could then suffer the appalling fate of being dissolved alive.

Yet all these risks were somehow worth it to the brave young souls whose dream of flight was to be the fastest men on Earth. It was ironic that in military terms, their aircraft was a total dud.

The Komet came upon its targets (usually US Flying Fortresses) so quickly the pilot had time to squeeze off only a few rounds before he shot past and found himself out of range again. Assuming he had the fuel to make another run, he would be forced to throttle back, losing his one great advantage – speed. An added problem was the return home. US Mustang fighters took to patrolling close to known Komet bases, picking off the fighters with ease as they glided down.

Despite all the plane's faults the rocket technology used impressed the conquering Allies and, no doubt, inspired more scientists into pushing back the frontiers of flight.

TAKE-OFF INTO THE UNKNOWN

Today, the Americans are known to have developed a top-secret reconnaissance plane that makes the Komet look positively snail-like. The Aurora aircraft uses a ramjet engine capable of taking it from London to New York in a little over 40 minutes. From take-off it can fly to anywhere in the world inside three hours. And the chances of any enemy shooting it down are too remote to even bother about. No bullet, no missile and certainly no other plane can catch it.

Thank goodness the world has scientists who dream. In under 200 years they have helped shepherd mankind from widespread disbelief that flight would ever be possible, to that first tentative take-off in a balloon and on to planes such as the Aurora.

Today there are those who insist inter-galactic travel is never on the cards. We could never reach the speeds required, they argue, never live long enough to see new worlds.

As the dream of flight proves, never say never.

THE AGONY WAS INDESCRIBABLE.

Below: *A Bleriot-style monoplane. Aircraft such as this may have looked as though the slightest gust of wind would blow them into matchwood, but many were surprisingly sturdy. The problem for the pilot, apart from keeping the thing under control with only basic equipment, was to counter the biting cold.*

THE PSYCHIC
DETECTIVES

Officially the police don't like to confess to it, but it happens more and more. An unsolved murder, a missing work of art, or an undiscovered corpse – when their investigations are fruitless, the officers of the law pick up their telephones and ask for the assistance of the psychic detectives.

Nella Jones walked to the bottom of the stairs. The whole world began to spin as she felt a sharp blow to the back of her head. She grabbed the banister to stop herself from falling. Terrible pain wracked her body and fear welled up inside her as she relived the final moments of an old lady's life only seconds before she was brutally murdered.

Nella, one of the world's foremost psychics, had been called in by police who needed help over an unsolved murder. A 75-year-old grandmother had been bludgeoned to death. The famous psychic had been called out of the blue by two detectives working on the murder case in only one of many occasions that she had been asked to use her special skill to help solve crimes.

Affectionately known as 'Witchy-poo' by police, Nella's discoveries as she steps back in time can never be used as evidence in a court of law. And police are often reluctant even to admit that they join forces with psychics.

When Nella, a grandmother from Bexleyheath, Kent, is called to assist, she 'becomes' the person involved in the crime, living each step of the events as they unfold. Often she takes on the person's mannerisms and voice. It was because of this that she was feeling the pain of the frail victim so acutely at the spot where the old woman was murdered …

Detectives had first contacted Nella two days earlier. They had visited her and had sat down at her dining table. Before they even had a chance to tell her who had been killed, Nella was able to give them the name of the poor woman and the names of two of the men the police had interviewed in connection with the horrific slaughter. She also described in minute detail the place where the grandmother met her death, including the furniture in the rooms.

Now she was standing in the very spot where the old lady was found dead. Nella felt ill. Working on murder cases always left her exhausted and disturbed. It would take many days before she would begin to recover from the trauma of working on such a violent crime.

Nella could 'hear' the woman's piteous cries: 'Somebody help me'. As she looked at the floor she could 'see' the woman. Known only as Mrs Box, the old lady stumbled into the living room, knocked to the floor by blows rained down on her by the callous murderer before he snatched a necklace from her neck. The pain was excruciating and the fear that she felt was paralyzing. Nella gasped. The psychic described the necklace to the police and later, once she had left the house, told them how the man had split the old lady's ear when he ripped out her earrings and how he had crushed her fingers so that they were black and blue.

Nella and the detectives returned to an unmarked police car, and she led them to a restaurant often visited by the man whom

Above: *The Vermeer painting stolen from Kenwood House in London. Nella helped police find the culprits and the psychic information she passed to detectives was so uncannily accurate that they wondered whether she was a member of the gang.*

SHE COULD HEAR THE OLD WOMAN'S PITEOUS CRIES, PLEADING FOR HELP.

Opposite: *Peter Sutcliffe with wife Sonia. The brutal acts of the Yorkshire Ripper made Nella Jones a household name after police turned to her for advice on catching their man.*

Above: *Police hunt for clues after another brutal Ripper murder. Officers quickly realized they were dealing with one of the worst serial killers on record but for months they failed to make any breakthrough. Then Nella had a vision of him while sipping a cup of tea with a WPC friend.*

she believed was the killer. Further along the road she pointed out a car she said was the same type the man drove. She also accurately predicted that the man worked in Dover and that he had dropped something at the scene of the crime.

When police eventually arrested the man and charged him with murder, they confirmed that everything Nella had described had been correct. As usual, she had been uncannily accurate.

TERRIFYING POWERS

Nella was born on 4 May 1932 into a family of Romany gypsies. As a child, she hid her psychic powers from everyone because she was terrified of being called a witch. It wasn't until she was 42 years old that she decided to make a career out of her talent as a clairvoyant after lying weakened and ill from overwork through her attempts to build up a cleaning business. Since then, she has built up an international following and is recognized not only for her psychic powers and ability to 'see' into the future and past, but also for her work as a healer.

For all the sterling work psychics like Nella and others have done to help combat crime and solve cases, the police are reluctant to acknowledge that they use mediums. An admission would be seen as a slur on their ability as police officers. The official line is that they are willing to take information from any source in the hope that it leads to the arrest and conviction of criminals. Usually psychics are called in when the case has reached rock-bottom and police have nowhere else to go.

Nella has worked with police forces for almost 20 years. She made her debut as a psychic detective when she told police where to find a rare stolen painting worth £2 million. The painting by Vermeer had been stolen by thieves from Kenwood House in London. Nella was watching a news report when she suddenly had a vision of where it was. She sketched out a map as the information came flooding into her mind, then rang the hotline set up by police.

Within hours, Nella was taken to Hampstead police station where she was grilled by two detectives. They took her to Kenwood and the three of them walked through the huge grounds until Nella led them to the spot where a burglar alarm lay hidden in the grass. Even the sniffer dogs had failed to find it. She also pinpointed the whereabouts of the huge gilt frame that was now empty of the painting 'The Guitar Player'.

When she returned to the incident room,

she met the man in charge of the investigation, Chief Superintendent Arthur Pike who, heartened by her success, asked her to lead on. She next took the detectives to the famous Highgate Cemetery, resting place of Karl Marx and a host of other illustrious names. On her way there she sketched the face of a man whom she said was the culprit.

As the three arrived at the gates to the cemetery, Nella immediately felt the man's presence. He was still there and had the priceless painting with him in the ancient catacombs. The two detectives left her to search the area, but she came back empty-handed.

As they left the graveyard, they showed the gatekeeper Nella's drawing. He immediately recognized the man as a well-known graverobber who was on police records. A quick comparison with a mugshot back at the station confirmed this.

By now the police were astonished at the accuracy of Nella's information, so much so that they even had her telephone tapped, just in case she may have been involved with the theft. It didn't help allay their fears when Nella accurately predicted the arrival of every ransom letter and their contents.

Not long after the first flurry of ransom notes, one of which even contained a piece of the painting, the desperate thieves got in touch threatening to burn the picture if the ransom wasn't paid. All involved were horrified at the prospect, but Nella knew the painting would be found safe and sound in a cemetery, as she had predicted all along. Not long after, it was discovered in a graveyard beside St Bartholomew's Hospital in London.

THE YORKSHIRE RIPPER

It was through her work on the Yorkshire Ripper case that Nella became a household name. Peter Sutcliffe was eventually jailed for life in 1981 for the gruesome murders of 13 women.

Nella had been having visions of the evil Ripper at odd times throughout the day. His wickedness pervaded her life and she felt frightened by the man. But it wasn't until

THE EVIL OF THE MAN STAINED HER LIFE AND SHE WAS HAUNTED BY VISIONS OF THE GRUESOME MURDERS.

Below: *Public pressure for the Ripper to be brought to book was intense – hence the willingness of detectives to try anything that might help. When conventional methods – such as the murder re-construction performed by this WPC – failed, they turned to psychics.*

SHE FELT THE KILLING URGE RISING IN HIM DAYS BEFORE HE TOOK HIS NEXT VICTIM, BUT SHE WAS POWERLESS TO STOP HIM.

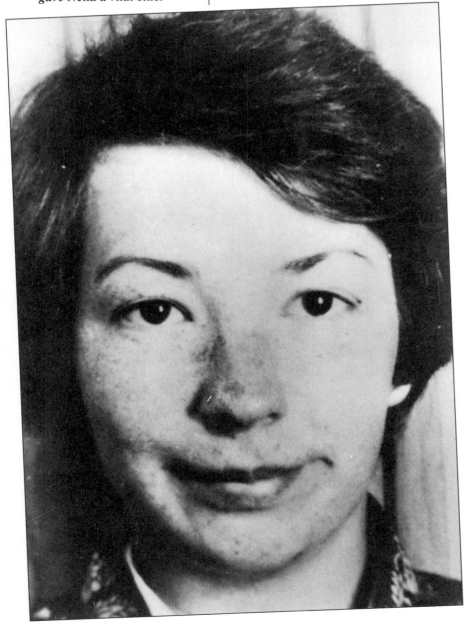

Below: *The Yorkshire Ripper's 13th victim – Jacqueline Hill of Leeds – who was found dead on 17 November 1980. The killing gave Nella a vital clue.*

she was having a cup of tea with a policewoman friend that she became involved publicly in the hunt for the murderer. As she sat sipping the warm brew, she suddenly had a vision of him with his bag full of tools near a cemetery, and as he walked down the road she described the surrounding countryside as though looking through his dark eyes.

The policewoman immediately recognized the scene as being a place near where she used to live in Yorkshire. Shortly afterwards Nella was phoned by Shirley Davenport, who worked on the *Yorkshire Post* and had come to hear of her powers. The journalist asked her if she could give an accurate description of the murderer, who by

now had been dubbed by the press the 'Yorkshire Ripper'.

Suddenly a man's face appeared in front of Nella. It hovered in mid-air just inches away from her, close enough for her to smell his bad breath and see the drops of perspiration on his skin. His eyes were blank and dark, like a shark's, and he had a fine white line above his lip and a dark beard. Nella relayed all this over the phone to the reporter until she could no longer bear to look at the vision.

She chillingly predicted that he would kill again and she described his next victim, even down to the clothes she wore. By now he had already killed 11 women and was Britain's most wanted man.

Through Shirley, Nella released as much information on the case as she was fed by her psychic powers. It took over her life for the next year: Sutcliffe's face haunted her almost daily. She also suffered horrific nightmares during which she saw him stalking women.

Throughout 1979 Nella put together the profile of the Ripper which was to prove amazingly accurate when they eventually captured the pervert.

She 'saw' that he was a long-distance lorry driver whom she was convinced lived in Bradford and was much older than the police thought.

When detectives handed her a photocopy of a letter they believed was written by the serial killer, she was immediately surrounded by a cacophony of voices who shouted the name 'Peter' over and over again. The voices instructed her to draw what they described, and she worked quickly, sketching a road with a flyover across it, a lorry depot and tall tower shaped buildings. She could see the initial 'C' on the side of the lorries. The names of two streets cropped up, Chapel Street and Charles Street.

She knew he was going to kill again, and the word 'Ainsworth' had something important to do with it. Shortly afterwards, the body of a naked young woman was found in the grounds of a house owned by a man called Peter Hainsworth. She had been strangled.

Every time the Ripper decided to kill, Nella could feel the urge rising in him in the days before he took his latest victim. Before he murdered his final victim, she accurately

saw that the poor woman's initials were 'J.H.'. She also knew it was going to be his last murder, and that soon after he would be caught.

On 17 November 1980 the Yorkshire Ripper murdered Jacqueline Hill in Leeds. Later, as Nella retraced his steps on the day of the murder, she found the street the spirit voices had told her about: Chapel Street. It was down this street that she found a bundle of papers which she passed on to the investigating officers. She was later told they contained pictures of naked women and one had a childish drawing of a man stabbing one of the women in the heart with a knife.

Not long before Christmas 1980 Nella had a vision that the Ripper would be caught very soon. She was relieved to hear that he was arrested by police on 3 January 1981.

As Nella's fame grew, so too did the demands on her time. Once she foresaw a double murder in Brighton. A man and a woman would be found dead in a flat above an antique shop. She vividly described how the couple were in a bedroom when another man suddenly entered wielding a knife. The victims were both drunk and the woman was out cold. After a terrible struggle both lay dead, the walls awash with blood.

When she told her local police contacts, they called their colleagues in Brighton and were told that there had been no such murders in the Sussex resort. It wasn't until two months later that two charred bodies were dragged from the smouldering remains of an antique shop exactly as Nella predicted.

STARTLING ACCURACY

Nella Jones is far from being the only psychic detective in Britain …

Anne Owen, a round-faced pleasant woman with an easy smile and laughing eyes, has also been called in by police to help with their cases. She has used her clairvoyance skills to find missing persons and dead bodies. In one case, she located the whereabouts of a man who had been missing for three months. When his body was found, he had been eaten by foxes.

Anne tunes into the events surrounding the crime almost like a radio station and is into the very heart of the person who has committed the deed.

Her first big murder case was the slaying of a nurse based at a hospital in Ashford, Kent. Anne walked through the hospital corridors trying to pick up information with

*Above: **Britain's most wanted man is finally brought to justice on 3 January 1981. After successfully eluding police for so long, the Ripper's reign came to an end suddenly, taking Fleet Street and TV by surprise. Nella says she had known since well before Christmas that the hunt for him was almost over, even though the arrest had a large element of luck.***

THE RESCUE TEAM ABANDONED THEIR SEARCH BUT THE PSYCHIC KNEW THAT THREE MEN WERE STILL TRAPPED IN THE HULL OF THE BOAT.

Below: *The wreck of the passenger ferry* **Herald of Free Enterprise** *lies just off the coast of Zeebrugge. Three survivors owe their lives to Anne Owen's visionary abilities.*

her psychic antennae. As she explored she 'reconstructed' the crime in her mind's eye. Anne felt that the body of the slaughtered nurse was not on the premises and that it would be found elsewhere. Not long after, it was discovered just as she had foretold: wrapped in a black bag in Epping Forest after being moved there in the boot of a car. A hospital porter was later convicted of the murder.

Anne's talents have taken her abroad to solve crimes. When a young student was killed in Wiesbaden, Germany, Anne told police who the murderer was.

After the Zeebrugge ferry sank with many dead, Anne helped to save the lives of three men. Divers had abandoned their search for survivors in the cold, murky water, convinced that they had managed to

rescue all of those who had not been killed. But Anne knew there were people trapped in the hull of the boat. She 'saw' three men who were miraculously still alive and quickly rang a contact at the BBC TV station who got a message through to the rescue teams. The men were found inside the ship, their lives saved by an air bubble.

Like Nella, Anne also received messages about Peter Sutcliffe as he carried out his grisly crimes. She 'saw' him as a lorry driver living in Bradford five months before his capture.

Some psychic detectives regard maps as a vital tool of the trade: the American Greta Alexander helped find the body of a young woman, Mary Cousett, simply by floating her hand above one. Mary had gone missing

after leaving her Illinois home with her boyfriend. She was thought to have been murdered, but police had drawn a blank when it came to finding a corpse. True, the boyfriend had been arrested and charged with her murder. Because of lack of evidence, however, the police could not bring the case to court.

As a final desperate measure they called in Greta, who concentrated on a map and told them to look in an area they had not previously searched. She also told them that the person who found the body would have a crippled hand. The body would be found in three pieces, the head and feet separated from the main torso. The letter 'S' would also be significant, she predicted. The body was found by a young policeman whose name was Steve and who had badly damaged his fingers in an accident earlier.

Nancy Czetli was called in by Maryland police to help solve the murder of 62-year-old stabbing victim, Leonetta Schilling. Nancy was shown police photo files and she picked out the picture of someone whom she believed was the killer. She said he had the same thought pattern as the murderer and predicted that police would find that Leonetta had been his babysitter at one point.

Nancy was startlingly accurate: she had chosen a picture of the old woman's nephew. Allen Glenn Finke was convicted of the brutal murder of Leonetta, who had indeed babysat for him when he was a child.

CAUGHT OUT

Sometimes psychic powers can backfire on both the medium and those who call for help. Poor Etta Louise Smith, an aircraft factory worker, had a vision in which she saw the dead body of a young woman. She rang the police and told them that she had 'seen' the corpse of a nurse who had gone missing the night before. It had been dumped in a canyon.

Etta told officers that she thought the nurse had been raped and that the killer had dealt her a fatal blow to the back of the head. Instead of heeding her warning, sceptical police arrested Etta on suspicion of murder. They had not released any details of the killing at that time, and concluded that she must have slain the nurse herself.

Etta was held for four days before three

men were charged with the killing. Later she was awarded $24,000 compensation from the Los Angeles police for wrongful arrest.

Owen Etheridge, meanwhile, was caught out when he rang a psychic radio broadcaster in California. He told Dixie Reterian that his father was missing and emotionally asked her if she could help find him.

Owen was told to come into the radio station with something belonging to his father. He handed over the man's watch and ring. As he did so, Dixie looked at the teenager's face and had a vision that he had killed his father.

She called the police and told them she believed Owen had shot his father and that the body would be found nearby wrapped in a green sheet and with a green cloth tied around its neck. A detective confronted Owen with these details and the boy broke

Above: *Sutcliffe's job as a lorry driver gave him the perfect cover to carry out his appalling crimes. No one thought it odd that he was away from home for long periods of time and Sutcliffe would while away the hours on long journeys by plotting his next attack.*

Above: *Digging up the Newall's garden. Dowser Brian Terriss was called in by police and informed them they were probably dealing with a murder inquiry.*

THEY DISCOVERED THE CLOTHING EXACTLY WHERE THE PSYCHIC HAD PREDICTED, BUT THE CORPSE HAD BEEN SWEPT DOWNSTREAM.

Opposite: *Roderick Newall after pleading guilty to murdering his parents. The case is one of only a handful on record in which a dowser has been used to assist detectives.*

down and confessed that they were all true. He led them to the body, exactly as Dixie had described it.

HORRIFIC CRIME

One specialist in 'seeing' missing people after handling their personal items is Gerard Croiset. It was because of his accuracy in this field that he was asked by police to help pinpoint the whereabouts of a missing teenager.

Pat McAdam was hitchhiking home to Dumfries, Scotland, with her friend Hazel Campbell. They had been to an all-night party in Glasgow in February 1967. A lorry driver picked both of them up and drove Hazel to a point near her house. As the two girls bid each other goodnight, Hazel was not to know that she would never see her chum again.

Pat did not arrive home. Police interviewed the driver but the girl's body had not been found and they had nothing to go on. Enter psychic detective Gerard. He picked up Pat's Bible and after a brief meditation declared that the young girl had been killed.

He 'saw' a bridge from which her body had been thrown into a river. He went on to describe the house next to the bridge. It had an advertising hoarding on the side wall; in the garden was a car with no wheels and a wheelbarrow propped up against it. He believed the girl's body was caught underwater in the gnarled roots of trees on the riverbank. Her clothes were trapped so that she could not float to the surface. There were also clothes hanging in the branches.

The investigating officers already knew that the driver's lorry was often seen close to a bridge. When they searched the area that Gerard pinpointed, they found the house exactly as he had predicted. They also found the clothing but no body. The river had flooded and it was thought the corpse had disappeared downstream.

Pat's body was never found and her murderer never brought to book. However, ten years later a lorry driver was jailed for a similar, horrific crime: the multiple rape and murder of another poor woman. Although the police could never prove it, they suspected that the same man killed Pat.

A more unusual aid for spiritual detectives is a pendulum. Brian Terriss, a 56-year-old harbour worker from Guernsey, uses his powers as a dowser not to find water or metals but to find people. Brian searches for them by the ancient pendulum method, dangling the device over a map.

The pendulum swings and jerks until the missing person is located. If the person is alive and well, the pendulum swings round and round. If it goes dead then that is where the search for a body must begin.

Brian has only once been called in by police: when wealthy underwriter Nicholas Newall and his wife Elizabeth went missing on the neighbouring Channel Island of Jersey.

The dowser held some items belonging to the couple: a glove, a lipstick and pieces of clothing. When he held his pendulum over the missing pair's mementos, he came to the conclusion that they were both dead. Finding them was to prove much harder. He travelled to a bay in Jersey, where the couple's boat had been moored. He picked up vibes from his map, but a search failed to come up with the bodies.

Long after they were declared dead, their murdered bodies were found buried in woodlands. Both their sons were charged in connection with the killings.

On another occasion, again using his dowsing technique, Brian pinpointed the body of a dead seaman who had gone missing. Police searched the area but found nothing – yet the body turned up seven weeks later, exactly where Brian said it would be. Rescuers had failed to find it because seaweed had anchored it to the seabed.

How could he have known?

DAVID ICKE

He wanted to be world famous but a cruel and crippling illness put paid to his football career. Then David Icke discovered his alternative destiny: he was to be the saviour of the world.

As a soccer league hopeful David Icke would bellow at team defenders and mutter about the judgement of referees. In the chair as a top sports commentator he remarked on the finesse and form of snooker or football heroes of the day. Later, he became an outspoken champion of environmental issues, fighting passionately to free the Earth of its choking pollutants and other hazards. But none of these activities prepared the world for what was to come: David Icke as the son of God.

His astonishing declarations and further exploits as 'the chosen One' made him and his family the laughing stocks of the nation.

But how could a one-time goalie and happily married father of two have turned so spectacularly into a mystic messiah – collecting a curious female entourage in the process? To see him perform on the pitch, few would have guessed the baffling future he had in store.

As a teenager in Leicester he displayed some stunning sporting skills. It seemed he was going to realize every boy's dream of playing soccer for a top British club when he was signed as an apprentice by Coventry City at the age of only 15. Dexterous David Icke was the master of the goal mouth, diving and leaping to make exciting saves.

But soon his athletic prowess was hindered by a series of injuries. The joints in his knees and elbows would balloon with painful swellings. Doctors were unable to say what was causing the string of problems. Courageously, he overcame the discomfort to continue playing, but by the time he was 19 it was clear something was critically wrong.

He was devastated when rheumatoid arthritis was diagnosed before he celebrated his 20th birthday. It cruelly ended his promising career with Coventry City. He moved to lower league Hereford United and was part of the team which won promotion from the fourth to the third division. His agility finally deserted him when he was just 21. It was a personal disaster for Icke. The trauma was compounded when, without an income, he and his wife Linda were virtually evicted from their home. He had to make some hard decisions about his future – and fast.

A HIGH FLIER

With his sporting pedigree he looked towards journalism, monitoring the action on the field instead of making it. Again it seemed certain he was headed for the big time.

From the launch-pad of his local newspaper in Leicester, Icke shot into sports broadcasting. He had a comfortably buoyant manner in front of the camera with expressive eyes and a ready smile playing around his generous mouth. His clean-cut good looks soon had him marked down as a high flier at the BBC.

When long-time anchorman Frank Bough left *Grandstand* it was thought by many that Icke would inherit the position. In fact, he did win the hot seat for a number of shows and proved himself a worthy recipient of the job.

But Icke had pushed noses out of joint at the BBC – which would spell his downfall. First, he refused to fly to international sports

HIS EXPRESSIVE EYES AND THE READY SMILE PLAYING AROUND HIS GENEROUS MOUTH ENSURED HIS APPEAL TO THE FEMALE AUDIENCE.

Above: *Icke was master of the goalmouth. He could make diving saves and leaping catches which left the crowds gasping in admiration. As a young keeper for top club Coventry, it seemed he might go all the way to the top and become goalie for the England team.*

Opposite: *He loved football. But he suffered a string of mystery injuries which hampered his performances. When rheumatoid arthritis was diagnosed it seemed Icke's glittering career had come to an end when he was aged only 21. It was the first hurdle of many in his life that he had to overcome.*

Above: *Icke became a first-class sports commentator. But above all he was a family man and didn't care who knew it. He preferred to stay at home with his wife Linda and their two children rather than jet off on overseas jaunts for work. His reluctance to leave them probably cost him a top job.*

Right: *Linda was devoted to her husband, and he to her. She stuck by him through thick and thin and refused to believe the gossips who linked his name to that of another woman. Even when the shameful truth emerged, she stayed loyally at his side.*

events. He was, he told bosses, too terror-struck by aircraft travel to work abroad. When he was eventually sent overseas to cover the 1986 World Cup in Mexico he grumbled about the heat and the working conditions, to the chagrin of those left behind in London.

Even in Britain, he disliked travelling to events if it meant being parted from his wife Linda and children for too long. As a devoted father and husband, he had no time for the drinking and wild affairs that often accompany working trips, which further added to his reputation for being out of step. One producer summed it up. 'As a presenter he knocked everybody else I had into a cocked hat but he wasn't a prima donna and perhaps you have to be if you're going to make it to the top.'

FALL FROM GRACE

For the second time in his working life, he was no longer a golden boy and fell from grace. Rival Desmond Lynam was finally picked for the *Grandstand* job, leaving Icke frustrated and bitter. His brilliant career was reduced to fill-in spots from sporting events around the country. He was left reflecting on

Don't let your world turn g

Vote Green.

THE GREEN PA

a lost opportunity and facing a future of bit-part broadcasting.

To fill the void he decided to move to the Isle of Wight, where he had spent happy holidays as a boy. In 1984 Icke, Linda and their children Kerry, 9, and Gareth, 2, moved from Aylesbury to a flat in a Victorian mansion block at Ryde, Isle of Wight.

There he entered some quick-fire campaigns to establish himself in island life. First, there was the Steam Railway Society. Icke had always been fascinated by steam trains and longed to see them return to puff and wheeze along the disused tracks crossing his adopted home island. But he was allied to the slow-moving campaign to reintroduce old time railway services for less than a year.

He cast around for another interest and found a role in the Special Olympics for the Mentally Handicapped, but again his association with the organization was brief.

After that he flirted with politics, first joining the Liberal Democrats. He was proposed as a prospective MP for the island but dropped out after being short-listed.

Then Icke looked to the Green Party, which he considered a true reflection of his beliefs at the time. Within six months he became national spokesman for the Green Party. He even talked about being Britain's first Green MP. His passionate beliefs in installing sound environmental sense in the rest of the nation was set out in a book,

It doesn't have to be like this: Green Politics Explained which sold 10,000 copies. But his abrasive style hallmarked by belliger-ence and barracking won him few friends. It was doubtful he would have won anything like the number of votes needed to make history and be Green in Parliament. The fact was, Icke never stood in an election to put his popularity to the test.

Residents in the close-knit community on the Isle of Wight finally lost faith in him following a noisy protest against the poll tax, the government's short-lived scheme to raise cash for local councils. The tax was about as popular and provocative as a fox in a hen house, so Icke found no shortage of supporters when he demonstrated against the introduction of the tax, pledging to go to jail rather than pay. When he defied the law, the BBC ended the dwindling number of contracts it had put his way. He was no longer a broadcaster but a live force in politics, if only for a brief spell.

But six months later it was revealed that he had paid up the money he owed, sidestepping the martyrdom – and discomfort – of a spell behind bars. Icke also faded from significance in the Green movement – which was still struggling to find a foothold in Britain's tightly run political scene. He finally resigned when he wrote to party leaders telling them of a book he was writing which would make his place in the party untenable.

Above: *Icke became absorbed by green politics. The world was waking up to the long-term havoc being wreaked on the environment by mankind. It seemed the Green Party was at last winning popular support and even had a chance of entering Parliament. Icke was at the heart of the movement as national spokesperson for the party in Britain and was one of the four people regarded as the leaders of the group.*

THE SAVIOUR OF THE EARTH

Above: *Icke won acclaim for his refusal to pay the poll tax, considered by many to be an unjust scheme. But his following dwindled when he quietly paid up rather than face jail.*

Behind the scenes, Icke had found a new cause which put everything else in the shade. He had been visiting medium and spiritual healer Betty Shine at her base in Brighton, ostensibly to find a cure for the arthritis which still plagued him.

But while he was visiting her for the third time in March 1990, she imparted some news from her contacts in the other world which made Icke sit up and listen. She communicated with a wise Chinese mandarin from the 12th century who was in the company of renowned philosopher Socrates. The message came back that Icke was in reality a healer who came to save Earth and was destined to be world famous. Before that could happen, he would have to abandon politics, the message relayed. For Icke, it was an eye-opener. His true purpose in life was at last exposed.

At the time Mrs Shine said she and Icke had undergone an amazing experience. 'I was giving him healing and suddenly this incredible person appeared and the whole room throbbed with the most tremendous power.

'It was just like a powerhouse and it shattered David. There were messages that he had got a job to do.'

Icke explained: 'Through Betty I received some astonishing revelations and predictions of fundamental importance to the future of humankind which set me on a journey of discovery that I would have found impossible to comprehend unless my path had crossed with hers.'

Aged 38, Icke felt the future of the world lay in his hands. He took his pivotal role seriously and set off around the world researching mystical religion, energy lines and the like.

At a Green Show held in the National Exhibition Centre in Birmingham, he met a group of people all committed to alternative beliefs, among them Deborah Shaw. Deborah was a teacher, born and brought up in Kenilworth, West Midlands. After qualifying, she taught deaf children in her home town until she moved to Calgary, Canada, on an exciting new contract.

In Canada, she had a plush apartment, a jeep and led a life-style which more befitted a wealthy executive than a humble teacher. That's because Deborah was a woman of means. Her shopowner father had died leaving a lump sum to his four children. Deborah was also a director of Toytown, a toyshop chain in the West Midlands.

After their initial meeting, Deborah wrote to Icke and invited him to Calgary. He went. It was there he became involved with women from a curious sect who took him to their hearts.

At a screening of a film about UFOs, he was introduced to Maia Trettler, a 48-year-old science teacher, who believes herself to be a reincarnation of St Francis of Assisi. Millions of years ago, she believes, she came from another planet and now she and fellow believers are known as the Brethren of the Flame.

She was known to dance naked with friends around a circle of stones in her garden and also to bow to the Sun.

Maia said of Icke later: "When he told me he was going to an Inca shrine in Peru I had to embrace him. After two minutes I said "I love you" and I gave him a psychic message. When David came back from Peru he asked me: "Did you know something passed between us when we embraced?"'

She went on: 'We are going to build a healing centre here in Calgary and I hope the entity you call David will play a major part. I've already put a £30,000 deposit on the land but I don't know where the money came from. Even the bank can't explain it. Sometimes it just seems to drop out of the sky. Everything we need will come the same way.'

In fact, the Brethren of the Flame is linked to the Church Universal and Triumphant. Its doctrine is based on the movement proclaimed in 1930 by engineer James Ballard after he had recounted a mountain top meeting with St Germain. Loosely explained, followers are urged to think and say positive, loving things to make the world a better place. It's often referred to as the 'I am' philosophy with its emphasis on phrases like 'I am feeling great'. When church leader Elizabeth Clare Prophet predicted the world would end in 1990, scores of believers trekked to her commune in Montana to seek refuge in a costly system of bomb shelters and defensive weapons.

Feeding off this intense spirituality, Icke and Deborah Shaw teamed up for trips across America and later around the world in the quest and thirst for greater understanding. While he was away Icke's father Beric died after a long illness and was buried before the wandering son – now apparently cured of his fear of flying – returned.

Deborah now changed her name to Mari Schawsun, explaining to friends she had always wanted to be called Maria after seeing *The Sound of Music*. And she seemed set to abandon the life she had made for herself in Canada in order to follow Icke

across the globe. In March 1991 she was due to host a seminar she had planned meticulously for weeks previously, aimed at helping the deaf children she taught. Instead of turning up for the prestige event, she came to England to be at Icke's side. Thousands of miles away inside her Calgary apartment were her two cats who had given birth to five kittens and were left to fend for themselves until site managers broke in. After forcing an entry they found a ring of rocks on the floor.

A PROPHET OF DOOM

On his return to Britain David Icke gave a press conference to unveil his new persona. A stunned audience listened as he announced: 'I am the conveyor of new truths … a messenger of the great Godhead. I am here to warn the world of pending terrible disasters.'

Among his predictions were floods in Tayside, Mull of Kintyre, Ireland, Japan, Holland and Denmark, with tidal waves hitting Greece and southern Italy; earthquakes in China, Salzburg, Austria, Cuba, Mexico, Los Angeles, New York, Las Vegas and the Texan oilfields; volcanoes erupting in Washington, Italy, Martinique, Japan and Sicily; and tornadoes hitting

---

IT SEEMED THAT ICKE SINCERELY BELIEVED THAT THE FUTURE OF THE WORLD LAY IN HIS HANDS.

Opposite below: *Spiritual healer Betty Shine helped Icke to recover from some of the ravages of rheumatoid arthritis. On his third visit to her, she imparted some startling revelations to him.*

Below: *A cyclone caused devastation in Bangladesh in May 1991, claiming as many as 200,000 lives. Icke infuriated the aid agencies battling to do relief work among the injured and homeless there when he announced that the catastrophe proved he was a prophet.*

FOR ONCE THE JOURNALISTS WERE SPEECHLESS: THE FORMER SOCCER WHIZZ-KID WAS CLAIMING TO BE THE SON OF GOD.

Above: *The Greek philosopher Plato, who revealed the teachings of Socrates. Betty Shine's communications with long-dead philosophers had a powerful influence on Icke.*

DAVID CLAIMED THAT A HIGHER FORCE HAD BROUGHT HIM AND MARI TOGETHER FOR SEX — AND THE PAIN WAS EXCRUTIATING!

Londonderry, Northern Ireland, and New Zealand. In addition, he forecast the collapse of the Channel Tunnel before its opening and the melting of the polar ice caps. Saddam Hussein was dead, he added for good measure, and later warned people not to wear black because of its damaging effects.

Revealing his strange predictions, Icke eventually returned to the soccer style parlance he knew his audience would understand. 'Nobody was more gobsmacked than me when my mission was revealed. Many people will not believe me. They have their free will. I'm laid-back about it.

'We have now reached a situation in time when our world is under threat. The Godhead itself has become imbalanced. The whole of creation could end. I am here, though, to tell you of these dangers. And there is still hope. Please believe, believe in the power of love. It's mankind's only escape.'

The world would end in 1997 unless more people issued loving thoughts and deeds, he insisted. Laudable his messages may have been, but they found little favour in the audience. The assembled journalists were virtually speechless at first and then began to openly ridicule Icke.

They found it bizarre beyond their wildest imagination that the former soccer whizz-kid was in front of them claiming to be the son of God.

A FAMILY AFFAIR

Even more strange was the appearance of Icke with his loyal wife Linda on one side and friend Mari on the other. Daughter Kerry, struggling to suppress nervous giggles, was also paraded for the press. All wore turquoise, Icke's chosen colour to symbolize love and wisdom.

Everyone wanted to know the extent of his relationship with Mari, labelled by Icke as the daughter of Christ. He would only declare: 'We have complementary energy patterns.'

Meanwhile, Linda would be known as Michaela, said Icke, being the earthly spirit of the Archangel.

His mother Barbara looked at all this askance. 'Any mother would be worried when her son starts behaving like this. I don't know what's happened to him, he never used to be religious.'

His brother Paul went further. 'Some of the things he has said sound totally far-fetched, suggesting he's flipped his lid and gone round the bend.'

As for Icke, he practically cut them off from his new spiritual life, telling them only they would understand more if they read his book.

Eyebrows were raised even further when it was clear Mari was living with Icke and his wife in their Isle of Wight flat between their jaunts around the world.

Within months, a massive cyclone devastated Bangladesh, killing 200,000 people. Icke claimed it was proof of his predictions. His comments provoked a furious response from British charities who helped mop up the after-effects of the catastrophe.

A spokesman for the Red Cross pointed out: 'Bangladesh is extremely disaster-prone and therefore it is very easy to predict cyclones there.'

Icke was then drawn to Britain's mysterious corn circles. The circular patterns which appear in farmer's fields are thought by some to be created by energy forces although others believe them to be an elaborate hoax.

After waiting until sightseers had left the circle which appeared in Alton Barnes, Wiltshire, in July 1991, he emerged from his car in customary turquoise tracksuit and ran around the circle in an apparently trance-like state, in the company of a woman.

By now the public were cautiously intrigued by Icke – not that many were rushing to sign up for his newly expounded religion. Most of all, they were compelled and perplexed to know what could cause an apparently stable man to act so weirdly. Was he mad or simply the centre of a publicity bonanza?

When he appeared on the TV chat show *Wogan*, the BBC received 241 calls in protest. Just 14 objected on the grounds of blasphemy. The rest thought it was quite wrong to allow someone showing sure signs of mental illness to appear on TV. And they weren't alone. Psychologists called in by newspapers were quick to diagnose Icke's mental state as being near collapse. Former colleagues struggled to find words to explain his outlandish behaviour.

People also freely speculated about Icke's relationship with heiress Mari Schawsun. A

Sunday newspaper revealed the pair shared a king-sized bed during one of their foreign visits. His wife, who stayed at home while they went around the world, insisted there was nothing between them. Savings were paying for the family's bills and the trips abroad, she told inquiring reporters. Any inner torment at the activities of her husband of more than 20 years was cleverly disguised.

Later she told a newspaper: 'I would love to have gone with them but we didn't have the money. There were also two children to look after – they have always come first.'

And she revealed how David finally admitted to illicit nights of passion.

'David was absolutely distraught, he couldn't bear to look at me. But Mari was cool. She just said, in a matter-of-fact way: "We thought you knew."'

David told her how a higher force brought him and Mari together for sex.

'I can't remember anything except the power of the energies that came through. The energy was unbelievable, like swhoosh, right through the top of my head. When Mari and I were doing this it was as if I was

not really there in the room. I was floating somewhere above, almost as if I was on the ceiling.

'I kept saying: "No way." I didn't want any part of that. I had never been unfaithful to Lin and the pain was excruciating. All I saw was her face. No one could love his wife more, everybody who knows me knows that. That woman is absolutely everything to me.

'At times I have felt so guilty I felt like walking into the sea and disappearing.'

Together, the pair picked up the pieces of shattered trust. During lengthy seafront strolls they vowed they would never part despite the affair. Somehow Linda found the strength to accept her rival's presence under the same roof.

'People will say I am mad or blind. But I am neither, Mari said it was a triangle that would last for ever but in my heart I knew she was wrong. We did not have rows even when it was all in the open.

'Part of me was thinking all the time, this is for the greater good and if we don't do it we might harm the Universe. The other part, a down-to-earth Midlands wife, was saying

Above: *At a press conference, journalists looked on open-mouthed as Icke declared he was a mystic messenger who had come to warn them of impending doom. Beside him were his wife Linda, daughter Kerry – and heiress Deborah Shaw, otherwise known as Mari Shawsun. All wore turquoise, the colour nominated by Icke to represent love and wisdom.*

ICKE REMAINS CONVINCED THAT HIS PROPHECIES WILL COME TRUE UNLESS MORE PEOPLE FOLLOW HIS TEACHINGS.

Above: *Despite their difficulties, Icke, his wife Linda and their children remain as close as ever. They are still committed to their strong spiritual beliefs. After Icke's affair was revealed, Linda said: 'Part of me was thinking all the time, this is for the greater good and if we don't do it we might harm the Universe.'*

to herself: "I wish she would pack her bags and go back to Canada."

'I have always been totally sure of David's love for me. There was never any suggestion of a romance despite what Mari has said.'

A FINAL GOODBYE

But it was with relief that she greeted the news that Mari was moving out. As autumn dawned she helped pack the bags and said a final goodbye to 'the other woman'.

For two months life in the Icke household bore some semblance of normality. Then came a telephone call which threatened to

throw their new-found happiness into chaos again. Mari said she was having David's baby.

Both David and Linda cared little what people thought about their activities. They only became concerned if the scorn and insults from others were aimed at their children.

David only spoke out about the arrival of Mari's child, called Rebecca, when he was accused of failing to provide the necessary financial support. It was, he asserted, patent nonsense to suggest he would turn his back on any child of his. He was even willing to bring up the child himself if that was what the mother wanted.

With the furore over Mari's baby still in the air, Linda became pregnant too. She was sensitive to suggestions that, at 42, she became pregnant in a tit-for-tat revenge on her rival which would keep her husband by her side.

'It was nothing to do with cementing our relationship because, despite all that has happened it has never been rocky. It sort of happened and I couldn't be happier.'

She gave birth to a boy at the start of 1993.

As for David Icke, his days are now spent reading the mountains of mail that come his way after writing four books, among them *The Truth Vibrations*, much of the mail being supportive.

He remains convinced more and more people will follow his teachings. As he writes in *The Truth Vibrations*: 'I am well aware of what the reaction to this book will be. The people reading it will fall into three main categories: those who laugh; those who condemn and those for whom it will change their lives forever ... And with every month and year that passes, the latter group will grow and grow until it is the largest.'

At weekends, he plays football again, either with his elder son Gareth or for a local team where he made his comeback two years ago.

Spiritual healing has improved his arthritis sufficiently for him to take his place in goal once more. Supporters were quick to test their wit on him. 'We want to make a profit, not sign one,' yelled one. 'No good on the cross, eh?' roared another. But Icke had enough commonsense to practice what he preached. He turned the other cheek.

CURSES, JINXES AND SUPERSTITIONS

PAST LIVES

Haunted by strange feelings and inexplicable terrors, many people are driven to explore the possibility that they may have lived – and have suffered – before. As they delve into memories of their past lives, the results can be extraordinary – and horrific.

Princess Diana fulfilled a burning ambition when she met Mother Theresa (above) *in Italy. Friends say Diana has tried to model her own life on the woman dubbed a living saint.*

In the cramped lounge of the modest semi in Surbiton, south-west London, a wide-eyed, attractive young woman listened intently to the gentle Irish brogue of her medium.

It was the unlikeliest of meetings. The medium, Betty Palko, was little known outside the circle of society figures who unburdened their souls to her. The young woman was Diana, Princess of Wales, and mother of a future king of England. And she was describing her past life as a nun.

Had fate not intervened, it is unlikely the world would ever have known about Diana's clandestine visits. It was only when taped phone conversations between the princess and a male friend – the so-called 'Squidgy Tapes' – were published in 1992 that the name Betty surfaced in connection with a discussion on astrology.

Diana says: 'Betty said it would be all OK, didn't she? The most fulfilling year [1990] yet.' She goes on to talk of her work with the sick and dying and speaks with venom about a meeting with the bishop of Norwich.

The princess tells her friend: 'In the end I said: "I know this sounds crazy, but I've lived before." He [the bishop] said: "How do you know?" I said: "Because I'm a wise old thing."'

In the context of the explosive nature of the tape these few lines were largely ignored as trivia. But as the dust settled several journalists with the right connections realized the Betty referred to had to be Betty Palko, medium to the rich and famous. Mrs Palko was duly doorstepped but loyally refused to reveal details of her private conversation. Eventually she gave a brief interview admitting that Diana did visit her, that she had the skills of a healer and believed she had lived a past life as a nun. She also sought to model herself on 'living saint' Mother Theresa.

Mrs Palko said: 'She will definitely be a person like Mother Theresa – she is so humble in her heart and is a wonderful healer. She knows she can heal. That's why she goes to all these places to help people.' The medium said Diana's aura (the glowing 'life force' psychics claim to see around all of us) suggested that in addition to her past existence as a nun she had been cruelly treated in an even earlier life.

The fact that such a high-ranking member of the British royal family should hold such unconventional beliefs is not as embarrassing as it might once have been.

Opposite: *Diana the bride. Her clandestine visits to the medium Betty Palko were hinted at in the so-called Squidgy Tapes. Diana told Betty she believed she had lived before as a nun.*

> THE RESPECTABLE WHITE SLAVE OWNERS SUBJECTED THE BLACK GIRL TO A HUMILIATING AND DEPRAVED INSPECTION — THEY CLAIMED THEY WERE TESTING HER SUITABILITY FOR FUTURE BREEDING STOCK.

For despite derision from the sceptics, 'past life regression' is rapidly gaining credence from the more open-minded psychologists and psychoanalysts.

The theory is that we have all lived before, a belief held for centuries by some Eastern religions that regard reincarnation as possible even between different species of animal. For most, memories of a past existence are said to be buried so deep in the psyche as to be barely recognizable. But for those who have suffered exceptional hardship, sadness or violence the mind can suddenly replay a series of events which burst out in a mass of confusion and contradiction.

FLOGGED TO DEATH

One of the experts leading the field is Dr Roger Woolger, a psychoanalyst who trained under well-established Jungian theories but decided to investigate regression therapy after practising meditation with a Buddhist teacher. He remembers coming out of one session to inform his teacher of some odd memories he had experienced. The mystic replied without surprise: 'But of course, those are your past lives.'

Dr Woolger says: 'That started me off on reincarnation. Now I wouldn't practise any other way. My success rate has doubled and I find patients' problems resolve themselves much faster. I've now treated more than 3,000 people and most of their stories, though very sad, were mundane. If these lives were invented they would be much more exciting.'

Attending one of his sessions means watching others appear to journey back in time. At one lecture hall in London in 1990 he regressed a number of volunteers under hypnosis. One woman who complained of depression and low self-esteem sat on stage, her head bent, hands together.

'Where are you?' asks Dr Woolger.

'In China. I'm about 14. My feet were bound when I was a child. Although I come from a poor family I have been chosen to be a bride of the emperor.'

The doctor moves her forward to a scene in which she is being forced to carry a large pitcher of water. 'I can't walk,' she says. 'It's very difficult. I've dropped the pitcher. It's broken. It's all my fault.'

Dr Woolger: 'What happens now?'

Woman: 'They're taking me to prison. I know I am going to be flogged.'

Dr Woolger: 'Is there any pain?'

Woman: 'It doesn't matter. I deserved it. I'm now above my body. I must have died. I can no longer feel any pain. I was too young. I deserved it.'

As the woman breaks down she is asked gently whether the age 14 was of particular significance in her present life. She replies: 'It was when I lost my virginity – unwillingly.'

HIDDEN FEARS

Other patients of Dr Woolger have experienced present-day problems that he can link to previous life trauma. One woman told him she couldn't bear the prospect of being ogled or sized up by strangers. Under deep hypnosis she told of her miserable former existence as a black slave, and of being prodded by slave owners. She was forced to undergo a humiliating inspection in which her masters claimed they were testing her suitability for future breeding stock. Once that experience was brought out of her psyche she was cured of her fears.

Another woman blessed with a superb voice sought counselling because she always froze with nerves at auditions. When she was put through hypnosis she told of living in an ultra-strict Amish community, a people she'd never even heard of. She remembered becoming pregnant at 18 and being hauled out in front of a kangaroo court of village elders. They whipped her and gang-raped her as 'punishment' before driving her out of the village. It was a logical explanation for her fear of being confronted by men who, of course, occupy most audition panels. Once she'd confronted her hidden memories, however, her career took off.

Past lives can cause physical as well as mental problems, according to Dr Woolger. Chest pain can be a link to a knife attack, asthma to suffocation. One young patient came to him suffering from inexplicable eye pains which surfaced from the moment he attended a new school at the age of 9. Hypnosis showed he had once lived as a street urchin who was forced into class by a

Left: *The kitchens, Glastonbury Abbey. Near this spot, so the legend goes, Arthur and Guinevere are buried side by side – ready to rise again when England is in peril.*

Below: *King Arthur and Queen Guinevere seen through the eyes of an early artist. Is Laurel Phelan a Guinevere reincarnation?*

truant officer. The boy remembered being bullied on his first day and a sadistic gang actually gouging out his eyes.

Though past lives are often filled with agonizing memories, most discoverers quickly come to terms with their legacy. Some even turn the whole experience into a reassessment of their present existence … and bounce off into a new career.

BLOOD AND GORE

One such is Canadian Laurel Phelan. She penned a movie film script on the Arthurian legends of old England with the working title *Guinevere: Truth of a Legend.* It was hawked around the Hollywood studios amid both scepticism and enthusiasm from producers, who inevitably asked where she'd got her research material. 'No need,' she'd reply. 'You see, I saw it all. I was Guinevere in a previous life.'

In early 1993, with Tinseltown's gimmick-alert now ringing loud and clear, Laurel arrived in England to explore her Arthurian roots properly. First stop was Glastonbury where, so the stories go, King Arthur and Queen Guinevere lie buried in a spot marked by a simple wooden cross.

'Knew where it was instantly. I didn't need a guidebook to tell me. I just came straight here,' said Laurel. 'It's hard to explain what it feels like to stand on your own grave. It's kinda intense. You hang around a bit after you die, in spirit form. You witness your own funeral. But after that, obviously, I don't know what happened to this place, or to England.'

Her recollection of life in 5th-century Britain was somewhat different from that

**THE MIDDLE-AGED ACTOR
QUICKLY DENIED ALL
KNOWLEDGE OF HIS LIFE AS
A LOVER OF THE SEXUALLY
RAMPANT GUINEVERE.**

Right: *The popular, angelic image of Arthur and his knights of the Round Table. But according to Laurel Phelan, Queen Guinevere was not as she is imagined.*

Below: *Glenn Ford. He was amazed when researchers showed that men he described in some of his past lives really did exist.*

recorded in classic historical works such as *Morte d'Arthur*. For a start, she said, Arthur was not a royal of ancient blood-stock, but a Roman nobleman charged with keeping out the northern and Welsh marauders when Rome recalled the main body of the occupying army. Merlin was, in fact, the resident historian and the only magic on show was produced with the help of some hallucinogenic mushrooms.

As for Guinevere herself – not for her the joys of jousting, feasting and looking queen-like in long white robes. Instead, claimed Laurel, she was an expert knife fighter with a reputation for being sexually rampant. In the film script Guinevere thinks nothing of beheading her sister-in-law and in one scene her taste for gore actually extends to chopping off the private parts of an unfortunate Saxon warrior. His testicles are then popped into a drinking cup and infused with boiling water like some kind of medieval teabag. 'Since people have read the script they have been rather nervous when they see me handling kitchen utensils,' she says.

Laurel told how her decision to begin past life regression followed a series of dreams laced with blood, gore and knives while she was in her early 20s. Under hypnosis she recognized herself as Guinevere but later described the whole process as extremely unpleasant – 'I didn't like myself. I kept seeing me killing Saxons.

'Up till about the age of 23 my life paralleled hers. I was raped. I had a strong relationship with my father. I used men to get what I wanted. You see, one's past life is stronger than genealogy. I don't look that much like her. She had higher cheekbones than me, curly hair, bigger breasts.'

Laurel claimed the film project produced an unforeseen spin-off in the shape of a reunion of several former Arthurian figures. She believed one of her major financial backers was a Pict ('when I told him he wasn't too happy') and a production assistant was one of her old 5th-century lovers. She even claimed to have identified a well-known middle-aged British actor who used to be Sir Lancelot. He was invited to take a role in her film although she admitted he seemed 'rather distant' in his reply. 'That's no surprise,' she said. 'There's a lot of misunderstanding

between us that needs to be worked through.'

PAST LIVES OF THE STARS

The idea of regression is hardly alien to Hollywood. Dozens of big stars have gone public with the belief that they once lived previous lives. One of the most publicized cases involved the actor Glenn Ford, who in 1978 was regressed first into a Colorado cowboy and then later into a piano teacher from Elgin, Scotland.

Ford was shocked to hear tapes of the hypnosis session – but even more amazed when researchers provided evidence that the men he described did indeed exist. The first, cowboy Charlie Bill, worked for a farmer called Charles Goodnight. He talked of his long hours at work in the saddle, of the rations he had to endure and of how he was eventually ambushed and shot dead by cattle rustlers. Students from the California State University in Los Angeles later established that both men had indeed been alive in the 19th century.

That regression was performed at the star's Beverley Hills home but for the second session he agreed to be hypnotized under carefully controlled conditions at the university itself. Almost immediately, one Charles Stuart spoke through Ford to reveal he taught the piano in Elgin to young 'flibbertigibbets' – a dialect term for naughty children. Ford even played the piano under hypnosis but admitted later: 'I don't know how. I cannot play a note.'

The research team flew to Scotland and discovered the grave of a Charles Stuart, who died in 1840. When they returned with a photograph of his earlier resting place Ford admitted: 'That shook me up really bad. I felt immediately that it was the place I was buried. I'm very confused about it all. It conflicts with all my religious beliefs. I'm a God-fearing man and proud of it but this has gotten me all mixed up.'

Other show-business figures who believe they've lived before are more philosophical. Country music star Loretta Lynn has spoken openly of the two lives she recalls clearly – even though she received unhappy images from both.

'It was like kind of being in a trance,' she said. 'The first time it happened I saw a rolling hill filled with horses and Indians.

All the Indians had their war paint on. I knew the Indian on the horse up front was my husband. My husband was the chief because he had long feathers all the way down his back – a head-dress.

'He and his braves were going out in the valley. I was standing beside his horse. I was wearing a long buckskin skirt and my hair was twisted in a braid. I was saying goodbye to my husband when all of a sudden a shot rang out. He slumped forward and started falling off the horse. I screamed and started running toward the teepees.'

In her second, later life Loretta saw herself married with three young children and living in terrible poverty as she tried to care for a sick husband.

'I saw myself running up an old gravel, muddy road,' she said. 'I was barefoot and wearing a dirty cotton dress. As I got to my house I realized it was a shack. I don't know how we ever lived in a place like that. My kids were around – triplets who'd just started walking. My husband was moaning and lying in a bed. All three of the babies were screaming and crying while I was feeding him.'

Above: *Martin Sheen. His most striking past life experience was of being a cruel cavalry soldier. The soldier was trampled to death under his horse and the experience left Sheen with one abiding legacy – he can't bear horses.*

Above: *Sly Stallone. Did he live four previous lives … two of which ended in violence?*

'I FEEL TREMENDOUS FEAR AND CAN HEAR HORSES' HOOVES COMING … HE HAS ONE OF THOSE CURVED KNIVES AND HE SLICES OFF MY HEAD.'

Right: *Helen Reddy. Her list of past experiences runs into hundreds and includes a vivid memory of decapitation.*

Memories of unhappiness are one thing, but some of the biggest names in Hollywood are on record as giving the most horrific accounts of their previous deaths.

Martin Sheen talks of being a cruel US cavalry soldier who died when he was trampled to a pulp by a horse. The experience has left him with an abiding fear of horses and panic attacks at the thought of any of his children going riding. Catherine Oxenberg believes stomach pains she suffered are caused by wounds inflicted in a previous life when she was tortured by Nazi doctors conducting concentration camp experiments. Singer Willie Nelson talks of being 'fried' in the electric chair after his career as a professional gunfighter was halted by the law. And Canadian actress Helen Shaver (Sheen's co-star in *The Believers*) reckons that in the year 579 BC she was a Greek high priestess who made love to her adopted son. He later strangled her.

Sly Stallone suspects he lived at least four previous lives, two of which ended in violence. In one incarnation he was a nobleman beheaded by the guillotine during the French revolution. In another he was a US boxer who died from a knockout punch during a fight in the 1930s.

As for Canadian pop star Helen Reddy – her list runs into hundreds. During regression sessions under hypnosis she has told of being a 13th-century page employed by an English knight, a duchess, a maid, a Romany palm reader living in Egypt and an Arab potter. She also vividly recalls life as a male trader crossing the Persian desert. A scene in which he is ambushed is burnt into her memory: 'I feel tremendous fear and can hear horses' hooves coming. The next thing I see is someone coming into my tent on horseback. He has one of those curved knives and he slices off my head.'

OUT OF THE MOUTHS OF BABES

A feature of previous lives is that they seem to transcend sexual orientation. In one well-documented case in England a little girl called Nicola Peart first alerted her mother to a past life when she was given a dog for her second birthday. With faltering words, a beaming Nicola said:

'I'll call it Muff, like the other dog I had before.' Her mother Kathleen dismissed her daughter's comment as the result of an over-active imagination. But later Nicola asked: 'Why am I a little girl this time, Mummy? Why aren't I a boy like I was before?'

Kathleen quizzed her further. Her daughter told how her 'other mummy' was a Mrs Benson and that they had lived at Haworth, Yorkshire, two miles from their present-day home in Keighley. Kathleen knew her daughter had never visited Haworth and was intrigued to hear her talk of the mid-terrace house she used to occupy with her two younger sisters and the mother whose first name, she thought, was Elsie. She remembered her previous mother wore a skirt and had hair 'all tied up funny'. Her father, a railwayman, always had a dirty face. The house was built of grey stone and was one of four built in a row.

Then Nicola told of her past death and how her mummy was always telling her not to play near the railway. 'I didn't used to listen to her,' she said. 'I was playing on

had described it – in Chapel Lane. Nevertheless, it could still have been a coincidence so Kathleen delved further.

In the parish records she discovered that a baby boy called John Henry Benson had been born there on 20 June 1875. His father had been a railway platelayer and his mother was called Lucey – desperately close to Nicola's recollection of Elsie. However, a national census in 1881 showed no mention of little John at the address, only his two younger sisters. The obvious conclusion was that he died before he was 6.

The amazing story defies modern-day logic. Nicola's recollection of her death remains as real as any memory of her present-day life. When she was 4 years old she was watching a TV drama in which a man was about to hurl himself from a bridge in front of an oncoming train. Nicola began to scream uncontrollably, throwing herself onto the carpet, fighting for breath and flinging her arms around wildly. She shouted down attempts to calm her and kept repeating 'the train, the train'.

The Nicola Peart case remains one of the strongest pieces of hard evidence for human reincarnation. Yet there are literally dozens of other children who have made similar claims. One such is Elspeth Lacey, from Newcastle upon Tyne, north-east England, who at the age of just 18 months suddenly began talking coherently about her memories of a convent.

the railway lines with Muff and a friend and I saw a man walking along swinging a lamp. After that a train came up fast and knocked me over. I got taken to hospital. Everyone kept asking me if I was all right but I couldn't walk or talk so I couldn't answer them.'

By now Kathleen was determined to get to the bottom of the mystery. She took Nicola with her for a walk over the moors to Haworth. They got lost … but Nicola was able to show her the way. She showed her mum her old home too – exactly as she

THE TODDLER'S EYES GLAZED OVER AS SHE TALKED COHERENTLY ABOUT HER LIFE IN A CONVENT CENTURIES BEFORE.

Left: *Nicola Peart. To date, no one has satisfactorily explained her extraordinary experience of another life. The detail she recalls is precise – and verifiable.*

Below left: *The kind of scene that was familiar to Nicola in her past life as John Henry Benson. Back in 1875 her father was a railway platelayer.*

Above: *The life of a nun is almost impossible to explain to a young child. Yet at 18 months little Elspeth Lacey began talking lucidly of her memories of a convent.*

Right: *Jonathan Pike: aged 3, he suddenly began talking of his wife.*

Below: *Was Jonathan a mechanic before he was born?*

Her mother Joan tells how the little girl's eyes glazed over as she pronounced: 'I'm not Elspeth now, I'm Rose, but I'm going to be Sister Teresa Gregory. I've got a long frock on and I'm walking up to the altar.' Later on she continued: 'I was an old lady once, Mummy. I always had a long black dress and I had a black cloth over my head and I was very, very old. It was when I was here before.'

Once, during another trance, little Elspeth told how she was in a convent in the countryside where, as Sister Teresa Gregory, she remembered having a lot of responsibility for running the convent. She described her simple, sparsely equipped room where she always said a lot of prayers. She even remembered how she died while saying prayers and recalled trying to call out. Then she awoke to find herself with old friends – nuns who had themselves died.

A third case involved a youngster called Jonathan Pike from Southend, England, who at the age of 3 suddenly began talking about his 'wife'. He and his parents had just moved to the town from Hull and were still finding their way around. Then one day during a bus ride Jonathan pointed at some white houses and pronounced: 'That's where my wife Angela lived.'

At first his mother, Anne, thought he was playing a make-believe game. He told her confidently: 'When I was here last time I grew up into a big man and Angela was

my wife.' He spoke of his son and curly headed daughter (also called Angela) and on one occasion became panicky and started weeping as he passed a particular crossroads in the bus. 'That's where my little girl got killed by a car,' he said, repeating the claim almost every time he saw the spot.

Jonathan also identified the garage where he used to work as a car mechanic – one of four in the town but easily the oldest and the only one which employed mechanics. Because he could never remember his previous name it has proved impossible to check his story. But there

was one tantalizing clue relating to the death of his 'daughter'.

Some time after Jonathan's case became public a long-serving traffic officer with Southend Police, Sgt Ernie Dark, remembered being called out to a fatal road accident at the crossroads Jon spoke of so much. Sgt Dark couldn't remember much; after all, the tragedy had occurred 30 years before. But he knew one thing. The victim was a little girl.

Another so-called 'memory child' is Carl Edon, brought up in Middlesbrough, north-east England. At 3 years old he was drawing perfectly formed Nazi swastikas – hardly a normal phase of child development – and telling anyone who would listen that it was the badge he used to wear on his uniform when he went flying. He could draw the cockpit of the plane, the position of all the controls and instruments and explained how each switch

worked and what each reading meant. He had never been near a cockpit and his parents knew there were no books on flight at home or at his playgroup.

His bewildered mother Valerie was even given an insight into how he died 'last time' on his final flight. 'It all went black for a moment,' said Carl. 'Then I saw this building rushing towards me. I smashed through a window and realized my leg had been torn off.' He put his age at around 23.

These examples all back up the theory that some of us retain memories from previous existences, much as our genetic make-up draws on the characteristics of ancestors going back hundreds of years. Interestingly there is little evidence that a reincarnated life stays in the family. However, as Nicola Peart and Jonathan Pike have discovered, there is a tendency for regenerated souls to return to their old haunts.

A HIDEOUS DEATH

One even more striking example of this concerns an Englishwoman called Avril Colvill, whose marriage to TV comedian Robin led her along a bizarre and inexplicable journey into her past.

Robin had long had an interest in hypnotherapy, particularly regression therapy. One day Avril asked him to try the technique on her and he successfully took her back to a life as a 17-year-old girl living in 1755. She poured out a long list of names, places, dates and events that meant nothing to Robin. He found it difficult to believe that this was his wife talking.

As the session continued she told how she was a very beautiful virgin who had pledged her troth to a wealthy, land-owning knight called Roger de Coverley. She was to move away from her father's estate in Northamptonshire to live with him and confessed to fears about the coming match. De Coverley was, she said, known to be a jealous man who spent much of his time drinking and gambling with his society friends in London.

As the session continued, Avril moved on to a time where she explained she was 'with child'. Robin coaxed more out of her and took her to the point where she gave birth. He recalls: 'The next thing I knew she was screaming and kicking; her whole face was contorted, her body twisted. It was as though she was going through hell. I brought her out of it straightaway. You must be able to do that – I don't recommend that people dabble with past regression. She was fine once she came round and begged to know what she had said. We were both intrigued but longed to know if it was historically accurate.'

The couple visited a historian, who was astounded at the accuracy of Avril's story. A man called De Coverley had indeed been a north country knight who married a young virgin, but the relationship broke down when he suspected her of having a fling behind his back. When he discovered

Above: *The bewildering array of controls in a World War 2 plane cockpit was faithfully reproduced by Carl Edon, aged 3.*

Above left: *The Nazi swastika remains a symbol of terror. Carl would tell how he wore it on his flying suit.*

HER FACE CONTORTED, HER BODY TWISTED: SHE WAS GOING THROUGH HELL AS SHE WAS FORCED TO GIVE BIRTH WHILE DYING FROM HER HUSBAND'S CRUEL PUNISHMENT.

his new bride was pregnant he flew into a terrible rage, walling up both her and her lover in a secret compartment he created in a local church. Later he was put on trial for his appalling crime and was executed.

Robin says: 'It came to me why Avril had become hysterical under her regression. When she was giving birth she was dying – walled up in that small stone church.'

The Colvills gradually forgot about their bizarre experience and didn't let it affect their marriage. But years later a strange twist of fate brought it all flooding back. Robin was working in a pantomime in Sheffield when he took a phone call from Avril. She wanted to talk about their plan to build their own home. She'd seen some land – a bit expensive perhaps – but she felt

Above: *Avril and Robin Colvill. Under regression Avril became hysterical – she was re-living the moment she gave birth while walled up inside a church.*

she had to have it. It was perfect for what they wanted.

On an impulse Robin told her it was OK with him. The plot was in Calverley, just outside Leeds. Then, some days later, he told Avril the name had a nagging familiarity. Wasn't it a bit like the Coverley of De Coverley fame? And hadn't he lived somewhere near Leeds? The couple dashed to their local reference library to check.

'Sure enough Calverley dates back to the De Coverleys,' says Robin. 'They had owned the land that we now live on. Our life had become a 200-year-old cycle … unbelievable but true.'

Sceptics say Avril Colvill and others like

her may indeed speak of unfamiliar stories and images under hypnosis. But they argue that the subconscious mind is more powerful and complex than modern medicine can even imagine. What regressed people are really doing, say the sceptics, is churning out information they never even remembered taking in. And the personalities they assume could be simply creations of their own imagination.

There certainly are some regressions which appear anything but believable. One 19th-century incarnation spoke of her 'boyfriend' in the modern sense – that is someone who had formed a sexual relationship with her. Then there was the man who was taken back in time to England in the early 1830s and claimed Queen Victoria was on the throne. In fact there were then at least four years of William IV's reign to go … and it was by no means cut and dried that Victoria would get the crown.

CONVINCING EVIDENCE

A well-respected Finnish pyschiatrist, Dr Reima Kampman, decided to test the theory that we can all produce multiple personalities while under hypnosis. One of the sample group, a 13-year-old girl, offered by far the most convincing evidence for reincarnation when she suddenly became Dorothy, daughter of an English innkeeper who was born in the Norwich area in 1139. She gave an in-depth account of life in the 12th century, including names and events she remembered. She even sang an obscure ditty in the old Middle English language – it was later matched to records in the British Museum and identified as the 'Cuckoo Song'.

At first her story seemed to offer more hard proof of a previous life. But when she was again hypnotized by Kampman some years later the session cast new light on her case. She recalled once leafing through a library volume called *The Story of Music* by Benjamin Britten and Imogen Holst. Part of the text referred to the 'Cuckoo Song' and though she only skipped her eyes across it briefly, her subconscious was able to file the whole thing away … even though it was in a language that meant nothing to her.

This said, there are a great many powerful arguments suggesting regression therapy is, for the most part, what it claims to be. For a start the dramatic accounts trotted out by subjects are often far in excess of their known acting abilities. For all the world it as though they are actually living out the mental images they project.

Secondly, there is the fact that a regressed patient will return to the same period in history without any effort and take on the speech and mannerisms of the same characters. When interviewers repeat a question from a previous session (to see if the subject answers it any differently) they almost inevitably get consistency.

Thirdly, there is the point that little-known facts of history are churned out in the most incredible depth. Often special research has to be commissioned before such facts can be checked and it beggars belief that a regressed subject can be so accurate about a matter barely covered by established works.

Finally there is the evidence of manners of speech. Even very common words can change drastically within a few years – the word 'gay' is the classic example – and yet people reliving a past life will talk in the language of the day and use words in a context they could surely not have picked up subconsciously. What scriptwriter or author would take the trouble to use the word 'slip' in its old Irish meaning – as a pinafore rather than the modern meaning, a petticoat?

Between November 1952 and October 1953 an amateur US hypnotist called Morey Bernstein regressed a 29-year-old Wisconsin housewife back to her previous existence in Cork, Ireland, where she was born on 20 December 1798. During these sessions housewife Virginia Tighe became Bridey Murphy and churned out a constant stream of highly detailed images of her life and times in a middle-class Protestant family. Her story is perhaps no more extraordinary than those above. But it drew headlines around the globe because of a celebrated film on her regression experience and an inflamed debate in the newspapers.

Mrs Tighe had neither visited Ireland nor had any close links with the Irish. Yet as Bridey (who was actually christened Bridget) she told in a clear Irish brogue

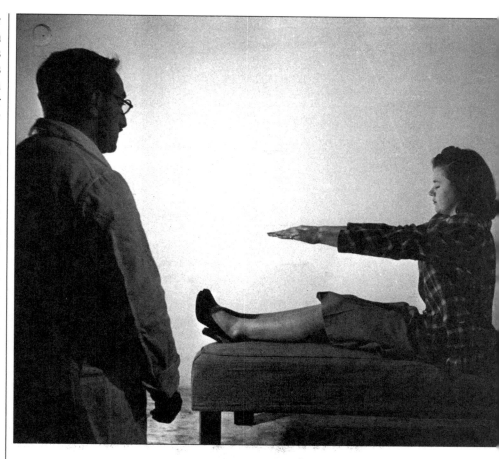

how she was the daughter of Duncan and Kathleen Murphy who lived at The Meadows, Cork. Her brother, also Duncan, was two years older than her and married Aimée, the daughter of one Mrs Strayne who was a mistress at Bridey's school. In around 1818 Bridey married Catholic Brian MacCarthy (whose relatives she could name as wedding guests). They took a stagecoach to start a new life in Belfast and she talks about passing through settlements on the way, though none of the names shows up on modern maps. She talks of shopping in named stores and worshipping at St Theresa's Church where the priest was a Father John Gorman. The shops – Carrigan and Farr – both proved to have existed. Of the good father and his church there was no trace.

But Bridey referred to the coinage of the day and used the correct language. It was she who used 'slip' for pinafore, 'linen' as the Irish word for handkerchief and talked of 'ditching' when she spoke of burying something. All were said without any hint that the language was contrived or forced. Bridey appeared to be talking naturally.

Above: *Science or stunt? This picture supposedly showing a woman in a hypnotic trance seems too staged to be authentic. Yet hypnotists can open barriers inside the mind.*

Some sceptics thought they'd caught her out when she made a reference to a metal bed. Metal beds, one historian stated confidently, were unknown in Ireland before 1850. Then someone unearthed an Irish advertisement for a metal bed. It was dated 1802.

In her final regressions Bridey told how she died aged 66 after falling and breaking her hip. She spoke of her own funeral and tombstone and even mentioned the uillean pipes that were played. The pipes were customarily played at Irish funerals because of their solemn and gentle tone. But how would Virginia Tighe have come across them in Wisconsin?

> THE SCEPTICS THOUGHT THEY HAD CAUGHT HER OUT — BUT THEY WERE TO BE PROVED WRONG.

MULTIPLE LIVES

There are dozens more case histories which have captivated the public throughout the 19th and 20th centuries. The celebrated Welsh hypnotist Arnall Bloxham performed many successful regressions, including that of a Jane Evans who revealed six different lives. The first was Livonia, living in AD 286. She was apparently the wife of Titus, a classics teacher who taught the future emperor of Rome, Constantine.

Then Jane emerged as a Jewish girl called Rebecca who lived in 12th-century York, England, at the time of a pogrom. She remembered being slaughtered in a church crypt and her descriptions quickly identified the church as St Mary's, in Cripplegate.

An analysis of her regression was conducted by Professor Brian Hartley, of Leeds University, an acknowledged expert on Roman Britain. He established that most of the names and facts she churned out were accurate, even though some were fairly obscure and unlikely to be gleaned by any except the keenest of students. But the St Mary's massacre of the Jews seemed less convincing. St Mary's had no crypt. Was Jane Evans making the whole thing up? A few months later workmen carrying out renovations in the church provided the answer. They discovered its lost crypt ... almost exactly as the Jewess Rebecca had described it.

Another of Bloxham's most celebrated patients was a young Welshman called Graham Huxtable. His lilting tones turned into a twangy south of England drawl as he told of his experiences on board a British man o' war during naval campaigns against France at the turn of the 18th century. He used an almost indecipherable slang and spoke of practices unheard of in the modern-day navy. However, most of the actions and equipment he described were later verified by the National Maritime Museum in south-east London.

Occasionally regressed patients are able to go into extraordinary detail about a large sample of their previous lives. In 1911 the hypnotist Colonel Albert de Rochas published an account of how he took a woman he called Madame J back step by step through her previous ten identities.

In the first one she died aged just 8 months. She then became a girl named Irisee, who lived near Trieste. From there she transformed into a man, Esius, who appeared to be plotting to kill the Emperor Probus on the grounds that Probus had taken his daughter Florina.

Then came Carlomee, a Frankish warrior chief captured by Attila at Chalons-sur-Marne in AD 449. From Carlomee it was a change of sex once more – this time to a sadistic abbess who took apparent pleasure in dominating and tyrannizing the teenage girls in her charge. Abbess Martha was replaced by a woman called Mariette Martin who described herself as the daughter of a man in service to the king around 1300.

Madame J then seems to have skipped almost 200 years to take on the psyche of Michel Berry, cut down aged 22 in the 1515 Battle of Marignano. Michel's life was described in minute detail, from his training in fencing at the age of 10 to his life in service as a pageboy in the courts of Versailles, a number of passionate affairs and his role in the Battle of Guinegatte, Normandy, in 1513.

From here Madame J jumps to 1702 where she talks of herself as a 30-year-old married woman. The next life placed her in 1776, once more as a man – sculptor Jules Robert. Jules reincarnated into the tenth, and last life – grocer's daughter Marguerite Duchesne, of Briancon.

The fact that Madame J remembered exactly ten lives is intriguing in the light of evidence given by the British psychic Joan Grant 26 years later. Joan became a national figure after writing a book called *Winged Pharoah*, said to be a historical novel. It received widespread praise from the critics as a highly accurate and descriptive account of the period it covered. According to Joan Grant the research was easy ... because she was there at the time.

From the moment she was a tiny girl she had been telling her family about what had happened 'before she was Joan'. As usual in such cases the adults around her decided she had an over-active imagination, refused to believe her and got on with their busy lives. Joan soon decided it was better to keep her knowledge to herself and she was well into her teens before she told a friend of her extraordinary experiences. In the meantime she tried hard to understand the bizarre dreams that filled her mind most nights.

It was not until 1936, however, that Joan found herself in a position to explore one of her past lives, almost as though she was living it again. She had been given a scarab – an Egyptian gem sculpted in the form of a sacred dung beetle – and whenever she held it she found herself entering a familiar trance state and heading back to the time of the pharoahs.

Over 200 separate regressions she dictated notes on her life as Sekeeta, the daughter of a pharoah and a woman who would later rise to become a priestess. The notes ran to 120,000 words, but perhaps the most fascinating section concerns her assertion that exploring past lives was a skill known and enhanced in Egyptian times. Anyone accepted for training in the

SHE STRUGGLED TO UNDERSTAND THE BIZARRE DREAMS THAT HAUNTED HER NIGHTS.

Below: *A mass-hypnosis session like this can be designed for almost any audience. But regression therapy, hypnotists agree, should be left in the hands of the experts.*

Right: *The well-known Harley Street hypnotist W.J. Ousby gathered a loyal following of patients undergoing psychoanalysis at his weekly clinics.*

art had to remember at least ten of their own deaths (perhaps Madame J was also a pupil) and then spend four days and nights locked in a tomb while they went through seven ordeals.

Sekeeta passed her test with flying colours and on her way to the 20th century seems to have lived out a string of separate existences. These include several in Egypt and others in 2nd-century Greece, medieval England and 16th-century Italy.

BEYOND THE GRAVE

Most of the cases in this chapter present powerful evidence for some kind of previous life phenomenon. If it does exist, how does it exist? And what are the implications?

Sadly, there are few answers to these questions, although the idea of regression has been around since primitive times. Indian Assam and Nagas peoples were taught that the soul moves into an insect after death. Borneo tribes believed the dead reincarnated into the bearcats that gathered around raised coffins. And in central Africa Kikuyu women used to worship at holy ground that they believed was haunted by ancestral souls because they thought a soul had to enter them before they could become pregnant.

Among the few who have attempted to explain regression are Buddhist and Hindu priests, who see nothing unusual or abnormal in the experience. According to some Hindu doctrines, people are reborn into creatures on the basis of the merits they have notched up during their lives. A particularly good citizen might rise further up the human social scale. A bad one could expect to slide down and become a toad, a lizard or even a cactus.

Buddhists take the view that every human being is composed of six basic elements – body, sensation, perception, impulse, emotion and consciousness – which all collapse at death. The person ceases to exist but then reincarnates into a new life, entering the world at a social scale dependent on previous actions. Put simply, good people move up; bad people move down, the purpose being that everyone has a chance to attain perfect bliss – the state of Nirvana.

Among the philosophers, Pythagoras asserted that the soul had tumbled into an earthly form and needed to reincarnate itself through a host of different creatures to be freed again. He made notes on what he believed were his own previous lives, including a spell as a soldier in the Trojan wars. Plato insisted the soul was immortal, that the number of souls was constant and that reincarnation occurred regularly.

One of the most fascinating studies in this area was conducted by the psychologist Dr Helen Wambach in her book *Life Before Life*. In a two-year investigation she regressed 750 subjects, under hypnosis, to a time before they were born. The subjects were offered the option of not experiencing their previous deaths, although hardly anyone took it. Dr Wambach reports: 'Ninety per cent of my subjects found that death was pleasant. Yet none of them reported that they had lost their zest for life. So I thought that they would find the return to life in another body a basically pleasant process. I was wrong.'

She says 81 per cent confirmed they had 'chosen' to be reborn, though often they made the choice reluctantly. Participants talked clumsily of consulting with advisers, of feeling some sense of duty to accept the new life offered to them on the grounds that there would be a new experience, or lesson, that would be an important part of their overall spiritual development. Only a quarter of the sample said they actually looked forward to the coming lifetime.

Dr Wambach writes: 'So death was experienced as pleasant by 90 per cent of these subjects, but being born – living another lifetime – was unhappy and frightening. What a strange reversal of what I had expected. Do we love and value life so much as we publicly profess in this culture?'

One thing is sure. No one in this world is going to prove her findings right or wrong.

We're all going to have to wait to find out.

HER FINDINGS OVERTURNED ALL THE CONVENTIONAL THEORIES.

Below: *Not all of those who claim to have regressed can be believed. One man taken back to a specific date in the 19th century claimed Queen Victoria was on the throne. In fact William IV was.*

CURSED PLACES

The beautiful old church and quaint cottages are the very picture of peace and tranquillity, yet this lovely village is cursed by a series of gruesome murders as law-abiding people are driven to destroy those that they once loved.

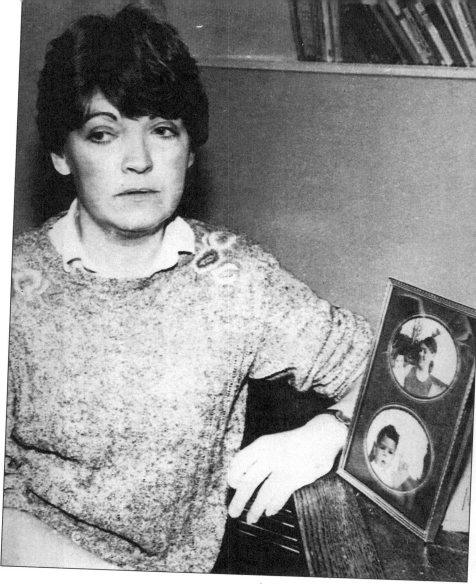

Cold-blooded murder is still rare in Britain today. Across England and Wales there are on average fewer than two slaughters every day. And you might reasonably expect those two unfortunate victims to be caught up in the drugs trade of a grimy inner city or on the receiving end of a ruthless armed robber.

But there's one green and pleasant corner of England which suffers more than its fair share of grisly killings. On the outside it looks leafy and affluent and sleepy enough for a speeding milk float to make the news. The lawns are manicured, the houses spruce and the streets worthy of a picture postcard. Yet in Coggeshall, Essex, there is an unexpected blip in the crime statistics, making it a chilling blackspot. In 1985 alone there were six murders here. And there are reports of other untimely deaths which make the spine tingle. For the past decade, observers have been prompted to ask: is Coggeshall cursed?

BATTERED TO DEATH

All eyes turned to Coggeshall in 1983 when doctor's wife Diane Jones was slain. Her killer has never been found.

Mrs Jones, aged 35, shared a magnificent home, the 16th-century Lees Farm, with her husband Robert, a GP in the village. She was last seen at the village pub before she went missing. It was nine days

before her husband reported her gone, believing she had walked out on him. Three months later, her battered body was found in a copse at Brightwell, some 35 miles from her home. Investigators discovered she was two months pregnant. It's thought she died on the night she disappeared.

Dr Jones, aged 40, was grilled for more than 60 hours about the disappearance of Diane, his third wife. The case continues to baffle detectives. By 1990 the doctor had married his fourth wife, Lorna, become a dad for a fifth time and moved away from Lees Farm to Stanway, some five miles distant. But new evidence brought sleuths to his door again. Early one morning a team of detectives turned up at his home and led him away to Ipswich police station for further questioning after new evidence emerged. He was there for seven hours before being allowed home.

His name was in the headlines again in 1992 when he was struck off for eight

Above: *Diane Jones was last seen in Coggeshall's pub. Nine days later her doctor husband reported her missing. It was three months before her body was found. Police scientists calculated she died only hours after she was last seen drinking at the Woolpack Inn.*

Opposite: *The Woolpack Inn, Coggeshall. Trippers believe Coggeshall to be in a quiet corner of rural England where the greatest crime is milk bottle theft. But some of the most notorious crimes in England have taken place here as well as one of the most vexing mysteries. Is an ancient curse causing acts of unseemly violence to occur?*

Above: *Dr Jones was prime suspect in his wife's disappearance and murder. Police grilled him for nearly 70 hours about the case. But he was never charged in connection with Diane's killing. He went on to wed again, for a fourth time, and moved away from Coggeshall, which held so many unhappy memories for him.*

months by the General Medical Council, who decided he had not been sufficiently vigilant in the case of a 47-year-old patient in failing to diagnose an appendix abscess. Dr Jones, facing the first complaint of his 20-year career, had prescribed indigestion tablets and pills for an ulcer.

A SORRY TALE

Tragedy struck the village less than two years after Diane's death when the body of Patsy Bull was found in the antiques warehouse she ran with her husband Wilfred. She had been shot in the head at point-blank range. Her dead body was discovered by her son Charles (known in the family by his pet name of Humphrey), who raised the alarm. At first police believed she was the victim of a bungled raid. Her tenacious fight forced her attackers to flee empty handed, they announced.

But within 24 hours, her husband was charged with the killing. The following year an Old Bailey court heard a sorry tale unfold.

Company director Wilfred Bull had spent years building up a successful business. He and his wife were familiar figures at the country's major antiques fairs and had a string of rich and sometimes famous customers. When Harold Wilson (now Lord Wilson) was prime minister, they sold him a set of chairs. They also numbered royalty among their customers. The couple, who had two children, were introduced to Princess Margaret and Princess Alexandra at shows they themselves had organized. Bull became an expert on ivories, respected the world over for his judgements about good, bad and indifferent pieces. In addition to her interest in antiquities, Patsy ran a fashion business selling top quality dresses to clients for as much as £1,500 apiece. A shotgun incident a quarter of a century earlier involving Bull, in which he accidentally killed his brother David while they were out bagging rabbits, was the only shadow which darkened their golden existence.

Mrs Bull was round and rosy; a vibrant

personality exuded from her ample bosom. She was the driving force of the duo, the one who inspired the business to the heights of success. After her death one friend remarked: 'Patsy was a larger-than-life personality and he [her husband] was terrified of her. But she didn't deserve to die.'

Bull appeared to have it all: a loving family, a £500,000 house, international recognition and ready cash. But it wasn't enough. He had a weakness for women and for one woman in particular. She was a 38-year-old widow, Carol Scotchford-Hughes, with whom he was infatuated. He would invent elaborate stories to win nights away from home which he would spend in intimacy with the woman he adored. Later, a family friend said: 'Wilfred was besotted with Carol. He was a bit of a soft touch with women and she always made a great fuss of him. He saw himself as a sugar daddy and called her his crazy Carol.'

For a while Bull believed he could keep everything – a wife, family and mistress. But Patsy found out about his 6-year-long affair and was furious. Facing a costly divorce that would wreck the livelihood he had built up so painstakingly over the years, he managed to convince his wife the fling was finished. For a while she believed him, but when she discovered the liaison was still flourishing, Patsy was furious. She asked her son to drive her to the flat in Chelmsford, Essex, used by the pair as an illicit rendezvous, where she confronted her love rival and threw her to the ground.

On the day of the shooting, the Old Bailey jury heard how Bull had endeavoured to meet his mistress in secret but that the plans had fallen through. The disappointment turned to frustration and anger. There was a confrontation with Patsy in the warehouse during which she demanded a divorce. It ended with Patsy being felled by a bullet from a .38 Smith & Wesson through the brain.

At first Bull tried to cover his tracks by faking a robbery. Then he quickly changed his story, telling police the killing was an accident. He described how the death of his brother – when Bull's finger was once again on the trigger – flashed through his mind like a TV film. He told the court he loved his wife and spoke of her as 'a

HE WAS DETERMINED TO HAVE IT ALL – BUT HIS HURT AND ANGRY WIFE WAS THREATENING HIM WITH DIVORCE AND RUIN.

Above: *Patsy Bull was a larger-than-life character who was a driving force in her family's business. When her body was discovered, shot at point-blank range, police believed she was the victim of an armed raid that went tragically wrong.*

Left: *Wilfred Bull had a loving family, a luxury house and a booming business. But he wanted more. He had a 6-year affair with an attractive widow. And when his wife discovered the infidelity, his comfortable life was threatened because she demanded a divorce.*

Below: Tolleshunt D'Arcy, the scene of one of Britain's most appalling crimes. Britain grieved with Bamber (bottom) as he wept at the funerals of his family. Yet his tears were phoney.

marvellous woman. Effervescent, volatile and tremendous fun … to kill her was the last thing I wanted to happen.' Both his son and daughter Suzanne gave evidence against him in court.

After he was found guilty of murder Mr Justice Jupp told Bull: 'The verdict of the jury is based on abundant evidence and this was clearly murder, though no doubt during a quarrel and it was not planned.' Bull was sentenced to life imprisonment.

GUN-CRAZY

Worse was to follow for the upright citizens of the area: a case that was to shock the nation, nearly the perfect crime. A couple, their daughter and twin grandsons, were found blasted to death at their home in Tolleshunt D'Arcy, barely two miles from Coggeshall. The nation grieved with their sole surviving son Jeremy Bamber as he mourned them at their funerals after it was revealed his sister went gun-crazy in a fit of depression.

But the massacre in August 1985 was not all it appeared. The slipshod police search had failed to identify vital evidence. It was left to the accused woman's cousins to find clues that would help to solve the crime. Christine Eaton and David Boutflour were unconvinced about the police theory. Two days after the shooting they carried out a search of the picturesque Georgian White House Farm, the Bamber family home. In a cupboard they found the silencer and telescopic sight belonging to the murder weapon. Later, forensic scientists discovered it bore a hair and minute specks of blood from the supposed killer. How did it find its way back to the cupboard if she had shot herself?

But if that wasn't enough to stir detectives into action, the bombshell evidence from student teacher Julie Mugford which came hot on its heels was. She was the long-time girlfriend of Jeremy Bamber in whom he had confided his hopes and dreams of executing his parents to scoop a massive inheritance. Only when

he set his sights on another girl did she decide to come clean to police with all she knew.

What went through the mind of Neville Bamber and his wife June as they faced their son down the barrel of a gun, one can only guess. It was the ultimate treachery. The son they had nurtured from babyhood, seen through childhood illness and teenage troubles, had now turned vicious killer and showed them no mercy.

Jeremy was the illegitimate son of a vicar's daughter and a married army sergeant who was adopted by the Bambers, as his sister Sheila had been two years before. It was a comfortable, middle-class existence, an excellent starting point in life. But it wasn't enough for Bamber. His father, ex-RAF pilot Neville, had high hopes of him going into farming, but Bamber couldn't settle. After returning from a tour of Australia and New Zealand financed by his father, Bamber stubbornly refused to entertain the idea. Instead, he worked in casual jobs – as a barman or waiter – living the life of a playboy on a pittance of wages. In desperation, his father gave him the job of farm manager on the

respectable income of £170 a week. It wasn't enough.

By now his debts had mounted and still the clean-cut, charming Bamber could not resist leading a life of luxury. Meanwhile his sister Sheila, known as Bambi, had made a name for herself as a model. Married with twins, she was not without troubles of her own. The marital relationship had collapsed, her name was linked with drugs and her future was on the skids. It led to depression; her brother even claimed she was seriously ill with schizophrenia.

Bamber chose his moment with care. During the early hours of 7 August he slipped into the family home clutching a semi-automatic rifle and opened fire at point-blank range. Neville Bamber died with nine bullets in his body and sustained a battering from a rifle butt. His 61-year-old wife was shot seven times, one bullet striking her between the eyes. Both children were shot in the head as they slept; one was found with a thumb still in his mouth. Sheila, 27, suffered two bullet wounds in the neck, one severing her jugular vein.

Above: *Neville Bamber was a former RAF pilot who had made a success of farming in the rich natural pastures around his mansion home. When his son drifted from one job to the next, he made him farm manager with a steady income. But it wasn't enough to finance the handsome charmer's lavish lifestyle. Young Bamber knew he would one day inherit the agricultural empire built up by his father. He simply couldn't wait to get his hands on the cash.*

THE CHILDREN WERE SLEEPING PEACEFULLY. THE MURDERER SHOT THEM IN THE HEAD AT POINT-BLANK RANGE.

Above: *The Bambers offered a secure home to their two adopted children. And there were good times too, when the family – including son-in-law Colin Caffell – laughed together. As he grew older, Jeremy Bamber lost respect for his hard-working father and loving mother. He planned to execute them, along with sister Sheila and her sons, to leave himself sole beneficiary of the estate.*

Right: *The twins, Daniel and Nicholas, died when they were just 6 years old. The handsome children were the sons of fashion model mum Sheila, known as Bambi, and her husband Colin Caffell. Bamber convinced police that Bambi was a schizophrenic who at times believed she was possessed by the devil. They swallowed his story that she carried out the massacre in a fit of depression after losing a custody battle with her estranged husband for the boys.*

Bamber had enough guile to alert the police with a mock-frantic phone call. He told them his father had rung him and begged him to come over because Sheila was going beserk with a gun. Police swooped and kept the house under siege for three hours before storming the place and discovering the grim scenes. They readily believed it was a case of murder followed by suicide. Bamber was quick to paint an unattractive picture of his sister as a desperate manic depressive with a working knowledge of guns. At any rate, a coroner was convinced she had fired the gun and the funerals were allowed to go ahead.

Bamber wept at the cremations, but the tears didn't last long. Soon after he was busy asset-stripping in the house he once shared with his family, selling off antiques and heirlooms. He travelled to Amsterdam with Julie Mugford, wining and dining in top restaurants. He even offered topless and semi-nude pictures of his by-now notorious sister for sale to national newspapers. His demands for a 4-figure sum were not met.

Then came the fall-out with Julie Mugford which would lead to his downfall. Their violent spat about his interest in another woman was enough to send her scurrying to the police to spill the beans just two weeks after the funerals. Bamber was arrested but the police, short of firm

man. He has asked the investigative organization Justice for All to help him prove his innocence. Of course, the cash bequeathed by his parents, amounting to some £430,000, as well as all the property no longer goes to him as the sole heir. Its fate, like Bamber's, is in the hands of the courts.

A JEALOUS HUSBAND

In 1986 farmer Jimmy Bell, a champion clay pigeon shooter, continued the pattern of carnage that besets Coggeshall. Bell was a violent and jealous man. He had served five weeks in prison in 1982 for dragging his first wife around an American airbase with a toilet seat around her neck, after he accused her of having an affair with a flier.

HE DRAGGED HIS UNFAITHFUL WIFE TO HER LOVER WITH A TOILET SEAT DRAPED AROUND HER NECK.

Left: *Before his conviction, Jeremy Bamber stood to gain more than £435,000 as well as property. He didn't get a penny.*

Below: *Peter Langan entertained diners at his fashionable London eating house with bouts of excessive behaviour.*

evidence, had to let him go after five days. He went off to the south of France and while he was away, police accrued enough forensic evidence to make the case against Bamber stick.

Julie Mugford revealed to the court: 'He told me his father was getting old and his mother was mad anyway. He said he would put her out of her misery. Bambi was mad as well and had nothing to live for. He said he would drug his parents' drinks, then burn the house down. Then he told me he had changed his mind. There were valuable things in the house that weren't insured. Later he said he would do it by shooting.

'I couldn't take him seriously. I just didn't want to believe it.'

Throughout his 19-day trial at Chelmsford Crown Court in 1986, Bamber maintained his innocence. He said his ex-girlfriend had made up the story which so damned him. The jury found him guilty of murder by a 10 to 2 majority.

Judge Mr Justice Drake said Bamber had killed out of greed. 'Your conduct in planning and carrying out the killing of five members of your family was evil almost beyond belief.'

In March 1989 Bamber was refused leave to appeal on the ground that he did not get a fair trial. The Police Complaints Authority has also thrown out Bamber's claim that there was a miscarriage of justice. Nevertheless, he still harbours hopes of being released as an innocent

His family and friends lived happily with his excesses, knowing him to be warm hearted and well meaning beneath his bluff exterior. But the high life and perpetual drinking put a strain on his relationship with his wife Susan. When the marriage started to fail, Langan bought a country restaurant at Coggeshall near their home in nearby Alphamstone. It was his recipe for reviving their romance. But months later it appeared his efforts were in vain.

He tried to woo her back with a champagne dinner. They ended up dividing up their belongings in preparation for a split and even talked about the possibility of them remarrying in the future.

Susan, aged 47, returned with him to

Above and right: *Susan Langan was wined and dined by her husband on the night of his death. Susan thought they would spend one more cosy night together. Langan had different ideas and produced two petrol bombs and a box of matches.*

When Langan sparked the fuel he was armed with, an explosion wrecked his luxury marital home. Susan was saved when she hurled herself from a balcony. Langan died seven weeks after suffering extensive burns. She believes it could have been a grand gesture to save their failing marriage.

He married for a second time, but when he took a young mistress, his wife fled to her parents taking with her their 18-month-old daughter. In a possessive rage Bell turned up at the house armed with a shotgun to confront her. Armed police besieged the house before storming it to find Bell and his wife lying dead side by side.

AN OPEN VERDICT

Next to feel the malevolent influence of Coggeshall was the flamboyant restaurateur Peter Langan. Irish-born Langan sprang to fame through his bizarre behaviour at the fashionable West End eaterie he owned jointly with film star Michael Caine. He was a convivial if boozy and blunt-talking host, prone to collapsing in drunken stupors at the tables of his diners.

their plush home on the fateful October evening in 1988 believing they were going to spend one last night together. But as she lay on their bed, her eyes widened in horror as Langan locked the bedroom door and produced matches and two bottles of petrol from a cupboard.

Fearing for her life, Mrs Langan rushed to the window and plunged from a balcony, breaking her heel in the fall. As she struggled to her feet she heard him calling her name in a strange, husky voice before witnessing an explosion. Langan suffered dreadful burns to the face, hands and back and died seven weeks later in hospital. The beautiful house was wrecked.

Before being rushed to hospital he told a policeman: 'I wanted to die but I didn't want her to die.'

At the inquest held in January 1989 Mrs Langan told the coroner: 'We had spent an extremely agreeable and happy evening, getting along better than we had for a long time. We had been making plans for the future. When I saw the matches and petrol I was panic stricken. I was terrified of being burned. After I jumped out of the window I heard him call my name twice in a low and unusual voice. I didn't answer because I was afraid he might throw the petrol after me. I still wonder if I had answered his call if it might not have ended this way.

'I find it hard to accept that he intended to end his life. I think he just lost control and wanted to make a grand gesture. He had made dramatic threats in the past when he was in a highly emotional state and debilitated by his excessive habits but he never carried them out and he never attempted to take his life.

'His last words to me in the ambulance were "Susan, are you staying?" I think it was a grand gesture to blackmail me into staying with him.'

Police experts, unable to interview him after the incident because he was too ill, found he had taken a combination of sleeping tablets and alcohol. Coroner Dr Charles Clark returned an open verdict.

Recent history has been peppered with other incidents of oddball suburban crime in the area, like the man who went beserk with a shotgun and wounded a local vicar cutting his lawn, and the woman who plotted with her lover to bump off her husband with the aid of their lawnmower.

Even thriller writer Ruth Rendell, who lives in the neighbourhood, has admitted: 'There's supposed to be a sinister atmosphere in this area.'

THE CURSE OF THE LAST WITCH

The region is steeped in history, with some of the oldest Christian graveyards in England. Coggeshall itself also falls on a junction of ley lines, claimed to be ancient routes connecting sites along which some mysterious Earth force operates.

It lies at the heart of the witches' domain in Essex. Witchfinder Matthew Hopkins, who rooted out sorcerers in medieval times, lived and worked in the area. The last witch to be burned at the stake in England was said to have died at Market Hill, Coggeshall, in 1651. Was it she in her dying breath who issued the curse which hangs over the village people today?

The village lies unnervingly close to the site of the celebrated Red Barn murder of 1827. At Polstead a local woman called Maria Marten vanished without trace. Her mother dreamed she had been buried by the Red Barn. And from the very site her

Above: *The ruins of Langan's house at Alphamstone, close to ill-fated Coggeshall.*

> HER EYES WIDENED IN TERROR AS HE LOCKED THE BEDROOM DOOR AND THEN PRODUCED PETROL AND MATCHES FROM THE CUPBOARD.

mother identified, Maria's body was exhumed. She had been shot and stabbed. William Corder, the father of her two children, was hanged for the grisly killing.

Could there really be an evil atmosphere in this tranquil setting compelling previously balanced and fair-minded folk to begin an orgy of killing and self-destruction? Or is it simply that greed and lust got the better of them and would have done no matter where they lived? The riddle of Coggeshall and its spate of killings will fascinate people for years to come.

UNTIMELY DEATHS

In Australia, Ayers Rock is best known as a popular tourist spot. The huge, sheer-sided feature erupts from a desert-like plain 100 miles south of Alice Springs. When the sun drops from the sky, the rock is transformed from its earth colour to a stunning pink, then a glorious red. This vivid spectacle of nature is enough to bring in visitors by the busload. Given the chance, many pluck a pebble from the rock to take home as a souvenir.

But now the looming landmass is gaining a reputation of a different kind. Trippers are returning the stones taken from the national park site, believing they have brought them bad luck.

One man from Arizona returned his Ayers Rock memento to the local ranger with a note saying: 'Please return it to its place of rest as I have suffered a lot of sickness since I removed it.'

An Australian woman who returned home with a sliver then developed diabetes and had a stillborn baby. She wrote: 'I just hope that by returning this rock that whatever evils I may have unleashed on myself may subside a little.'

Some of the stones which have found their way back to the national park weigh several pounds and they have been posted from all over the world. Ayers Rock is considered a sacred site by the aboriginal community, who call it Uluru. But the spirits they attribute to the area are mostly friendly.

But Ayers Rock has also been a site of tragedy. During the past 15 years five trippers have fallen to oblivion in one spot. Could these untimely deaths be the source of the curse which so many people from different corners of the world now feel is jinxing them?

THE HOUSE OF DEATH

Wealthy businessman David Wilson laughed off claims that his Victorian home was cursed. But the accountant died in terror, the victim of two masked assassins. His death revived claims by villagers that the hill-top house he lived in was fatally jinxed.

Mr Wilson bought the four-bedroomed house at an auction in 1976, paying £140,000 for the property, built in around 1840. Neighbours in the quiet village of Brinscall, Lancashire, warned him about its unhappy past. Five of its previous occupants had died prematurely. Two of the owners of pretty, gabled Withnell Villa

Below: *Thomas Paycocke's House in Coggeshall, built in 1500.*

died while having a bath – one fell and cracked his head. Another suffered a heart attack while chasing poachers in a disused quarry. A fourth perished in a road accident, while the fifth victim also had a heart attack.

All the deaths were linked to the ghost of an old drover which appeared clad in black shortly before the deaths.

Mr Wilson paid no heed to talk of a curse and went ahead with renovations worth some £80,000. But five years later he was the centre of a hate campaign with every window of his home being smashed. On the evening of 5 March 1992 two gunmen forced their way into the house and lay in wait for Mr Wilson, who was out with his wife and younger daughter. After he arrived, Wilson was frogmarched to the garage, where he was shot twice in the head.

Detectives investigating the killing found Wilson was involved in some business intrigues overseas and may have even been connected with some shady underworld characters who wreaked a terrible revenge when a scam went wrong.

One officer said: 'He was out of his depth. He seems to have dabbled with the big boys and paid the price.'

Meanwhile, despite all the evidence of earth-bound forces which claimed Mr Wilson's life, nearby residents still insisted the curse of Withnell Villa was behind the killing. The mystic force would surely strike again, too. No matter how desirable the house seems, none of the villagers acquainted with the old story of the curse would live there for a king's ransom.

One local declared: 'There is a jinx on that house. Only an outsider would want to buy it.'

THE ABORIGINES CONSIDER THE ROCK SACRED, BUT FOR THE WHITE PEOPLE IT HAS BECOME A PLACE OF DEATH.

Below: *Tourists flock to Australia's Ayers Rock. But visitors who chipped mementoes from the famous landmark suffered a string of mishaps. Many sent their souvenirs back in the hope of escaping further misfortune. Is the rock really responsible for illness and death?*

VOODOO IN HAITI

The voodoo priests ruled the island of Haiti with fear and terror. Westerners dismissed the peasants' tales of the living dead with scornful smiles – until they came face to face with the truth.

The woman's name was Felicia Felix-Mentor and she was in an appalling state when she was found wandering in Haiti's Artibonite Valley in October 1936. Her face was blank, her eyes glassy and unseeing and her eyelids looked as though they had been scorched. She seemed to have suffered some brain damage.

There was no doubt about her identity. Several reliable witnesses swore it was her. The problem for the Haitian authorities was that Felicia Felix-Mentor had died two years previously and some of the witnesses now identifying her had been there to watch her being laid in the ground.

The first documented case of a zombie – one of the living dead – was about to make headlines around the globe.

Felicia was interviewed in depth by the black ethnographer Zora Hurston, who had been trained in America by the highly respected Franz Boas. Hurston spent hours at the woman's bedside trying to coax the truth out of her and a painstaking job it proved. Hurston described her patient as having 'a blank face with dead eyes' and eyelids 'white as if they had been burned with acid'. She concluded that Haitian people risked being 'zombified' with quick-acting poisons if they betrayed the secrets of the island's voodoo religion. Her views were greeted with ridicule in the scientific community. Recent research suggests she was closer to the truth than they.

Haiti is an island synonymous with the voodoo (sometimes called voodoun) religion. For hundreds of years the high priests, or *houngan*, of this bizarre sect were able to dominate the people to the point that almost every aspect of their lives was dictated by magic. Even today there are many Haitians who bow to the old sorcerer's art and believe its power implicitly.

To understand how such a grip has persisted historians have pointed to the centuries of violence, slaughter and dictatorship which effectively prevented the population from educating themselves. Almost from the moment Christopher Columbus landed on Haiti – originally the central mountainous region of the Spanish colony Hispaniola – the bloodshed got underway.

Opposite: *The notorious voodoo priestess Mamaloi with three of her aides. The billy goat nestling against her is a sacrifice to the gods.*

Below: *This voodoo painting shows the goddess of love with the chief of the gods, Leyba.*

CAPTURED RUNAWAY
SLAVES WERE SMEARED
WITH MOLASSES AND TIED
DOWN IN THE BURNING HEAT
OF THE DAY TO BE EATEN
ALIVE BY ANTS.

SADISTIC EXECUTIONS

The original inhabitants, Arawak and Carib Indians, were massacred to extinction over 50 years by the Spanish. The colony became so depopulated as to revert almost to a desert island, but then European growers saw its potential for sugar cane production and began shipping in slaves sold in the newly emerging African markets. These poor unfortunates very often arrived with nothing, not even clothes. But they retained a legacy of their culture. They had a belief in magic and the occult – the roots of voodoo.

In the international power plays of the 17th and 18th centuries Hispaniola was eventually handed to France and re-christened Haiti. By the French Revolution there were 40,000 Frenchmen living there with a lower class of 30,000 mixed-race settlers and upwards of half a million slaves existing in abject poverty. The ambitious Emperor Napoleon had once nurtured plans to turn the island into a gigantic naval base from which to retake his empire's lost territory in North America. But once the oppressed blacks saw how the ordinary, poor French had overthrown a powerful ruling class they decided they could do the same. A savage war of independence began.

The slaves had a lot of hatred to work out of their system. They had been treated sadistically by their French masters and stories abound of some of the appalling methods of execution. These included smearing 'offenders', particularly captured runaways, with molasses and tying them down to be eaten by ants. Another horrific custom was to ram gunpowder into the slave's body orifices and set it alight, a practice the French referred to as 'blasting black ass'.

Despite being forced to witness such sanctioned murder, many slaves were prepared to take the risk of escaping into the mountains to join the rapidly expanding resistance. Marshalled by voodoo leaders such as the inspirational priest-warrior Boukman, they quickly turned most of the high ground into a no-go zone for the French. Inflamed by Boukman's bizarre rituals, and given medicines said to turn them into fearless, unfeeling zombie warriors, they revisited some of the past horrors of colonialism on the French.

One slave in particular, Macandel, played a crucial role in the uprising by teaching his fellow rebels the art of poisoning. First the cattle of the whites were targeted, then the farmers and growers themselves. Even when Macandel was betrayed, and ordered to be burned at the stake in the manner the French then treated suspected werewolves, rumours persisted that magic had helped him escape.

From the 1740s the voodoo sects started to flourish and by the 1790s French authority was in tatters. Napoleon restored order with predictable savagery but even he failed to wrest away the mountains from the control of the witch-doctor emperors. From the early 19th century anarchy and dictatorship became the order of the day under a shaky declaration of independence.

ZOMBIE SLAVES

History shows that even the worthiest revolutions have a darker side and Haiti was to prove no exception. From being their champion, the voodoo religion became the people's new enslaver. Their lives were totally ruled by it and those who practised the secret art were treated like living gods. No one dared challenge these witch-doctors, people whose spells could raise a corpse from its grave and put it to work as a zombie slave.

One story which has survived without the

Below: *A shot taken from the filming of Wes Craven's* **The Serpent and the Rainbow,** *which portrayed the journey of a Harvard anthropologist in Haiti and his experiences with Haitian voodoo – including his encounters with Papa and Baby Doc's secret police force.*

Left: *The wild, staring eyes of this woman show she is close to the trance-like state adopted by some voodoo priests and their followers.*

Above: *On Haiti voodoo was more than a way of life … it was big business. Shops such as this would have been officially licensed by the priests in return for a cut of the profits. Woe betide any shopowner who set himself up without permission.*

usual embellishments dates from the summer of 1918 when the island was preparing to gather a record sugar cane crop. Growers were desperate for labour and were willing to take almost anyone who turned up. At one plantation, owned by the Haitian-American Sugar Corporation, a group of tatty, shuffling peasants arrived under the leadership of a well-known village headman, Ti Joseph. The HASCO manager didn't rate the workers but he was willing to give them a try under the circumstances. Ti Joseph told him the men were from a remote mountain near the Dominican Republic border. They were withdrawn and nervy because they only spoke a little-known dialect. However, they would work well provided the others stayed away from them.

Ti Joseph agreed pay rates and his gang set to work. That first day they easily harvested the plantation's biggest quota of cane, and paused only for an evening supper of watery millet porridge. They carried on in similar style for the whole week, with other labourers occasionally pausing to marvel at Ti Joseph's tireless team. The headman was rarely seen without a wide smile on his face. He spent most of his time adding up his bonuses.

On Sunday all work stopped and Ti Joseph headed for the Haiti capital Port au Prince to drink away some of his earnings. His wife, Constance, felt sorry for the sullen harvesters and decided to round them up for an outing to a nearby church festival. She hoped they would cast off their frowns for the day and make merry.

The reality was just the opposite. The men hung together uncertainly, not knowing what to do or say and refusing to take part in the fun. Constance decided they should have a special treat in the hope it might liven them up. Each man was handed a packet of biscuits, made with brown sugar and salted nuts. One by one they began to eat, absent-mindedly it seemed at first. But within minutes the transformation was dramatic. They began crying and screeching and started heading back to their village en masse.

There they were regarded with disbelieving horror by friends and family. Each member of that gang had died and been buried within the last few months. They had been raised from the grave and zombified – but the sudden change in their diet appeared to have reversed the spell. The extraordinary story was later published by

Above: *At first glance the bizarre symbols in this room might appear to be the work of a graffiti spray-can artist. In fact the scrawling was brushed on in blood.*

THE VOODOO PRIEST WARNED HIM TO IGNORE THE ZOMBIE'S PLEAS FOR FOOD AND WATER.

Right: *Papa Doc Duvalier never took any chances with his personal safety. It wasn't so much the people he feared – they held him in awe – as a possible CIA-sponsored assassin.*

US explorer and author William Seabrook, who made his home on Haiti.

Other Western writers have noted similar accounts. Alfred Metraux's fascinating study *Voodoo in Haiti*, first published in 1959, advised: 'There are few, even among the educated, who do not give some credence to these macabre stories.'

He goes on to mention the experience of an island society figure who sought shelter in the home of a voodoo priest. The pair discussed the art of magic and the white man found it difficult to contain his scepticism. He swallowed his words, though, when the witch-doctor asked him when he'd last seen one of his best friends, a man called M Celestin. At the crack of the priest's whip Celestin hobbled into the room, and held out a trembling hand as if pleading for a drink of the visitor's water. As the goblet was handed over the witch-doctor angrily intervened, warning his visitor that nothing could be more dangerous than to give victuals to a dead man in zombie form. Apparently Celestin had been murdered through a spell and then sold by the magician responsible for $12.

WEREWOLVES

In his book Metraux makes it clear that he believes voodoo to be the stuff of superstition. He finds no scientific evidence to explain how corpses are raised to live again as zombies. However he is at pains to stress just how entrenched voodoo has become as the island's principal religion. In one section he describes how the islanders prepare to defend their children from the werewolves summoned up by the witch-doctors.

'The peasants are not always entirely helpless in face of their children's danger from werewolves. Since the numerous available talismans are not always effective, it is thought wise to immunize new-born babies by "spoiling their blood". This is done as soon as possible during pregnancy.

'The mother must drink bitter coffee laced with clairin and flavoured with three drops of petrol. Then she bathes in water infused with garlic, chives, thyme, nutmeg, bois-caca leaves, manioc mush, coffee and clairin. Some time after its birth the child is plunged into a similar bath. It is also given a tisane made of various herbs. For good measure of precaution, clairin is burned in a plate and the child passed through the resulting flames. The exorcizer who is drugging it asks three times: "Who wants this little one?" The mother replies: "I do." In these words she affirms her determination to resist any werewolf who may take advantage of her sleep to come and demand her child.

'Then the calabash used in the ablutions is buried open side downwards. If a *loup-garou* [French for werewolf] turns up near the house and tries by deceitful utterances to obtain the mother's consent to her own loss, the calabash must answer it. In some families the children's blood is made bitter by feeding them with cockroaches – first trimmed of their legs and wings and fried in castor oil, syrup, nutmeg and garlic. Some children have blood that is naturally salty or bitter and these therefore have nothing to fear from werewolves. The werewolf who drinks "spoilt blood" is seized with violent vomiting.'

Metraux says his studies showed no inclination among the island's voodoo werewolves to eat their own children, as such creatures are rumoured to do in other parts of the world. But he warns: 'If no other prey is available, then it [the beast] knows no scruple.

'Even less does it hesitate if it cherishes a secret grudge against the child's mother or father. One of the laws of the supernatural world requires that no werewolf may "eat" a baby unless its mother has expressly "given" it. Such a gift is obtained by the following trick: having gone up close to the house where the child they want to eat is sleeping they find out their chances of success by shuffling clover leaves together like playing cards. Success is certain if all the leaves fall shiny side down but if only three fall thus it means there will be some snag and the attempt is usually abandoned.

'When the signs are favourable the werewolf first goes into the kitchen which, in the country, is a small shelter not far from the dwelling place. From there she calls the child's mother. The latter, half asleep, hears her name and answers "yes". The werewolf then asks: "Will you give me your child?" If then, drowsy and only half awake, she still replies "yes" then that's that, the child is lost.'

AN EVIL DICTATOR

With fears such as this rife across the country for much of the 20th century the chance for leaders to use voodoo as a means of control was too tempting. A cunning physician, Dr François Duvalier, saw his chance of power and seized it in a 1957 *coup d'état*. Within seven years his rule had turned into a corrupt dictatorship with the mysteries of voodoo and zombieism used to quell any opposition that dared raise its head.

Duvalier, known at home and abroad as 'Papa Doc', hit on the idea of presenting voodoo as a unique piece of cultural heritage which bound all Haitians together, both in this world and the next. Those who stepped out of line would suffer the curse of the witch-doctors and, naturally, the chief witch-doctor was Papa Doc himself.

In a sense the island was turned into one huge cult fortress, similar to the types established by crazed preachers Jim Jones and David Koresh. Duvalier bestowed upon himself all the privileges of a voodoo high priest and formed a personal bodyguard-cum-enforcement agency called the Tonton

Above and top: *Voodoo boasted some bizarre rituals, prominent among which was the process of mud purification. Devotees would immerse themselves in one of the 'holy' mud baths and meditate until they believed the gods were satisfied they had been cleansed.*

Above: *The monster in his lair. Papa Doc Duvalier with his wife Simone at a function for visiting Church leaders. Behind him stand members of his hated mafia – the Tonton Macoutes.*

UNDER THE DICTATOR'S EVIL RULE EVEN DEATH WAS NO ESCAPE – THE PRIESTS WOULD DISINTER THE BURIED BODIES AND USE THEM FOR THEIR CORRUPT PURPOSES.

Macoutes. This collection of bullying scum revelled in a carefully fostered image as both state police and official witch-doctors. All the time Papa Doc encouraged the belief that any who challenged him and his cronies would be turned into zombies. Horrific tales were deliberately spread about the dictator's awesome occult powers.

The tactic worked. By the early 1960s nothing moved on Haiti without the voodoo implications being considered first. Peasants were obsessed by the zombie threat and devised extraordinary rituals to keep the magicians at bay. Even the poorest would save up to buy heavy stones, which would be laid over their graves on death to dissuade some voodoo priest from disinterring them and transforming them into the living dead.

Many families drew up rotas to watch a new grave day and night until they could be sure the body underground had decomposed to the point where the witch-doctors could do nothing with it. In extreme cases poisons were injected into the veins of a corpse, or it was mutilated or sprayed with machine-gun bullets – all practices which, it was believed, ensured the dead stayed put.

By 1962 the USA had lost patience with Duvalier. It was clear to the White House that Haiti's charismatic leader was engaged in a long-term nest-feathering exercise in which his people were doomed to live lives akin to the slaves that were their forebears. President Kennedy led the way, announcing that he had cut off all US economic aid to Haiti and would not resume the link until it became clear democratic rule was being pursued.

Papa Doc responded by placing a voodoo curse on Kennedy and gleefully claimed the credit when the president was assassinated the following year. His people believed him and, to the horror of US senators and congressmen, the evil Duvalier tightened his grip still further.

Another Democratic president, Jimmy Carter, also tried to take on the Duvaliers. He warned that unless he saw signs of civil rights emerging on the island he would also review his foreign aid budget. Voodoo leaders reacted with horror at the D-word 'democracy' and Duvalier's widow (he died in 1971) convened a meeting of the Tonton Macoutes to decide how to strike back.

Soon afterwards in Port au Prince the voodoo enforcers dug a huge pit in the centre of town into which was placed a live bull. The animal was then buried alive, together with a photograph of President Carter.

With the curse in place, Haiti's believers watched impatiently for it to take effect. They were not disappointed with the 'proof' that followed. A year later Carter launched his Special Forces débâcle to free American citizens held hostage in the US embassy in Tehran. On the night chosen, blinding sandstorms swept into the Iranian desert and many of the US commandos were killed in collisions between their helicopters. The miserable affair was too closely linked to Carter and the humiliation lost him another chance of a shot at the White House. Unsurprisingly, widow Mama Doc Duvalier claimed it was all down to her.

By now control of Haiti had passed to Papa Doc's 19-year-old son, Jean Claude, who was predictably dubbed 'Baby Doc' by the press. For a while Western politicians, who had wrung their hands in despair at the regime, were hopeful that at last Haiti would be dragged into the 20th century. It was not to be. The principle of 'government by voodoo' remained as strong as ever.

Yet all was not lost. Where the military might and economic muscle of the USA had failed to convert Haiti, careful scientific research would succeed. One man, Harvard anthropologist Dr E. Wade Davis, must claim at least some of the credit.

CERTIFIED DEAD

In 1980 he made the astonishing declaration that: 'Zombieism actually exists. There are Haitians who have been raised from their graves and returned to life.'

Dr Davis had been given the task of studying the zombie mystery by the head of the Port au Prince Psychiatric Center, Dr Lamarque Douyon. Together they carried out exhaustive examinations of an alleged zombie called Clairvius Narcisse. In 1962 Clairvius, then aged about 40, had been taken in to the island's Albert Schweitzer Hospital in the Artibonite Valley with all the symptoms of high fever. Within 48 hours he was certified dead and was buried the following day.

Then in 1980 a man approached Narcisse's sister Angeline claiming to be her deceased brother. She recognized Clairvius and with a mixture of horror and delight listened to his incredible story. He had, he said, been zombified by order of their brothers after he refused to agree to their plan to sell off family land. He couldn't remember how long he had lain in his coffin but he was eventually restored to life by a voodoo witch-doctor. He was then taken to work the fields with a gang of other zombies.

Two years later his master had died and he managed to get away, wandering the country as a beggar and casual labourer for 16 years. He only dared reveal his true identity once he was sure the brother who had led the plot to zombify him was dead.

The authorities managed to confirm Clairvius's claims from hospital records. He showed them a scar on his cheek caused by a nail driven through his coffin and even insisted his grave – clearly undisturbed for years – be dug up so that the empty coffin could be inspected. As final confirmation a group of 'zombies' was found trailing aimlessly across the north of Haiti, where Clairvius said he had been put to work. They remembered him and backed up his story of escape.

To Douyon and Davis he was priceless research material as the first authenticated, and fully recovered zombie. Then two others were brought to their attention. The first, a 30-year-old woman called Francena Illeus, also known as Ti Femme, had been certified dead in 1976. Yet in 1979 she was found alive by her mother and recognized by an unmistakable scar on her forehead. Ti Femme believed her jealous husband had ordered her to suffer the curse of the zombies. When her coffin was raised it was full of rocks.

The third case concerned a woman called Natagette Joseph, aged 60, who was recognized as she walked near the village of her birth. Many villagers had been at her funeral in 1964.

THE POWER OF POISON

Dr Davis's investigations concentrated on the possibility that witch-doctors used little-known poisons to turn their victim into a

WHEN THEY DUG UP HIS COFFIN IT WAS EMPTY.

Below: *On Haiti voodoo even managed to worm its way into mainstream religions such as Catholicism. This shrine or 'emblem' was set up in a Catholic cemetery to Baron Samedi, the voodoo god of the dead.*

state approaching suspended animation. Once the unfortunate zombie had been buried, his theory ran, the coffin would be exhumed a couple of days later and an antidote administered to the body. Brain damage might well occur, but this would be to the advantage of the witch-doctor who would be able to sell on a more malleable slave.

The poison theory had first been advanced by anthropologist Zora Hurston in the 1930s but ridiculed up until now. Davis concentrated on the use of toxins from the plant *Datura stramonium*, called jimsonweed by Americans and 'zombie's cucumber' by Haitians. He also looked at extracts from a certain toad – *Bufo marinus* – and at toxins recovered from two types of puffer fish. The fish, so named because they can blow themselves up with water as a defence mechanism against predators, are regarded as a superb delicacy by the

Japanese. They are eaten raw as *sashimi*, but only after the most fastidious preparation in which the lethal liver is carefully cleaned before being boiled.

Davis knew that past victims of puffer fish poisoning included Captain Cook, who suffered terribly after wolfing down the liver and roe of a puffer ... and the lethal chemicals they contained. He noted that two Japanese victims had case histories which 'read like classic accounts of Haitian zombification'. These both involved men who had been certified dead by doctors but recovered before funeral services could be arranged.

Further evidence for his theory emerged when he paid $2,400 for eight different samples of 'zombie powder' used by Haitian sorcerers. These proved to contain bits of human corpse, nettle, toad and puffer fish.

Dr Davis observed: 'Zombies are a Haitian phenomenon which can be explained logically. The active ingredients in the poison are extracts from the skin of the toad *Bufo marinus* and one or more species of puffer fish. The skin of the toad is a natural chemical factory which produces hallucinogens, powerful anaesthetics and chemicals which affect the heart and nervous system. The puffer fish contains a deadly nerve poison called tetrodotoxin.'

He went on: 'A witch-doctor in Haiti is very skilled in administering just the right dose of poison. Too much poison will kill the victim completely and resuscitation will not be possible. Too little and the victim will not be a convincing corpse.'

As part of his study Davis went to great lengths to look at the motives of witch-doctors in placing zombie curses. Surprisingly he discovered they were not quite the crazed murderers they were sometimes made to appear. Clairvius Narcisse, for instance, was not selected for zombification purely on the say-so of his brother. Apparently he had been something of a ladies' man and had left a trail of illegitimate children – for whom he provided no maintenance – in his wake. His transformation into one of the living dead was seen as a righteous punishment by many.

Intriguingly Davis also concluded that administering zombifying potions, though

Below: *Baby Doc pictured in the days when he still wielded power on Haiti. If he ever returns, say those who still follow the voodoo way, he will become a zombie.*

SOME BELIEVED THAT HIS TRANSFORMATION INTO ONE OF THE LIVING DEAD WAS A JUST PUNISHMENT FOR HIS SINS.

the root of the whole voodoo religion, was not the sole skill of the witch-doctors. So-called 'magical' powers have some vital role to play in reviving a zombie from the grave, over and above the antidotes themselves. There is also an art to mixing further, stupefying drugs which effectively turn the victim into a walking vegetable.

Davis's findings sounded the death knell of the Duvalier regime. In 1986, seeing which way the wind was blowing, Baby Doc slipped out of his Port au Prince palace by cover of night and fled the country for political asylum in France. With the mystique of voodoo laid bare he could no longer wield any power over the peasants and his position was hopeless. The high priests and witch-doctors had long grown disillusioned with his leadership.

It is unlikely Baby Doc ever seriously contemplated returning, but the voodoo priests who still practise the old arts took no chances. They placed a curse on him to take effect the moment he set foot in the country.

If he dared to do so, he would be turned into a zombie.

Above left: *A voodoo dancer, probably in a drug-induced state, performs for the absorbed villagers around her. Dance is a crucial part of the voodoo cult and is associated with most of the 'magic' ceremonies.*

Shown below is another ritual dance, performed to the background of mournful bamboo horns and a voodoo drum.

EVIL GEMS

When the headstrong American heiress bought the inappropriately named Hope Diamond, she thought her money could erase three centuries of tragedy. She soon discovered that curses, like diamonds, are for ever …

The sight of a giant glittering diamond, frozen blue and as large as a bird's egg, is enough to make any heart flutter.

Surely such a gem would not only bring riches beyond reason but also satisfaction and happiness to any person lucky enough to have it in their clutches?

Not if this fantastic jewel was the Hope Diamond, a stone notorious for the calamities suffered by its string of owners. Even sceptics are hard pushed to describe the woes which occur in the wake of the gem as nothing more than coincidences.

A VENGEFUL GOD

The diamond is believed to have been plundered from the eye or forehead of an idol in an Indian temple some 350 years ago. It is thought to have been mined to provide lavish adornment for the Rama-Sita temple near Mandalay. Rama-Sita was a powerful and vengeful god who put a curse not only on anyone who robbed the temple of his earthly riches, but also on successive owners of the stolen goods.

No one knows how, but the diamond came into the hands of a French trader called Jean-Baptiste Tavernier towards the end of the 17th century. Possibly he plucked the stone from its ordained resting place or maybe he stumbled on it in a dusty, fragrant Indian market. It was a flawless gem of stunning beauty, an incredible 112 3/16 carats. He instantly recognized its rare quality and once back in France sold it to King Louis XIV.

There are various stories about how Tavernier subsequently died but there is no doubt he met an untimely and nasty end. Some say he went on a trip to Russia and vanished without trace until his skeleton was found in the snowy wastes of Siberia, the flesh having been eaten by wild animals. Others claim he fell on hard times, embarked on a trip to India where he had found treasures so readily before, and died from a horrible illness en route.

The French king had the gem cut into the shape of a heart and gave it to a

Above: *The legendary Hope Diamond. Even sceptics are pushed to explain the woes it brings its wearers.*

Opposite: *Heiress Evalyn Walsh McLean fell in love with the diamond when she saw it in Cartier's Paris showroom. She later bought it for £64,000.*

THE GEM MERCHANT HAD THE STOLEN DIAMOND RETURNED TO HIM – BUT THE PRICE WAS HIS SON'S LIFE.

Below: Louis XIV of France. He had the diamond cut into the shape of a heart for his mistress.

mistress, Madame de Montespan. But she fell from royal grace when it was discovered her body was being used as an altar for black magic rituals, including the killing of babies. She was closely linked with a group of women later burned for supplying poison to bump off husbands in the French court. Ousted from her charmed life, Madame de Montespan was forced to hand back the gift before leaving Paris to die in obscurity.

It didn't bring much better fortune to Louis XIV or his descendants. The autocratic king brought his country to the brink of economic ruin and laid the ground for the French revolution.

Two generations later, the stone finally came to rest on the neck of Marie Antoinette, the wife of Louis XVI. Renowned for her unworldly attitude towards her country's peasants – she wondered why, if they were hungry and had no bread, they did not eat cake instead – she was tried for treason along with her husband and guillotined in 1792.

TREACHERY

Mystery surrounds the fate of the diamond for the next 40 years – it is believed to have been kept for some time by the then king of England, George IV – until it appeared again in Amsterdam in the custody of Dutch gems merchant Wilhelm Fals. He carved it into its present shape – at 45.5 carats, less than half its original size. It was then the source of treachery between father and son as young Hendrick Fals stole the gem and spirited it to London in search of the wealth he knew it would bring. But when he got to Britain's capital he committed suicide, plagued by guilt or perhaps under the evil influence of the gem.

The unlucky stone was returned to his grief-stricken father who was glad to sell it. London banker Henry Thomas Hope splashed out £18,000 for the diamond and it thereafter took his name. Perhaps because he bought it fair and square the curse of the diamond appears not to have touched Hope himself.

However, when it passed to his cousin Lord Francis Hope, the hex began its work once more. Suddenly, Hope found his marriage to singer May Yohe dogged by quarrels until it finally collapsed. She refused to look at the gem, claiming it brought bad luck, and stuck to the story until she died in poverty.

Hope was also hit by financial hardship and sold the diamond to continental jeweller Jacques Colot. The Frenchman probably thought he was making the deal of his lifetime. In fact, he was to lose his mind and eventually committed suicide in an asylum.

But not before he sold it on to Russian playboy Prince Kanilovsky. He proudly draped the jewel around the neck of his mistress, Mademoiselle Ladue. But as the actress took to the stage at the Folie-Bergeres in Paris, he produced a gun and shot her from the box where he was to have watched the show. Even today, no one can explain the apparently unprovoked assassination.

His miserable fate was sealed only days later: he was murdered in the street by an angry mob.

A merchant by the name of Habib Bey next held the Hope Diamond. He drowned before realizing the riches he had hoped the gem would make him. Greek dealer Simon Montharides bought it from Bey's estate and soon sold it to Abdul Hamid II, the sultan of Turkey. Montharides together with his wife and child then died as his car plunged over a cliff.

Meanwhile the brutal and unpopular sultan was deposed in 1909. Pierre Cartier, from the famous jewellery dynasty, was the next owner; he sold it to the American family perhaps worst hit of all by the jinx of the diamond.

A MALEVOLENT SPELL

Heiress Evalyn Walsh McLean first saw the fabulous gem when she visited Cartier's Paris showroom in 1910. She was warned about the curse and was riveted by the tale of disastrous luck following the path of the stone. More than that, she was spellbound by the beauty of the Hope Diamond. She decided it had to be hers.

Above: *Sultan Abdul Hamid Khan II of Turkey. He bought the cursed diamond from Greek gems dealer Simon Montharides. Montharides and his family were killed in a car crash soon afterwards. The sultan was overthrown in 1909.*

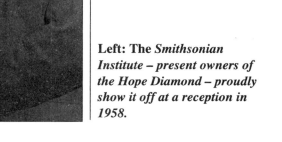

Left: The *Smithsonian Institute – present owners of the Hope Diamond – proudly show it off at a reception in 1958.*

worries, shook Ned McLean to the core. The grieving father took to drink and was finally taken into an asylum where he died.

Evalyn continued to dismiss stories about the evil powers of the stone. But her daughter, who had worn the necklace at her wedding, went on to commit suicide in 1946 with an overdose of pills.

When Evalyn died the following year, there were so many debts outstanding on the estate that the jewellery had to be sold and did not pass to her grandchildren as she had hoped.

Even without the possession of the gem, the spell lingered on the McLean family, with one of Evalyn's granddaughters dying in her Texas home in 1967 full of drink and drugs.

New York jeweller Harry Winston was the next owner. He was the man who purchased the entire McLean gem collection reputedly for a million dollars. 'It's a Cinderella world,' he once said of the diamond business. 'It has everything – people, drama, romance, precious stones, speculation, excitement. What more could you want?'

Above: *The Victoria-Transvaal Diamond. This 67.89-carat champagne-coloured gem was one of a clutch of priceless stones donated to the Smithsonian Institute.*

Right: *The Hope Diamond on display.*

WHEN THE DIAMOND WAS TESTED SCIENTIFICALLY IT WAS SHOWN TO HAVE STRANGE POWERS.

Opposite: *Nina Dyer and Baron Henri von Thyssen. She killed herself by a drug overdose at the age of 35.*

After purchasing it for £64,000 Evalyn quickly visited a priest for a blessing that she was sure would rid the gem of any lingering curse. After that, she revelled in owning one of the world's most astonishing diamonds. She put it on the collar of her beloved great dane, Mike, and even allowed her son Jock to chew it over while teething. She herself often wore the blue stone surrounded by 16 alternating pear- and cushion-cut white diamonds set on a diamond-studded chain, sometimes alongside some of her other costly jewels.

Soon her mother-in-law and two members of staff died. Then, in 1918 while she and her husband were at the Kentucky Derby, their 8-year-old son Vinson eluded his minders, ran out in front of a car and was killed.

The tragedy, along with business

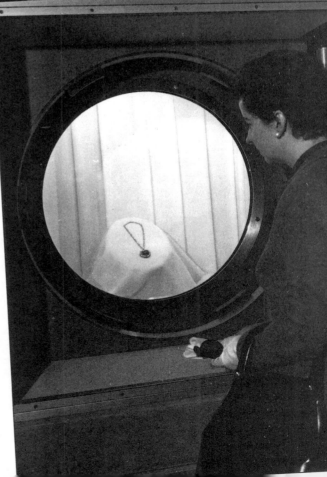

Happily, he put the stone in a travelling jewellery show, sent it around the world raising thousands of pounds for charity and was never scarred by its ownership.

In 1958 he donated it to the prestigious Smithsonian Institute in Washington DC, posting it to the gallery in a plain brown wrapper. Its arrival promoted a flood of donations of fine and unique stones, including the 423-carat Logan Sapphire, the size of a goose egg and mounted with 20 sparkling white diamonds, and the Napoleon Necklace, a 275-carat diamond piece given by the French emperor to his wife in 1811 on the birth of their son. The sight of the Hope Diamond on its rope of 62 matching stones thrilled a stream of visitors who feasted their gaze on the glorious stone and wondered at its chequered history. The institute was even more excited when it discovered in 1965 that the gem glowed burning red when tested under ultra-violet light, a quality never known before among diamonds. Today the stone is believed to be worth £53 million.

Of course, most of the time it is kept securely in its vault. But in 1990 socialite Georgette Mosbacher donned the gem saying: 'I don't believe in bad luck. I'd wear it in my navel for a million bucks.'

She wore it to celebrate the million-dollar donation by the Harry Winston Foundation which paid for the renovation of the room which houses the gem.

Who can say if the curse has finally diminished? After all, when Georgette insisted she didn't want to take off the gorgeous jewel, husband Robert was US commerce secretary. Two years later the Republicans were ousted from office by victorious Democrats …

The Hope Diamond is not alone among gems carrying a malevolent spell. Various pieces of Cartier jewellery seem to evoke bad luck.

There was the Kokoshnik tiara made in 1908, resplendent with strings of gracefully dangling diamonds, worn by beautiful American singer Lillian Nordica. She perished in a shipping tragedy off New Guinea in 1914.

In 1906 the Lavalliere necklace was created, resembling a ribbon on a bow. It was made for feted actress Eve Lavalliere.

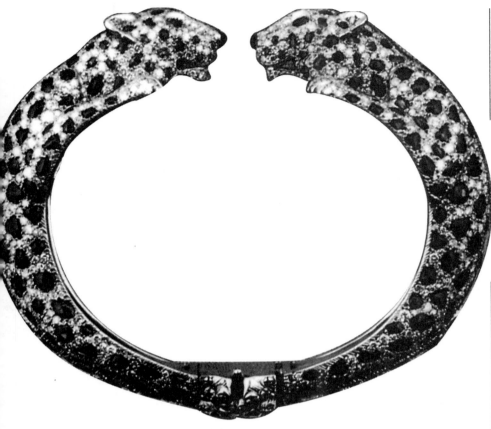

THE JEWELS VANISHED IN MID-AIR.

Above and right: Beautiful women delight to adorn themselves with eye-catching jewellery such as the diamond-encrusted bracelet and brooches shown here. Whether they ultimately bring them happiness is open

But she later quit at the height of her popularity to live out her days closeted in a convent.

Perhaps the most notorious items in the Cartier collection were those once owned by eminent society goddess Nina Dyer. She was married to Baron Henri von Thyssen but the glittering couple parted after only months together.

She was then wooed and won by Prince Sadruddin Aga Khan who presented her with a set of jewellery cut in the shape of panthers on their wedding. It amused her to wear the panther bracelet while walking her own live panther called Ti Amo around her glossy apartments in Geneva and Paris.

Once again the marriage failed, probably because the prince was bitterly disappointed when their union failed to produce children. At the age of 35 Nina Dyer killed herself with an overdose of pills.

Her father claimed the jewellery and sold it at an auction. Manufacturer Cartier was the buyer. In 1978 the jewels were put on a flight to Hong Kong, destined for a private exhibition – and vanished. A team of top sleuths was put on the case. They visited virtually every country in the world during the decade after the theft in a bid to track the stolen jewels down. The detectives were successful, although they refused to reveal the tricks of their trade. Now the encrusted panthers with the melancholy past are under lock and key, seen only occasionally during exhibitions.

Publicity about jinxes on jewels has done much to add to the aura of ancient stones. It was just such an eerie feeling that put thief Bob Lavington back on the straight and narrow.

Bob stole £14,000 worth of Egyptian amulets from Bristol museum when he was 16. But he believed the charms used to ward off evil spirits were cursed and became haunted by fear of unearthly reprisals. Within five years he had turned to God, become a voluntary worker and confessed to the police about the theft, which they had no idea he had done.

Defending him at Bristol Crown Court in February 1992, James Tabor said the thought of stealing the trinkets made him almost suicidal. Lavington was ordered to do 150 hours' community service and seems unlikely to ever offend again.

THEATRICAL
SUPERSTITIONS

The theatre was once considered an evil domain, and assuming another's character was believed to be unholy and dangerous work. Perhaps that is why, even in the late 20th century, the actor's world is still a minefield of superstitions, where even wishing someone good luck can lead to disaster ...

Actors are the most superstitious bunch in the world. It's a minefield for the theatre-goer who doesn't wish to send the cast of a production scurrying away with crossed fingers in search of some wood to touch.

A well-meaning granny, for example, who sat in the audience clickety-clicking away on knitting needles as she watched, could single-handedly bring the curtain down on a tour. In one ill-starred play which folded after only six weeks, an unfortunate actress was blamed for being a knitter during rehearsals.

Absent-minded parents who turn up still humming 'Three Blind Mice' which they sang to their children at bedtime can also evacuate the stage. It's one of a number of tunes which, once heard, will scare performers out of the spotlights.

Like so many of today's superstitions, nobody knows how most of the folklore sprang up. The theatre was once thought of as the devil's domain. This was probably because impersonating someone else was believed to be unholy, and work for shady characters.

TREADING CAREFULLY

Of course, the attitude towards the theatre has changed down the years and it is now a respected profession. But over-dramatic actors who pay heed to omens must be in a permanent spin. Anyone who wants to wish a close pal all the best on a first night had better tread warily.

Never utter the seemingly innocent phrase 'Good luck'. It's believed those few words can tempt fate and damn a player and production to ill fortune. Instead, it is considered good form to say 'Break a leg' or 'Snap a wrist' or even 'Fall down backwards'. Better still, give a pinch for good luck. Any actor *au fait* with theatre good-luck charms will forgive a small bruise.

Don't send flowers before the start of the play. This is also thought to invite trouble, as is the appearance of fresh flowers on stage during a play.

If you must visit the dressing room, ensure you step over the threshold with your right foot first. And for the actors' sakes, never wear blue, yellow or green. Blue is thought to be unlucky in theatres all over the world. Only a generous smattering of silver is likely to lift the curse it brings. Yellow is the colour of envy, treachery and cowardice. It was the hue worn by actors in medieval plays who appeared as the devil. Yellow roses sent to an actor indicate the impending death of a

Below: *Peacocks are beautiful birds. But they and their stunning plumage are loathed by actors who believe them to be an evil influence. One stuffed peacock which stood in the lobby of a theatre was blamed for the bankruptcy of its owner.*

'THE MISERABLE BIRD OF
MALIGNANT FATE' WAS
HELD RESPONSIBLE FOR
THE THEATRE OWNER'S
BANKRUPTCY.

Left: *Enter a dressing room right foot first to ensure good fortune for its occupant. And actresses should stick to fake gems* (below) *to get good reviews.*

friend. Also, golden-coloured dogs are not welcome in theatres because they are thought to bring with them misfortunes. An orchestra leader once barred a musician from the pit for playing a yellow clarinet. Green is a similar colour to limelight, sought by most members of the profession. But forest-coloured costumes merge with the spotlight which is intended to mark them out and the actor becomes almost invisible. Green is also the colour of the fairies who become jealous if humans don it, and wreak a terrible revenge.

No matter how close it is to Christmas, never mention the word 'turkey' backstage. This is because an early play called *Cage Me a Turkey* closed after only one act was performed.

Should you be wearing a peacock feather in your hat, remove it hastily unless you want to reduce the aspiring star to a gibbering jelly. Both peacocks and peacock feathers are considered extremely unlucky in theatres. So feared by theatre folk is the poor creature that it was once branded 'the miserable bird of malignant fate'. That was by a theatre owner who went bankrupt in the 1870s and entirely blamed a stuffed peacock which stood in the theatre lobby. Another theatre in the same era fell on hard times but prospered again when the peacock motif painted in the auditorium was covered up.

Be careful where you tread. A cat which makes a mess backstage is welcome in the theatre for the good fortune it brings, but the feline is never allowed on stage for

Above: *Nowadays the sound of whistling in the theatre is rare as it means someone will soon be fired. That's because stage hands in Elizabethan times were often sailors who communicated to each other with a shrill whistle. If their call signs were misunderstood, staging would collapse around the heads of the actors and the unfortunate matelots involved were instantly dismissed.*

there it would bode badly. Large quantities of champagne are drunk on opening nights – or any night – in the theatre, purely in the interests of attracting good fortune. Any spilled on the first night should be dabbed behind your ears, a habit first started by legendary American actress Tallulah Bankhead.

Nervous actors will be taking note of certain other traditions to ensure the success of their play. Don't be surprised to find them donning make-up with a rabbit's foot. Unsavoury though it might appear, a rabbit is born with its eyes open and therefore has special powers over the evil eye. In fact, the rabbit's foot in question should be the left hind paw from an animal which has been killed at a full moon by a cross-eyed person if it is to be truly effective in warding off evil spirits. The rabbit's strong back legs touch the ground before its front ones when it walks, signifying magical powers. There will be panic if an actor opens the make-up box to find the rabbit's foot applicator missing. The loss of the lucky paw is associated with a loss of talent. Expect a grubby, well-worn make-up box on the dressing-room table, as well. It is not only unlucky to break in a new box of grease-paints on the first night, it is also a bad sign ever to clean it out.

Would-be actors might have already tried their luck at standing on the stage and throwing a piece of coal into the gallery which should ensure a successful career.

They will have been bucked by a bad rehearsal. That's a sure-fire way to achieve a successful opening night. And all being well, the performance will start 13 minutes

Right: *A scene from* **Babes in the Wood.** *The play is often passed over in favour of other productions, like the well-liked* **Cinderella,** *because it is thought to be a problem panto.*

late. If their luck is in, they will stumble as they go on stage. If it's a woman who trips over her dress, she would do well to spare the few seconds it would take to kiss her hem, to generate good fortune. Falling on stage while the play is in progress signifies a long engagement. Squeaky shoes worn by an actor on the very first entrance, no matter how irritating, is thought lucky. If, when he kicks the footwear off after treading the boards, they land upright, it means even more luck will follow. But he will lose the advantage if the shoes fall on to their sides or are put on a chair.

A hunchback in the cast is also considered a happy omen.

TEMPTING FATE

There's unlikely to be a real mirror among the props and woe betide the cast if there is. If one actress peers over the shoulder of another into a looking glass, it brings misfortune to the person overlooked. Fake jewellery is also chosen above the real thing by superstitious actors – who would never open an umbrella on stage. This stems from 1868 when an orchestra leader by the name of Bob Williams pushed up his brolly on stage before leaving the theatre in pouring rain. He immediately boarded a

ship for a trans-Atlantic crossing, only to be killed when the engine of the liner exploded. Nor will you find tense performers peeping through the stage curtains at their audience as it is a certain forerunner of doom. Actors may invest their time wisely and devote a few moments to checking the clothes of their cohorts in the cast. Picking a length of cotton off a fellow actor and winding it around your finger is supposed to bring about a contract.

Any actor must be forgiven for fluffing the final line of the play on the first night. For among a superstitious cast it will never have been uttered during all the preceding rehearsals until that moment. Completing the play in such a way before the run starts is yet another way by which to tempt fate.

Theatre visitors are unlikely to find anyone whistling as it is a sure sign that someone will get fired. There are two reasons for this. First, whistling carries and may be heard on stage. Second, in Elizabethan times when theatre flourished in Britain, stagehands were commonly former sailors who communicated to each other in shrill whistles. The only trouble

Above: Macbeth *is never referred to by name. It's known only as 'the Scottish play' and considered to bring bad luck to its cast. The curse is linked to the witches' chant. It is thought Shakespeare borrowed the words from an actual sorcerer's spell.*

Left: *Laurence Olivier scored a triumph in the 1937 production of* **Macbeth.** *But in the process, its curse nearly killed him. Not only did he lose his voice but he was brushed by a 25lb weight which plummeted from the stage lights.*

Right: *Paul Scofield himself escaped unscathed when he performed in a 1946 production of* Macbeth *but it did some damage to his reputation. In his haste to return to the stage one night, he appeared in front of an audience minus his wig and smoking a cigarette.*

Below: *The Drury Lane Theatre boldly decided to produce* The Bohemian Girl, *which was notoriously unlucky, in 1843. Its production was normally an indicator of an impending death.*

was that a misinterpreted note could bring the curtain down on the actor's head and the hapless fellow responsible for the blunder would be kicked out there and then.

There are a few plays thought to be lucky, the pantomime *Cinderella* is among them. But conversely, there are those believed to be disastrous choices, including *Robin Hood*, *Babes in the Wood* and above all, *Macbeth*.

THE KISS OF DEATH

Such is the fear and awe in which this Shakespearian work is held among actors, they never breathe its name. Only the term 'the Scottish play' is reverentially whispered by those respectful of the power it possesses. Apparently, the story that the play was condemned by a curse sprang up on its opening night in 1606. The actor

who was playing Lady Macbeth became mysteriously ill and Shakespeare himself had to step into his shoes. It was commissioned by the king, James I, who attended the opening night and loathed it. Fifty years passed before it was performed again. It's thought the witches' song incorporated by Shakespeare has its foundation in sorcery and this is what causes all the trouble.

There have been a string of deaths and misfortunes associated with productions of *Macbeth*. During the 18th century some unfortunate actors discovered at the end of the run that someone had absconded with all the takings and there would be no wages for them. In 1849, there was a riot in which 31 people died at the Astor Place Opera House when *Macbeth* was playing. Years ago, when passionate fights were enacted with real weapons, one Macduff came away without his thumbs, hacked off by the fiery Macbeth. In the 1937 production at the Old Vic in London, the director was killed in a car crash, the producer's dog died, star Laurence Olivier lost his voice – and almost died himself when a 25lb weight fell from the stage lights. The tale of horror was compounded when the theatre boss breathed his last on the opening night.

The play brought bad luck of a more light-hearted vein to actor Paul Scofield when he played Malcolm in a *Macbeth* production at Stratford. Chatting in a fellow thespian's dressing room, he was oblivious that his cue was imminent until a

"I DREAMT THAT I DWELT IN MARBLE HALLS,"

Song,

SUNG BY

Miss Rainforth.

At the *Theatre Royal Drury Lane,*

In the Opera of

THE BOHEMIAN GIRL,

Written by Alfred Bunn Esqre

Composed by

M. W. BALFE.

Ent. Sta. Hall.   Price 2/-

LONDON,

Published by CHAPPELL, *Music Seller to Her Majesty, 50 New Bond Street.*
And in Paris by Bernard Latte.

This Song may also be had a Third lower.

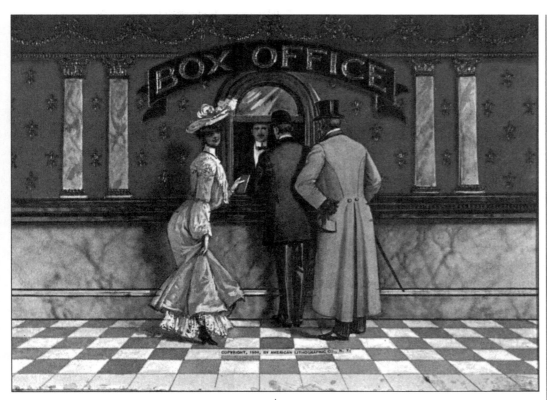

TRADITION RELATES THAT
THE PLAY HAS ITS
FOUNDATION IN SORCERY,
AND ACTORS REFUSE TO
EVEN WHISPER ITS NAME
FOR FEAR OF THE
CONSEQUENCES.

Left: *Box office staff get a production off to a good start if they sell the first ticket to an elderly person. Alternatively, it signifies early closure if the all-important first customer is a youngster.*

Below: *If they never let a lady's cash cross their palms, programme sellers are giving a new play its best chance. Nor should they spend their first tip, but keep it in a pocket where they can rub it against their leg to induce further good fortune.*

breathless stage manager alerted him. In his haste to get on stage, Scofield not only appeared before the audience with a cigarette sticking out of his mouth, he'd also forgotten to put his wig on.

Quoting from the play is also bad form. Actors subjected to bursts of it from literary show-offs are compelled to leave the room, turn around three times, spit over their left shoulder and knock three times before re-entering. Music from *Macbeth* is similarly avoided at all costs by actors, who fear it will have devastating consequences. Other musical numbers are hated by superstitious players. 'I Dreamt that I Dwelt in Marble Halls' from *The Bohemian Girl* is supposed to indicate an impending death. Not only is 'Three Blind Mice' hated, but so is the 'Barcarolle' from *The Tales of Hoffman*.

Lobby staff have a part to play in the success of a play. The first ticket should always go to an elderly person, which signifies a long run ahead for the production. If that key customer is a young woman, the play is doomed.

On the big night, the theatre will be filled with foreboding if the first person to be seated holds ticket number 13. Ushers should do their bit and always stay for the first few words of the play if they want to ensure a successful run. In their own interests, the first tip they receive in the new season should never be spent. In order that it is followed by plenty more, it should be rubbed hard against the leg and kept in a pocket. Tips should never be accepted from women buying programmes if the sellers want to stay lucky. Fortunately for them, a token from a man is quite acceptable.

CURSED FAMILIES

Wealth, position and power – some families seem to have everything and are envied from afar. But the envy soon turns to pity when it becomes apparent that succeeding generations have also inherited something that is far less desirable ...

Hers should have been a fairy-tale existence of lace and luxury. Christina Onassis, the only daughter of a Greek shipping tycoon, was pampered like a goddess. At her fingertips were diamonds and designer clothes, lavish parties and limos. But lonely, overweight and unhappy, she died in a hotel bathroom aged just 37, leaving the daughter she cherished without a mother's love.

It was the last in a long line of tragedies to hit the massively wealthy clan, prompting widespread speculation about the existence of a curse dogging their fortunes. Certainly, the Onassis family was proof – if any were needed – that money doesn't buy happiness. Christina, her brother Alexander, mother Tina and aunt all died prematurely. Her father died in misery and pain after a life of wheeler-dealing which brought him fabulous riches. If a curse was indeed placed on the Onassis family it may well have been by one of the unfortunate business people who felt the sharp end of his business practice.

Aristotle Onassis was born on 20 January 1920 in the Anatolian port of Smyrna, now known as Izmir, in Turkey. He was the son of Socrates Onassis, head of a burgeoning tobacco business in the region. But when he was no more than a boy, Aristotle's mother Penelope died, opening a wound which never fully healed. He refused to accept the stepmother brought into the house by his father – a pattern which was to be repeated by his own children many years later when he married America's former first lady Jackie Kennedy.

Aristo, as he was affectionately called by his family, was no scholar. He flunked school after school and his bad behaviour became more excessive with each explusion. His father wasn't unduly concerned. He had a career in commerce in mind for his son and believed education could muddle a good business brain. But that didn't spell an easy life for Aristotle at home. He was frequently subject to barbarous beatings from his father, a stern disciplinarian. Yet neither was his life endless toil. Away from the tyranny of his father, he discovered leisure and pleasure.

By day he would row, swim or sunbathe on the picturesque shoreline. At night he would visit prostitutes in the red-light district. But this all came to a sudden end when the ambitious Turkish leader Kemal Ataturk marched into Smyrna with his forces, bringing murder and mayhem. The Onassis family were lucky to escape with

Opposite: *Grace Kelly was the glamorous queen of Hollywood who became a princess when she married Prince Rainier of Monaco. Hers was a fairy-tale story which thrilled the world. She died in a mystery car crash in 1982.*

Below: *As a boy, Aristotle Onassis was grief-stricken when his mother died. He never accepted the woman his father later married. Although he failed school exams, his place in the family firm was assured – until Turkey invaded his home town.*

Right: *To the outside world, Onassis appeared a soft-hearted family man when he was with wife Tina and children Alexander and Christina. In fact, he was a ruthless and devious businessman guilty of criminally sharp practice who thought nothing of cheating on his wife. Some of his success was rooted in work he carried out for Europe's Fascist leaders between the wars.*

HE RISKED HIS LIFE TO RESCUE HIS FATHER, AND HOPED FOR AN EMOTIONAL WELCOME — BUT HE WAS GREETED WITH FURY AND CONTEMPT.

their lives. While Socrates was jailed, the womenfolk were transported to a camp on the island of Lesbos. Aristotle, meanwhile, discovered a new talent in the art of diplomacy. He so charmed the Turkish general who requisitioned the Onassis family house that he was even allowed to stay on in the safety and comfort of those four walls while scenes of slaughter and pillage were occurring outside.

AN ASPIRING MILLIONAIRE

Aristotle didn't waste his opportunity. Furtively, he emptied the business safe and eventually bought himself a passage on an American destroyer heading for Lesbos where he located his stepmum and sisters. Using the money from his father's business, he helped them escape to the Greek capital of Athens before bravely returning to Smyrna for his father. But if he had imagined a grateful, emotional welcome, he was sadly mistaken. Socrates's primary interest was where the money taken by Aristotle had been spent and he was furious about the none-too-satisfactory replies given by his confused and disappointed son. After they clashed, young Aristotle decided to go-it-alone by moving to Argentina.

At 17 years of age and alone in the Argentinian capital, Buenos Aires, he happened on the perfect job for an aspiring millionaire. He became a telephone operator, ideal because he could listen into high-powered business calls and use the insider knowledge he sneakily gained to give a good account of himself on the stock market. Onassis tried to repeat his father's success by breaching the tobacco market. Obligingly, his father sent over some Turkish leaf tobacco, unavailable elsewhere in the South American country and in demand by young high-society types. But his covert business activities revealed the streak of ruthlessness which was to become so glaringly apparent when he was a tycoon. He injected chemicals into rival cigarette brands which made them smell revolting. In addition, he adopted the brand name already used by someone else, only Aristotle cut the price to make his product seem more appealing. Once he even arranged with local mobsters to have a shipment of tobacco ruined by seawater while it was in Genoa, Italy, so he could claim the insurance. To bump up his earnings, he traded in opium.

His new-found power base was threatened when Greece proposed new surcharges against countries like Argentina with whom it had no trading agreement. Horrified, Onassis flew to Greece to put his case to the government. The arguments worked – and he was appointed deputy Greek consul in the Argentine for his trouble. It was a position of authority he exploited for his own ends by launching a currency scam.

The next step was to start supplying his South American interests using his own tankers, registered, of course, in Panama to steer clear of the usual shipping regulations. At first, the new venture struggled, thanks to the Depression which still gripped Europe. But a new brand of leader emerged around the world and Onassis found there was money to be made from the regimes run by Hitler and Mussolini as well as from Imperialist Japan. While they were all busy arming themselves for certain conflict, Onassis was kept busy. So too was the world's first supertanker, the *Ariston*, which he built and launched from Sweden in 1938. War proved more an inconvenience than a disaster.

In July 1940 he left Argentina for New York and spent the rest of the conflict in the safety of the US. His fortunes continued to blossom. It was time, he decided, to find himself a wife. For 12 years he had been involved with Ingeborg Dedichen, a divorced Norwegian heiress to an important whaling business. She was captivated by the brooding Greek even though he was physically unappealing. He proposed several times and thrilled her with wildly romantic gestures. But he was also jealous and brutal, beating her for imagined flirtations.

When Onassis made the decision to end his bachelor days, it wasn't to the faithful Ingeborg that he turned. He became attracted to a pretty and eminently suitable schoolgirl, Athina Livanos, the daughter of a London-based Greek shipowner, Stavros Livanos. Aristotle finally won her father's approval and the pair wed in New York's Greek Orthodox Cathedral on 28 December 1946. He was 40, she was 17. They had two children, Alexander and Christina.

Tina's sister Eugenie married Stavros Niarchos, at that time a friendly business adversary of Onassis. Aristotle swiftly capitalized on the US government's desire to rid itself of surplus ships following the war. Operating from behind a smoke-screen to sidestep regulations, he cashed in on the bargains. Also he found new profits were to be made in whaling – as long as the stiff rules imposed by the International Whaling Commission were flouted.

COURTING DISASTER

The double misdemeanours led to his arrest in New York in February 1954 on fraud charges – which later fizzled out – and an embarrassing fine from the whaling authorities of some $700,000 the following year. But if Onassis thought the worst had come, he was wrong.

He plotted to become the sole shipper of Saudi oil with a multi-million pound deal which undermined the hold on the oil trade in America engineered by a consortium of US companies. The business community in the US was outraged, and so was the government. Working for the government, brother-in-law Niarchos began a long-term feud by probing the business affairs of Onassis; he uncovered a bribes scandal which was enough to scare off the Saudi king. Meanwhile, the retaliatory boycott instituted by US oil producers left the Onassis fleet idle. It seemed the Midas touch had finally deserted him and he was to be fed to the lions.

Fate was kind, however. The Suez Crisis blew up, and as Egyptian leader Nasser blocked shipping from the short-cut canal which linked the Gulf of Persia to the Mediterranean, Onassis found a new market for the services of his ships. Western governments were desperate to get oil from the Arab nations, even if it meant tankers travelling around the tip of South Africa. In the space of five months, Onassis had realized profits upwards of $70 million. A business disaster had quickly been transformed into a raging success. It gave

ONASSIS HAD SAILED TOO CLOSE TO THE WIND – AND HIS JEALOUS RIVALS WERE DETERMINED TO SCUPPER HIS FLEET AND HIS FORTUNE.

Below: *Jackie Kennedy sat only inches from her husband President John F. Kennedy when he was shot and killed. Onassis was among the mourners at the funeral. Five years later she wed tycoon Onassis, to the horror of his children. Her extravagance and cagey behaviour soon convinced him the union was a terrible mistake.*

Above: *As heiress to her father's riches, Christina Onassis had fabulous wealth. But money failed to buy her happiness. She lost her brother and mother in tragic circumstances and suffered four broken marriages before her untimely death in 1988.*

Right: *Alexander Onassis was a skilled pilot who yearned to run his own private airline. He was at the controls of a rogue seaplane which crashed soon after take-off from Athens airport and died soon after in hospital.*

him enough cash to purchase the Greek national airlines, Olympic Airways, from a troubled government.

Onassis enjoyed all the trappings of enormous wealth. There were foreign apartments, social events at which he and Tina rubbed shoulders with European royalty and Hollywood stars, and the lavish *Christina*, at the time the world's largest and most luxurious yacht.

But despite the glorious indulgences, Onassis was unable to find personal contentment. His marriage to Tina didn't stop him from having affairs when he chose. None of them proved a major distraction for Onassis until he met opera singer Maria Callas.

The diva was wooed relentlessly by Onassis – despite the fact she was married. He welcomed the Americanized Greek Callas and her husband aboard the *Christina* in July 1959 for a cruise on which war-time premier Winston Churchill was also a guest. It was during the trip that the opera star's husband, Giovanni Meneghini, discovered the relationship which had developed between Callas and Onassis. He was told by a fretful Tina who blurted out that she had discovered her husband and his wife making love.

Tina filed for divorce which was won by June 1960. She had custody of the children and soon went on to wed the Marquess of Blandford, a relative of Churchill. Meneghini would only reluctantly agree to a separation, warning his wife that Onassis would never marry her. His prophecy was correct. There is little doubt the passionate Callas longed to wed Onassis, but the man who loathed opera began to distance himself from his mistress when she continued to pursue her career. He had plans for her to become a major film star. She dismissed his efforts in favour of her devotion to the classics.

Little did Callas realize he had already met a woman he desired more than her. She was Jackie Kennedy, wife of US President Kennedy. Jackie was cruising with Onassis in the Mediterranean during the summer before her husband was assassinated. Onassis attended Kennedy's funeral and the courtship of the dead man's widow began in earnest. They met regularly in the ensuing five years, but Jackie was unwilling to go public with the relationship for fear of it

harming the political ambitions of her brother-in-law Robert. When Bobby Kennedy was killed in June 1968, the last obstacle was removed.

Jackie Kennedy married Aristotle Onassis in October 1968 on the tiny island of Skorpios which he owned. Although they attended the service, his children were tight-lipped with fury. Even after the wedding they always referred to her with distaste as 'the Widow'.

But the 1970s were to prove disastrous for Onassis – it was the decade the hex on the family took root. A string of business woes put his undisputed claim of being the richest man in the world in jeopardy. As his fortune started to ebb away, he was faced with mounting bills from his free-spending wife. Jackie spent most of her time in America where she was close to her children and to the expensive New York shops which she patronized so often. She saw her husband infrequently and rarely welcomed him at her apartment. When a letter written by Jackie on honeymoon to an old flame was published in 1970, Onassis realized he had made a serious mistake. In 1973, after a public spat with Jackie, he consulted a lawyer with a view to a divorce.

A STRING OF DEATHS

Christina wed for the first time and felt the full force of her father's wrath because her chosen partner, American property magnate Joseph Bolker, was 29 years older than her and already a father of four. Onassis cut off her income and despatched go-betweens to talk her out of the marriage. When that failed he resorted to typically underhand tactics of vicious anonymous telephone calls during which Bolker was made a subject of loathing and ridicule. The marriage was finished within the year.

In May 1970 Eugenie Niarchos died aged 44 in her Greek island home in mysterious circumstances. She had taken an overdose of 25 tablets but was also covered in bruises. Her husband Stavros explained that in attempting to revive her he had inflicted the knocks. There were no fewer than three inquiries into her death, one of which found Stavros's energetic efforts to bring life back to his wife probably caused internal bleeding and amounted to involuntary homicide. The case was never brought because a judge ruled she in fact committed suicide.

The family was appalled at the events. But their shock was replaced by horror

when Eugenie's sister Tina divorced her English nobleman husband and wed the widower Niarchos.

Alexander Onassis was an able pilot who took over a segment of Olympic Airways and successfully controlled it on behalf of his father, but his love of flying was a kiss of death. He was piloting a Piaggio seaplane which he hated on 22 January 1973 when it crashed shortly after taking off from Athens airport. Although he survived the smash, doctors discovered he was brain dead. After Christina had rushed to his bedside to say farewell, the life support machine which kept him alive was switched off.

It was a body blow to Tina. Her grief was compounded when Christina took a massive drugs overdose in August 1974. On 10 October Tina was found dead in Paris aged 45. Christina quickly initiated an investigation and a post-mortem found

Above: *Connected by marriage but with little warmth between them, Christina and Jackie Onassis in a rare photograph of the two.*

Left: *Businesswoman Christina let her heart rule her head when she met Russian company director Sergei Kauzov. Romance quickly blossomed and the pair were married. Like her first two marriages, the third was doomed to failure.*

*Above: **Husband number 4 was Thierry Roussel, and together they had a much loved daughter, Athina. Yet once again her marriage broke down, leaving Christina despairing of fulfilling her dream of lifelong romance.***

barbituate-addict Tina had died from acute oedema of the lung.

The grief-stricken heiress to the Onassis millions was then forced to watch her father's health decline. He was suffering from a wasting disease which left him increasingly incapacitated and extremely bad tempered. The man she once worshipped as a god had to have his eyelids held open with tape. His spirit was finally broken when he lost Olympic Airways to

the government. After a painful operation to remove his gall bladder and a bout of bronchial pneumonia, Aristotle Onassis died on 15 March 1975 aged 69. Christina mourned as she watched him relinquish his hold on life.

His body was taken from Paris where he had died to the island of Skorpios to be buried alongside his son. Jackie attended the funeral, accompanied by her brother-in-law Edward Kennedy.

Christina was then alone to make what she could of the business, now in real danger of collapse. In the same year as her father died she married Alexander Andreadis, the son of a Greek banker and shipyard owner. The union lasted only a matter of months.

Before it was dissolved in 1977 she had met and fallen in love with Sergei Kauzov, the director of a Russian company with which she was doing business. Again, the marriage lasted no more than a year.

With three swiftly broken marriages behind her. Christina sought refuge in food and drink. While she had a choice of dishes, she plumped for burgers and chips time and again. She swigged Coke by the crateful. Cruel observers called her 'Thunderthighs' or 'The Greek Tanker', which sent her further down the spiral of depression. She finally managed to conquer her eating habits and slim with the help of a clinic and

*Right: **The Kennedy clan in 1934. They were the American equivalent of the royal family, with all the trappings of wealth and success. But tragedy dogged the lives of the nine children born to Rose and Joe.***

Left: US ambassador to Britain Joseph Kennedy proudly linked arms with his handsome sons Joe and John in 1937. He saw both men cut down in their prime. Joe died in wartime service in 1944 after volunteering to fly a plane loaded with high explosives against the Germans. John was sensationally assassinated in 1963.

emerged svelte and happy. It was this vision that enchanted wealthy French bachelor Thierry Roussel. The pair fell in love and married in March 1984. Within a month she was pregnant and her daughter Athina arrived in January 1985.

But once again marital troubles plagued her and the pair split. In misery, she visited Buenos Aires, the South American city which had once proved so lucky for her father. But despite a new and promising romance, drug-dependent Christina was found dead on 19 November 1988. A coroner decided she had died of natural causes.

Her death has left Athina a wealthy child but as cursed as her mother. The risk of kidnapping is so high she is guarded constantly and will never be like other children her age, despite the best efforts of her father, with whom she now lives. When she comes of age, her biggest concern will surely be not how to spend her fortune but more importantly how to shatter the curse.

A FAMILY OF TRAGEDY

Jackie Kennedy emerged a survivor from the Onassis curse just as she escaped unscathed from her links with the famous Kennedy clan, America's first family. And if

any family bore the scars of a jinx, surely it was this one.

Joe Kennedy was the man who started the dynasty, earning piles of money although no one is quite sure how. Rumours that he was involved in bootlegging or booze smuggling during a government alcohol ban during the 1920s have been given credence. After striking it rich so early in life, this highly motivated man didn't sit on his laurels. He moved into property speculation and found success on the stock market. By the time he reached his 30th birthday, he was a multi-millionaire.

Above: J.F.K. pictured with his wife Jackie in Dallas on the morning of his assassination. He was adored by millions who knew nothing of the seedy, sleazy lifestyle he led behind closed doors at the White House.

Top: *Despite frantic efforts to revive him, J.F.K. couldn't be saved. Marxist Lee Harvey Oswald (above) was charged with the assassination. Two days later he was killed while in police custody by Jack Ruby. It's now widely accepted that Oswald was not acting alone.*

Below: *The world came to a respectful halt when Kennedy was buried with full honours.*

The cash allowed him to pursue his political aspirations. He became US ambassador to Britain, some achievement for a man staunchly loyal to his Irish Catholic roots. He was recalled in 1940 after publicly opposing America's entry into the war, having unwisely declared: 'Democracy is finished in Britain. If the US gets into the war with England, we'll be left holding the bag.'

In a marriage of minds and empires, he wed Rose Fitzgerald, the formidable daughter of Boston's first Irish mayor, in 1914. Together they had nine children. Each was offered a financial incentive not to drink or smoke until he or she was 21. She once told how she encouraged them to do homework. 'I told the boys to study hard and maybe they'll be president one day.' Joe was more forceful about it. He was convinced one of his boys would be top cat and he groomed them carefully for the demanding role.

But Joe was faithless throughout his 55-year marriage, a habit also learnt by his sons. The most famous liaison he had was with Hollywood goddess Gloria Swanson, who was also married, for whom he even considered leaving his wife. Only the prospect of opposition from the Church cooled the affair.

This, however, was perhaps the least of Rose's agonies during the unfolding years. Their third child, Rosemary, was born with mental handicap and has lived almost all her life in a home.

In 1944 their eldest son, Joe Junior, died aged just 29 when the bomber aircraft he was flying exploded over the English Channel. It gutted his father who couldn't even grieve at the graveside of his hero son: the body was never found. The husband of daughter Kathleen, the Marquis of Harting-ton, was killed in action during the same year. Kathleen herself perished in a plane crash in 1948. She was just 28 years old.

For more than a decade, the effects of the Kennedy curse subsided and the family basked in the reflected glory of John F. Kennedy, elected 34th president of America in 1960. However, the Kennedys were rocked when J.F.K.'s son Patrick was stillborn in 1963.

Jackie had barely recovered from the trauma when she accompanied the president on a tour of Dallas, Texas, in November. As she sat next to her 46-year-old husband, receiving cheers and appreciation from the

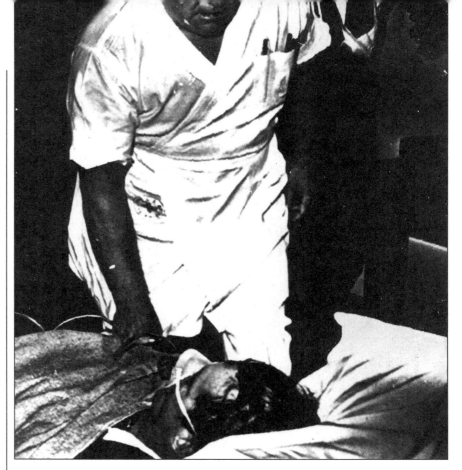

crowds, bullets from a gun fired by assassin Lee Harvey Oswald racked his body. The presidential car sped off to hospital with Jackie Kennedy cradling the head of her husband, blood from his head wound pouring on to her coral-pink suit. Within 25 minutes, the president was dead. Jackie was wearing the same suit still bearing bloodstains when Lyndon B. Johnson was sworn in as president hours later aboard Air Force 1, the plane which then took off to return the president's body to Washington.

J.F.K. was the first of the clan to be murdered – but not the last. Robert Kennedy, on whom the political hopes of the ageing Joe Kennedy were now centred, was felled by a bullet as he campaigned for the presidency in 1968. The assassination happened on 5 June just hours after he was successful in clinching the California Democratic primary election after an acrimonious campaign. Senator Kennedy was meeting his supporters at the Ambassador Hotel in Los Angeles close to midnight when the shots rang out. There were five bullets fired from a gun levelled by Palestinian immigrant Sirhan Sirhan before he was pounced on by security men. Despite a 20-hour battle at the Good Samaritan Hospital in the city, the senator died of his wounds aged just 42.

IMMORAL CONDUCT

The series of untimely deaths was subsequently followed by dishonour. Rumours that had been whispered about the Kennedys while they lived were discussed openly after their deaths. Soon the whole world knew about the astonishing sexual appetites possessed by both Kennedy men, which they satiated as often as possible. Both appeared to be clean-cut, wholesome American boys who had worked hard to make good. On the surface they were both happily married – John to Jackie and Robert to Ethel – with handsome young families.

But their conquests were legion and their quest for sexual fulfilment even compromised national security on occasions. As a navy officer, John had a fling with a known Nazi spy and later became involved with a German woman with communist sympathies. In between there were infatuations with Hollywood stars like Angie Dickinson and Jayne

Mansfield, as well as affairs with a host of other women, including members of staff and friends of his wife.

The most infamous relationship was with voluptuous film star Marilyn Monroe, a woman he shared with brother Bobby. Later, their connection with her became public when she was found dead and the world's press speculated about what had happened. The rest of the family could only suffer in

Above: *Medics tried in vain to save the life of Robert Kennedy, shot in Los Angeles while campaigning for the presidency in 1968.*

Left: *Senator Edward Kennedy might have succeeded in his quest to reach the White House had it not been for the death of Mary Jo Kopechne, a capaign worker who died when the car he was driving plunged into a fast-flowing river. Kennedy himself escaped unscathed.*

THE CAR SPED TO THE HOSPITAL AS THE BLOOD SPURTED FROM HIS WOUNDS, STAINING JACKIE'S PINK SUIT BRIGHT SCARLET.

He denied drinking, he denied fornicating — but he didn't deny the curse of the Kennedys.

Below: *Senator Kennedy with his son Teddy Junior, who was also struck down by the family curse. He lost a leg when he was stricken with cancer aged just 12. He has also been accused of drugs misuse despite his healthy lifestyle – he tackles many sports.*

silence as the golden boys of American politics were ripped from their pedestals, victims of their own hungry personalities. The pair were branded hypocrites for using drugs behind the bedroom door while maintaining a tough public stance against pot and pills. But the indignity of public debate about the private lives of the Kennedys didn't end there.

In 1969 youngest brother Edward, by now a senator and the last political hope in the fold, sacrificed his path to the presidency in one night of fatally flawed judgement. After a day spent sailing with friends off the Cape Cod coast, the 37-year-old Democrat headed for a select party on the island of Chappaquiddick. There were six men and six women, all of whom spoke animatedly about the forthcoming race for the presidency.

Shortly before midnight Teddy Kennedy left the gathering to return to the mainland. In the car was campaign worker Mary Jo Kopechne, aged 29, a veteran of Bobby's political camp. Instead of taking the road back, Kennedy inexplicably directed his car down a bumpy track towards the beach. Disaster struck as his 2-year-old vehicle toppled from the 85-foot-high wooden bridge and sank into the waterway below. Kennedy fought his way free and broke the surface of the fast-running water gasping for air. There was no sign of Mary Jo.

Later he told how he repeatedly dived in

a bid to save her. He crawled out of the water but instead of rushing to raise the alarm, lurched back to the party where he urged close colleagues to keep quiet about the incident. It wasn't until the next morning that the police became involved after they were alerted by a resident near the scene of the crash.

Astounded cops discovered the body of a girl inside the car, learned the car belonged to Senator Edward Kennedy and were then told that the politician was sitting in their police station waiting to talk to them, all in the space of a few shocking moments.

Kennedy's accounts of the evening were veiled and unilluminating. He went to Mary Jo's funeral in the company of his pregnant wife Joan and Bobby's widow Ethel. Soon after, he was given a suspended 2-month jail sentence and a driving ban for leaving the scene of the accident.

The press speculated at length about the destination of the car and the reasons behind the crash. Kennedy appeared on TV in a bid to calm the public rumourmongering. 'There is no truth whatsoever to the widely circulated suspicions of immoral conduct that have been levelled at my behaviour and hers regarding that evening. There has never been a private relationship between us of any kind … Nor was I driving under the influence of alcohol.

'All kinds of scrambled thoughts – all of

them confused, some of them irrational, many of them which I cannot recall and some of which I would not have entertained under normal circumstances – went through my mind during this period. They were reflected in the various, inexplicable, inconsistent and inconclusive things I said and did, including such questions as whether the girl might still be alive somewhere out of that immediate area, whether some awful curse did actually hang over all the Kennedys, whether there was some justifiable reason for me to doubt what had happened and to delay my report, whether somehow the awful weight of this incredible incident might in some way pass from my shoulders.'

The incident put an end to any chance Edward Kennedy had of reaching the White House. It was a feat merely to hold on to his Massachusetts seat. His father Joe died the same year, knowing as much. But if the heavyweight ambition had been knocked out of the famous family, the hex attached to their name certainly hadn't.

In 1983, Robert Kennedy Junior was arrested for possessing heroin. A year later his brother David died of a drugs overdose. The body of the 28-year-old was discovered in a rundown motel following a week of high living.

Teddy Junior, son of the troubled Edward and his wife Joan, was struck down with cancer and had to have one leg amputated in order to save his life. His name was also later linked with drugs misuse. His parents had divorced in 1983 amid gossip about her dependence on alcohol and his philandering.

The most recent swipe the family has endured was a rape claim following a party at a Kennedy mansion in Palm Beach at which many of the menfolk made merry. William Kennedy Smith was arrested over the allegation and later cleared.

Once again, it is difficult to decide if the family is really cursed or whether in truth they are the victims of their own avarice and ambition.

PURSUED BY DEMONS

High-kicking Kung Fu star Bruce Lee was a match for any earthly foe. Few opponents held fear for him, whether they were karate, boxing or judo champions. But he lived in terror of confronting demon spirits who

would wreck his life and even threaten his very existence. So convinced was he about the power of the demons that he was reluctant to have children in case the lurking evil was passed on to them.

Many now believe his fears were justified. He died aged 32 of a mystery brain haemorrhage. His son Brandon was killed aged 27 when a Hollywood stunt went tragically awry. Could the pair have evoked a mystic curse through the ancient martial art of Kung Fu in which they were both schooled?

Bruce Lee was christened Li Yuen Kam, meaning 'protector of San Francisco' after his birth in November 1940. His Eurasian mother Grace gave birth to her fourth child in America while his father Li Hoi-chuen worked as a comedian and singer. Within

Above: *After they married, Princess Grace and Prince Rainier had three children: Caroline, Albert and Stephanie. Their unity was shattered when the former Hollywood star was killed in a car crash. Her early death at 52 scarred her children as they entered adulthood.*

HE WOULD BE RICH FOR THE REST OF HIS LIFE – WHAT WAS LEFT OF IT.

IT WAS A SIMPLE STUNT THAT WENT HORRENDOUSLY WRONG.

three years, little Li was reunited with three older brothers and sisters who had been left with relatives in Hong Kong. His parents decided to return to the British colony where their youngest child would soon forge a reputation as a child actor in the Chinese film industry.

As he matured Bruce, as he was then known, spent more time on the streets instead of in the studios. Virtually all of the young, male population found themselves struggling to find an identity in the system of gangs which operated in the throbbing, overcrowded city. He and his friends attacked and were attacked with varying degrees of success.

It wasn't until he was a college boy that he realized there could be so much more to fighting than an undignified scuffle. He alighted on the art of Kung Fu, a strenuous but also spiritual form of self-defence dating back to around AD 600, learning the finer points from an enthusiastic grandmaster.

In 1958 Lee returned to America, seeking fame and fortune. He graduated from the Edison Vocational School and enrolled at Washington University. It was there he met medical student Linda Emery who later became his wife.

During his spare time he ran Kung Fu classes and found there was plenty of interest among young Americans. It wasn't long before he dropped out of university to start the country's first Kung Fu school, soon followed by a second. At a martial arts competition, dominated by exponents of karate rather than Kung Fu, Lee was spotted by a talent scout. It led to a bit part in a TV series called *Green Hornet*, to Lee's immense delight. He played the part of Kato, an Oriental houseboy and chauffeur. Alas, the show folded after only 30 episodes were made, but it helped establish a reputation for him in America which led to other appearances in the *Batman* series and several films. More importantly, the series was exported to the East where Lee became a cult figure.

When he returned to Hong Kong on tour he received an offer from a local film company but turned it down because he still dreamed of the ultimate achievement: star status in America. Back in the States, he began lessons again and his pupils included actors Steve McQueen, James Coburn and James Garner. But Lee received a crushing

blow when Warner Brothers signed up David Carradine for the role of a Kung Fu fighter in a series called *The Warrior*. Lee accepted what he considered to be second-best – a revised offer from a Hong Kong film-making company. His first picture with them – *The Big Boss* in 1972 – was a smash hit in his home city. His fans gasped at the speed and dexterity Lee showed in combat. The new-born celebrity had a fresh philosophy of fighting which was to respond to the moves of the opponent rather than pounce with set pieces.

Within months the Kung Fu cult and its hero became big news in the USA as well. His next film, *Fists of Fury*, grossed over \$3 million. It was enough to win him an offer from Warner Brothers that would keep him in comfort for the rest of his days. Little did he realize how short those days would be.

In 1973 he made the films which most people identify with the enigma of Bruce Lee: *Enter the Dragon* and *Return of the Dragon*. At last he was heaped with recognition across the world. His base remained Hong Kong where he lived in luxury with his wife and their children Brandon and Shannon. His only vice was vanity. While he did not drink or smoke, he cared passionately about how he appeared on screen. He even went so far as to have his underarm sweat glands removed to improve his looks on film.

By May 1973 there were the first signs of impending doom. He collapsed on set and was diagnosed as having a convulsion. Two months later he complained of a headache during a business meeting about his next film. A friend, Taiwanese actress Betty Tin Pei, gave him a mild drug to help. He went to lie down – but hours later when the actress came to rouse him, she could not get a response. Lee was rushed to hospital but died despite efforts to resuscitate him.

Doctors claimed a brain haemorrhage killed him, but it wasn't long before rumours of a sinister assassination plot to finish Lee were rife with Hong Kong gangsters as chief suspects. Lee himself was still living in fear of demons who he felt sure would claim his life one day.

At his funeral tough guy actor James Coburn said: 'Farewell my brother. As a friend and teacher you brought my physical, spiritual and psychological being together. Thank you and peace be with you.'

Little more would have been said about demons and dragons if son Brandon had not followed in his father's footsteps. He also made a name for himself in a handful of roles – and then died in mysterious circumstances at a young age.

Brandon, star of hit film *Rapid Fire*, was killed in 1993 on a film set when a stunt went horrendously wrong. A gun supposed to fire blanks apparently contained a .44 calibre magnum slug which ripped into his stomach. Despite attempts to save him, including the transfusion of some 14 pints of blood, Brandon died. The tragedy occurred just two weeks before he was due to wed his fiancée Lisa Hutton, a production worker.

After his death, the extent of Brandon's belief in a Kung Fu curse haunting his family was revealed by friends and relations. Morbidly obsessed with death, he chose to drive around in an old hearse. And he refused to appear in a film as his father in case it riled the demons he was convinced had claimed the life of his dad.

Bruce's brother, Brandon's uncle, Robert Lee said: 'I don't know if our family is cursed but I am seriously starting to think about it.

'Bruce is dead, my brother Peter is divorced and I am divorced. Now Brandon is dead. It seems like a never-ending story.'

British actor Peter Russell, a friend of Brandon's, told how the budding star feared the demons. 'He would talk about "The Dragon" as he called it. I used to laugh at him but now it has given me food for thought.

'He believed they were always there, waiting to get him. He was convinced they killed his father. He would not accept a rational explanation for his dad's death at such a young age.'

The death of Brandon Lee was the culmination of a sequence of misfortunes which plagued the production of the film *The Crow* in which Brandon played a rock musician who returns from the dead to avenge his murder. Carpenter Jim Martishius, aged 27, suffered severe burns on his face, chest and arms when live power lines hit the crane on which he was working. Film publicist Jason Scott was hurt in a car accident and an equipment truck caught fire.

A sculptor with a grudge went beserk and drove his car through a studio building while filming was in progress. Also, a construction worker slipped and drove a screwdriver through his hand. Even before Brandon's death, the film crew thought they were working under a curse. It was left to police to try and discover how the bullet found its way into the gun.

A Chinese expert warned Lee's family that they would be haunted with bad luck because Bruce was buried next to a 12-year-old boy. Robert Lee explained: 'He said it was a bad omen to be next to a kid who died so young and that if he isn't moved, or if a wall isn't built between them, that there will be more death and divorce in our family.'

UNHAPPILY EVER AFTER

All families suffer from tragedy, but members of Monaco's first family seem to be inflicted with more than their share of death and disaster. Could it be the result of a curse issued by an ancestor? Legend has it that one of the Grimaldi family vowed that not a single descendant should enjoy a happy marriage. His wish, it seems, has come true.

Yet despite the dramas, the family retains a fairy-tale feel. The tiny principality on the French Riviera excited the imagination of

Above: *While Princess Stephanie had a series of unstable relationships, sister Caroline met and fell in love with Italian businessman Stefano Casiraghi. Three children later in 1990, he was tragically killed in a speedboat accident.*

Left: *Prince Albert graduated from Amherst College, Massachusetts, USA, after studying for a BA in political science. His parents looked on proudly as he received his diploma in 1981.*

Above: *The first earl of Craven. His family has lived under a curse for 300 years.*

caused a major family upset. And the divorce which followed just two years later was devastating for her Roman Catholic parents.

In 1982 the happy marriage of Grace and Rainier was abruptly ended when she died in a car crash, aged 52. She was killed when the car plunged 120 feet down a Monaco mountainside. Beside her was her daughter Stephanie, then 17, who suffered only minor injuries but was severely shocked. Rumours were rife that the under-age Stephanie had, in fact, been at the wheel.

Stephanie grew up to forge a string of unsuitable liaisons, including a bizarre relationship with a convicted sex offender 17 years her senior. Her wayward behaviour caused more heartache for the grieving prince but he took solace in the secure and happy marriage Caroline had found with Italian Stefano Casiraghi. Together they had three children and provided a dignified, refreshing family image to complement the kingdom.

But their happiness was ripped to shreds when Stefano died in a speedboat accident off the Monaco coast in 1990. He was aged just 30. Caroline appeared almost paralysed with grief. The death of the speedboat racing champion deprived her of the man she adored and left her a lone mother with three children aged 6 and under. Monaco mourned with her as he was buried in the stunned principality. It's now left to Rainier's son and heir Albert, as yet unwed, to put the curse to the test.

THE GIPSY'S CURSE

It was tragic when 28-year-old Simon Craven died in a car crash, but the premature death came as no great surprise. For Simon was the eighth earl of Craven and latest victim of a doomed dynasty.

None of the holders of the title in the past 200 years has died of old age. It's all down to a gipsy curse uttered 300 years ago. Folklore tells how a 17th-century baron, William Craven, made a servant girl pregnant and refused to wed her, turning her away from his door. Little did he know the girl was part gipsy. She used her Romany roots to summon up a spell to get revenge for her public disgrace, declaring that no male heir of the cold-hearted baron would live out a full life.

the world when screen beauty Grace Kelly was wooed and won by Prince Rainier III. The stunning blonde who had starred in *High Noon* and Alfred Hitchcock's *Rear Window* was filming *To Catch a Thief* in 1955 when the pair met.

They wed the following year and Grace gave up her Hollywood career, bowing out with a memorable performance in the aptly named musical *High Society*. The couple had three children – Caroline, Stephanie and Albert – and the prince became head of state.

But the cracks in the model family began to show when Caroline lost her heart to playboy Phillipe Junot. Their marriage

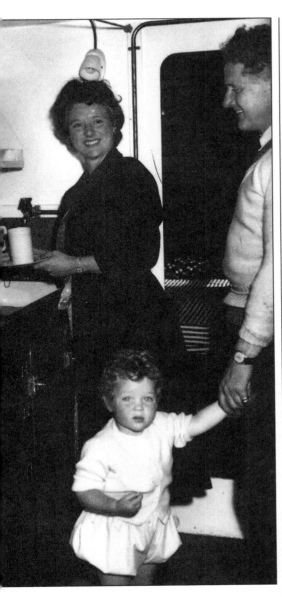

The eighth earl was killed in 1990 when his car was crumpled in a road smash. He inherited the title from his brother Thomas, who was so obsessed by the curse and depressed by a run-in with the law over drugs that he committed suicide. He shot himself when he was just 26 years old.

Their father, the sixth earl, died of leukemia aged 47 in 1965. Before him, his father fell off a boat after a riotous party and drowned aged 35. It's been the same sorry story since 1801 when the family were awarded an earldom.

Simon's mother Lady Elizabeth Craven said: 'Simon used to laugh at the idea.' The title passed on to his 16-month-old son, Benjamin.

Observers believed the curse tainted everything surrounding the family. Superstitious villagers believed it had struck

again when the new owner of a Craven manor house was found gassed in his car.

Dr Robert Reid, a former science editor at the BBC, bought Morewood House in Hamstead Marshall, Berkshire, from the tragic seventh earl. It was the picture of English grandeur, set in 500 acres and overlooking the beautiful River Kennet. He committed suicide in his Range Rover parked in woods nearby after his wife Penelope left him.

Afterwards a villager said: 'We felt ill at ease for Dr Reid when we knew he was moving into the manor house. We weren't surprised when we heard he had died.'

Another declared: 'The curse got him. The house and everything that the Craven family has is tainted by it. I would no more live in that place, grand as it is, than drink a bottle of poison.'

'I WOULD NO MORE LIVE IN THAT PLACE THAN DRINK A BOTTLE OF POISON.'

Left: *As a curly-headed toddler, Simon Craven knew nothing of the fate that awaited him. He died at the wheel of his car in 1990. Another victim of the Craven curse was the fifth earl (below), great-grandfather of today's young title-holder. He drowned during a party.*

SUPERSTITIONS

In the age of computers and high technology, surely it is hard to believe that superstitions, rooted in folklore and fear, have any power over lives in the 20th century?

'Good luck will rub off, if I shakes hands with you. Or blow me a kiss, 'cause that's lucky too.' So sang Dick Van Dyke, playing Bert the chimney sweep in the classic musical fairy-tale *Mary Poppins*.

Few of the millions of excited children – and their mothers and fathers – who watched that enchanting film would dispute his words.

Even today, when sweeps are a dying breed, most Westerners are familiar with the idea that somehow chimney sweeps manage to spread good fortune wherever they travel.

A sweep remains a popular figure at weddings (more of which later) and indeed some reckon to earn just as much from brushing past the church door on cue as they do brushing soot. But how did this intriguing snippet of folklore start? And how has it managed to persist into an age in which fewer and fewer houses depend on wood and coal?

Like many superstitions it stems from ancient beliefs in the sacred nature of ordinary everyday objects or features of nature, in this case the household fire and hearth. Fire has always been a phenomenon to respect – even worship – and for thousands of years it has been a symbol of life and survival across the world.

Tradition has it that a sweep should be greeted warmly or bowed to. Some say that you should also spit and make a wish. But there are drawbacks. It is essential that you first catch sight of him walking towards you. If he's walking away it is a sign of bad news to follow.

To spread his luck he must also be in full work gear, sporting a blackened and grimy face. A clean sweep, pressed and dressed, is no use to the superstitious because his powers are said to fall off with the clothes he uses on the job.

Superstitions, by their very nature, cover an enormous range of everyday items and events. They may be irrational, but it doesn't follow that they are valueless. They may be taken too seriously, yet it is rare for them to do any serious psychological harm. The comforting thing about them is that for every action that brings bad luck, the chances are there is a 'charm', or antidote, to send it away again.

HOUSEHOLD CHARMS

Many of these beliefs are rooted in ways of thinking that existed long before our existing civilizations. They unveil glimpses of the hopes and fears of past peoples, their religious beliefs and long-forgotten rituals and their ways of trying to bring certainty into an uncertain world. That said, the most common superstitions could rule your life if you let them. You wouldn't even need to step out of doors to feel the bad vibes.

Spilling salt is one obvious example. This is an omen of the very worst kind: some say it brings the devil himself peeking behind you. You should immediately grab a pinch and throw it over your shoulder to blind him. If you don't the consequences could be dire.

Above: *For such an everyday item, salt is credited with an amazing range of strange powers. Spilling it brings the devil spying over your shoulder while knocking over a salt cellar can cause two friends to squabble.*

Opposite: *The chimney sweep in traditional dress. It's essential that you first catch sight of him walking towards you.*

**A SCORNED WOMAN
COULD TAKE HER REVENGE
WITH NINE PINS –
AND INFLICT CONSTANT
TORTURE ON THE MAN WHO
HAD REJECTED HER.**

Right: *Eclipses of the Sun
are thought to have been the
cause of many early
superstitions.*

Below: *Some can shrug off
superstition. Others go out of
their way to defy it. Here the
Queen Mother proves a
point.*

One old saying talks of 'a tear shed for every grain spilled', while knocking over a salt cellar placed between you and a friend is a sure sign that a quarrel is looming.

Household uses of salt – aside, of course, from cooking – go on almost indefinitely. Dairymaids should drop a pinch in their pails before milking (it wards off witches' spells), unbaptized children can be protected from the evil eye by scattering it in their cradles, and stirring a glass of salt and water three times is the perfect antidote to bad luck (the idea is you sprinkle the mixture over the unlucky item in question).

The salt water remedy is often brought out to counter the effects of a typical minor domestic accident, such as dropping a pair of scissors. If a pair falls point downwards it predicts a death shortly in the house or near neighbourhood. Likewise, scissors given as a gift are a sign that the friendship will be cut.

Suppose you've spilled the salt and dropped the scissors. You go to make a pot of reviving tea confident that nothing else can go wrong. Then, as you stir the pot, you realize the teapot lid has been left off. That's a double dose of misfortune – the lid is a sign of imminent bad news while a stirred pot means quarrels are about to descend on the family or dwelling.

Seeking solace in housework may heap even more woes upon you. Making a bed, according to folklore, can be fraught with dangers. If you turn a mattress on a Sunday whoever sleeps on it will get bad dreams all week. Turn it on a Friday and you'll turn your sweetheart away. As for inviting the rest of the family to help, forget it. A bed made by three people means someone will die in it within the year.

With such a maze of superstitions to navigate at home it's surprising hardened believers don't just get into bed (as soon as they've finished making it properly) to seek refuge in sleep. The important thing for all diehards to remember here though is that they must be sure to climb out the same side they climb in. Otherwise they might get out of bed the wrong side – and we all know that does to people.

The big problem with superstitions is that there's often a catch. You think you've got them all worked out and then …

Take pins. The well-known rhyme runs

'See a pin, pick it up and all day long you'll have good luck.' Fine, just as long as you pick the pin up immediately and it's pointing away from you. If it points towards you you're in danger of picking up unhappiness.

Pins are a bit more consistent when they're used as charms, especially for women whose lovers have somehow let them down. Spurned spinsters are supposed to take 12 new pins and throw them on a fire at midnight chanting:

''Tis not these pins I wish to burn,
But my man's heart I wish to turn,
May he neither sleep nor rest,
Until he's granted my request.'

In some parts of England a woman scorned could be even more sadistic in exacting revenge. It was – and still is – believed that simply by wearing nine pins concealed in her dress she could torture her husband or lover through his every waking moment.

Any item capable of cutting or inflicting a wound does seem to attract more than its fair share of superstition. This is particularly true of knives, at one time a very personal and much loved possession used for fighting, hunting and eating.

The steel shaft was thought to protect against fairies and witches and a knife thrust into a front door protected the entire house. Even today, knives should never be crossed on a table (a sign of arguments and bitterness) or sharpened after sunset (a burglar could then be expected to enter the house). Making toast on the tip of the blade is seen as tempting fate, and if a knife must be given as a present it should always be accompanied by a coin – the price of ensuring the friendship remains intact.

It is also thought unlucky to spin a knife on the table, though sometimes this is done to establish the hair colour of a spinster or bachelor's future spouse. If it falls with blade towards the questioner, the partner will be dark. If it finishes handle first a fair-haired lover is due to arrive.

LOVE NOTIONS

Which brings us to courtship and marriage and the mass of superstition that drifts like mist around both events.

For women the world over there are many ways to 'see' a future husband. One of the most popular is through dreams and, before getting into bed, a girl can perform the following magic spell. She pins her garters to the bedroom wall, arranges her shoes in a T-shape and recites quickly:
  'I pin my garters to the wall,
  And put my shoes in the shape of a T,
  In hopes of my true love for to see,
  Not in his apparel, nor in his array,
  But in the clothes he wears every day,
  If I am his bride to be,
  If I am his clothes to wear,
  If I am his children to bear,
  I hope he'll turn his face to me,
  But if I am not his clothes to wear,
  If I am not his children to bear,
  I hope he'll turn his back to me.'
She then had to dash between the sheets quickly, without saying another word. A similar version of the dream charm is used

MEN HAD DEVIOUS WAYS OF DISCOVERING WHETHER THEIR CHOSEN BRIDE WAS STILL A VIRGIN.

Below: *Household spiders are generally good omens. Twirling one three times around your head by its thread is supposed to bring a cash windfall.*

Above: *Was the origin of this ceremony rooted in the belief that the shaft of a knife or sword helped ward off fairy mischief? The guardsmen are careful not to cross blades. If they did, bad luck would dog the happy couple.*

by betrothed girls whose loved ones are far from them. In this the lovesick girl must knit her left garter around her right stocking while reciting the following poem (knitting a knot at every comma):

'This knot I knit, to know the thing,
  I know not yet,
That I may see, the man that shall
  my husband be,
How he goes, and what he wears,
  and what he does,
All days, and years.'

Among men eyeing up a future bride there were – and are – plenty of equally bizarre beliefs and practices. In the days when marrying a virgin was far more important than it is today there were, apparently, reliable ways to tell how careful she had been with her favours. For instance, could she walk through a swarm of bees unharmed? (She would be undoubtedly pure if so.) Had owls been heard repeatedly hooting near her house? (A sign her virginity had been taken.)

Predicting future marriage partners is a popular pastime at Halloween, the old Druid festival at which the forces of magic and witchcraft are said to issue from the deepest caves and darkest forests to wreak chaos and mischief upon mankind. One version of this game is for all the single people to fasten an apple on a string and twirl it before a blazing fire. Whoever's apple falls first will be first to wed while the poor unfortunate whose fruit hangs on longest will die unwed. An adaptation of this is to peel an apple in one strip and then toss it backwards over the left shoulder. The shape it assumes on the ground is said to be the initial of a future spouse.

There is also the use of apple pips for those hoping to discover whether the man or woman of their dreams will be faithful. A pip is placed on the bars of a fire or given the name of the loved one in question. The fortune-seeker then asks: 'If you love me, bounce and fly; if you hate me, lie and die.' If the pip explodes the love affair is sound. If it just blackens and burns quietly, the courtship is doomed.

Some superstitions to establish the identity of a future husband are decidedly racy and distinctly unappealing. One such method was common on

Christmas Eve, Halloween and St Agnes's Eve (20 January).

In the days when dresses were held together with pins it was the custom for three young spinsters to get together to bake a cake which they would share in a downstairs room on the stroke of midnight. They would then walk backwards upstairs to bed but before taking the first step every pin had to be removed from their clothes and every part of their dress loosened. If the charm had been strictly followed the girls' future husbands would appear in ghostly form, pursuing them to snatch off their clothes.

As these were already loose the theory was that the women could slip out of them as they were being pawed and fondled and, once safely in bed, the apparitions would vanish. It was never explained exactly what would happen if the ghostly husbands caught their brides-to-be – but the implications are obvious.

WEDDING SPELLS

As every bride knows, wedding days are fraught with tension at the best of times. If you stir in a generous measure of superstition as well, it could be worth staying single. Bad news for brides includes a lizard crossing the path on the way to church (a bad omen), breaking something at the wedding feast (sign of an unhappy married life) or failing to be first to cut the cake (the marriage will be childless).

Worst of all is if she catches a glimpse of herself in a mirror while clad in her bridal gown. This means something is about to happen preventing the marriage from taking place.

The colour of the dress, of course, is vital. Grey, stone colours or fawn are all OK. Black is a complete no-no, green is dodgy – it has too many links with the fairies – purple is unlucky because it is a mourning colour, while brown means the married couple will never make it rich. Blue is considered an important accessory (every bride knows she should approach the aisle wearing something old, something new, something borrowed and something blue), but yellow is frowned upon because in rural areas it signifies the girl's heart may already have been lost to a stranger.

Going to and from church demands enormous care from the superstitious. It is, these days, unlucky for the bride and groom to see each other on the wedding morning, though strangely this never used to be the case among ordinary folk who generally opted for a 'walking wedding'.

The bride should always leave her front door right foot first and if the Sun shines upon her or a rainbow appears it is an excellent omen. Bizarrely, elephants are considered extremely lucky but a pig running across the bride's path is unfortunate. As for the wedding procession which meets a funeral, well, the best advice

IF THE RING ROLLED TOWARDS THE GRAVE, THE IMPLICATIONS WERE DIRE.

Below: *Pregnancy attracts more than its fair share of superstition. Mums-to-be apparently put the unborn child at risk if they so much as glance at the wrong kind of animal.*

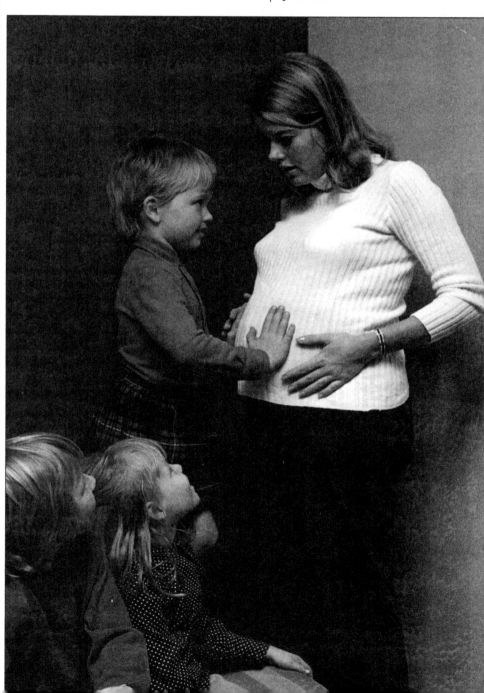

from the folklore experts is to consult a solicitor immediately and call the whole thing off. Otherwise certain personal trauma lies ahead.

Grey horses are desirable to draw the bridal carriage, though if they don't start trotting on request it is another unlucky omen. Equally, a car which conks out just before or after the service is a warning of trouble ahead. Dropping the wedding ring was a sign that the clumsy spouse

Above: *Wedding bells ring out the joy of marriage. But for the superstitious bride and groom the big day is fraught with danger.*

responsible would die first. If it rolled away from the altar bad news was due, and if it stopped on a grave one of the happy couple would die young.

Times of marriage were also steeped in tradition. May is a particularly bad month,

perhaps because in pagan times it was the start of the warm season and a very busy time for young men driving cattle out to grass. Was it thought that they would have less time for their new wife? Even days of the week have significance. One old rhyme, still repeated around the world, goes:

'Monday for wealth, Tuesday for health, Wednesday the best day of all, Thursday for losses, Friday for crosses, and Saturday no luck at all.'

Hardly does the superstitious bride get through her big day than worries start to surface about her next big life event – pregnancy.

BIRTH RITES

Many ancient civilizations believed that both a pregnant woman and her unborn child lived in great peril and needed special protection from evil spirits. It was said that she made those around her equally susceptible and sometimes she would be forced to go and live in isolation for the good of her neighbours.

Less drastic beliefs prevented her from touching pork or washing clothes in a river (she would drive away the fish). She would only be accepted back into the community once her baby was born.

There are many charms to protect the poor mum-to-be from the pain and anxiety of childbirth. One of the most common is the wearing of a brown semi-precious stone, called an eagle stone, imported from the Far East. This can be worn around the neck as a protection against miscarriage or tied around the thigh during labour to ensure a quick and easy delivery. The stones were said to be found in or near the nests of eagles, who could not lay their eggs without magical assistance.

If a pregnant woman steps over a grave, however, not even an eagle stone can save her child. Folklore says the baby will die before, or soon after, birth. A cord tied around the mother's waist is enough to make the unborn child unlucky. If she washes in dirty water the baby will grow up to have coarse hands. And if she picks and arranges flowers too much the child will have have no sense of smell.

In many parts of Europe no pregnant woman would ever act as godmother to a friend's child. Such folly would sentence the babe to certain death.

Babies born with unusual physical markings or other disabilities are said to have suffered because of something seen by their mother during her pregnancy. For instance, a harelip means the mum must have seen a hare (often the animal form assumed by witches). Children with eyes offset, or of unusual colour, are a sign that their mother must have encountered a snake or lizard while carrying them. Both animals are also well known as witches' familiars.

Pregnant women who follow these superstitions will still make three slits in

Below: *No sailor would ever kill an albatross at sea. The bird, it is believed, has the soul of a dead mariner.*

Above: *The American vampire bat. This bizarre-looking creature at one time convinced many that human vampires were a reality ... and that they sucked the blood of their fellow men and women.*

their clothing if they see such an ominous beast. The charm apparently wards off any curses that happen to be flying about.

Birthmarks are another source of great speculation. By far the most popular 'cure' – common the world over – is to lick the mark 9, 21 or 30 times or until it disappears. There are reports, dated as late as the 1950s in southern England that this remedy works.

Days of birth are also important. Most Western schoolchildren know the rhyme:

'Monday's child is fair of face,
Tuesday's child is full of grace,
Wednesday's child is full of woe,
Thursday's child has far to go,
Friday's child is loving and giving,
Saturday's child works hard for a living.
But the child that is born on the
    Sabbath Day,
Is blithe and bonny and good and gay.'

Times of day have significance too. Twilight, midnight and the hour immediately following, and the chiming hours of 3, 6 and 9 o'clock are all times of great influence on the child's psychic nature. Children born at these times are said to be able to see ghosts and fairies and may also have the ability to look into the future. They enjoy full protection against witches' spells.

OVER THE RAINBOW

As we've seen, animals and birds hold enormous sway over the lives of the superstitious. No sailor would ever kill an albatross at sea (it is the reincarnation of a dead mariner) because of the inevitable bad luck that would descend upon him. On land the cuckoo carries the can for many and varied superstitions. In Europe weighty matters can be deduced depending on the circumstances in which you hear the first cuckoo-call of spring.

If it comes from the left or behind, evil is dogging your path. If from the right or in front, the omens are excellent. Whichever direction you happen to be looking in at the time the call rings out, that's the direction you'll be exactly a year to the day. If you're careless enough to be looking down at the ground you'll be dead and buried within the year.

In Germany a call from the north is a death omen, from the south means a good butter year and from either east or west means general good fortune. Almost everywhere the cuckoo flies it is thought lucky to have money in your pocket when the first call of spring sounds. A coin should always be turned over at once while making a wish. Those caught without money on them can expect a year of poverty. As for a girl seeking a husband, the number of notes the bird calls denotes how many years she must wait to wed.

Cats, perhaps because of their traditional role as familiars, are credited with many secret powers. Unfortunately they provide another good example of the inconsistency of some superstitions. In Britain a black cat is considered lucky while a white one is to be avoided at all costs. Yet just the opposite view prevails in Belgium, Spain and America.

It is thought to be lucky (provided the colour is right) for a cat to come into a house or on board ship uninvited. If you do encounter the wrong colour fur you can see

CHILDREN BORN AT SUCH TIMES WERE GIFTED WITH SECOND SIGHT.

Below: *A waterspout on land. The desire of primitive peoples to predict bad weather sparked off a whole string of appropriate superstitions.*

Above: This collector was making sure good fortune was at close hand. He needed a ladder to inspect the upper reaches of his heap of lucky horseshoes.

EVEN THE BRIDGE FOR THE DEAD WAS FRAUGHT WITH DANGER.

off the bad omen by stroking the animal three times and talking to it politely. Ill fortune is worse if the cat crosses your path from left to right, or runs away from you. Similarly if puss leaves the house of a sick person, and won't be coaxed back, that poor soul will die.

Miners and sailors avoid using the word 'cat' at all. In some of the old Cornish tin mines of south-west Britain men would walk out if one was discovered among them and refuse to return until it had been killed. Yet with seamen the animals were treated almost reverentially. Many has been the shipwreck in which the cat has been first to be saved.

Cats which run about wildly forecast a high wind coming; washing ears means rain, while sitting with their back to a fire predicts a storm.

Weather-lore of this kind is perhaps the oldest superstition of all. The desire of primitive tribes to know when bad weather lay ahead was understandable, given that it could mean the difference between life and death in the coming winter.

Rain is the source of more bizarre beliefs than any other single weather event. For those who want it, burning fern, sprinkling water on stones amid magical incantations (an old Indian witch-doctor speciality) and stirring flour into a spring with a hazel rod (popular in northern France) are all supposed to produce the required result.

In northern Europe, given the climate, such elaborate methods must have a fair chance of success at almost any time of year. But trying to keep rain away is a different matter – perhaps the reason why not much time has been wasted devising complicated charms.

The best-known survivor is still sung by children and optimistically pleads:

'Rain, rain go away,
Come again another day,
When I brew and when I bake,
I'll give you a piece of cake.'

If that seems a waste of time, spare a thought for the hundreds – if not thousands – of simple souls who used to graft away digging for pots of gold where they thought they'd seen a rainbow end. In fact, of all the phenomena mentioned here, the rainbow provides some of the most absorbing and evocative images.

In Burma and southern Africa it is a dangerous demon. In Finland it is the bow used by the mighty thunder-god. In Germany and Austria it is the soul bridge along which little children are ushered into heaven by their guardian angels. In Norway it is a bridge for the dead … and those that don't make it to paradise are consumed by the red vein of the bow.

It's probably all nonsense, this sacred ancient power attributed to the weather, birds, animals and trees.

But better touch wood, just in case.